# Spatial Demography and Population Governance

This series aims to strengthen the development of spatial demography in Asia, accelerate the application of new spatial analysis and spatial econometric methods in population research, and promote modern population governance in numerous developing countries. To achieve these goals, the series focuses on different important demographic phenomena, including internal migration and talent flows, urbanization, fertility change, population aging, labor force change, population-environment interactions, and regional population projections. By applying different methodologies from different perspectives, the relationship between demographic change, population policy, and economic development is further explored, thus providing policymakers with theoretical support for modern population governance.

Jiafeng Gu

# Wealth Management Report for Mid-High Net Worth Families

Springer

Jiafeng Gu
Institute of Social Science Survey
Peking University
Beijing, China

ISSN 2731-7579 ISSN 2731-7587 (electronic)
Spatial Demography and Population Governance
ISBN 978-981-97-0386-9 ISBN 978-981-97-0387-6 (eBook)
https://doi.org/10.1007/978-981-97-0387-6



This Springer imprint is published by the registered company Springer Nature Singapore Pte Ltd.
The registered company address is: 152 Beach Road, #21-01/04 Gateway East, Singapore 189721, Singapore

# Contents

# Chapter 1
# Introduction

**Abstract** To find the "blue ocean market," the financial industry has been concerned about the extension of customers from high net worth to mid-net worth individuals. There is no universally accepted standard for defining mid-high net worth individuals, as the purpose of the study varies by country and region. In terms of operational definition, the size of investable assets is generally taken as a measure. This book conducts research on six aspects, namely, the behavioral characteristics, financial asset management, non-financial asset management, commercial insurance allocation, commercial health insurance allocation for children, and retirement and insurance of mid-high net worth families. This research is an attempt to provide a comprehensive and accurate panoramic analysis of China's mid-high net worth families and individuals and provide an important reference basis for the government, financial institutions, and other related institutions.

The term "Mid-High Net Worth" was coined in the late twentieth century. Generally, mid-high net worth people refer to a social group comprising affluent individuals with a certain amount of personal assets or wealth. In terms of social class, mid-high net worth people generally refer to the middle and upper middle classes and higher social classes. The concept of mid-high net worth did not attract the attention of financial institutions immediately after its introduction because they were more focused on high net worth clients at the time, and the concepts of high net worth and mid-high net had not yet merged into the middle and high net worth concept. However, the financial services industry encountered considerable difficulties after the global financial crisis in 2008, and financial institutions needed to adjust their business processes and services to adapt to the new environment. Financial institutions that were unable to do so risked being marginalized by their customers (especially mid-high net worth individuals) [1]. At the time, the business focus of financial institutions started gradually extending from high net worth customers to mid-high net worth customers, and middle and high net worth customers gradually entered the strategic and operational levels of financial institutions and became important targets for the financial industry. This period was called by some people in the industry "A Crucial Moment in the Fight for Mid Net Worth" [2]. Since then, middle and high net worth individuals

 
J. Gu, *Wealth Management Report for Mid-High Net Worth Families*, Spatial Demography and Population Governance, https://doi.org/10.1007/978-981-97-0387-6_1

have become an important customer group over which financial institutions compete as well as an important basis for building their core competencies. Therefore, it is necessary to analyze the mid-high net worth population and its development trend from a global perspective and understand and grasp the characteristics, scale, and future changes of banks' mid-high net worth customers in a holistic manner.

## 1 Background of the Study

The rise of mid-high net worth families and individuals has drawn the attention of people from all walks of life, and it is an inevitable consequence of social and economic development reaching a certain stage. In the financial field, the development and competition of private banking has inevitably extended the target customers from high net worth families and individuals to mid-net worth families and individuals, leading to the battle for mid-high net worth customers. With the development of the social economy, the scale of the middle-income group is growing, and they have become an important pillar of society. The middle-income group is bound to be an important part of the mid-high net worth population. At the same time, with the increasing popularity of financial knowledge and the upgrading of the family financial management concept, the concept and way of creating, maintaining, transmitting, and enjoying the wealth of families are undergoing profound changes. These factors are driving the development of mid-high net worth families and individuals, making the understanding of these families and individuals a common need of the government, industry, and academia.

### *1.1 Development of Private Banking*

Since the emergence of modern banking, the banking industry has undergone several stages of development, and banking services have become increasingly diversified. The development history of private banking can be traced back to the sixteenth century. At the time, private banking emerged in Geneva, Switzerland, to provide private and exclusive financial services to some French nobles who had been exiled from their country. Private banking refers to a comprehensive operation in which a commercial bank or international financial institution and a specific client sign a relevant investment and asset management contract on the basis of full communication and consultation, and the specific client fully entrusts the aforementioned bank or financial institution to carry out the relevant investment and asset management in accordance with the investment plan, scope, and method agreed upon in the contract. Private banking is characterized by high barriers to entry, integrated services, and a strong focus on client relationships.

According to the classification of services in the Western banking industry, banking services can be divided into different types. The first is mass banking services, which do not limit the size of client assets; the second is very important person (VIP) banking services, which require client assets above USD 100,000; the third is private banking services, which require client assets above USD 1 million; and the fourth is family office services, which require client assets above USD 80 million. Of course, these thresholds vary by country and region. In terms of banking services, private banking services are mainly reserved for high net worth clients [3–5], while family office services target the middle and upper classes of high net worth clients, especially ultra-high net worth clients [6]. Ultra-high net worth clients generally have family businesses and face the problem of family wealth inheritance [7]. Clearly, the third and fourth categories of services in the Western banking industry are oriented to customers who are high net worth individuals (HNWIs).

However, with the rapid increase of wealth in society at large, the service strategy followed by banks of focusing on high net worth clients has been questioned by some. Some experts have pointed out that banks focus more on serving the wealthy, but this strategy does not really reflect the strength of banks, and the wealth management needs of the mass affluent are often ignored by banks, despite this segment being where banks should seek future growth [8]. The mass affluent market is a marketing term that generally refers to individuals or households with ¥100,000 to ¥1 million in liquid financial assets [9]. The so-called mass affluent population is the mid net worth population. Although the concept of the mid net worth population was not explicitly introduced at the time, the mass affluent population referred to was synonymous with the mid net worth population. In terms of banking services, VIP banking services are mainly targeted at the mass affluent, that is, the bank's mid net worth customers. The expansion of the private banking business is bound to intensify competition among banks. Given the limited number of high-net-worth clients, banks will extend their services from high net worth to mid net worth to maximize profit.

The middle-income group comprises individuals with a relatively generous income, and its income level is between that of the low-income and high-income groups. Overall, it is a group of people with more stable jobs, more affluent material life, and a medium level of income. In urban areas, the National Bureau of Statistics defines the annual household income standard of China's middle-income group as 60,000–500,000 yuan. According to this definition, households in the urban middle-income group accounted for 14% of all urban households as of 2010 and 45% of all urban households as of 2020 [10]. In recent years, the middle-income group in China has shown a trend of continuous expansion, and the assets owned by them have continued to grow. Before 2005, one study pointed out that the proportion of the middle-income group to the total population in China was decreasing [11]. However, after 2005, there has been a consensus that the share of the middle-income group in the total population has been on a continuous upward trend. According to the estimation, the middle-income group in China would comprise approximately 417 million people in 2020, accounting for 29.5% of the country's total population. Approximately 42.2% of urban residents are in the middle-income group, as are approximately 15.1% of rural residents [12]. Although there are still some differences in the specific values of the current estimates of the size of the middle-income group in China, it is agreed that its size exceeds 400 million people.

The rapid development of the middle-income group has resulted in a continuous increase in social consumption [13]. Compared with low-income groups, middle-income groups have stronger purchasing power, greater willingness to consume, and more urgent needs for family wealth management. With the general growth of household income and continuous accumulation of household wealth in China, household consumption capacity has been increasing, household consumption structure has been continuously improving, and mass consumption, mainly among middle-income groups, has become one of the important driving forces for expanding domestic demand and transforming the mode of economic development. In addition to the consumption of tangible goods, middle-income groups also consume intangible goods, including financial services and insurance, which have been growing continuously. In terms of family investment and financial management, middle-income groups have distinctive personalities, which are mainly reflected in the following aspects: in terms of investment objects, they develop from single to diversified, that is, from traditional single savings investments to diversified investments, such as stocks, funds, bonds, real estate, and gold; in terms of investment cycle, they develop from traditional emphasis on short-term investment to medium and long-term investment, and the investment time frame becomes longer. From the perspective of investment risk, the growth rate of financial products is significantly higher than that of traditional financial assets, the scale of non-monetary risky financial assets is gradually increasing in the total financial assets of households, and there is a trend of evolution in savings from monetary savings to value preservation and capital savings.

With the rise of the middle-income group, China has gradually formed an "olive-shaped" social structure with a large middle and small ends. The change in social structure will inevitably lead to structural changes in social consumption and family financial management. In terms of economic value, the expanding middle-income group will help increase the demand for financial and insurance products and build a benign family financial culture. The higher demand of the middle-income group for financial and insurance products and services in terms of price, quality, design, service, and even efficiency has strongly contributed to the innovation and improvement of the supply side of financial institutions. This helps promote the innovative development of China's financial industry from the demand side. Financial institutions are keenly aware of the huge opportunities and market space contained therein and actively adjust their financial product design and service strategies in an attempt to attract middle-income groups and thus obtain customers. A prerequisite for achieving this goal is a comprehensive and systematic study of the middle-income group. Since the middle-income group is often the main component of mid-high net worth households, financial institutions can effectively grasp the main characteristics and development trends of the middle-income group, especially their demand for financial and insurance products and services, through the study of mid-high net worth households. This is extremely important for a competitive advantage in the financial industry in this new era.

## 1.2 Rise of the Middle-Income Group

The middle-income group comprises individuals with a relatively generous income, and its income level is between that of the low-income and high-income groups. Overall, it is a group of people with more stable jobs, more affluent material life, and a medium level of income. In urban areas, the National Bureau of Statistics defines the annual household income standard of China's middle-income group as 60,000–500,000 yuan. According to this definition, households in the urban middle-income group accounted for 14% of all urban households as of 2010 and 45% of all urban households as of 2020 [10]. In recent years, the middle-income group in China has shown a trend of continuous expansion, and the assets owned by them have continued to grow. Before 2005, one study pointed out that the proportion of the middle-income group to the total population in China was decreasing [11]. However, after 2005, there has been a consensus that the share of the middle-income group in the total population has been on a continuous upward trend. According to the estimation, the middle-income group in China would comprise approximately 417 million people in 2020, accounting for 29.5% of the country's total population. Approximately 42.2% of urban residents are in the middle-income group, as are approximately 15.1% of rural residents [12]. Although there are still some differences in the specific values of the current estimates of the size of the middle-income group in China, it is agreed that its size exceeds 400 million people.

The rapid development of the middle-income group has resulted in a continuous increase in social consumption [13]. Compared with low-income groups, middle-income groups have stronger purchasing power, greater willingness to consume, and more urgent needs for family wealth management. With the general growth of household income and continuous accumulation of household wealth in China, household consumption capacity has been increasing, household consumption structure has been continuously improving, and mass consumption, mainly among middle-income groups, has become one of the important driving forces for expanding domestic demand and transforming the mode of economic development. In addition to the consumption of tangible goods, middle-income groups also consume intangible goods, including financial services and insurance, which have been growing continuously. In terms of family investment and financial management, middle-income groups have distinctive personalities, which are mainly reflected in the following aspects: in terms of investment objects, they develop from single to diversified, that is, from traditional single savings investments to diversified investments, such as stocks, funds, bonds, real estate, and gold; in terms of investment cycle, they develop from traditional emphasis on short-term investment to medium and long-term investment, and the investment time frame becomes longer. From the perspective of investment risk, the growth rate of financial products is significantly higher than that of traditional financial assets, the scale of non-monetary risky financial assets is gradually increasing in the total financial assets of households, and there is a trend of evolution in savings from monetary savings to value preservation and capital savings.

With the rise of the middle-income group, China has gradually formed an "olive-shaped" social structure with a large middle and small ends. The change in social structure will inevitably lead to structural changes in social consumption and family financial management. In terms of economic value, the expanding middle-income group will help increase the demand for financial and insurance products and build a benign family financial culture. The higher demand of the middle-income group for financial and insurance products and services in terms of price, quality, design, service, and even efficiency has strongly contributed to the innovation and improvement of the supply side of financial institutions. This helps promote the innovative development of China's financial industry from the demand side. Financial institutions are keenly aware of the huge opportunities and market space contained therein and actively adjust their financial product design and service strategies in an attempt to attract middle-income groups and thus obtain customers. A prerequisite for achieving this goal is a comprehensive and systematic study of the middle-income group. Since the middle-income group is often the main component of mid-high net worth households, financial institutions can effectively grasp the main characteristics and development trends of the middle-income group, especially their demand for financial and insurance products and services, through the study of mid-high net worth households. This is extremely important for a competitive advantage in the financial industry in this new era.

## *1.3 Changes in Household Wealth Patterns*

With the adjustment of China's economic structure, the way families create, maintain, transmit, and enjoy wealth is quietly changing. Property investment is the main way families create and enjoy wealth. Over the past 20 years, housing prices have soared, enabling many families to rapidly increase their wealth. The rapid development of the Internet has given rise to several "online businesses" and "internet celebrities," creating new opportunities for many families to become rich. With the continuous improvement and development of China's financial market, the government is actively guiding the direct flow of funds into the financing market, thus reducing the financing costs of the real economy and "releasing water to feed the fish," so that enterprises can thrive. Subsequently, the favorable development of enterprises will drive the investment sentiment of the capital market, thus forming a virtuous and efficient financial asset allocation cycle. Under these circumstances, some families have seized the windfall of using financial assets to become rich by continuously obtaining financial knowledge and applying it to financial management to increase their family wealth steadily. As the country continues to support and promote the "double creation" (mass entrepreneurship and innovation), many families have become rich through entrepreneurship. Of course, families have different ways of creating wealth and becoming rich at different times, and one obvious development trend is to move from a relatively single to a diversified way.

As the economy continues to develop at a high rate, family assets in China show a steady growth trend. After accumulating a certain amount of wealth, many families begin to consider how to maintain their hard-earned wealth and smoothly pass it on to the next generation. However, marriage, taxation, education of children, high inflation rate, improper management, investment failure, and growth risks may all pose threats to family wealth, making "maintaining and passing on wealth" even more difficult than "creating wealth." Wealth transmission has become an urgent concern not only for mid-high net worth families and individuals, but also for society in general. If this problem is not resolved adequately, there will be a situation in which "wealth cannot be passed on to three generations." The problem is more urgent for mid-high net worth families because of their greater wealth. After more than 40 years of rapid development, China now has many mid-high net worth families and individuals who are the "first to become rich" in the context of our specific era, the "wealth creation generation." Moreover, with the passage of time, the "second generation of the wealthy" has gradually emerged, injecting new blood into mid-high net worth families, which have a natural need for wealth inheritance.

Buying financial and insurance products is often one of the more convenient ways for mid- high net worth families to maintain their wealth. Their willingness to invest in insurance products is second only to their willingness to invest in financial products, and they excel at striking a balance between asset preservation and insurance protection. According to many mid-high net worth families, insurance products, including commercial insurance, can not only manage unexpected risks but also bring good investment returns. For example, financial products such as whole life insurance and annuity insurance can meet the needs of wealth management and inheritance of mid-high net worth families. Of course, with the wave of globalization and the impact of financial literacy on the investment philosophy of mid-high net worth families and individuals, their needs are gradually changing. Hence, financial institutions need to keep pace with the times, continuously strengthen their research and understanding of mid-high net worth families and individuals, accurately grasp the changing trends of their needs, and develop relevant financial products in a targeted manner.

## 2 High Net Worth Individuals

The banking industry's focus on mid-high net worth individuals began with high net worth clients. High net worth customers have the typical characteristics of being relatively few in number but having more assets. Therefore, services for this group can increase the profitability of the banking industry. Internationally, the focus on high net worth individuals (HNWIs) began in the 1990s. A typical example of this focus is the release of the 1997 World Wealth Report. This report clearly introduced the concept of HNWIs. However, at the time, China had not yet joined the World Trade Organization, and China's banking industry had not yet opened to the outside world. Therefore, the World Wealth Report did not attract much attention from domestic industries at the time, and the concept of HNWIs went unnoticed by bankers and academics.

In 2001, China joined the World Trade Organization, and in 2006, China's banking industry was officially opened to the outside world. As foreign banks continue to enter China's market, the business management concepts and methods of foreign banks are being introduced as well. Chinese bankers and academics have begun to pay attention to the high net worth customers of banks. An online search of relevant literature in Chinese journals revealed that the earliest literature mentioning banks' high net worth customers was published in 2008 [14]. Moreover, it is a translation of an article originally published in the August 2007 issue of The Banker magazine [15]. The original article, which has a long title, highlights the impact of high net worth clients on the wallet share of private banks and the strategic adjustments needed by private banks. The article cites data from Merrill Lynch and Capgemini's 2007 World Wealth Report, which showed that in 2006, the number of high net worth clients with ¥1 million in investable assets grew by 8% to 9.5 million worldwide, and their total assets under their control swelled to ¥37.2 trillion. As can be seen, the criterion for bank high net worth clients at the time was ¥1 million in investable personal assets. Converted to RMB at the average exchange rate of 7.97 between RMB and USD in 2006, the standard for bank high net worth clients at the time was ¥7.97 million, or nearly ¥8 million, in personal investable assets.

## *2.1 Global Situation*

Merrill Lynch and Capgemini began publishing the World Wealth Report in 1997 with the title "Changing HNWI Behaviors." Since then, Merrill Lynch and Capgemini have published an annual World Wealth Report on the changing wealth of HNWIs. In 2008, Merrill Lynch and Capgemini jointly published Wealth, a summary and review of the previous World Wealth Reports, which was a more systematic study of the changing wealth of HNWIs worldwide from 1996 to 2006 (Lynch and Capgemini, 2008). The data in this book show that the number of HNWIs worldwide increased from 4.5 million in 1996 to 9.5 million in 2006, i.e., a net increase of 5 million people during this period. In terms of the wealth of the world's HNWIs, it increased from ¥16.6 trillion in 1996 to ¥37.2 trillion in 2006, a net increase of ¥20.6 trillion.

Merrill Lynch was acquired by Bank of America in 2008, but this did not immediately affect the release of the World Wealth Report. The 2009 World Wealth Report was still jointly published by Capgemini and Merrill Lynch, as was the 2010 World Wealth Report. They differed only in the addition of a line stating "Bank of America Corporation (BAC)" under "Merrill Lynch." This joint venture continued for the 2011 World Wealth Report, which was the last World Wealth Report to be jointly published by Capgemini and Merrill Lynch. Capgemini then chose to partner with Royal Bank of Canada, which jointly published the 2012, 2013, 2014, and 2015 editions of the World Wealth Report. The World Wealth Report was then restructured and published independently by Capgemini. As can be seen, the world has changed dramatically since the first World Wealth Report was published in 1997, and the partners have changed repeatedly; the only aspect that has remained the same is the research on HNWIs. In the 24 years from 1997 to 2020, the World Wealth Report has successfully captured the attention of the financial industry with its research regarding the population size, wealth size, asset allocation, and wealth management needs of the world's HNWIs. Thus, the World Wealth Report has become the definitive report in this field.

In addition, the Credit Suisse Research Institute (CSRI) has published the Global Wealth Report since 2010, and it has gradually become an important report for systematically monitoring changes in global wealth. The Global Wealth Report mentions that the personal net worth of HNWIs ranges from ¥1 million to ¥50 million, whereas the personal net worth of ultra-high net worth individuals (UHNWIs) is ¥50 million and above. As a latecomer, the Global Wealth Report clearly references the World Wealth Report, and its structure and content are similar in many ways. The Global Wealth Report's analysis of HNWIs also draws on the World Wealth Report, dividing them into HNWIs and UHNWIs. Nevertheless, the Global Wealth Report is richer than the World Wealth Report in its analysis of the UHNWI population. The number of HNWIs and UHNWIs mentioned in the Global Wealth Report from 2010 to 2020 are shown in Table 1.

As shown in Table 1, the number of HNWIs worldwide increased from 24.5 million in 2010 to 51.9 million in 2020. In other words, the global HNWI population more than doubled from 2010 to 2020. Looking at the UHNWI population, the number of global UHNWIs increased from 81,000 in 2010 to 176,000 in 2020, also more than doubling. Clearly, the overall increase in this population is still relatively rapid.

## 2.2 *Situation in China*

The Global Wealth Report also pays close attention to changes in China's high net worth population. In the relevant part of the report, data are generally provided separately for China. This is related to the increasing size of the HNWI population created by China's continuous economic growth and the fact that this segment of the population in China accounts for an increasingly high proportion of its global counterpart. Consequently, China has become one of the countries on which the Global Wealth Report focuses. The number of HNWIs and UHNWIs in China from 2010 to 2020 listed in the Global Wealth Report is shown in Table 2.

As shown in Table 2, the number of HNWIs in China has increased from 800,000 in 2010 to 5.71 million in 2020, a rate higher than the rate of increase in global HNWIs during the same period. In terms of the size of the UHNWI population, the number of UHNWIs in China increased from 4,000 in 2010 to 21,090 in 2020. Clearly, the size of China's UHNWI population in 2020 was more than five times that in 2010. Additionally, this growth rate significantly exceeded that of the global UHNWI

**Table 1** Number of HNWIs and UHNWIs, 2010 to 2020

| | 2010 | 2011 | 2012 | 2013 | 2014 | 2015 | 2016 | 2017 | 2018 | 2019 | 2020 |
|---|---|---|---|---|---|---|---|---|---|---|---|
| HNWIs | 24.5 | 29.6 | 28.5 | 31.4 | 35 | 33.6 | 33 | 35.9 | 42 | 46.8 | 51.9 |
| UHNWIs | 0.081 | 0.085 | 0.085 | 0.099 | 0.128 | 0.124 | 0.141 | 0.148 | 0.150 | 0.168 | 0.176 |

**Table 2** Number of HNWIs and UHNWIs in China, 2010 to 2020

| | 2010 | 2011 | 2012 | 2013 | 2014 | 2015 | 2016 | 2017 | 2018 | 2019 | 2020 |
|---|---|---|---|---|---|---|---|---|---|---|---|
| HNWIs | 0.8 | 1 | 1 | 1 | 1.2 | 1.3 | 1.6 | 2 | 3.5 | 4.68 | 5.71 |
| UHNWIs | 4000 | 5400 | 4700 | 5830 | 7600 | 9600 | 11,000 | 18,100 | 16,510 | 18,130 | 21,090 |

population during the same period. This shows that with the strong development of China's economy, its HNWI population is rapidly expanding, accounting for an increasingly high proportion of the global HNWI population. In other words, China's fast-growing economy is highly efficient in creating HNWIs.

In China, China Merchants Bank (CMB), through a partnership with Bain & Company, has been conducting a study of HNWIs and releasing a China Private Wealth Report every two years from 2009. The 2009 China Private Wealth Report defined individuals with investable assets over 10 million RMB as HNWIs and individuals with investable assets over 100 million RMB as UHNWIs [16]. Investable assets include the individual's financial assets and investment properties. Individuals' financial assets include cash, deposits, stocks, bonds, funds, insurance, bank wealth management products, offshore funds, and other investments (commodity futures, gold, etc.) and exclude assets such as home ownership properties, equity in non-listed companies, and consumer durables. To date, China Merchants Bank and Bain & Company have released seven China Private Wealth Reports. The relevant profiles of China's HNWIs from 2008 to 2020 obtained from these seven reports are shown in Table 3.

As shown in Table 3, the number of HNWIs in China surged from 300,000 in 2008 to 2.62 million in 2020, an expansion of more than 7.7 times. The total amount of investable assets owned by this group increased rapidly from 8.8 trillion yuan in 2008 to 96 trillion yuan in 2020. This growth rate was very fast. The per capita investable assets of HNWIs reached 36.6 million RMB in 2020. According to the data in the 2021 China Private Wealth Report, the number of Chinese HNWIs exceeded 3 million in 2021.

The 2017 China High Net Worth Population Data Analysis Report, jointly released by Minsheng Wealth, the National Finance and Development Laboratory of the Chinese Academy of Social Sciences (NLFD), analyzed the general characteristics, asset allocation preferences, current living conditions, and travel and consumption preferences of China's high-net-worth population [17]. In this report, HNWIs refer to the group with a net asset value of 6 million RMB or more, which is also the social group with more investable assets, such as financial assets and investment properties.

**Table 3** HNWIs in China, 2008 to 2020

| | 2008 | 2010 | 2012 | 2014 | 2016 | 2018 | 2020 |
|---|---|---|---|---|---|---|---|
| Number of HNWIs (10,000) | 30 | 50 | 70 | 100 | 158 | 197 | 262 |
| Investible assets per capita (million dollars) | 29 | 30 | 31 | 30 | 31 | 30.9 | 36.6 |
| Total investable assets (trillion yuan) | 8.8 | 15 | 22 | 32 | 49 | 61 | 96 |

If the group's net asset value were converted to U.S. dollars at the average exchange rate of 6.75 between the RMB and the U.S. dollar in 2017, HNWIs are a group with a net asset value of ¥890,000 or more. In addition, this definition includes investment properties among investable assets. After defining HNWIs, the 2017 China High Net Worth Population Data Analysis Report mentioned that the total number of China's HNWIs reached 1.97 million in 2017, with total investable assets of approximately 65 trillion yuan. Overall, this report is slightly more optimistic than the 2019 China Private Wealth Report. The data in the 2019 China Private Wealth Report show that in 2018, China's high net worth population numbered 1.97 million people, with total investable assets of 61 trillion yuan.

This situation suggests that the reports released by China Merchants Bank (CMB) and Bain & Company are relatively more conservative in their estimates of China's HNWI population and assets. Since the 2019 China Private Wealth Report was released in June 2019 and the 2017 China High Net Worth Population Data Analysis Report was released in December 2017, it cannot be ruled out that the former referred to the latter's relevant content before its release. Both reports estimate the number of HNWIs in China to be 1.97 million. It is difficult to consider this a coincidence. However, this perspective suggested that China's HNWI population would exceed 2 million by 2020. This conclusion is supported by the two aforementioned reports.

However, the data in the 2018 Global Wealth Report show that China's HNWI population numbered 2 million in 2017 and 3.5 million in 2018. Although the criterion for HNWIs in the 2018 Global Wealth Report is US¥1 million in investable assets, a figure much higher than the US¥890,000 in the 2017 China High Net Worth Population Data Analysis Report, both reports estimate essentially the same number of HNWIs. This suggests that the estimates in the 2017 China High Net Worth Population Data Analysis Report are more optimistic than those in the 2018 Global Wealth Report. By comparison, it is easy to see that different studies have different measurement standards for China's HNWI population, and the estimated population size is also different.

## 2.3 Debate on Measurement Criteria

The definition of HNWIs has not been standardized in the financial industry owing to differences in business. For example, Citibank's private banking division requires members to have assets in excess of ¥3 million, while Chase Manhattan Bank's private banking division requires members to have assets in excess of ¥1 million. These are the asset thresholds for high-net-worth clients. However, different institutions have different perspectives regarding this. Data regarding marketing financial services for HNWIs compiled by Datamonitor, an independent London-based strategic management consulting firm, show that the high-net-worth portfolio size is ¥500,000 to 750,000 in assets, not more than ¥3 million [18]. In other words, the asset threshold for high-net-worth clients is ¥500,000, not ¥3 million. Clearly, the criteria of independent research institutions and financial institutions differ.

In China, the "Guiding Opinions on Regulating Asset Management Business of Financial Institutions" issued by People's Bank of China, China Banking and Insurance Regulatory Commission, China Securities Regulatory Commission, and State Administration of Foreign Exchange in 2018 stipulates that the entry threshold for qualified individual investors is: family financial net worth of not less than 3 million yuan, family financial assets of not less than 5 million yuan, or an average annual income (of the individual) of not less than 400,000 yuan in the last 3 years. This is an official standard that emphasizes financial assets and income and does not involve investment properties. If we refer to this standard, individuals with household financial assets of 5 million RMB and above are HNWIs.

Although the aforementioned document stipulates the threshold for individual investors, many banks currently do not use the aforementioned criteria when identifying high net worth customers. For example, when customers subscribe to financial products, one of the threshold criteria of banks is: natural persons whose individual or family financial assets total more than 1 million RMB and natural persons whose individual annual income exceeded 200,000 RMB in the last three years or whose combined spousal income (annual) exceeded 300,000 RMB in the last three years. Obviously, this standard is lower than the officially released standard for qualified individual investors. Operationally, banks emphasize the joint income of an individual and their spouse. An important reason for banks to adopt this criterion is their realistic business needs. If the standard for HNWIs is set too high, the size of this group of customers will be smaller for some bank branches according to the principle of "local management and hierarchical responsibility" followed by banks for their customers, in which case banks will be unable to achieve economies of scale in their services. According to the actual situation of the bank's business and local customers, the bank adopts a lower standard for high net worth customers, which helps ensure a considerable scale of high net worth customers and achieve scale benefits in management and service. In fact, the bank's standard for high-net-worth clients is closer to that for medium-net-worth clients.

The issue of defining high net worth clients from the bank's perspective is emphasized here. Nowadays, there are different standards for defining HNWIs in society, and they are generally established according to the theory of wealth stratification, which is a standard in the theoretical sense. However, banks need to establish operable criteria for defining high-net-worth customers based on objective reality. These criteria, based on business needs, are established in direct accordance with the characteristics of local customer stratification. Generally, such criteria are more relevant to a bank's specific business. Therefore, when studying the criteria for defining the high-net-worth customers of banks, it is important to distinguish between the bank's business perspective and the theoretical one.

Generally, in theoretical studies, the standard for defining HNWIs is slightly higher. The Global Family Business Research Center of the Wudaokou School of Finance of Tsinghua University, in cooperation with the Private Banking Professional Committee of the China Banking Association, conducted a survey study of its standing committee (27 commercial banks) and 1,056 private banking clients from 21 of them from 2018 to 2019. The survey study showed that the statistical caliber of the asset size of HNW clients of private banks was 6 million yuan [5]. This standard is higher than the standard of ¥5 million RMB for qualified individual investors, but somewhat lower than the international standard of ¥1 million US dollar. Of course, some studies set the standard higher than USD 1 million, such as a study on the consumption characteristics of HNWIs and their lifestyles, in which HNWIs refer to those with investable assets of USD 10 million and above [19]. In addition, in 2019, HNW and Wu Xiaobo Channel jointly launched the 2019–2020 China HNW Wealth Report, which proposed that family assets of 6 million to 10 million RMB is the threshold for HNWIs and that approximately 60% of high-net-worth families have investable assets in this range. Of course, some studies and reports point out that HNWIs generally refer to the group with net assets of more than 10 million RMB, which is also the social group with more investable assets, such as financial assets and investment properties.

Taikang Insurance Group and Hurun Report have jointly published the annual "China High Net Worth People's Medical and Health Care White Paper" since 2015. In the 2015 White Paper on Medical Care for China's High Net Worth Individuals, HNWIs were defined as those with total personal assets of more than 10 million RMB. The assets of HNWIs include fixed and liquid assets owned by individuals. Fixed assets include listed or unlisted equity, owner-occupied properties, and investment properties owned by individuals, while liquid assets include stocks, funds, bonds, deposits, and insurance. It is worth noting that the assets of HNWIs explicitly include owner-occupied properties. This indicates that owner-occupied properties can also be included among the assets of HNWIs. Following the 2015 paper, Taikang Insurance Group and Hurun Report released the "2016 China High Net Worth People's Medical and Health Care White Paper" and "2017 China High Net Worth People's Medical and Health Care White Paper" consecutively. However, the collaboration between Taikang Insurance Group and Hurun Report did not continue past three years. By the time the 2020 White Paper on Medical Care for China's Mid-High Net Worth Individuals was released, the theme of the report had changed, and Hurun Report was no longer partnered with Taikang Insurance Group. Thus, many things are changing quietly.

## 3 Mid-High Net Worth Individuals

There are three main trends in the study of the social distribution of wealth. The first trend focuses on the study of individuals at the top of the wealth pyramid, such as the study of the number, characteristics, consumption patterns, and investment and financial needs of ultra-high net worth individuals [20]. Of course, the public regards this group with ambivalence, and sociologists focus more on studying the social roles played by this group [21]. The second trend focuses on the bottom of the wealth pyramid, such as the "wealth at the bottom of the pyramid," as emphasized by C. K. Prahalad, who stressed the importance of serving more than 4 billion poor people [22]. This trend has been reinforced in the area of financial inclusion. For example, Muhammad Yunus, the Bangladeshi economist known as the "banker of the poor," was awarded the Nobel Peace Prize. The third trend focuses on middle-income groups [23]. In the West, the term commonly used is the middle class. For example, in the United Kingdom, the middle class began to rise as early as the Victorian era with a large amount of social wealth [24]. As an important force for social stability, the size of the middle class or middle-income group and its wealth are topics of general interest to all sectors of society. The three trends mentioned above are the three main directions of the current study on the social distribution of wealth.

As competition in the banking industry continues to intensify, its competition for customer resources with a relatively high net worth has become more intense. Since the size of the high net worth group is limited, banks will adopt the strategy of tilting and extending their services to the mid net worth group according to their business needs to actively pursue this group, consolidate and expand the size of their customers, and improve their competitiveness. Compared with high net worth clients, mid net worth clients have fewer investable assets, but the size of this group is much larger than that of the high net worth group. Moreover, in terms of the wealth appreciation trend, this group has the highest probability of growing into a high net worth group. Therefore, on one hand, banks extend their services from the high net worth group to the mid net worth group to expand the scale of customers and achieve the scale benefit of financial services. On the other hand, to cultivate more high net worth customers, they try to nurture the mid net worth group deeply to help them achieve wealth preservation and appreciation, and thus transform them into a high net worth group. Clearly, serving the mid net worth group is not only a tactical need for banks, but also a strategic one.

In practice, banks generally integrate middle and high net worth customers to provide targeted financial services and refer to them collectively as mid-high net worth customers. The reason for such an arrangement, apart from gaining economies of scale in financial services, is that mid-high net worth individuals are dynamic and changing. In reality, high net worth individuals may become mid net worth individuals owing to investment mistakes, etc. A mid net worth individual may become a high net worth individual through wealth appreciation. Therefore, both high net worth individuals and mid nct worth individuals are in a dynamic state of change. This requires banks to serve mid-high net worth individuals dynamically according to the reality, and therefore, they usually study and provide services to mid-high net worth individuals as a whole.

## 3.1 Global Situation

As a latecomer in the field of mid-high net worth research, the Global Wealth Report has surpassed the World Wealth Report. For example, the Global Wealth Report generally publishes a data report (Databook) along with its publication, so that relevant institutions and people can easily access relevant statistics. Additionally, although the Global Wealth Report does not directly present the concept of the mid net worth group, it implicitly contains statistics and information on the wealth of this group. For example, the Global Wealth Report presents the distribution of wealth among different groups in the form of a wealth pyramid. The report ranks individual assets from high to low, forming a four-level wealth pyramid structure from top to bottom. The first tier (top tier) comprises individuals with ¥1 million or more in assets, the second tier, individuals with ¥100,000 to ¥1 million in assets, the third tier, individuals with ¥10,000 to 100,000 in assets, and the fourth tier (bottom tier) comprises individuals with less than ¥10,000 in assets. In this report, the third tier is referred to as the middle class, and the second and first tiers are referred to as the high wealth class, which can be considered to comprise mid-high net worth individuals, respectively.

The Global Wealth Report collectively refers to the segment with personal assets of ¥100,000 and above as the high wealth segment. Although the report does not explicitly define this class as mid-high net worth individuals, it provides very detailed statistics (see Table 4) and analysis of this class. From the perspective of personal assets, this class comprises middle and high net worth individuals.

As shown in Table 4, the number of individuals with personal assets of ¥100,000 and above increased from 358.2 million in 2010 to 641.9 million in 2020. Overall, there was a clear trend of increase, especially from 2016 to 2020, during which time there was a continuous increase. Of course, in 2012 and 2015, the size of this population decreased from the previous year. This was closely related to the overall global economic development at the time. Related to the change in population size is the change in the proportion of people in this group in the global adult population. The share of the number of people in the high wealth class in the global adult population from 2010 to 2020 is shown in Table 5.

As shown in Table 5, the share of the global adult population with personal assets of ¥100,000 and above increased from 7.9% in 2010 to 12.4% in 2020. In other words, by 2020, about 1 in 9 people worldwide had assets of ¥100,000 or more.

**Table 4** Number of people in the high wealth class, 2010 to 2020

| Number of people | 2010 | 2011 | 2012 | 2013 | 2014 | 2015 | 2016 | 2017 | 2018 | 2019 | 2020 |
|---|---|---|---|---|---|---|---|---|---|---|---|
| First layer | 24.2 | 29.7 | 29 | 32 | 35 | 34 | 33 | 36 | 42 | 47 | 51.9 |
| Second layer | 334 | 369 | 344 | 361 | 373 | 349 | 365 | 391 | 436 | 499 | 590 |
| Aggregate | 358.2 | 398.7 | 373 | 393 | 408 | 383 | 398 | 427 | 478 | 546 | 641.9 |

**Table 5** Number of individuals in the high wealth class as a share of the global adult population, 2010 to 2020

| Proportion of people | 2010 | 2011 | 2012 | 2013 | 2014 | 2015 | 2016 | 2017 | 2018 | 2019 | 2020 |
|---|---|---|---|---|---|---|---|---|---|---|---|
| First layer | 0.5 | 0.5 | 0.6 | 0.7 | 0.7 | 0.7 | 0.7 | 0.7 | 0.8 | 0.9 | 1 |
| Second layer | 7.4 | 8.2 | 7.5 | 7.7 | 7.9 | 7.4 | 7.5 | 7.9 | 8.7 | 9.8 | 11.4 |
| Aggregate | 7.9 | 8.7 | 8.1 | 8.4 | 8.6 | 8.1 | 8.2 | 8.6 | 9.5 | 10.7 | 12.4 |

Overall, there was a clear upward trend, especially during the 2015–2020 period, which showed a continuous rise.

The change in the size of this population is closely related to the change in its total wealth. In general, the larger the population size, the more total wealth it has. The total wealth owned by the high-wealth class from 2010 to 2020 is shown in Table 6.

As shown in Table 6, the total wealth owned by the high-wealth class increased from ¥154.2 trillion in 2010 to ¥335.1 trillion in 2020. Excluding 2012 and 2015, there was a continuous upward trend from 2010 to 2020. In other words, 2012 and 2015 were the exceptions in which the total wealth owned by the high wealth class decreased slightly from the previous year. A comparison of Tables 4 and 6 shows that the change in the total wealth owned by this class is consistent with the change in the number of people, and the total wealth decreased in 2012 and 2015, while it increased in the remaining years. The total wealth owned by the high-wealth class as a share of the total world wealth shows a similar trend (see Table 7).

As shown in Table 7, the proportion of total wealth owned by the high wealth class to the total world wealth increased from 79.3% in 2010 to 83.9% in 2020. Looking at the top two tiers of the wealth pyramid, the share of total wealth owned by the first tier in the world's total wealth is generally on the rise, from 35.6% in 2010 to 43.4%

**Table 6** Total wealth owned by the high wealth class, 2010 to 2020

| Total wealth | 2010 | 2011 | 2012 | 2013 | 2014 | 2015 | 2016 | 2017 | 2018 | 2019 | 2020 |
|---|---|---|---|---|---|---|---|---|---|---|---|
| First layer | 69.2 | 89.1 | 87.5 | 98.7 | 115.9 | 112.9 | 116.6 | 128.7 | 142 | 158.3 | 173.3 |
| Second layer | 85 | 100.6 | 95.9 | 101.8 | 108.6 | 98.5 | 103.9 | 111.4 | 124.7 | 140.2 | 161.8 |
| Aggregate | 154.2 | 189.7 | 183.4 | 200.5 | 224.5 | 211.4 | 220.5 | 240.1 | 266.7 | 298.5 | 335.1 |

**Table 7** Total wealth owned by the high wealth class as a share of the total world wealth from 2010 to 2020

| Proportion of total wealth | 2010 | 2011 | 2012 | 2013 | 2014 | 2015 | 2016 | 2017 | 2018 | 2019 | 2020 |
|---|---|---|---|---|---|---|---|---|---|---|---|
| First layer | 35.6 | 38.5 | 39.3 | 41 | 44 | 45.2 | 45.6 | 45.9 | 44.8 | 43.9 | 43.4 |
| Second layer | 43.7 | 43.6 | 43.1 | 42.3 | 41.3 | 39.4 | 40.6 | 39.7 | 39.3 | 38.9 | 40.5 |
| Aggregate | 79.3 | 82.1 | 82.4 | 83.3 | 85.3 | 84.6 | 86.2 | 85.6 | 84.1 | 82.8 | 83.9 |

in 2020. However, the share of total wealth owned by the second tier in the world's total wealth shows a slight downward trend, from 43.7% in 2010 to 40.5% in 2020. This shows that these two tiers of the wealth pyramid generally show a trend of "the rich getting richer," which indicates that wealth is further concentrated among the richest people.

## 3.2 Situation in China

There are relatively few studies on the middle- and high-net-worth group in China. However, in recent years, some organizations have started to pay attention to research on this group. On August 20, 2019, Xinhua, together with Taiping Life, released the "Blue Book on Insurance Protection Needs of Mid-High Net Worth People" in Beijing. The survey in this report targets the middle- and high-net-worth population, comprising middle- and high-net-worth individuals and high-net-worth individuals [25]. In terms of specific definitions, the report uses total personal investable assets as a criterion for identifying mid-high net worth individuals. Those with total personal investable assets of ¥3 million to 6 million are defined as mid-high net worth individuals, while high net worth individuals have total investable assets of ¥6 million or more. However, the report does not clearly define what comprises investable assets. The age of the survey respondents ranged from 25 to 55 years. In terms of survey city distribution, first-tier cities are the main ones, while second-tier and third-tier cities are covered. Clearly, this report targets the MHNWIs in urban areas.

Compared with past reports that have studied HNWIs, this report has several distinctive features.

First, according to the information I have so far, this is the first research report on MHNWIs in China, and the research object is no longer high net worth people, which is very innovative. This indicates that the insurance industry is no longer only focusing on the high net worth group, but has started to consider and study the overall situation of the mid-high net worth group, including the mid net worth group, and its needs in terms of insurance protection in a more systematic manner. From this perspective, this report represents an important milestone.

Second, as the title of this report, "Returning to the Origin and Exploring the Blue Ocean," suggests, this report begins to recognize the origins of HNWIs and mid net worth individuals and emphasizes research based on "origin." In exploring the origin of the demand for insurance coverage, the report no longer focuses only on the study of the HNWI population, because the size of this segment of society is limited, but extends focus to the study of the broader mid-high net worth population, which may be the "origin" of society's demand for insurance coverage. This is one of the basic assumptions in this report. Although this hypothesis may not be fully valid (for example, the low income segment of society also has corresponding insurance protection needs), the realistic basis of this hypothesis becomes more solid as the research population is extended from the high net worth group to the mid-high net worth group.

Again, this report aims to find and explore the "blue ocean" of the insurance industry, and the research is strategic and forward-looking. This indicates that competition in the HNWI market is already very intense and is becoming increasingly fierce. The products and services offered by the banking industry to HNWIs are becoming increasingly homogeneous, and profits in this market are decreasing. Therefore, the banking industry needs to find and explore new markets, the so-called "blue ocean markets" [26]. Compared with the HNWI market, the mid net worth market has not received sufficient attention from the traditional insurance industry. Therefore, the insurance industry considers this market a "blue ocean market" that needs to be explored, and exploring the mid-high net worth population is an important way for the insurance industry to move from a "red ocean strategy" to a "blue ocean strategy."

Finally, although this report is not very long (44 pages), it is relatively complete, including not only the current situation and basic characteristics of MHNWIs, their pursuit of wealth, and wealth inheritance, but also their specific needs and preferences for insurance coverage. This report also distinguishes between male and female MHNWIs when analyzing MHNWIs, resulting in a more in-depth and detailed analysis. Therefore, except for the lack of information regarding asset allocation of MHNWIs, this report is relatively complete, and the logic of its analysis and ideas are also clear.

A comparison of the "Blue Book on Insurance Protection Needs of Mid-High Net Worth Individuals" and the "2020 White Paper on Medical Care for China's Mid-High Net Worth Individuals" shows that they have different criteria for defining mid-high net worth individuals. The "Blue Book on Insurance Protection Needs of Mid-High Net Worth People" classifies a person with investable assets above 3 million RMB as a mid-high net worth individual, while in the "2020 White Paper on Medical Care for China's Mid- High Net Worth Individuals," a mid-high net worth individual is defined as a person with investable assets above 1 million RMB and aged 30 years or above. Investable assets include cash, deposits, funds, stocks, bonds, insurance, and other relatively liquid assets, but do not include fixed assets, such as real estate. From this definition standard, the following two points are worthy of attention: one is that the assets are held as a household unit, not as an individual unit, and the other is that investable assets do not include investment properties. This indicates that there is no universally accepted standard for defining mid-high net worth individuals. Different studies have proposed suitable and actionable definition criteria according to their respective needs.

Regarding the sample distribution in the "2020 White Paper on Medical Care for China's Mid-High Net Worth Individuals," it adopts a stratified random sampling method for 29 first-tier to third-tier cities, including Beijing, Shanghai, and Tianjin, and selects 1,185 mid-high net worth individuals as survey respondents. Therefore, the survey study focuses on urban areas and does not involve mid-high net worth individuals in rural areas. In other words, the criteria for defining mid-high net worth individuals in this report are applicable to urban areas; however, whether they are applicable to rural areas requires further research. Overall, a common feature of the report is that it focuses on MHNWIs in urban areas of China and lacks research on MHNWIs in rural areas.

In terms of content, this report focuses on the status, needs, and challenges of mid-high net worth individuals and their families in terms of healthcare and retirement, including their perception of longevity, choice of retirement life, and health. In terms of wealth, this report includes the income and financial characteristics of mid-high net worth individuals. The report points out that the main sources of income for mid-high net worth individuals are salary and financial income. The share of rental income increases with age, and it becomes the main source of income for those aged 60 years and above. However, this report has the issue that property is not included among investable assets when defining mid-high net worth individuals, but not only rental income but also income from buying and selling property is considered when calculating the income of mid-high net worth individuals. In other words, investment properties are an important source of income for mid-high net worth individuals. Most mid-high net worth individuals own investment properties. For example, for mid-high net worth individuals aged 60 and above, their combined income from rentals and buying and selling properties accounts for 62% of their total income. Clearly, this is a departure from this report's criteria for classifying mid-high net worth individuals. This report's exclusion of investment properties from investable assets is open to question.

In terms of asset allocation, this report points out that mid-high net worth individuals allocate 26% of their funds to bank wealth management products and 22% to bank deposits. These are the two main allocation products for this group. Stocks, insurance, and funds are the three categories of secondary allocation products. This raises another question about the criteria for classifying mid-high net worth individuals, which is whether to include the value of the financial products held in investable assets. Many definitions of investable assets do not consider the value of financial products. However, mid-high net worth individuals generally have strong financial management skills and own a large number of financial products. Therefore, this is an issue that needs further study. In terms of insurance protection, this report points out that mid-high net worth individuals have a high allocation ratio in life and health insurance, but there are still problems of omission and mismatch in specific types of insurance, especially when the allocation ratio of annuity insurance is low. Even though this report focuses on health care issues, it also analyzes the asset allocation and insurance protection issues of mid-high net worth individuals.

It is worth noting that the appendix section of this report covers country and industry studies. It summarizes and compares the experience of each country in terms of health care by examining the policies and developments in Japan, the United States, Germany, the United Kingdom, and China, and then complements the research on mid-high net worth individuals. Although the relevant country studies are relatively brief, qualitative, and do not provide relevant data, the idea of analyzing and exploring healthcare issues through international comparison is of value. In particular, the evaluation of specific policies and their effects in different countries is an important part of the research on mid-high net worth individuals.

## 3.3 *Development of the Concept of Mid-High Net Worth*

In September 2004, Insurance Brokers Monthly published a supplement entitled "High Net Worth." The last article in this supplement was "Mid Net Worth." The article was written by Saunders Adrian, the then head of Zurich Insurance Group's mid net worth business. As the title indicates, Zurich was already providing financial insurance services to the mid net worth population. The Datamonitor data cited in this article indicated that the number of mid net worth individuals in the UK with liquid assets of £30,000 to £200,000 would reach 7 million by 2007 [27]. If we consider the exchange rate of RMB to GBP at the time, then the corresponding RMB assets would have been 450,000–3 million RMB. This was the asset criterion provided by Datamonitor at the time regarding the mid net worth population in the UK. According to Datamonitor, the number of mid net worth individuals in the UK was 7 million in 2007, and as the total population was 61.3 million at the time, it can be estimated that the proportion of mid net worth individuals in the UK was about 11% of the total population, which means that approximately 1 in 10 British people were in the middle-income group.

The per capita GDP in the UK at the time was approximately £50,600, equivalent to ¥357,000. According to the international per capita GDP ranking at the time, the UK ranked 16th, ahead of the US (18th). China's per capita GDP at the time was only ¥2,693, ranking 129th worldwide. As you can see, the UK was a relatively wealthy country at the time. By 2020, according to data published by the International Monetary Fund, China's per capita GDP had reached US¥10,484, ranking 63rd in the world. Thus, as China's economy continues to grow rapidly, the size of its mid net worth population continues to grow and its share in the total population continues to increase. However, further research is required to determine the current share of the mid net worth population in the total population. Since China's per capita GDP is still far below that of the UK in 2007, a basic assumption is that the current share of MNAs in China is lower than the share of MNAs in the UK in 2007. In other words, there should be less than 1 MNA per 10 people in China.

In the aforementioned article, Adrian Saunders described the defining criteria of Zurich Insurance Company. He pointed out that Zurich Insurance Company integrated mid-high net worth clients with an asset threshold of £80,000 [27]. In other words, Zurich Insurance Company served mid-high net worth customers with personal assets of £80,000, which is equivalent to ¥1.2 million. As can be seen, this criterion differs from Datamonitor's, which has an entry threshold of ¥450,000. An important reason for this difference is the difference in research perspectives. Zurich Insurance Company defined mid-high net worth clients from a business perspective, while Datamonitor defined mid-high net worth individuals from a social monitoring perspective. The difference between the two reflects the difference between the two concepts of mid-high net worth population and mid-high net worth client. The term mid-high net worth population emphasizes the objective existence of such a group in society with a potential demand for specific financial and insurance services. Mid-high net worth customers are the direct service targets of banks, insurance companies, and other financial institutions, as customers who not only have potential needs but also have realistic and urgent needs. In other words, a part of the mid-high net worth group will be transformed into mid-high net worth customers of banks, insurance companies, and other financial institutions. Therefore, in general, the definition standard of mid-high net worth customers will be slightly higher than that of mid-high net worth individuals.

In 2008, Insurance Brokers Monthly published an article entitled " Mid-high Net Worth: Merging the definitions". The article was written by David Sweeney, head of personal and commercial insurance at Sterling Insurance Group [28]. The article presents an important point: Today's mid net worth clients are tomorrow's high net worth buyers. Therefore, there is a need to merge the mid net worth and high net worth populations. It should be said that David Sweeney clarified the motivation behind the focus of banks, insurance companies, and other financial institutions on the mid net worth population and the concept of mid-high net worth clients. Of course, Sweeney mentioned that although the merger of these two concepts brought opportunities to the insurance industry, it also raised some problems and challenges. However, insurance players would not give up in the face of new business opportunities. An article in the February 5, 2015 issue of Reaction revealed that Brit Insurance had launched a new Managing General Agent (MGA) called Horizon, which would underwrite business for the mid-high net worth markets [29]. According to the paper, Horizon would offer two products: longitude (for mid net worth clients) and latitude (for high net worth clients). This suggests that the insurer had targeted exclusive services for mid net worth and high net worth clients. Of course, in this example of Brit Insurance, not only are the mid net worth and high net worth clients separate from each other, but the services are also separate, and the clients are not combined into a group comprising mid-high net worth clients.

In addition to life insurance, insurers have begun to offer targeted and customized services in property insurance based on the characteristics of the mid-high net worth individuals. According to a report published in the March 2013 issue of Insurance Age, Legal & General Group in the U.K. launched a home insurance product for mid-high net worth clients. The coverage available to mid-high net worth families through the new policy included coverage in excess of £800,000 for buildings and £80,000 for property. High-value items, such as jewelry and watches valued at less than £10,000 or other valuables valued at less than £15,000, were standard and would not need to be specifically listed (IFP, 2013). A very important reason for the success of this family insurance product was that it met the needs of mid-high net worth customers. What mid-high net worth customers really value is the personalized service that the insurance provider provides to them, which means that the insurance provider understands and is able to provide truly valuable and customized services for mid-high net worth customers. Mid-high net worth clients are welcomed by financial institutions, and an increasing number of financial institutions are focusing their business on mid-high net worth individuals [30]. This is a major trend in the development of the financial services industry.

# 4 Criteria and Research Arrangements for Mid-High Net Worth Clients

## *4.1 The Sorting of Relevant Standards*

To define the criteria for mid-high net worth clients, it is necessary to refer to the relevant definition criteria for high net worth and mid net worth individuals. For comparison purposes, this chapter summarizes the asset definition criteria for mid-high net worth individuals from different studies and reports in Table 8, based on the literature research mentioned above.

As shown in Table 8, investable assets are commonly defined for mid-high net worth individuals, but family assets, personal wealth, etc., are defined as well. Investable assets generally include cash, deposits, stocks, bonds, funds, insurance, and other financial assets. There should be no dispute regarding the definition of this aspect, which is commonly adopted. In addition, investable assets generally do not include owner-occupied properties; this is a more general consensus and is not controversial. However, there are different ways to determine whether investment properties need to be included in investable assets. Some studies do not classify investment properties as investable assets; however, some studies do include investment properties among investable assets. Therefore, there are two completely different approaches to the treatment of investment properties.

An investment property is a property held to earn rent or realize capital appreciation (the difference between the purchase and sale of a property), or both. Investment properties should be able to be measured for value and sold separately. In China, the strong demand for investment properties is an important reason for the continuous increase in housing prices, and for this reason, the government has introduced a series of policies to reasonably guide this demand [31]. Of course, the demand for investment home purchases should be viewed dialectically, and from the perspective of household asset management and financial management, investment home purchases are an important strategy to ensure the appreciation of household assets [32]. For long-term investors, the property market is less risky than the stock market. This is because the expectation of long-term appreciation of real estate is recognized by almost all investors [33].

Investable assets should include investment properties for several reasons.

First, the investment property has an important holding value, both for businesses and households as well as individuals, mainly for investment purposes [34]. From the household perspective, investment property is an important way to invest in household assets in China. According to the data in Trends in Wealth Change of Chinese Households under the Epidemic: The China Household Wealth Index Research Report published by Survey and research center for China Household Finance of Southwest University of Finance and Economics (SRCCHF), and Ant Group Research Institute (Ant), factors that influence changes in the wealth of

**Table 8** Asset definition criteria for mid-high net worth individuals in different studies

| | | |
|---|---|---|
| Zurich insurance company | Mid-high net worth | Personal assets of £80,000, equivalent to RMB 1.2 million |
| Datamonitor, Inc | Mid-high net worth | 450,000 RMB |
| Blue book on insurance protection needs of middle and high net worth individuals | Mid-high net worth | Personal investable assets above 3 million RMB |
| White paper on medical care for China's middle and high net worth individuals in 2020 | Mid-high net worth | Individuals with family investable assets above 1 million RMB and aged 30 or above, where investable assets include cash, deposits, funds, stocks, bonds, insurance and other relatively liquid assets, excluding fixed assets such as property |
| Global wealth report | Mid-high net worth | Personal assets of USD 100,000 and above |
| Anderson [9] | Mid-high net worth | Personal assets of USD 100,000 and above |
| White paper on health care for China's high net worth individuals | High net worth | People with total personal assets of ¥10 million or more. The assets of HNWI people include fixed assets and liquid assets owned by individuals. Fixed assets are divided into: listed or unlisted equity owned by oneself, home ownership property, investment property; liquid assets include stocks, funds, bonds, deposits, insurance, etc |
| Gao and Xu [5] | High net worth | The statistical caliber of asset size is uniformly 6 million RMB |
| Zhou et al. [19] | High net worth | Investable assets of RMB 10 million and above |
| China high net worth individuals wealth report, 2019–2020 | High net worth | Family assets of 6 million and above |

(continued)

**Table 8** (continued)

| | | |
|---|---|---|
| Zurich insurance company | Mid-high net worth | Personal assets of £80,000, equivalent to RMB 1.2 million |
| Guiding opinions on regulating asset management business of financial institutions | High net worth | Family financial assets of not less than 5 million RMB |
| Global wealth report | High net worth | Investment assets of USD 1 million |
| 2017 China high net worth individuals data analysis report | High net worth | Net asset value of RMB 6 million or more |
| China private wealth report | High net worth | Investable assets of more than RMB 10 million, investable assets include personal financial assets assets and investment properties. Among them, financial assets include cash, deposits, stocks, bonds, funds, insurance, bank financial products, offshore funds and other investments (commodity futures, gold, etc.), excluding assets such as home ownership property, equity in non-listed companies and consumer durables |

Chinese households cover four major categories: housing assets, financial investment, industrial and commercial operations, and disposable cash. Housing assets and financial investment are the main factors among them, contributing 69.9% and 21.2% to the increase in household wealth, respectively [35]. A considerable portion of housing assets is investment properties. As an important contributor to China's household wealth, household investable assets should not exclude, but include, investment properties.

Second, property is not only the most important component of household wealth, but also the most critical core factor driving the growth of residents' wealth. According to the data in the China Household Wealth Survey Report (2018) released by the China Institute of Economic Trends in the Economic Daily, in terms of growth, the net value of household property in China grew by 15.56% in 2017, a growth rate higher than that of household wealth. For national residents, the increase in net property value accounted for 68.74% of the increase in per capita household wealth in 2017 [36]. Hence, it can be surmised that investment properties contribute similarly to the growth of household investable assets, with a contribution rate of 60–70%. Therefore, the role of investment properties as a core factor driving the growth of household investable assets cannot be ignored. Only by including investment properties in the scope of household investable assets can the size of household investable assets in China be objectively measured.

Third, an active second-hand property transaction market allows investment properties to be quickly liquidated in a short period through their sale or rental and their conversion into a more liquid capital. According to the second-hand property transaction data from BEKE, the average transaction cycle of second-hand properties in Guangzhou is 25.9 months, Shenzhen is 24.8 months, Beijing is 11.4 months, Shanghai is 9.5 months, and Hangzhou is 19.5 months. As you can see, houses can generally be sold in as little as one year or as much as two years. If the selling price of the property is reduced appropriately, the sale can be realized even faster. The liquidation of investment properties is faster, and the liquidity of capital is higher. For household investors, the property and stock markets are interchangeable, and capital tends to flow between them. In other words, there is substitutability between investing in property and investing in equities. This suggests that investment properties and stocks have similar investment characteristics from the household investment perspective. Therefore, the calculation of household investable assets must include both financial household assets, such as stocks, and non-financial household assets, such as investment properties and assets with some liquidity.

Based on the above rationale, in this book, investable assets include financial assets, such as cash, deposits, stocks, bonds, funds, and insurance, and investment properties, but not homeownership properties. This book defines high-net-worth clients in banks based on the value of their household investable assets. Specifically, with reference to the criteria of other similar studies, the book defines the criteria for medium- and high-net-worth households as having household investable assets of ¥450,000 and above. It should be noted that such a criterion is consistent with many similar studies and is in line with the objective situation of households in China.

Investment properties are generally measured using an indicator of the market value of properties other than owner-occupied properties [37]. Of course, there are some other measures; for example, in regional and urban studies, the indicator used is the number of second and multiple homes purchased by households as a proportion of property sales [38]. To capture the household investment property situation, studies are generally conducted using random sampling. For example, in 2004, a questionnaire survey conducted in 25 property companies and 1,000 households in 11 districts of Shanghai found that the proportion of investment property purchases was close to 17% [39]. In the study of regional investment property purchases, "hot money speculation" can have a significant impact on the local housing market. For example, in as early as 2010, Chongqing used the coefficient of investment in off-site housing purchases (the ratio of the size of "hot money speculation" to the size of off-site housing purchases) to measure investment housing purchases and found that 70% of these were concentrated to mid-high level residential properties (Yang et al., 2014). A study also used the Urban Household Sample Survey database of the National Bureau of Statistics to select data from 12 representative large and medium-sized cities from 2002 to 2009 as the study sample and used the presence of multiple homes in the household as a dummy variable to study the demand for household investment home purchases, which were found to be one of the three major intrinsic motivations for household re-purchase [40]. Based on the above study, this book uses the indicator of market value of properties other than owner-occupied ones to measure the value of households' investment properties.

## 4.2 The Standard and Content Arrangement of This Book

After considering the research objectives of this book and the characteristics of the current middle-income group in China, the criterion adopted in this book for mid-high net worth households is a household investable asset size of 450,000 RMB. A household with investable assets greater than or equal to 450,000 RMB is a mid-high net worth household; otherwise, it is a non-mid-high net worth household. In this book, household investable assets include the investment properties held by the household as well as the household's cash, deposits, stocks, bonds, funds, insurance, and other financial assets. In the calculation, the total market value of the additional properties held by the family is the value of the family's investment properties. Based on this criterion, this book focuses on the following six research aspects.

The first is the behavioral characteristics of mid-high net worth families. This book analyzes the psychology and behavior of mid-high net worth families and related individuals in a panoramic manner in the areas of mid-high net worth family relationships, network and information, body and health, working conditions, religion, law and politics, spirituality and values, etc., to comprehensively describe and portray the characteristics of this type of family and related individuals, especially regarding their thoughts and behavior.

The second aspect is the financial asset management of mid-high net worth families. This book analyzes and portrays the characteristics, distribution, and development trend of household financial asset allocation of mid-high net worth households and related groups in terms of household participation in financial market investment and management, value of financial products held, proportion of risky financial assets, and household leverage.

The third aspect is the non-financial asset management of mid-high net worth families. This book provides a panoramic portrayal and description of the non-financial assets of these families through the analysis of their allocation of business assets, real estate, consumer durables, etc., and explains the patterns and trends in the allocation process to provide a reference for optimizing household non-financial asset allocation.

The fourth aspect is the allocation of commercial insurance by mid-high net worth families. This book describes the allocation of mid-high net worth families in terms of commercial insurance by analyzing family commercial insurance coverage, family commercial insurance expenditure, and per capita family commercial insurance expenditure.

The fifth aspect is the allocation of children's commercial health insurance by mid-high net worth families. Since children's health is a common concern and is important for mid-high net worth families, we study children's commercial health insurance, analyze the investment of mid-high net worth families in children's commercial health insurance, and then analyze the allocation of children's insurance protection by mid-high net worth families in a comprehensive manner.

The sixth aspect is retirement and insurance in mid-high net worth families. Pursuing a high quality of life in old age is a common characteristic of mid-high net worth families. This book analyzes the allocation of mid-high net worth families in terms of retirement and insurance from the perspective of the number of divorces/pensions or pensions received by families, family pension insurance, and commercial pension insurance coverage.

## *4.3 Features of the Book*

Compared with similar existing studies, this book has several distinctive features, as follows:

First, this book focuses on mid-high net worth families and analyzes the characteristics of these families and individuals in terms of asset allocation and insurance protection from the perspective of families, making this the first systematic work in this field. In the past, most relevant studies focused on high net worth families, and studies on mid net worth families are lacking. Unlike previous studies, this book provides a comprehensive and systematic study and analysis of mid-high net worth families and the population from the perspective of families, resulting in an empirical research report with a quantitative basis, thus providing a new perspective and new evidence to promote the study of mid-high net worth families and the population.

Second, this book uses nationally representative micro-household survey data, and the research results are more objective. This book uses data from the 2020 China Family Panel Studies (CFPS), a nationwide, large-scale, multidisciplinary social tracking survey project that aims to reflect the social, economic, demographic, educational, and health changes in China by tracking and collecting data at three levels: individual, household, and community [41]. The CFPS sample covers 25 provinces, districts, and cities, with a target sample size of 16,000 households, and it includes all members of the sample households [42]. The CFPS questionnaire is divided into four main questionnaire types: the community, household, adult, and pediatric questionnaires, and on this basis, it has continuously developed. The CFPS project is implemented by the Chinese Social Science Survey Center of Peking University. The project uses computer-assisted survey technology to meet diverse design needs, improve interviewing efficiency, and ensure data quality, and it is a major project funded by Peking University and the National Natural Science Foundation of China. Most of the data of previous studies on middle- and high-net-worth populations are not nationally representative. By analyzing the data from the household and adult questionnaires in the 2020 CFPS questionnaire, this book analyzes and studies middle- and high-net-worth households for the first time from the perspective of national scope and level, and it shows the overall picture of middle- and high-net-worth households and individuals in China.

Third, this book delves deep into the family and reveals the micro-decision-making mechanism and influencing factors of mid-high net worth families and individuals in terms of asset allocation and insurance protection. The family is the basic component unit of society and plays a fundamental role in economic and social activities. As a direct result of the growing economy, the annual disposable income of households is increasing, the desire and demand for financial investment and insurance protection are becoming stronger, the demand for diversified financial and non-financial products is increasing, and the asset allocation and insurance protection of mid-high net worth households are becoming increasingly important to the government, industry, and academia. This book finds that factors such as the community in which the household is located and the size of the household affect the financial and insurance decisions of middle- and high-net-worth households and individuals. In addition, the gender, education level, health status, and marital status of the head of the household are also important factors that influence these decisions. This book delves deep into the household and systematically examines and reveals the influence of these factors within the household on the financial and insurance decisions of middle- and high-net-worth households and individuals using research methods including empirical models, which provide important empirical evidence to reveal the decision-making mechanisms of mid-high net worth households and individuals.

## 5 Summary

The main contents of this chapter are as follows.

First, most of the current research focuses on the high net worth group, which has shown a trend of gradual increase in recent years; the proportion of wealth owned by them is rapidly expanding, and their financial investment and management needs have obvious individuality. This is an important market for which banks, insurance companies, and other institutions compete. Currently, competition in this market is becoming increasingly intense, and the problem of homogenization of products in the financial industry is becoming increasingly obvious.

Second, to find the "blue ocean market," the financial industry has been concerned about the extension of customers from high net worth to mid net worth individuals; hence, the concept of mid-high net worth people has been created. This is the inevitable result of market extension and refinement of financial services. Of course, this is related to the increasing wealth of this group. In addition, the rise of the middle-income group, the changes in family wealth patterns, and the profound changes in the way families create, maintain, transmit, and enjoy wealth all drive the further development of asset allocation and the insurance protection needs of mid-high net worth families and individuals.

Third, there is no universally accepted standard for defining mid-high net worth individuals, as the purpose of the study varies by country and region. In terms of operational definition, the size of investable assets is generally taken as a measure. The criterion in this book is household investable assets of 450,000 RMB and above, and the book defines individuals meeting this criterion as mid-high net worth individuals. This definition is in line with the current national conditions in China. Household investable assets are primarily investment properties and financial assets. Of course, it is possible to exclude investment properties from the calculations in some studies. This book argues that considering the specific situation regarding investment properties in China, they should be included among investable assets.

Fourth, this book conducts research on six aspects, namely, the behavioral characteristics, financial asset management, non-financial asset management, commercial insurance allocation, commercial health insurance allocation for children, and retirement and insurance of mid-high net worth families. This research is an attempt to provide a comprehensive and accurate panoramic analysis of China's mid-high net worth families and individuals and provide an important reference basis for the government, financial institutions, and other related institutions.

## References


1. David, A.: Tailored strategies key to servicing mid to high-net-worth investors. Prof. Plan. (48), 60–61
2. Trott, B.: MID NET WORTH: A crucial moment in the fight for MNW. Insurance Brokers' Monthly **58**, 14 (2008)
3. Drig, I., Ni, D., Cucu, I.: Private banking and wealth management services offered by banks. Ann. Univ. Petrosani Econ. **9**, 10–10 (2009)
4. CITIC, CUFE.: *China Private Banking Report 2012*. CITIC Private Banking Center, Central University of Finance and Economics (CUFE), Beijing (2012)
5. Gao, H., Xu.L.: Report, P.B.I.D. Wealth management for high net worth individuals. Tsinghua Finance Rev. **2020**, 107–112 (2018)
6. Gross, D.: Creating value for business owners and ultra-high-net-worth families. Forbes **196**, a2–a2 (2015)
7. CBA, Tsinghua.: China Private Banking Development Report 2019:and White Paper on Family Wealth Management and Inheritance in China;, China Finance Press: Beijing (2020)
8. Conrad, L.: In pursuing HNW investors, banks ignore mass affluent. U.S. Banker **117**, 42 (2007)
9. Anderson, B.: Mass affluent market: just right' for today's producer? Life Insurance Sell. **88**, 8 (2013)
10. NBS.: 60,000–500,000 Yuan: Exploring the middle-income group in urban. Data 39–41 (2005)
11. Long, Y.: Dynamic change of middle-income group size and income polarization in China: statistical description and measurement. Res. Finance Trade 92–99 (2012)
12. Wei, Y.: Targeting key populations and expanding the middle-income group. China Econ. Trade Rev. 73–74 (2022)
13. Latif, A.M., Hanif, M.: Impact of price hike on the standard of living of middle income people: a study on sylhet city, Bangladesh. Manag. Stud. Econ. Syst. **2**, 279–286 (2016)

14. Wang, Q.: The battle for the high net worth client's "Share of Money". China Urban Finance 71–73 (2008)
15. Trovato, E.: Wealth management: the fight is on for high net worth wallet share–the phenomenal expansion of the world's super-rich requires a parallel growth in specialist advisers–a development that has private banks rethinking their recruitment and retention Str. The Banker **8**, 1–5 (2007)
16. CMB; Bain: 2009 China Private Wealth Report. China Merchants Bank, Bain & Company, Beijng (2009)
17. Minsheng, N. L. F. D.: China high net worth individuals data analysis report. Minsheng Wealth, National Laboratory for Finance and Development of the Chinese Academy of Social Sciences Beijing Oriental Guoxin Technology Co., Beijing (2017)
18. Clayton, M.: Optimal high net worth portfolio size is mid-range. Am. Commun. Bank. **7**, 7 (1998)
19. Zhou, C., Wu, Q., Zou, J.: Exploring the consumption characteristics of high net worth individuals and their lifestyles. Soc. Sci. Res. 82–91 (2019)
20. Morison, S., Lincoln, D., Kinnard, B., Ng, Z.Y.: The changing nature of global wealth creation: shifts and trends in the ultra high net worth (UHNW) community. J. Wealth Manag. **16**, 9–14 (2013)
21. Kelly, V.: The rise of the super-rich. Am. Sociol. Rev. **77**, 679–699 (2012)
22. Prahalad, C.K.: The Fortune at the Bottom of the Pyramid: Eradicating Poverty Through Profits. Wharton School Publishing (2004)
23. Yuan, Z., Wan, G., Khor, N.: The rise of middle class in rural China. China Agric. Econ. Rev. **4**, 36–51 (2012)
24. Rubinstein, W.D.: The victorian middle classes: wealth, occupation, and geography. Econ. Hist. Rev. **30**, 602–623 (1977)
25. Xinhua, Taiping.: Blue Paper on the Insurance Protection Needs of Middle and High Net Worth Individuals. Xinhua News Network, Taiping Life, Beijing (2019)
26. Kim, W.C., Mauborgne, R.: Blue Ocean Strategy: How to Create Uncontested Market Space and Make the Competition Irrelevant. Harvard Business Review Press (2015)
27. Adrian, S.: MID-NET WORTH. Insurance Brok. Month. **4** (2004)
28. Sweeney, D.: MID-HIGH NET WORTH: Merging the definitions. Insurance Brok. Month. **58**, 16 (2008)
29. EII.: Brit launches Horizon to cover mid-high net worth market. Reactions 1/5 (2015)
30. Matt, A.G.: Firm opens, plans to pamper mid-rich clients. Am. Bank. **169**, 9 (2004)
31. Li, C.: Countermeasures to the high demand for investment property purchases. The Banker 38–39 (2017)
32. Chen, B.: Investment property purchases can't be killed with a stick. Real Estate World 18–19 (2005)
33. Yang, H.: Talking about investment property purchase. China Real Estate Mark. 62–63 (2009)
34. Cowley, A.: Investment Property. Accountancy **158**, 59–61 (2017)
35. SRCCHF.: Ant. Wealth Change of Chinese Households under the Epidemic: The China Household Wealth Index Research Report Survey and research center for China Household Finance of Southwest University of Finance and Economics (SRCCHF). Ant Group Research Institute (Ant), Chengdu (2020)
36. CIET.: China household wealth survey report 2018. Economic Daily News, Beijing (2018)
37. Huang, J., Cui, G.: Monetization of housing allocation, rising house prices and differentiation of urban residents' housing property gap: an analysis based on household micro survey data. Contemp. Econ. Res. 57–64 (2013)
38. Zhang, H., Yuan, X., Chen, Z., Guo, H.: An empirical analysis of the degree of influence of investment demand on China's house prices. Soft Science **25**, 24–30 (2011)
39. Xiao, Y., Shen, S.: The status of investment property purchase in Shanghai. China Statist. 32–33 (2004)
40. Yang, Z., Zhang, H., Chen, J.: How do potential incentives to repurchase affect the wealth effect of housing?—A micro-level analysis based on large-sample survey data of urban households. Res. Finance Econ. 55–65 (2014)

41. Gu, J., Ming, X.: Perceived social discrimination, socioeconomic status, and alcohol consumption among chinese adults: a nationally representative study. Int. J. Environ. Res. Public Health **17**, 6043 (2020)
42. Gu, J., Zhu, R.: Social capital and self-rated health: empirical evidence from China. Int. J. Environ. Res. Public Health **17**, 9108 (2020)

# Chapter 2
# Behavioral Characteristics of Mid-High Net Worth Families

**Abstract** This chapter provides a panoramic analysis of mid-high net worth families and people through an analysis of the psychology and behavior of different people in the total sample, presenting a viewable and comprehensive picture of the mental and behavioral characteristics of mid-high net worth people, effectively filling the gap in this field and providing important clues for understanding and mastering the situation of mid-high net worth families and people. The results show that the proportion of mid-high net worth households using mobile networks and online learning is higher, but the proportion of online shopping is lower; the average height of mid-high net worth households is slightly higher than that of the total sample; mid-high net worth individuals are more concerned about politics, and the percentage of party members, league members, and union members is higher among mid-high net worth households.

Understanding mid-high net worth families and populations is a common concern among the government, industry, and academia. However, systematic empirical research on mid-high net worth populations is still lacking. The reasons are manifold, such as the fact that high net worth individuals (HNWIs) are increasingly straying from traditional surveys, which leads to the emergence of so-called missing HNWIs [1, 2]. Consequently, patching techniques have emerged for HNWIs [1]. Through these patching techniques, researchers hope to restore the profiles of HNWIs. At the same time, in order to further grasp the characteristics of the HNWI population, more and more "portraits" of this population have been created [3–5]. These "portraits" aim to reveal the characteristics of the mid-high net worth population in order to grasp their needs and thus provide decision support for the introduction of targeted products and services [6]. In 2006, Shenzhen Junrong Wealth Management Institute started to publish the HNWI-China Affluent Wealth Management Index, which provides a 27-dimensional "portrait" of the HNWI population. In 2009, China Merchants Bank and Bain & Company jointly released the 2009 China Private Wealth Report, which systematically tracked the HNWI population and its changing trends. Since then, more and more studies and reports have emerged, making the "portrait" of the



J. Gu, *Wealth Management Report for Mid-High Net Worth Families*, Spatial Demography and Population Governance, https://doi.org/10.1007/978-981-97-0387-6_2

HNWI population blossom. However, most of the current "portraits" of this group focus only on HNWIs, while neglecting the study of mid net worth individuals.

The fact that research on mid-high net worth populations is a gradual process that adopts a behavioral model that goes from the external population characteristics to the internal ones also contributes to the lack of empirical research [7]. Most of these studies start from the behavior of the HNWI population; summarize the general characteristics of this population's behavior and the resulting consumption preferences in finance, financial management, and insurance protection; and propose strategies for customer engagement and marketing of financial institutions [8, 9]. However, existing studies define the behavioral patterns of this population too narrowly, mainly in terms of financial and financial behaviors, while ignoring general social behaviors. This results in a narrow and one-sided perception of the behavioral patterns of the mid-high net worth populations, which are prone to biased judgments. In addition, there is a serious shortcoming in existing research: it rarely explores the thoughts, concepts, and spirituality of mid-high net worth individuals (MHNWIs), making it difficult to truly grasp the spiritual world of mid-high net worth individuals. Only by delving into the spiritual world from behavioral patterns can we reveal the psychological-level influences and behavioral motivations of mid-high net worth individuals, and we can better grasp their needs [10]. Therefore, it is necessary to comprehensively and systematically study the psychological and behavioral characteristics of the mid-high net worth individuals, and to conduct a comprehensive "portrait" in order to gain a comprehensive, objective, and accurate understanding of this group.

This chapter analyzes the psychology and behavior of mid-high net worth individuals in the areas of family relationships, networks and information, physical conditions and health, working conditions, religion, law and politics, and spirituality and values to provide a comprehensive picture of the characteristics of this group, especially what they think and how they behave. This information is an important reference point for the implementation of policies targeting mid-high net worth individuals. Some countries have introduced policies to attract the migration of mid-high net worth individuals [11]. The effective implementation of such policies depends largely on the understanding of the target group. In addition, having this information helps financial institutions design and provide exclusive products and services for this population, thus further gaining their trust and having a greater advantage in fierce competition.

## 1 Family Relations

The family is the basic building block of society, a carrier of family wealth, and the essential foundation of all social relationships. Intrafamily relationships and family perceptions have an impact on the behavior of mid-high net worth individuals. Family relationships, also known as family interpersonal relationships, are inherent in family members. Family relationships are expressed in different ways of contact, communication, and mutual assistance between family members and are the links between family members. Family relations are characterized by marriage and descent, where people related by marriage and descent live together and are manifested by the special mutual behavior of the members of the family.

## 1.1 Distribution of Household Chores

In family relationships, the allocation of time for household chores reflects relationships within the family as well as the division of labor [12, 13]. The statistical results of the allocation of household chores are summarized in Table 1.

As shown in Table 1, 71.98% of mid-high net worth households agreed that men should be responsible for half of household chores. This percentage of mid-high net worth households is significantly lower than that of the total sample (73.59%). This indicates that women are likely to be the primary homemakers within the mid-high net worth households, i.e., the traditional "male heads the household, female heads the household" approach. In mid-high net worth households, men are likely to focus on work as the main labor force and the main generator of household wealth. In addition, it is common for mid-high net worth families to have full-time housewives because of the abundance of family wealth. All of these factors may lead to women in mid-high net worth families to take on the majority of the household chores.

There was no significant difference in childcare between mid-high net worth families and average families, with fathers and mothers devoting time and energy to care for their children. Both parents have equal responsibility in caring for their children in mid-high net worth and ordinary families in total sample. Moreover, there is no substitute for parental status, and parents play an indispensable role in caring for their children. Therefore, there was no significant difference in the care of children between parents in both mid-high net worth families and ordinary families.

In addition, 86.79% of mid-high net worth families agreed that parental care when their children were 0–3 years old had a significant impact on their children's

**Table 1** Statistical results of household chores distribution

| Attributes | Mid-high net worth households | Total sample | Absolute value of the mean difference |
|---|---|---|---|
| Agree that men should take on half of the household chores | 71.98 | 73.59 | $1.61^{**}$ |
| Agree that fathers should invest as much in the care of their children as mothers | 74.99 | 75.48 | 0.49 |
| Agree that how parents treat their children between the ages of 0–3 Have a significant impact on the long-term development of their children | 86.79 | 84.04 | $2.75^{***}$ |

*Note* $^{**}$ $p < 0.05$, $^{***}$ $p < 0.01$

long-term development compared to 84.04% of the total sample. The difference between the two was 2.75 percentage points, which is significant. This indicates that mid-high net worth families place more importance on providing their children with good care during infancy and early childhood to promote healthy and strong growth. For mid-high net worth families, children are the future heirs of family wealth, so they pay special attention to the cultivation of their children. In order not to let their children lose at the beginning, MHS families emphasize on investing in their children's upbringing during infancy.

## *1.2 Relationship Between Children and Parents*

Child-parent relationships are an important component of family relationships. It calculates the mean difference between the mid-high net worth families and the total sample regarding the child-parent relationship, and performs significance tests. The statistical results of the child-parent relationships are summarized in Table 2.

As shown in Table 2, 87.66% of parents are close to their children in mid-high net worth households, which is slightly higher than the 84.64% of the total sample. In this regard, there was a gap; however, the difference was not significant. Overall, the relationship between parents and children was closer in mid-high net worth families.

In terms of parents providing financial help to their children, parents of mid-high net worth families rarely provide financial support to their children, accounting for only 3.62%, which is 12.19 percentage points lower than the total sample of 15.81%, which is a significant gap. This suggests that children who grow up in good financial conditions may receive better education and can pave and prepare for higher-paying jobs and thus become financially independent; therefore, parents of mid-high

**Table 2** Statistical results of children's relationship with their parents

| Attributes | Mid-high net worth Households | Total Sample | Absolute value of the mean difference |
|---|---|---|---|
| Being close to your children | 87.66 | 84.64 | $3.02^{*}$ |
| Providing financial help to children | 3.62 | 15.81 | $12.19^{***}$ |
| Helping children with household chores or childcare | 54.86 | 40.07 | $14.79^{***}$ |
| Financial help from children to parents | 43.82 | 46.65 | 2.83 |
| Child helps parent with household chores or childcare | 36.9 | 34.43 | 2.47 |

*Note* $^{*}$ $p < 0.1$, $^{***}$ $p < 0.01$

net worth families do not have to pay much attention to their children's financial problems. Another possible reason is that parents of mid-high net worth families have already provided good financial protection for their children through family wealth management and have prepared the necessary education money in advance; therefore, they generally do not need to provide financial help to their children.

In addition, parents in middle net worth households are more likely to help their children with household chores or take care of their grandchildren, and this percentage is 54.86%, which is 14.79 percentage points higher than the total sample of 40.07%, which is a significant difference. Because parents of mid-high net worth families invest more in pension insurance coverage than average families, they can generally maintain good health after retirement and have the energy and ability to help their children with some of their household chores or take care of their grandchildren.

There was no significant difference between mid-high net worth households and the average household in terms of children helping their parents financially and children helping their parents with household chores or childcare. The proportion of children helping their parents with household chores or childcare is about 1/3 for both mid-high net worth households, meaning that 2/3 of children generally do not help their parents with household chores or childcare.

## 1.3 Parents' Expectations of Their Children

Parents' expectations of their children can indicate the future direction of family relationships. The statistical results for parents' expectations of their children are summarized in Table 3.

As shown in Table 3, 70.36% of mid-high net worth households agree that having children is for retirement, which is 9.92 percentage points lower than 80.28% of the total sample, which is a significant difference. In other words, approximately 30% of mid-high net worth families do not think that having children is for retirement. Because mid-high net worth individuals generally have adequate pension insurance and protection, they are less likely to retire with the help of their children. In ordinary families, parents tend to focus more on retirement when pension insurance and protection are insufficient.

The percentage of mid-high net worth households agreeing that having children is necessary to continue the family lineage is 64.17%, which is 8.84 percentage points lower than the total sample of 73.01%, a significant difference. This indicates that mid-high net worth individuals are more modernly conscious and differ from traditional society's idea of continuing the family lineage, with about 1/3 of them disagreeing with this idea. Mid-high net worth families, even in terms of passing on family wealth, are likely to give back to society rather than to their children by setting up funds, for example. These concepts are more modern and have changed considerably compared with traditional societies. In addition, a large function of traditional society's concept of a continuing legacy is to solve the problem of retirement. For mid-high net worth individuals, modern insurance and protection systems can not

**Table 3** Statistical results of parents' expectations of their children

| Attributes | Mid-high net worth households | Total sample | Absolute value of the mean difference |
|---|---|---|---|
| To have children so that you can have someone to help you in your old age | 70.36 | 80.28 | 9.92*** |
| Agree to have children in order to continue the family legacy | 64.17 | 73.01 | 8.84*** |
| Agree to have children to help the family financially | 40.61 | 55.24 | 14.63*** |
| Agree to have children for the joy of watching them grow up | 93.33 | 93.87 | 0.54 |
| Agree to have children for the joy of having children around | 93.27 | 94.28 | 1.01** |
| Agree to have children to feel the joy of having a baby | 93.38 | 93.85 | 0.47 |
| Agree to have children to make the family more important | 86.46 | 89.6 | 3.14*** |
| Agree to have children in order to increase the sense of responsibility | 89.17 | 91.52 | 2.35*** |

*Note* ** $p < 0.05$, *** $p < 0.01$

only provide for their retirement but also enable them to have a high quality of life after retirement. As a result, the perception of perpetuating their families gradually changed in relative terms.

The percentage of mid-high net worth families who agreed that they had children to help their families financially was only 40.61%, much lower than the 55.24% of the total sample, a difference of 14.63 percentage points. Overall, the scores in this area were low. More than half of the sample felt that having children was a way to help their families financially. Nowadays, the cost of having children is increasing, and it may not only help the family financially but may also become a heavy financial burden for the family. Consequently, many families are reluctant to have children. About 60% of mid-high net worth families do not believe that having children helps their families financially. Mid-high net worth families are better off financially and do not expect their children to bring more financial benefits to their families.

Parents often have children based on their natural bonds with them. This can be seen in the percentage of those who agree that they have children for the joy of watching them grow up, feeling the joy of having children around them, and feeling the joy of having a baby. In all three areas, the percentages were high (above 93%) for both mid-high net worth families and ordinary families. That is, parents have children not purely based on utilitarian considerations but more based on kinship considerations and needs. This joy in the family is not something that can be measured in terms of financial gain. This differs from Becker's description in the field of family economics.

A total of 86.46% of mid-high net worth households agree that having children is about making the family more important, 3.14 percentage points lower than 89.6% of the total sample, which is a significant difference. This suggests that a smaller percentage of mid-high net worth households hold the idea that having children is a way to highlight the importance of the family, compared to the average household. In addition, 89.17% of mid-high net worth households agree that having children is a way to increase responsibility, compared to 91.52% in the total sample, a significant difference of 2.35 percentage points. In both these aspects, the proportion of mid-high net worth families was lower than that of the total sample. There are various reasons for this phenomenon, one of which may be that mid-high net worth individuals are good at balancing their career and family; family is a part of life, and career is quite important. Therefore, it is not necessary to highlight the importance of the family and the responsibility of having children. That said, there are many ways for mid-high net worth individuals to express their responsibilities to their families.

## 2 Network and Information

In the era of big data, the Internet has become an important and indispensable tool in people's lives and work. As early as 1995, Nicholas Negroponte, a professor at MIT, predicted in his book Digital Survival that "while traditional media such as radio, television, and newspapers are vigorously promoting the Internet, they are not aware that they are cultivating their own gravediggers". With the popularity of smartphones and wireless networks, and the continued increase in Internet speed, the Internet has become an important part of today's social time and space. Internet virtual space–time is already an inseparable part of real space–time.

### *2.1 Network Use*

The books were grouped to calculate different network usages, and the statistics are summarized in Table 4.

As shown in Tablc 4, mid-high net worth households are more likely to use mobile networks than computer networks, and their proportion of Internet access is significantly higher than that of the total sample. The mid-high net worth individuals generally owned high-end smartphones and installed commonly used applications. Smartphones can not only overcome time and space constraints but can also be more convenient. The mid-high net worth individuals will have more time and convenience requirements and are therefore more likely to use mobile networks.

For those who use the Internet, the data in Table 4 show that the proportion of online learning among mid-high net worth households is 31.5%, which is 7.11 percentage points higher than the total sample of 24.39%. Mid-high net worth individuals value education and knowledge more and continue furthering their education and enrich

**Table 4** Statistical results of network usage

| Attributes | Mid-high net worth households | Total sample | Absolute value of the mean difference |
|---|---|---|---|
| Mobile Internet | 79.93 | 64.24 | 15.69*** |
| Computer Internet access | 39.04 | 20.7 | 18.34*** |
| Play online games | 27.34 | 25.32 | 2.02 |
| Online shopping | 36.9 | 56.12 | 19.22*** |
| Watch short videos | 77.55 | 80.77 | 3.22** |
| E-learning | 31.5 | 24.39 | 7.11*** |
| Using WeChat | 98.73 | 97.98 | 0.75 |

*Note* ** $p < 0.05$, *** $p < 0.01$

their cultural knowledge through online learning and other means outside of work. However, for practical reasons, those with regular jobs need to commute to work on time, so they need a more flexible way of learning through the Internet. Among the mid-high net worth households, the proportions of online shopping and watching short videos were 36.9% and 77.55%, respectively, which were significantly lower than those of the total sample of 56.12% and 80.77%; 19.22 and 3.22 percentage points lower, respectively. This shows that mid-high net worth individuals are more likely to use the Internet for learning rather than for entertainment and shopping. However, this does not mean that mid-high net worth individuals do not like online shopping. Some studies have shown that mid-high net worth individuals purchase luxury goods through online platforms [14].

As shown in Table 5, mid-high net worth households spend 28.58 more points per day online on mobile devices than the total sample and 18.178 more points per day online on computers than the total sample. The above results show that mid-high net worth individuals have a higher frequency of Internet access and use the Internet significantly more hours than the total sample. People with good economic conditions can afford the costs associated with using high-speed Internet (e.g., hardware equipment, traffic costs, broadband costs, etc.), which may be one of the reasons for the significant differences between the samples. People with higher economic status may spend more time using the Internet for work and communication. For example, agricultural workers may not spend their labor time mainly on the Internet, but those working in enterprises. For example, agricultural workers may not spend their labor time mainly on the Internet, but employees working in enterprises use the Internet to work more frequently, which is also the reason for the above differences. In conclusion, mid-high net worth individuals are more dependent on the Internet and more likely to use it for communication and cooperation.

Next, the book's statistics on the weighting of high net worth households and the total sample in terms of the perceived importance of the Internet for work, leisure, and entertainment; staying connected with family and friends; studying; and daily life are summarized in Table 6.

**Table 5** Statistical results of network usage hours

| Attributes | Mid-high net worth households | Total sample | Absolute value of the mean difference |
|---|---|---|---|
| Mobile device Internet hours | 207.759 | 179.179 | 28.58*** |
| Computer Internet access time | 176.015 | 157.837 | 18.178*** |

*Note* *** $p < 0.01$

**Table 6** Statistical results of network importance

| Attributes | Mid-high net worth households | Total sample | Absolute value of the mean difference |
|---|---|---|---|
| The importance of the Internet for work | 61.44 | 55.12 | 6.32*** |
| The importance of the Internet for leisure and entertainment | 57.02 | 49.8 | 7.22*** |
| The importance of the Internet in keeping in touch with family and friends | 81.95 | 82.28 | 0.33 |
| The importance of the Internet for learning | 72.95 | 65.92 | 7.03*** |
| The importance of the Internet in daily life | 69.86 | 62.39 | 7.47*** |

*Note* *** $p < 0.01$

As shown in Table 6, overall, mid-high net worth households are more certain of the importance of the Internet and attach more importance to its role. The importance of the Internet for work was 61.44%, 6.32 percentage points higher than the 55.12% of the total sample; the importance of the Internet for leisure and entertainment was 57.02%, 7.22 percentage points higher than the 49.8% of the total sample; the importance of the Internet for learning was 72.95% and 7.03 percentage points higher than the 65.92% of the total sample; and the importance of the Internet for daily life was 69.86% and 7.03 percentage points higher than the 65.92% of the total sample. The proportion of those who think the Internet is important for learning is 72.95%, which is 7.03 percentage points higher than the total sample of 65.92%, and the proportion of those who think the Internet is important for daily life is 69.86%, which is 7.47 percentage points higher than the total sample of 62.39%. In addition, both samples affirmed the importance of the Internet in keeping in touch with family and friends, and the difference between them was not significant. This shows that mid-high net worth individuals value the role of the Internet more and are more efficient in their reliance on and use of the Internet.

## 2.2 Access to Information

Common ways to obtain information include television, newspapers, periodicals, radio, cell phone, text messages, and referrals from others. This book counts the importance of these as ways of information acquisition according to different sample groups of people, scores them from 1 to 5, where 1 means very unimportant and 5 means very important, and calculates the average of the scores; the statistical results of the methods of information acquisition are summarized in Table 7.

As shown in Table 7, the importance of newspapers and periodicals are more important for mid-high net worth households, with mean scores significantly higher than the mean scores of the total sample. This type of access is characterized by more formal and reliable sources of information. However, this type of information medium generally requires readers to have a high level of literacy and strong information processing and digestion skills. Mid-high net worth individuals are more likely to be well educated, have a broader perspective, and know how to use newspapers and periodicals to find the information they need; therefore, they will attach more importance to this type of information media.

In addition, the importance of traditional information media such as TV, radio, cell phone text messages, and referrals from others are all lower and more significant for mid-high net worth households than for the total sample. This indicates that, relatively speaking, the importance of these channels is, on the contrary, lower for the mid-high net worth individuals. This shows that there is often a difference in information access between the mid-high net worth populations and the general population. This difference may also be related to the fact that mid-high net worth individuals use the Internet more to obtain information. However, this difference cannot be simply labeled and stereotyped by the "digital divide," as different people's information access habits and preferences lead to different evaluations of the importance of their access to information.

**Table 7** Statistical results of the access to information

| Attributes | Mid-high net worth households | Total sample | Absolute value of the mean difference |
|---|---|---|---|
| Importance of television | 2.947 | 3.154 | 0.208*** |
| Importance of newspapers, journals and magazines | 2.149 | 2.102 | 0.047** |
| Importance of broadcasting | 2.199 | 2.261 | 0.062*** |
| Importance of cell phone text messages | 2.883 | 2.93 | 0.047** |
| Importance of referrals from others | 2.746 | 2.856 | 0.11*** |

*Note* ** $p < 0.05$, *** $p < 0.01$

# 3 Body and Health

Height and weight are important characteristics in judging a person's physical appearance. A person's height and weight can be influenced by many factors such as congenital genes, acquired dietary conditions, and geography. People often have different heights and weights, based on different genes, diets, and regions.

## *3.1 Body and Diet*

The mean height and weight of the different samples were calculated in the groups, and the statistical results are summarized in Table 8.

As shown in Table 8, in terms of height, the average height of mid-high net worth households reached 165.753 cm, which was 1.224 cm higher than the total sample of 164.529 cm, and this difference was significant. In other words, the heights of the mid-high net worth individuals were significantly higher than the average. In addition to genetic factors, the reason for this difference may be that people with better economic conditions draw more nutrients, such as meat and dairy products, during their physical development; people with high income have the financial ability to enroll in some fitness courses; and reasonable physical exercise during teenage years promotes strong bones and muscular development and increases height.

In terms of weight, the average weight of mid-high net worth households was higher than that of the total sample. That is, compared to the total sample, the mid-high net worth individuals were slightly fatter. This may be related to the good diet and nutrition of mid-high net worth individuals. Based on the above data, we can calculate the Body Mass Index (BMI) of the mid-high net worth individuals and the total sample, which are 23.61 and 23.266, respectively, both of which are less than 24 and within the normal range. The BMI of mid-high net worth individuals were slightly higher than that of the total sample.

Smoking is detrimental to health. However, smoking also has a social aspect, sometimes as part of social interaction. This book analyzed the smoking behavior of adults in different types of households, and the statistical results are summarized in Table 9.

As shown in Table 9, in terms of smoking behavior, the percentage of mid-high net worth households who have ever smoked is 10.81%, which is slightly lower than

**Table 8** Statistical results of average height and weight

| Attributes | Mid-high net worth households | Total sample | Absolute value of the mean difference |
|---|---|---|---|
| Current height (cm) | 165.753 | 164.529 | $1.225^{***}$ |
| Current weight (pounds) | 129.711 | 125.96 | $3.752^{***}$ |

*Note* $^{***}$ $p < 0.01$

**Table 9** Statistical results of smoking behavior of adults in the family

| Attributes | Mid-high net worth households | Total sample | Absolute value of the mean difference |
|---|---|---|---|
| Ever smoked (%) | 10.81 | 11.04 | 0.23 |
| Smoked in the past month (%) | 24.98 | 27.95 | 2.97*** |
| Smoking per day (sticks) | 13.81 | 14.119 | 0.306 |

*Note* *** $p < 0.01$

11.04% of the total sample. The difference between the two is not significant. Among those who smoked in the past month, the number of cigarettes smoked per day for the mid-high net worth households was 13.81, which was lower than 14.119 for the total sample, and the difference between the two was insignificant. It can be seen that there is no significant difference between the smoking behavior of the mid-high net worth households and the total sample in these two aspects.

However, looking at the percentage of smokers in the past month, the mid-high net worth households are 24.98%, which is lower than 27.95% of the total sample, a difference of almost 3 percentage points, which is a significant difference. This indicates that in terms of recent smoking rates, mid-high net worth households were significantly lower than the total sample. The results of the adult tobacco prevalence survey in each region show that in 2020, the smoking rates of people aged 15 years and older were less than 20% in the Shanghai and Tibet Autonomous Regions and higher than 30% in Yunnan and Guizhou provinces. In addition, 18 provinces, autonomous regions, and municipalities accounted for 20–24.9%, and nine provinces, autonomous regions, and municipalities accounted for 25–29.9%. The average national smoking rate is estimated to range from 23 to 30%. These data are generally similar to those obtained in this study. According to the estimates in this book, the total sample smoking rate was approximately 27.95%. However, there is still some way from achieving the tobacco control target of reducing the adult smoking rate to below 20%, as required by the Healthy China Initiative (2019–2030). Therefore, emphasis should be placed on not smoking and smoking less, both for the mid-high net worth populations and for the non-mid-high net worth populations.

Exercise and diet are related to health. This book groups the statistics on exercise and diet in different populations, which are summarized in Table 10.

As shown in Table 10, there was no significant difference in the number of hours per exercise session in the past year between mid-high net worth households and the total sample. This was an era of exercise for all people. Many exercise facilities have been installed in communities. Therefore, exercise is a universal activity, and mid-high net worth households do not appear to be unique in terms of exercise duration. Of course, the environment and conditions for exercise were slightly better than average. For example, mid-high net worth people will choose to go to higher-end gyms for exercise and choose more professional and higher-level coaches to guide exercise and fitness.

**Table 10** Statistical results of exercise and diet

| Attributes | Mid-high net worth households | Total sample | Absolute value of the mean difference |
|---|---|---|---|
| Length of each exercise session in the past year (minutes) | 57.302 | 58.342 | 1.04 |
| Ate meat in the past week (%) | 94.48 | 86.42 | $8.06^{***}$ |
| Ingested fruits and vegetables in the past week (%) | 99.15 | 98.19 | $0.96^{***}$ |

*Note* $^{***}$ $p < 0.01$

In terms of diet, the proportion of mid-high net worth households that had eaten meat and fruits and vegetables in the past week was significantly higher than that of the total sample. Mid-high net worth households have higher income levels to afford meat, fruit, and vegetables, and those with higher income levels may be more conscious of a balanced nutrient intake. Therefore, the mid-high net worth individuals not only consume more meat, but also consume more fruits and vegetables to ensure that dietary fiber is more abundant.

## 3.2 *Self-Health Assessment*

This book divides the assessments into self-subjective and objective. Self-subjective assessment is a common health assessment method in which individuals evaluate their health based on their subjective feelings. This book counted the self-assessed health of different populations, and the results of the self-subjective assessments are summarized in Table 11.

As shown in Table 11, 78.79% of mid-high net worth households considered themselves to be very healthy, compared to 73.09% of the total sample. The difference between the two was 5.7 percentage points, which was significant. In addition, the percentage of mid-high net worth households who think their health has improved

**Table 11** Results of subjective self-assessment

| Attributes | Mid-high net worth households | Total sample | Absolute value of the mean difference |
|---|---|---|---|
| Health status: very healthy and very healthy | 78.79 | 73.09 | $5.7^{***}$ |
| Changes in health: getting better | 9.96 | 9.19 | $0.77^{***}$ |

*Note* $^{***}$ $p < 0.01$

is 9.96% compared to 9.19% in the total sample. The difference between the two was 0.77 percentage points and is significant. It can be seen that from a self-assessed health perspective, the health status or health change status of the mid-high net worth individuals is significantly better than that of the total sample.

First, mid-high net worth families with good economic conditions can afford regular medical checkups and health care products, so they can maintain their own health. Second, mood may also be a key factor affecting health. People with high net worth and higher economic status have less anxiety about life, at least they do not need to worry about food, clothing, housing, and transportation. Their optimistic mental state can also encourage them to maintain a good mental state and reduce the risk of illness. In contrast, the average family has a weak financial base, and when facing a major illness, it is difficult to pay for the high cost of treatment because there is no commercial medical insurance to reimburse them. Therefore, their health is not optimistic after the illness. These factors are why the self-assessed health of mid-high net worth individuals was relatively good.

The book group statistics on the injuries and medical visits of different populations are summarized in Table 12.

As shown in Table 12, the percentages of mid-high net worth households with discomfort and serious illness or injury in the past two weeks were 23.44% and 22.45%, respectively. Both were lower than the total sample, with a difference of 2.7 percentage points and 5.24 percentage points, respectively, and both were significant. The proportion of mid-high net worth households who have seen a doctor in the past two weeks is 55.22%, which is 8.69 percentage points lower than the 63.91% of the total sample, and the difference is significant. Overall, these results indicate that the mid-high net worth groups are slightly healthier in all three areas.

Mid-high net worth individuals with better financial conditions undergo regular medical checkups and have a better grasp of their own health status. As the proportion of mid-high net worth individuals who buy high-end commercial medical insurance is higher, they will choose to seek timely medical treatment at high-level hospitals when they feel unwell and will not worry too much about medical expenses,

**Table 12** Statistical results of injuries and medical visits

| Attributes | Mid-high net worth households | Total Sample | Absolute value of the mean difference |
|---|---|---|---|
| Physical discomfort in the past two weeks | 23.44 | 26.14 | $2.7^{***}$ |
| Had a serious illness or injury in the past two weeks | 22.45 | 27.69 | $5.24^{***}$ |
| Have seen a doctor in the past two weeks | 55.22 | 63.91 | $8.69^{***}$ |
| Chronic illness within six months | 14.87 | 14.96 | 0.09 |

*Note* $^{***}$ $p < 0.01$

while those who are less well off may have their conditions aggravated due to long-standing illnesses, limited regional medical standards, and inability to afford medical expenses. At the same time, the proportion of middle- and high-net worth people seeking medical treatment was significantly lower than that of low-income people, which also reflects that the illnesses of mid-high net worth people are less serious and generally do not need to be treated in hospitals.

However, in terms of the proportion of patients with chronic illness within six months, the difference between the mid-high net worth households and the total sample was small and insignificant. This suggests that there is nothing special about the occurrence of chronic diseases among the mid-high net worth individuals. Some chronic diseases are more likely to be suffered by people who are well-off; that is, the so-called "diseases of the rich". Therefore, the risk and probability of chronic diseases are not lower for mid-high net worth individuals because they are better off.

## 4 Working Conditions

Salary income is an important source of household wealth for both mid-high net worth individuals, as well as the general population. Data from the "HNWI Values and Lifestyle Research Report 2022," jointly released by Bojangles Lifestyle Research (Shanghai) and the Hurun Report, show that the proportion of salary income in the assets of HNWIs has steadily increased over the past seven years.

### *4.1 Work Income*

The book is grouped to calculate the wages and benefits of different populations, and the statistical results are summarized in Table 13.

As shown in Table 13, the after-tax per capita wage income for all jobs in the past 12 months for mid-high net worth households is ¥71,609.4, which is ¥25,646.48 higher than the total sample of ¥45,962.92, which is a significant difference. It can be seen that the income of the mid-high net worth individuals is significantly higher than that of the general population. Mid-high net worth families with better economic conditions have more quality connections and social capital, which can provide them with certain convenience when looking for jobs. Children who grow up in good economic conditions tend to receive more quality education, make knowledge reserves for finding higher-paying jobs, and are more likely to find jobs with higher income levels. People from mid-high net worth families have a certain economic foundation, and may choose to start their own businesses, manage a family business, and so on, which will also bring them higher salaries.

Mid-high net worth individuals receive more cash benefits at work, such as transportation and housing subsidies. High-income jobs tend to have high work intensity and long working hours, so employees often reap higher levels of benefits. Companies

**Table 13** Statistical results of wages and benefits

| Attributes | Mid-high net worth households | Total sample | Absolute value of the mean difference |
|---|---|---|---|
| After-tax wage income from all work in the past 12 months | 71,609.4 | 45,962.92 | 25,646.48*** |
| Monthly cash benefit amount: transportation allowance | 465.169 | 420.691 | 44.478* |
| Monthly cash benefit amount: meal allowance | 411.395 | 421.567 | 10.172 |
| Monthly cash benefit amount: housing allowance | 765.675 | 633.895 | 131.78** |
| Monthly cash benefit amount: other allowance | 629.342 | 586.399 | 42.943 |
| 12 months cash benefit amount | 2438.857 | 1629.34 | 809.517*** |

*Note* * $p < 0.1$, ** $p < 0.05$, *** $p < 0.01$

with higher-income jobs may be located in more developed cities, such as Beijing, Shanghai, and Guangzhou, where housing prices and prices in general are higher, and therefore offer more housing and transportation subsidies. However, for meal subsidies and other subsidies, the difference between the mid-high net worth households and the total sample was not significant. However, it is worth noting that the 12-month per capita cash benefit amount for mid-high net worth households reaches ¥2438.857, which is significantly higher than the total sample's ¥1629.34, with a difference of ¥809.517, which is significant. This indicates that, overall, both wages and benefits are higher for mid-high net worth households than for the total sample. In other words, the jobs of mid-high net worth individuals should be more competitive and have good financial returns.

Different units tend to have different levels of job security. This book calculates the relevant situations in groups, and the statistical results for job security and unit size are summarized in Table 14.

As shown in Table 14, the monthly individual insurance contributions and monthly CPF contributions of the mid-high net worth households are significantly higher than those of the total sample. First, since the "five insurance and one fund" contributions are proportional to individual wages, the mid-high net worth individuals tend to have higher income level jobs, so their monthly individual insurance contributions and monthly CPF contributions are significantly higher than those of the total sample. Second, the difference between the size of work units and the size of managers of the mid-high net worth households and the total sample is not significant, which indicates that although the average size of the work units is not very different, there is a big difference in the positions, which can be seen by the salary level.

**Table 14** Statistical results of job security and unit size

| Attributes | Mid-high net worth households | Total Sample | Absolute value of the mean difference |
|---|---|---|---|
| Monthly individual insurance contribution amount (yuan/month) | 737.888 | 545.438 | 192.45*** |
| Monthly provident fund contribution amount (yuan/month) | 700.273 | 565.248 | 135.025*** |
| Size of work unit (people) | 983.304 | 733.125 | 250.178 |
| Size of management staff (people) | 21.756 | 17.125 | 4.631 |

*Note* *** $p < 0.01$

## 4.2 Work Characteristics

Differences in job characteristics cause people to have different characteristics in specific jobs. In this book, group calculations are based on job characteristics, and the statistical results of the job characteristics are summarized in Table 15.

As shown in Table 15, the proportion of mid-high net worth households with executive management positions in enterprises and institutions is 20.4%, which is 8.01 percentage points higher than the 12.39% of the total sample; this gap is significant. Additionally, the proportion of mid-high net worth households with direct subordinates in enterprises and institutions is 23.94%, which is 8.98 percentage points higher than the total sample of 14.96%; this gap is significant. This indicates that a higher percentage of mid-high net worth individuals hold middle and senior management positions in enterprises and institutions and are more likely to be leaders. Mid-high net worth individuals tend to have higher education, and many have overseas study experience, so the possibility of job promotion is also higher compared to the average person. Second, people who grow up in good economic conditions are more confident and have better communication skills, which indirectly improves their work efficiency and makes them get better job opportunities. In addition, mid-high net worth individuals have stronger interpersonal networks and social capital, which help them gain an edge in workplace competition.

**Table 15** Statistical results of workplace characteristics

| Attributes | Mid-high net worth households | Total sample | Absolute value of the mean difference |
|---|---|---|---|
| Have executive management positions | 20.40 | 12.39 | 8.01*** |
| Have direct reports | 23.94 | 14.96 | 8.98*** |

*Note* *** $p < 0.01$

The use of foreign languages at work and on computers is an important reflection of workplace characteristics. This book analyzes these characteristics by group, and the statistical results of the workplace characteristics are summarized in Table 16.

As shown in Table 16, the percentage of jobs held by mid-high net worth households that use a foreign language is 13.2%, which is 5.58 percentage points higher than the total sample of 7.62%. This indicates that the jobs of mid-high net worth individuals are more likely to be foreign-related or to work in foreign companies. The percentage of jobs held by mid-high net worth households that used computers was 62.62% compared to 45.58% for the total sample. The difference between the two was 17.04 percentage points, which is significant. This indicates that the jobs of mid-high net worth individuals are somewhat foreign-related and modern. The jobs held by economically privileged mid-high net worth individuals require a higher level of literacy and the use of foreign languages and computers in their work. First, high-paying jobs require overseas business development and research in foreign markets, thus requiring higher foreign language skills; second, nowadays, enterprises and institutions need to use computers for data analysis and report writing. This shows that mid-high net worth people are more likely to be "white collar" and less likely to be "blue collar."

Job satisfaction is a measure of how satisfied employees are with their jobs. Job satisfaction can be measured using cognitive (evaluation), affective (emotional), and behavioral measures. This book here uses a multidimensional measurement approach to rate job satisfaction on a scale of 1 to 5, where 1 means very dissatisfied and 5 means very satisfied. Job satisfaction was counted in the groups in this book, and the results are summarized in Table 17.

As shown in Table 17, the job satisfaction of the mid-high net worth households is 3.757 compared to 3.715 for the total sample, with a significant difference of 0.042. This indicates that mid-high net worth individuals have higher job satisfaction. The better-off mid-high net worth individuals are overall the more satisfied with their jobs. Generally speaking, mid-high net worth people are more likely to work in high-quality enterprises, so income, work environment, and job security, among others are reasonably guaranteed; employees working in such enterprises and institutions will have higher job satisfaction.

Looking at the specific dimensions of job satisfaction, the job income satisfaction of middle- and high-net-worth households was 3.525, which was 0.077 higher than the total sample of 3.448, and the difference was significant. This indicates that

**Table 16** Statistical results of job characteristics

| Attributes | Mid-high net worth households | Total sample | Absolute value of the mean difference |
|---|---|---|---|
| Work in a foreign language | 13.20 | 7.62 | $5.58^{***}$ |
| Use of computers in the work performed | 62.62 | 45.58 | $17.04^{***}$ |

*Note* $^{***}$ $p < 0.01$

**Table 17** Statistical results of job satisfaction

| Attributes | Mid-high net worth households | Total sample | Absolute value of the mean difference |
|---|---|---|---|
| Job income satisfaction | 3.525 | 3.448 | 0.077*** |
| Job safety satisfaction | 3.975 | 3.906 | 0.07*** |
| Job environment satisfaction | 3.782 | 3.729 | 0.052*** |
| Satisfaction with working time | 3.689 | 3.673 | 0.017 |
| Job promotion satisfaction | 3.412 | 3.508 | 0.096*** |
| Job satisfaction | 3.757 | 3.715 | 0.043*** |

*Note* *** $p < 0.01$

middle- and high-net-worth individuals are more satisfied with their job income. In terms of job security satisfaction, mid-high net worth households are 3.975, which is 0.069 higher than the total sample of 3.906, which is a significant difference. This indicates that mid-high net worth people are more secure in their jobs, and therefore, more satisfied. In terms of work environment satisfaction, the difference between the mid-high net worth households was 3.782, compared to 3.729 for the total sample, which is a significant difference. This finding indicates that the working environment is better for mid-high net worth individuals. However, in terms of work-time satisfaction, the gap between the two was not significant. This indicates that mid-high net worth individuals are not significantly different in terms of work time satisfaction.

In terms of job promotion satisfaction, mid-high net worth households are 3.412, which is 0.096 lower than the total sample of 3.508, and the difference is significantly difference. This indicates that mid-high net worth workers are less satisfied with job promotions than the general population. People with weak economic conditions often need to work harder to get job promotions, so they are more likely to be satisfied with the opportunities they get through their own efforts, while the mid-high net worth people with superior economic conditions tend to have higher requirements and expectations for themselves because their professional backgrounds are better and the competition among them is more intense; therefore, for job promotions, they often face the situation that the ideal does not match reality. In addition, this also indicates that mid-high net worth individuals have greater attempts to promote jobs.

## 5 Religion, Law, and Politics

Politics is the act of parties and other parties governing a country. It is a social activity and social relationship concerning authoritative governmental decisions and their implementation and is closely related to everyone is life, so people cannot help but pay attention to it. Politics are wind vanes that affect the daily lives of people. People care about politics in different ways.

## 5.1 Pay Attention to Current Affairs

The level of political concern of the mid-high net worth households and the total sample is calculated here separately. The statistical results are summarized in Table 18.

As shown in Table 18, mid-high net worth individuals with better economic conditions are more concerned about political issues, and they learn about politics more frequently through the Internet than TV stations. Managers of an enterprise or institution need to be highly sensitive to policies that can affect the business behavior and operational performance of the enterprise or institution at a deep level. With the gradual improvement of the socialist market economy system, the social and market environments in which enterprises and institutions are located have also changed. To perceive the relevant signals from political changes in time and provide further guidance to the operations of enterprises and institutions, leaders and management need to pay attention to politics.

At the same time, mid-high net worth individuals were more willing to make political statements on websites, which may also be due to their jobs. Managers of enterprises and institutions should grasp the latest market dynamics and make their own estimations and considerations of the impact of policy implementation. Therefore, they are more willing to express their views on these policies. Of course, in general, the percentage of political speeches through websites in the past year was very low: 4.42% for mid-high net worth households and 3.18% for the total sample. Thus, the vast majority did not make political statements on their websites.

**Table 18** Statistical results of the degree of concern about politics

| Attributes | Mid-high net worth households | Total sample | Absolute value of the mean difference |
|---|---|---|---|
| Learn about politics through TV stations (days/week) | 2.611 | 2.393 | 0.218*** |
| Learned about politics via the internet (days/week) | 4.941 | 4.338 | 0.602*** |
| Political statements via website in the past year (%) | 4.42 | 3.18 | 1.24*** |

*Note* *** $p < 0.01$

## 5.2 *Affiliated Organizations*

Individuals belong to diverse organizations. These organizations are either complementary or exclusive to one another. This book groups statistics on the organizations and beliefs of different populations, and the results are summarized in Table 19.

As shown in Table 19, the proportion of mid-high net worth households whose political outlook was party or league membership was significantly higher than that of the total sample. Mid-high net worth individuals with better economic conditions have received good education, are more ideologically active, mostly take the initiative to pursue progress, understand the historical and practical significance of joining the party and league, and are willing to take on the responsibilities of the party and league members. In addition, this also indicates that party and league members will have somewhat stronger personal qualities and abilities, will perform better in all walks of life, and are therefore more likely to become MHPs.

Additionally, mid-high net worth individuals who are financially better off also choose to become union members, and this percentage is significantly higher for mid-high net worth households than for the total sample. Joining these organizations helps mid-high net worth individuals gain more social capital, which is very beneficial for individuals and their career development. However, in terms of being members of an individual worker's association, the proportion of mid-high net worth households is only 4.49%, which is 0.64 percentage points lower and significant than the total sample of 5.13%. This may be related to the occupations and positions held by mid-high net worth individuals.

In terms of religious affiliation, although the proportion of members of religious affiliation groups among mid-high net worth households is slightly higher than the total sample. However, this difference was not statistically significant. That is, there is nothing special about mid-high net worth households in terms of membership of religious faith groups.

**Table 19** Statistical results of organizations and beliefs

| Attributes | Mid-high net worth households | Total sample | Absolute value of the mean difference |
|---|---|---|---|
| Member of the communist party of China | 2.11 | 1.5 | $0.61^{***}$ |
| Member of the Chinese communist youth league | 14.90 | 13.98 | $0.92^{*}$ |
| Members of religious faith groups | 2.50 | 2.36 | 0.14 |
| Members of trade unions | 17.79 | 8.37 | $9.42^{***}$ |
| Members of individual workers' associations | 4.49 | 5.13 | $0.64^{*}$ |

*Note* $^{*}$ $p < 0.1$, $^{***}$ $p < 0.01$

# 6 Spirituality

Mental state is a psychological term that refers to the temporary orientation of a person's mind, that is, the psychological situation of the person at that time. A person's mental state can ebb and flow in both positive and negative states.

## *6.1 Mental State*

In this book, mental states are divided into seven categories, and the percentage of "often" and "most of the time" mental states are counted separately.

As shown in Table 20, 9.28% of mid-high net worth households felt depressed, 3.8 percentage points lower than the total sample of 13.08%; 8.66% felt it was hard to do anything, 6.5 percentage points lower than the total sample of 15.16%; 18.76% felt sleep-deprived, 2.14 percentage points lower than the total sample of 20.9%. The percentage of those who felt lonely was 5.47%, which was 4.11 percentage points lower than the total sample of 9.58%, and the percentage of those who felt sad was 4.67%, which was 2.78 percentage points lower than the total sample of 7.45%. All these gaps are significant. This indicates that the mid-high net worth individuals scored generally lower than the total sample for these negative emotions.

In addition, 77.57% of mid-high net worth households felt happy in their lives, 4.37 percentage points higher than the 73.2% of the total sample. The percentage of mid-high net worth households who feel happy is 74.1%, which is 6.2 percentage points higher than the 67.9% of the total sample. Differences were considered statistically significant. This indicates that mid-high net worth individuals have more positive emotions and a good mental state. Therefore, in terms of the overall mental outlook, the mid-high net worth individuals are sunnier, more positive, and more spirited.

**Table 20** Statistical results of the proportion of mental status

| Attributes | Mid-high net worth households | Total sample | Absolute value of the mean difference |
|---|---|---|---|
| Feeling depressed | 9.28 | 13.08 | $3.8^{***}$ |
| Feeling overwhelmed with everything you do | 8.66 | 15.16 | $6.5^{***}$ |
| Not sleeping well | 18.76 | 20.9 | $2.14^{***}$ |
| Feeling lonely | 5.47 | 9.58 | $4.11^{***}$ |
| Feeling sad and upset | 4.67 | 7.45 | $2.78^{***}$ |
| I live a happy life | 77.57 | 73.2 | $4.37^{***}$ |
| Feeling happy | 74.1 | 67.9 | $6.2^{***}$ |

*Note* $^{***}$ $p < 0.01$

It follows that mid-high net worth individuals have more positive emotions and are less likely to experience negative emotions. For example, income is a major hurdle for low-asset households, and there are expenses everywhere in life, such as children's education, medical care, food, clothing, housing, and transportation. Second, economic conditions may affect the level of socialization. Social activities, such as going out to dinner with friends, incur costs, and people with average economic conditions consider such reasons and therefore try to reduce their social costs, and they may feel lonely. Long-term anxiety and depression may further affect sleep quality and the psychological state. Mid-high net worth individuals are more optimistic and positive. For example, they have financial support for education when they want to pursue further education, they have the courage to quit a job they do not like because they can afford the financial burden of the window period, and they have enough money to support their own life and entertainment. In terms of life and entertainment, they have sufficient money to support their favorite fields. In summary, middle- and high-net-worth individuals who are financially well-off are more likely to maintain positive and optimistic attitudes.

A positive mental outlook is derived from all aspects of life. It further explores interpersonal relationships and happiness by grouping different people to calculate the mean of their scores in these two areas, where 0 represents the lowest and 10 the highest. The statistical results are summarized in Table 21.

As shown in Table 21, the interpersonal relationships of the mid-high net worth families were slightly better than those of the total sample; however, the difference was not significant. Mid-high net worth individuals from wealthy families have a stronger sense of superiority, are more confident in interpersonal interactions, and dare to present themselves. Because of the complexity of interpersonal relationships, the interpersonal relationships of mid-high net worth individuals are not necessarily better than those of the general population.

In terms of happiness, the average score for mid-high net worth households was 7.69 and the average score for the total sample was 7.534, a significant difference of 0.156. This indicates that mid-high net worth individuals consider themselves happy. Mid-high net worth people with better economic conditions receive a good family education and are more willing to share with others because they do not experience material deprivation, and those who know how to share are more likely to feel happy. In addition, people with high family income levels have better housing conditions and living environments, and a good living environment can enhance one's sense

**Table 21** Statistical results of interpersonal relationships and well-being

| Attributes | Mid-high net worth households | Total sample | Absolute value of the mean difference |
|---|---|---|---|
| How well connected I am to people | 7.146 | 7.106 | 0.041 |
| How happy I am | 7.69 | 7.534 | $0.156^{***}$ |

*Note* $^{***}$ $p < 0.01$

of happiness and security. People in good economic conditions will receive better education, and society will give more respect to those who have received higher education; this respect will also enhance happiness to a certain extent.

## 6.2 *Life Satisfaction*

The present is a dialogue between the past and the future. The mental state is related to life satisfaction and confidence in the future. This book then calculates the mean value from these two groupings, in scoring, 1 means very dissatisfied and 5 means very satisfied; 1 means no confidence and 5 means very confident, and the results are summarized in Table 22.

As shown in Table 22, the life satisfaction score for mid-high net worth households is 4.04, which is 0.036 higher than the total sample of 4.004, and the difference is significant. This indicates that mid-high net worth individuals are more satisfied with their current state of life. First, mid-high net worth people with good economic conditions generally have better jobs, and a sense of career achievement and social security will make this group of people more satisfied with their lives. Second, higher income levels can improve the quality of people's leisure activities, such as doing fitness and reading, and these activities will also improve people's satisfaction with their lives.

However, for confidence in the future, the score for mid-high net worth households is 4.128, which is somewhat lower than 4.148 for the total sample. Although this gap is insignificant, it is easy to see that the mid-high net worth individuals have more to think about and worry about the future. The more fear you have, the more fear is lost. The mid-high net worth individuals have more resources and advantages than the general population. However, things are always in flux. Uncertainty about the future can make mid-high net worth individuals more apprehensive about losing what they possess. Comparatively speaking, the general population is more likely to be content with what they have and will instead expect to live better in the future.

**Table 22** Statistical results of life satisfaction and confidence in the future

| Attributes | Mid-high net worth households | Total sample | Absolute value of the mean difference |
|---|---|---|---|
| Satisfaction with your life | 4.04 | 4.004 | $0.036^{***}$ |
| Degree of confidence in one's future | 4.128 | 4.148 | 0.019 |

*Note* $^{***}$ $p < 0.01$

## 6.3 Trust

An individual's mental outlook is associated with a or sense of trust. A sense of trust is an emotional experience in which an individual feels safe, reliable, and trustworthy regarding the people, things, and objects around him or her. A sense of trust arises when an individual feels that someone, something, or an object is consistent, predictable, or reliable. In this book, the sense of trust of different people is counted in groups and scored, with 0 representing very distrustful and 10 representing very trustful. The statistical results are summarized in Table 23.

As shown in Table 23, the level of trust in different objects is the highest for parents, which is obvious because they are the dearest people to them and have gifts for nurturing. Then comes the level of trust in doctors because they are professionals who not only take care of people's health but may also decide their life and death. Then comes the level of trust in neighbors. This was followed by the level of trust in local government officials, who were very important. The level of trust in strangers and Americans scored lower.

In terms of trust in parents, mid-high net worth households scored significantly higher than the total sample. This indicates that mid-high net worth individuals are more likely to trust people close to them. It is worth noting that the scores for trust in neighbors were significantly lower for mid-high net worth households than for the total sample. In terms of trust in doctors and local government officials, the scores of mid-high net worth households were significantly lower than those of the entire sample. This indicates that mid-high net worth individuals are more skeptical, prefer to think independently, and are more likely to question professional authority.

Interestingly, mid-high net worth households scored their trust in strangers at 3.729, which is 0.133 higher than the total sample's 3.596, and the difference is significant. This suggests that for strangers, mid-high net worth individuals are also likely to give greater trust. This may be related to the fact that mid-high net worth

**Table 23** Statistical results of trustworthiness

| Attributes | Mid-high net worth households | Total sample | Absolute value of the mean difference |
|---|---|---|---|
| Level of trust in parents | 9.441 | 9.369 | $0.072^{***}$ |
| Level of trust in neighbors | 6.66 | 6.796 | $0.137^{***}$ |
| Level of trust in Americans | 3.708 | 3.689 | 0.019 |
| Level of trust in strangers | 3.729 | 3.596 | $0.133^{***}$ |
| Level of trust in local government officials | 5.862 | 6.041 | $0.179^{***}$ |
| Level of trust in doctors | 7.113 | 7.239 | $0.126^{***}$ |

*Note* $^{***}$ $p < 0.01$

individuals place more emphasis on contractuality. For example, in financial management, mid-high net worth individuals are more likely to manage their wealth through trust, which may relate to their emphasis on contractuality [15].

# 7 Values

Values are cognition, understanding, judgment, or choice based on certain human thinking senses; that is, a kind of thinking or orientation in which people identify things and recognize right and wrong, thus reflecting a certain value or role of people, things, and objects. Generally, a person's values have a guiding effect on his/her motivation. Motivation for human behavior is governed and regulated by values that have an important influence on motivational patterns.

## 7.1 *Personal Values*

This book examines the values of mid-high net worth individuals from multiple perspectives. After grouping the statistics, the statistics regarding the percentage of values are summarized in Table 24.

As shown in Table 24, 74.91% of mid-high net worth households agree that wealth reflects personal achievement; however, this percentage is 3.09 percentage points lower than 78% of the total sample, and the difference is significant. This indicates that, although the majority of mid-high net worth individuals agree on the role and status of wealth in personal achievement, the percentage of agreement is

**Table 24** Statistical results on the proportion of values

| Attributes | Mid-high net worth households | Total sample | Absolute value of the mean difference |
|---|---|---|---|
| Agree that fair competition leads to harmonious interpersonal relationships | 84.88 | 85.45 | 0.57 |
| Agree that wealth reflects personal achievement | 74.91 | 78 | $3.09^{***}$ |
| Agree that hard work can be rewarded | 83.24 | 87.55 | $4.31^{***}$ |
| Agree that intelligence and talent can be rewarded | 83.93 | 86.66 | $2.73^{***}$ |
| Agree that having connections is more important than having ability | 69.36 | 71.49 | $2.13^{***}$ |
| Agree that there are great opportunities to improve living standards in today's society | 81.54 | 82.61 | 1.07 |

*Note* $^{***}$ $p < 0.01$

slightly lower than that of the general population. In other words, some mid-high net worth individuals agree that wealth reflects personal achievement, and others agree that indicators other than wealth reflect personal achievement.

A total of 83.24% of mid-high net worth households agree that hard work pays off; however, compared to 87.55% of the total sample, it is 4.31 percentage points lower, and the gap between the two is significant. Mid-high net worth individuals tend to hold higher positions and have relatively more difficulty changing positions at work, so their perception of being rewarded for hard work will be significantly lower than those in low-asset households. Another important reason is that a significant portion of the family wealth of mid-high net worth individuals is passed down through the family, making the contribution of individual efforts relatively less important.

A total of 83.93% of mid-high net worth households agree that being smart and talented pays off; however, compared to 86.66% of the total sample, this is 2.73 percentage points lower, and the difference is significant. This indicates that while the vast majority of mid-high net worth individuals believe in the role of intelligence and talent, some believe that factors other than personal intelligence and talent cannot be ignored as factors that affect how individuals are rewarded, such as family background and interpersonal relationships. In other words, mid-high net worth individuals have a more thorough view of the complexity of personal rewards in the real world. The rewards that an individual can receive are highly related to their hard work and intelligence, but not to a simple linear relationship.

Of the mid-high net worth households, 69.36% agreed that having connections is more important than having competence; however, this is 2.13 percentage points lower than 71.49% of the total sample, and the difference is significant. This indicates that while mid-high net worth individuals value the power of social connections and social capital, there is also a significant portion that affirms the importance of personal competence.

In addition, for those who agree that fair competition is necessary for harmonious relationships and that there are many opportunities to improve living standards in today's society, the gap between the mid-high net worth households and the total sample is not significant. In other words, more than 80% of both mid-high net worth individuals and the general population affirm the importance of fair competition and agree that there are still more opportunities in today's society. Opportunities often go hand-in-hand with challenges.

## 7.2 *Assessment of Success Factors*

The book is grouped to calculate the scores of influencing factors of personal achievement, where 0 indicates the least important and 10 indicates the most important, and the statistical results of influencing factors of personal achievement are summarized in Table 25.

As shown in Table 25, the level of effort of a child is the most important to one's achievement in all factors, both for middle- and high-net-worth families and for

**Table 25** Statistical results of the factors influencing individual achievement

| Attributes | Mid-high net worth households | Total sample | Absolute value of the mean difference |
|---|---|---|---|
| Family social status is important to a person's achievement | 6.333 | 6.486 | 0.152 |
| Family economic conditions are important to a person's achievement | 6.542 | 6.724 | 0.182 |
| Educational level is important to one's achievement | 7.9534 | 8.025 | 0.071 |
| Talent is important to a person's achievement | 6.328 | 6.364 | 0.036 |
| How hard a child works is important to a person's achievement | 8.115 | 8.214 | 0.099 |
| A child's luck is important to a person's achievement | 6.26 | 5.874 | 0.385*** |
| Family connections are important to a person's achievement | 6.8012 | 6.745 | 0.057 |

*Note* *** $p < 0.01$

average families, with scores above 8. This suggests that this is a general consensus and that any family would encourage their children to work hard. Of all the factors, children's luck is the least important to achievement for both mid-high net worth and average families. This is the consensus. This suggests that neither middle nor high net worth families, or average families believe luck will play a key role in a child's future achievement. Both mid-high net worth families and ordinary families emphasize the importance of personal effort and struggle. The score for "children's luck is important to one's achievement" is 6.26 for mid-high net worth families, which is 0.386 higher than the total sample's score of 5.874, and the difference between the two is significant. In other words, mid-high net worth families do not completely ignore the role of luck but even value it more than the total sample.

In addition, the perceptions of the importance of social status, economic conditions, educational attainment, talent, level of effort of children, and having connections in the family for personal success were largely consistent and did not differ significantly, regardless of whether the family was a middle to high net worth family or an average family. This suggests that they shared common perceptions and ideas. That is, all these factors affect personal success in general, as perceived by all. This shows that the factors that influence personal success and achievement are multi-faceted and multidimensional and that this is the result of a combination of effects. This also shows that the factors that determine personal achievement are complex and cannot be described in a few words. Children from mid-high net worth families have an advantage over children from ordinary families in terms of social status, economic conditions, education level, and family connections. As a result, children from mid-high net worth families are likely to be more successful in the future. However, this is not necessarily universal, as children from poor families may also achieve something through persistent personal effort. These are common examples. Therefore, predicting whether a person will be successful in the future cannot be generalized but requires specific analysis of specific issues.

## 8 Summary of This Chapter

This chapter provides a panoramic analysis of mid-high net worth families and people through an analysis of the psychology and behavior of different people in the total sample, presenting a viewable and comprehensive picture of the mental and behavioral characteristics of mid-high net worth people, effectively filling the gap in this field and providing important clues for understanding and mastering the situation of mid-high net worth families and people. Based on the analysis presented in this chapter, the following conclusions can be drawn.

For example, when it comes to family relationships, mid-high net worth families are much less likely to agree that men should take on half of the household chores, that parents provide financial help to their children, that children are born to help the family financially, and that children are born to continue the family legacy.

Second, in terms of networks and information, the proportion of mid-high net worth households using mobile networks and online learning is higher, but the proportion of online shopping is lower; the proportion of those who think the network is important for work, leisure, entertainment, study, and daily life is higher; and the importance of obtaining information through traditional information media is lower.

Third, in terms of body and health, the average height of mid-high net worth households was slightly higher than that of the total sample, the percentage of ever smokers was lower, the percentage of having eaten meat and consumed fruits and vegetables in the past week was higher, the percentage of very healthy and very healthy health was higher, and the percentage of injuries and medical visits was lower.

Fourth, in terms of working conditions, mid-high net worth families had higher after-tax per capita salary income and 12-month per capita cash benefits for all jobs in the past 12 months, higher monthly personal insurance and provident fund contributions, higher percentages of administrative positions in enterprises and institutions and direct subordinates in enterprises and institutions, higher percentages of jobs using foreign languages and computers, and higher job satisfaction.

Fifth, in terms of religion, law, and politics, mid-high net worth individuals are more concerned about politics, and the percentage of party members, league members, and union members is higher among mid-high net worth households.

Sixth, in terms of mental outlook, the proportion of mid-high net worth individuals who feel depressed, find it hard to do anything, sleep poorly, feel lonely, and feel sad was significantly lower. However, the proportion of participants who felt happy and enjoyed life was significantly higher. Mid-high net worth families have higher happiness, higher life satisfaction, and higher trust in parents and strangers, but lower trust in local government officials and doctors.

Seventh, in terms of values, the percentages of mid-high net worth individuals who agree that wealth reflects personal achievement, hard work pays off, being smart and talented pays off, and having connections is more important than having abilities are all somewhat lower, but the percentage of those who believe that a child's luck is important to a person's achievement is somewhat higher.

## References

1. Wan, H.: New advances in tinkering technology for high net worth individuals. China Popul. Sci. 91–105 (2020)
2. Westermeier, C., Grabka, M.: Significant statistical uncertainty over share of high net worth households. DIW Econ. Bull. **5**, 210–219 (2015)
3. Liu, N., Shao, M.: Anhui high net worth individuals portrait. Huizhou Merch. 62–63 (2017)
4. Lv, J.: Family Office, "Chinese Style"—A "Portrait" of China's High Net Worth Individuals. Financ. Expo. 34–40 (2018)
5. Zhao, L.: A "Portrait" of China's high net worth individuals. Financ. Expo. 34–40 (2018)
6. Wang, X.: Overview of the characteristics of high net worth individuals in China and the implications for commercial banks. Wuhan Financ. 30–32 (2012)
7. Zhou, C., Wu, Q., Zou, J.: Exploring the consumption characteristics of high net worth individuals and their lifestyles. Soc. Sci. Res. 82–91 (2019)
8. Chen, Y.: Analysis of the characteristics and needs of high net worth clients. China Technol. Expo 297 (2012)
9. Liao, Z.: A Brief discussion on private banking customer engagement and marketing strategies—based on analysis of behavioral characteristics and financial consumption preferences of high net worth individuals. Zhejiang Financ. 44–46 (2014)
10. Schroeder, T.: Understanding the mind of a high net-worth donor. Major Gift. Rep. **22**, 8 (2020)
11. Ramtohul, R.: High net worth' migration in Mauritius: a critical analysis. Migr. Lett. **13**, 17–33 (2016)
12. Alenezi, M., Walden, M.L.: A new look at husbands' and wives' time allocation. J. Consum. Aff. **38**, 81–106 (2004)
13. Qi, L.: The effect of changes in bargaining power on time allocation for household chores - empirical evidence from two-income Chinese households. Econ. Res. 78–90 (2005)
14. Shin, D., Darpy, D.: Rating, review and reputation: how to unlock the hidden value of luxury consumers from digital commerce? J. Bus. Ind. Mark. **35**, 1553–1561 (2020)
15. Marrache, B., Vinet, F.: The use of trusts for high net worth individuals. Trust. Trust. **10**, 9–10 (2004)

# Chapter 3
# Financial Asset Management for Mid-High Net Worth Families

**Abstract** Financial asset allocation, an important part of family wealth management, plays an important role in preserving and appreciating family wealth. Under such circumstances, studying household financial asset allocations is of great theoretical value and practical significance. Based on CFPS data for 2020, the main findings of this study are as follows: the coverage rate of financial products among mid-high net worth households is significantly higher than that of non mid-high net worth households; the total price of financial products held by mid-high net worth households is significantly higher than that held by non mid-high net worth households; financial market participation and the share of risky financial assets are significantly higher for mid-high net worth households than for non mid-high net worth households.

Financial Assets exist in the form of values owned by a unit or individual as opposed to physical assets. Accordingly, family financial assets refer to all types of assets held by families in the form of value, which are an important part of a family's wealth. With the continuous development of China's economy, the scale of the financial assets owned by residents has shown a continuous growth trend. Since entering the twenty-first century, China's household wealth has been increasing. From 2000 to 2019, China's total household wealth grew from US¥3.7 trillion to US¥78.08 trillion, a full increase of more than 20 times, and now ranks second in the world [1]. Thus, the allocation of financial assets has become a common problem faced by households when making financial investments. Even in rural areas, household allocation of financial assets is receiving increasing attention. A survey based on several rural areas in Nanjing showed that risky financial assets accounted for 13.4% of the financial assets of rural households in Nanjing [2]. Then, for households, how to achieve optimal allocation of household wealth by purchasing financial products and other means? This is an important topic in the study of family financing.

This issue is particularly important for mid-high net worth households because of the large amounts of investable assets they hold. The size of the assets held by mid-high net worth households and their allocation to financial assets have traditionally been topics of concern for the government, as well as the banking and insurance

 
J. Gu, *Wealth Management Report for Mid-High Net Worth Families*, Spatial Demography and Population Governance, https://doi.org/10.1007/978-981-97-0387-6_3

industries [3]. For the government, knowing the allocation of financial assets of mid-high net worth households can help introduce relevant policies to optimize the allocation of financial assets in mid-high net worth households, improve their ability to resist financial risk, and achieve household wealth appreciation. For banks and insurance industries, analyzing the financial assets and other allocation strategies of mid-high net worth families can help them grasp the wealth management characteristics of mid-high net worth customers. Furthermore, developing targeted business strategies, designing, and providing corresponding financial products/services will encourage mid-high net worth families to allocate more financial assets to these financial products/services, thereby improving the retention rate of mid-high net worth customers. Further research on this topic is required.

## 1 Analysis of Household Financial Product Ownership Rates

Household participation in financial investments and markets is an important indicator of a country's financial market coverage and literacy. The CFPS questionnaire already includes the question, does your household currently hold financial products, such as stocks, funds, government bonds, trust products, and foreign exchange products? This variable consisted of one and zero. One means that the household holds at least one of these financial products, and zero means that the household does not hold any financial product. Accordingly, it is possible to calculate the proportion of household participation in financial market investments.

### *1.1 Family Level*

It calculates the coverage of financial product holdings for the full sample of households by grouping them according to the nature of the community, and the results are summarized in Fig. 1.

According to Fig. 1, the coverage rate of financial products held by households whose community structure is a neighborhood committee is 16.27 percentage points higher than that of households whose community structure is a village committee, and the difference between them is significant. According to the data from the 2018 China Household Income Survey (CHIP), the participation rate of risky financial assets is only 8.5%, including only 3.6% for stocks and 2% for funds [1]. Overall, this rate is similar to the results of the present study. In addition, the findings of this book show that the coverage rate of financial products held by households living in village councils is relatively low at 3.64%. The financial market participation rate of households in rural areas is relatively low, and the proportion of rural households

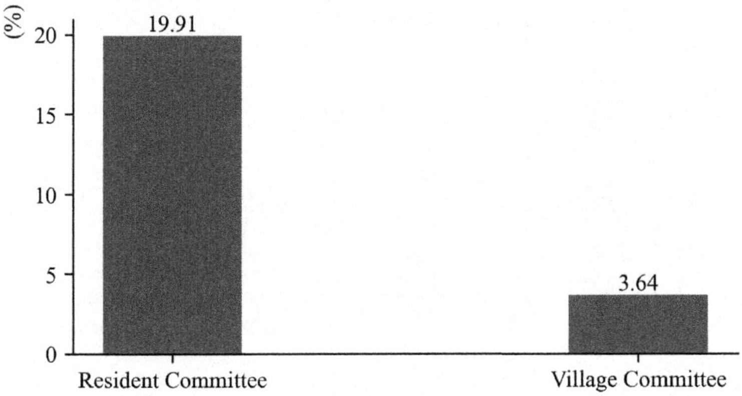


**Fig. 1** Coverage of financial products held by the full sample of households (community-based)

making investments in financial management is not yet high. Indeed, there are some differences between rural households in different regions.

According to Fig. 2, in general, the coverage rate of financial products held by mid-high net worth households is significantly higher than that of non mid-high net worth households in both neighborhood and village committees. In neighborhood committees, the coverage rate of financial products held by mid-high net worth households was 42.92%. In the neighborhood committee, the coverage rate of financial products held by mid-high net worth households is 30.47 percentage points higher than that of non mid-high net worth households. In the village committee, the coverage rate of financial products held by mid-high net worth households is 13.09 percentage points higher than that of non mid-high net worth households. As can be observed, the gap between the two is evident, especially in the neighborhood councils.

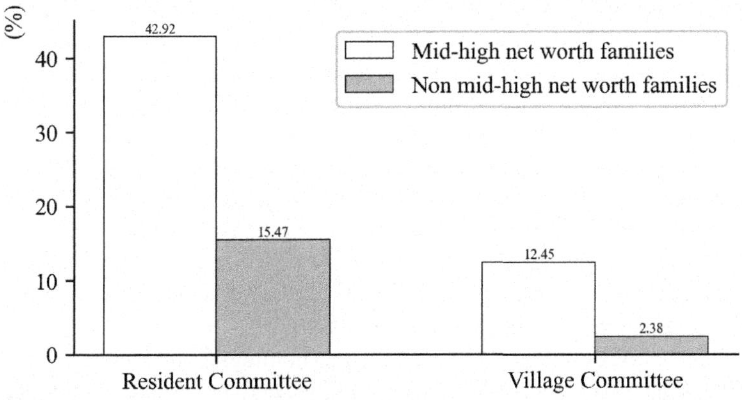


**Fig. 2** Coverage of financial product holdings (community-based) among mid-high net worth households and non mid-high net worth households

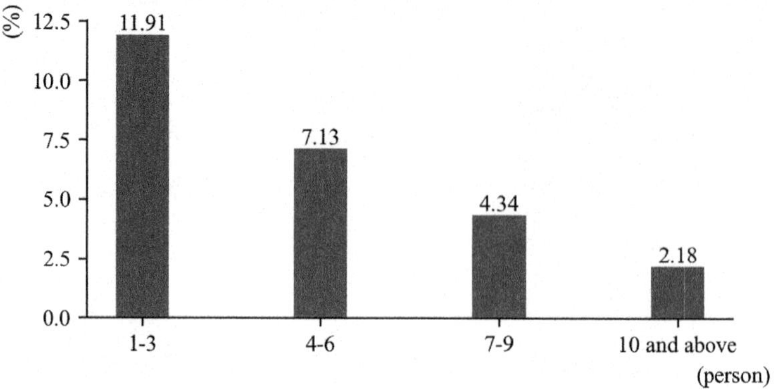


**Fig. 3** Coverage of financial products held by the full sample of households (household size)

It calculates the coverage of financial product holdings for the full sample of households based on household size groupings, and the results are summarized in Fig. 3. As Fig. 3, as the number of people increases, the coverage of financial products by households tends to decline in a stepwise manner. Specifically, the larger the household, the lower the proportion of financial products held. One reason for this is that the larger the household size, the greater the pressure to provide for the family resulting in less household money available for investment in financial products. Therefore, the household is less likely to participate in financial market investment activities. Essentially, there is a negative relationship between household burden and households' financial market participation rate.

According to Fig. 4, in general, the coverage rate of financial products held by mid-high net worth households is significantly higher than that of non mid-high net worth households regardless of household size. Specifically, the coverage rate of financial products held by mid-high net worth households is 32.26 percentage points higher than that held by non mid-high net worth households when the household size is 1–3 persons, 21.32 percentage points higher than that held by non mid-high net worth households when the household size is 4–6 persons, 18.88 percentage points higher than that held by non mid-high net worth households when the household size is 7–9 persons, and 18.88 percentage points higher than that held by non mid-high net worth households when the household size is 10 persons or more. The coverage rate of financial products held by mid-high net worth households is 3.59 percentage points higher than that of non mid-high net worth households when the household size is 10 or more. It is evident that the smaller the household size, the larger the difference between the coverage rate of financial products held by mid-high net worth households and non mid-high net worth households.

It calculates the coverage of financial product holdings for the full sample of households based on urban and rural district groupings, and the results are summarized in Fig. 5.

According to Fig. 5, the coverage of financial products held by urban households is significantly higher than that held by rural households. In urban areas, the coverage

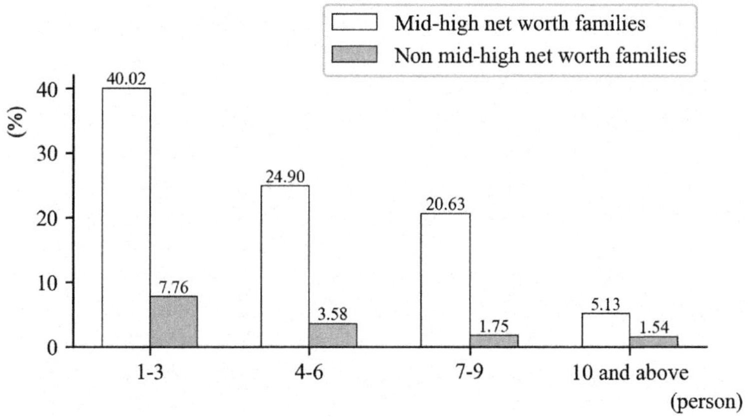


**Fig. 4** Coverage of financial product holdings (household size) for mid-high net worth households and non mid-high net worth households

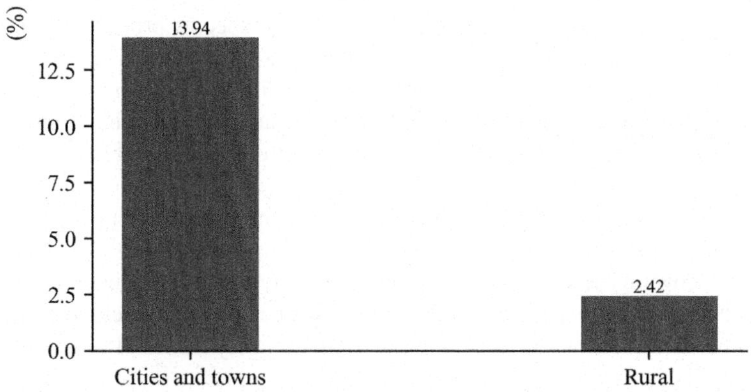


**Fig. 5** Coverage of financial products held by the full sample of households (urban–rural divisions)

rate of financial products held by households is 13.94%, whereas it is only 2.42% in rural areas. The difference between the coverage rates of the financial products held by urban and rural households is 11.52 percentage points, which is significant. Previous studies show that the gap in the choice of financial asset allocation between urban and rural residents in China is large, especially for risky financial products, and that the share of urban residents is much higher than that of rural residents [4]. This study verifies this view. This also implies that rural areas have great market potential for developing financial investments. Financial institutions should provide regular financial literacy lectures to potential investors in rural areas and promote financial products in a targeted and reasonable manner to enhance rural residents' acceptance of access to products. Simultaneously, the government should also widely publicize financial knowledge, especially in rural areas, and use various channels, such as the Internet, WeChat, and SMS, to publicize and popularize financial knowledge for rural residents, improve their understanding of financial products, and optimize and enhance their investment concepts. This is important for building a harmonious society and the smooth development of the market economy, which is also conducive to the preservation and appreciation of the wealth of rural families and stimulates their enthusiasm of rural families to participate in financial market investment.

According to Fig. 6, the coverage rate of financial products held by mid-high net worth households is significantly higher than that of non mid-high net worth households, in both urban and rural areas. Specifically, there is a difference of 28.79 percentage points between the coverage rate of financial products held by urban MHP households and non-MHP households and a difference of 11.28 percentage points between the coverage rate of financial products held by rural and non-MHP households. It is observed that the gap between different types of households in urban areas is significantly higher than that in rural areas in terms of the coverage rate of financial products held by households.

The results can be compared with previous results for neighborhood and village councils (community-based). Overall, the results were consistent between the two groups. However, there was a slight difference in the specific proportions. This was due to the existence of "urban villages" in urban areas. Meanwhile, in rural areas, some village committees have been converted into neighborhood committees because of the construction of new rural areas. Thus, there are crossover situations between them. However, in general, this did not affect the differences between urban and rural areas.

It calculates the coverage of financial product holdings for the full sample of households based on city type. The results are summarized in Fig. 7. According to Fig. 7, the coverage rate of financial products held by households decreases stepwise as the city rank decreases. The coverage rate of financial products held by households in first-tier cities reaches 32.24%. That is, approximately a third of households hold

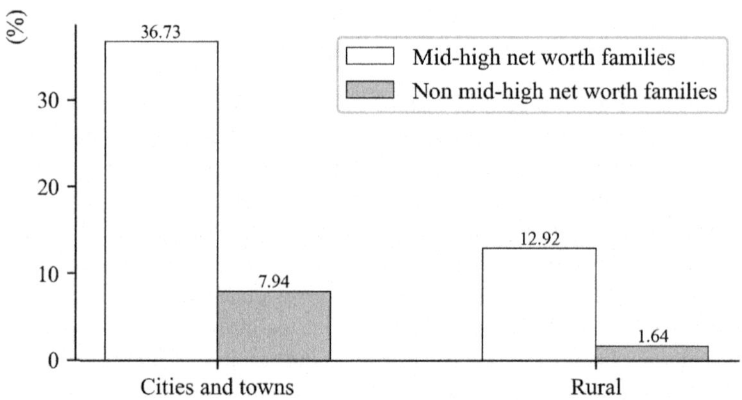


**Fig. 6** Coverage of financial products held by mid-high net worth households and non mid-high net worth households (in urban and rural areas)

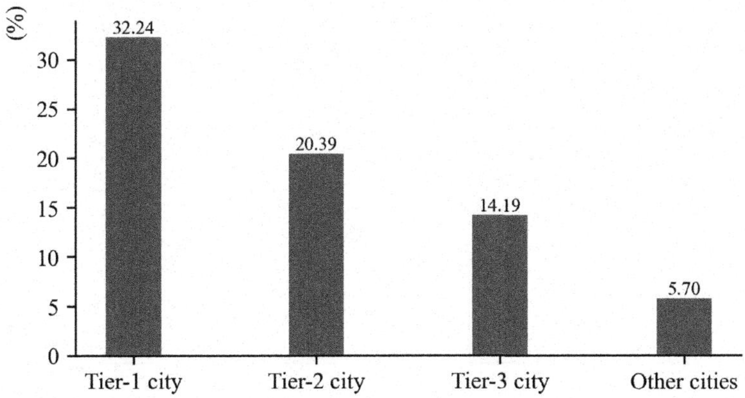


**Fig. 7** Coverage of financial products held by the full sample of households (city type)

financial products. The coverage rate of financial products held by households in second-tier cities dropped to 20.39% or about a fifth of households held financial products. The coverage rate of financial products held by households in third-tier cities is 14.19%, whereas that of financial products held by households in other cities is only 5.7%.

According to Fig. 8, the coverage rate of financial products held by mid-high net worth households is significantly higher than that of non mid-high net worth households regardless of the city tier. Specifically, there is a 35.5 percentage point difference between the coverage rates of financial products held by mid-high net worth households and non mid-high net worth households in first-tier cities, a 28.75 percentage point difference between the coverage rates of financial products held by mid-high net worth households and non mid-high net worth households in second-tier cities, a 22.66 percentage point difference between the coverage rates of financial products held by mid-high net worth households and non mid-high net worth households in third-tier cities, and a 17.66 percentage point difference between the coverage rates of financial products held by mid-high net worth. The difference between the coverage rate of financial products held by high-net-worth (HNW) households and non-high-net-worth (non-HNW) households in other cities is 17.07 percentage points. In summary, the gap between the coverage rates of financial products held by households with different economic conditions gradually increases as the city level increases. In addition, in tier 1 cities, the coverage rate of financial products held by mid-high net worth households reached 53.31%, and more than half of the mid-high net worth households hold financial products.

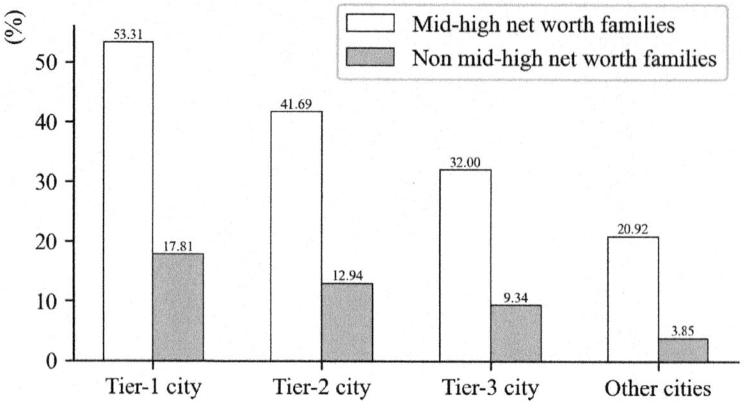


**Fig. 8** Coverage of financial product holdings by mid-high net worth households and non mid-high net worth households (city type)

## *1.2 Head of Household Level*

In addition to household-level factors, head-of-household-level factors can affect household holdings of financial products. It calculates the coverage of financial product holdings for the full sample of households by grouping them according to the education level of the household head, and the results are summarized in Fig. 9.

As shown in Fig. 9, the coverage rate of financial products held by households gradually increases as the education level of the household head increases. When the household head's education level is secondary or tertiary, there is a significant difference between the coverage rate of household holdings of financial products and households whose head's education level is at or below primary education. It has

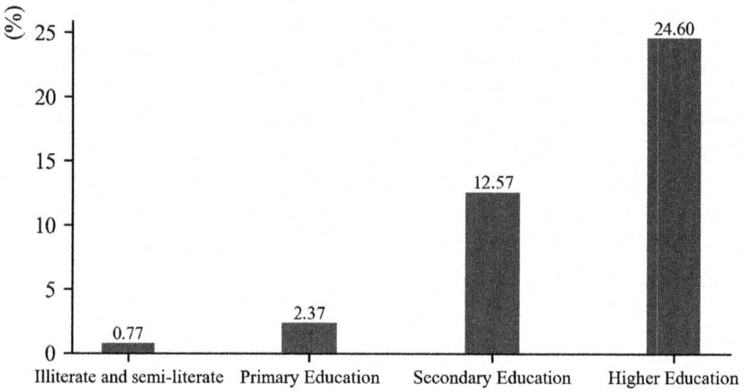


**Fig. 9** Coverage of financial products held by the full sample of households (education level of household head)

been shown that the education level of the household head has a positive effect on the participation and the holding ratio of risky financial assets [5]. The increase in education not only increases employment opportunities and residents' income, but also improves individuals' cognitive ability, avoids irrational investment and financial behavior, increases the probability of individuals' participation in the stock and other risky asset markets, and changes the ratio of risky to risk-free household assets. Foreign studies have shown that an additional year of education for the household head increases the household's stock market participation by two percentage points and the share of financial wealth allocated to stocks by 10 percentage points [6]. These findings indicate that education boosts financial market participation.

According to Fig. 10, the coverage rate of financial product holdings is significantly higher for households with medium and high-net-worth than it is for non-medium and high-net-worth households, regardless of the education level of the household head. Specifically, for illiterate/semi-literate heads of households, there is a 5.2 percentage point difference between the coverage rates of financial products held by mid-high net worth households and non mid-high net worth households. For primary education, there is a 12.06 percentage point difference between the coverage rates of financial products held by mid-high net worth households and non mid-high net worth households and for secondary education, there is a 26.11 percentage point difference between the coverage rates of financial products held by mid-high net worth households and non mid-high net worth households. When the education level of the household head is secondary, there is a difference of 26.11 percentage points between the coverage rate of financial products held by mid-high net worth households and non mid-high net worth households. When the education level of the household head is higher, there is a difference of 22.51 percentage points between the coverage rate of financial products held by mid-high net worth households and non mid-high net worth households. In summary, when the education level of the household head is secondary education, the difference between the coverage rate of financial products held by mid-high net worth households and non mid-high net worth households is the largest. When the education level of the household head is illiterate/semi-literate, the difference between the coverage rate of financial products held by mid-high net worth households and non mid-high net worth households is the smallest. Notably, the higher the education level of the head of household, the greater the differentiation of household holdings of financial products. The more educated the household head, the more they have a unique judgment on the allocation of risky assets. Resultantly, the more likely it is that the household's financial thinking is different and the greater the difference in the proportion of financial products held by the household.

Due to the innate biological and psychological differences between males and females, different decision patterns within households regarding asset allocation often lead to different decision outcomes. It is grouped according to the gender of household heads to calculate the coverage of financial products held by mid-high net worth households and non mid-high net worth households. The results are summarized in Fig. 11.

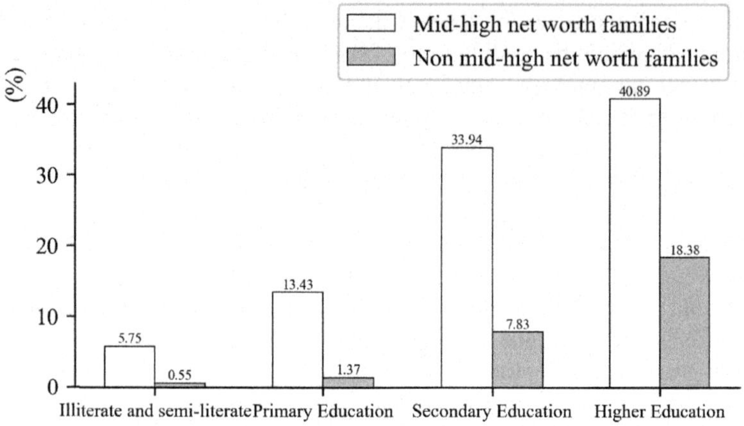


**Fig. 10** Coverage of financial product holdings of mid-high net worth households and non mid-high net worth households (education level of household head)

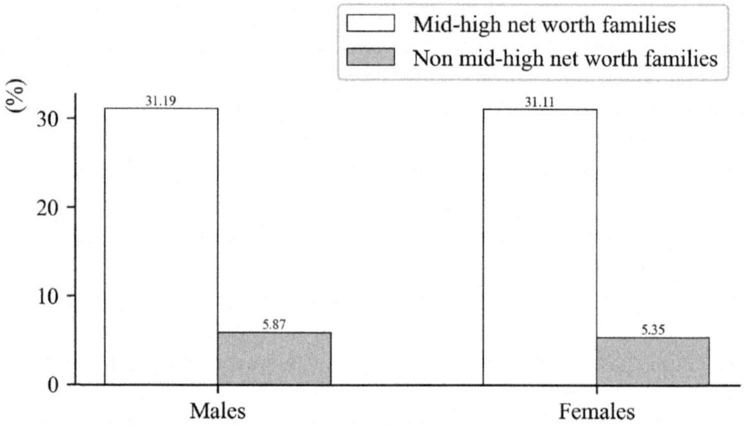


**Fig. 11** Coverage of financial products held by mid-high net worth households and non mid-high net worth households (gender of household head)

According to Fig. 11, overall, the overall coverage rate of financial products held by households with male heads is slightly higher than that of households with female heads. When the head of household is male, there is a difference of 25.32 percentage points between the coverage rate of financial products held by mid-high net worth households and non mid-high net worth households. When the head of household is female, there is a difference of 25.76 percentage points between the coverage rate of financial products held by mid-high net worth households and non mid-high net worth households. In summary, the difference between the coverage rate of financial products held by mid-high net worth households and non mid-high net

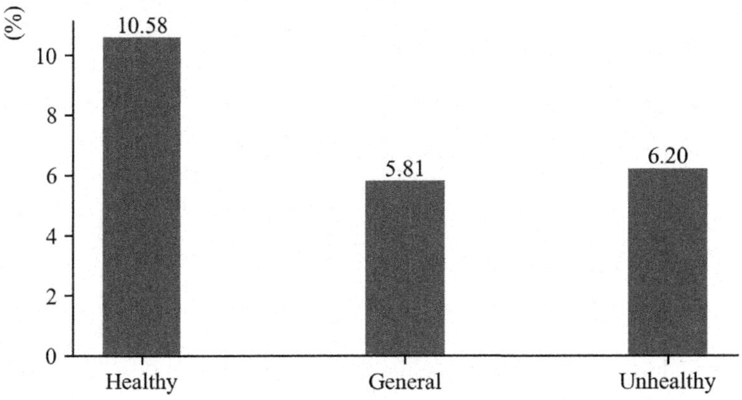


**Fig. 12** Coverage of financial products held by the full sample of households (health status of household head)

worth households is larger when the head of household is female. Female decision-making empowerment has a significantly negative effect on both the probability of household participation in financial markets and the share of risky financial assets [6]. Conversely, households headed by males are more likely to participate in risky asset markets, because males have higher risk preferences [7]. Consequently, a higher proportion of households headed by men held financial products.

It is grouped according to the health status of the household head and calculates the coverage of financial products held by the full sample of households. The results are summarized in Fig. 12.

According to Fig. 12, the coverage of household holdings of financial products is highest when the household head is healthy and lowest when the household head is in fair health. When the head of a household is healthy, they tend to be more energetic and can participate in investments and transactions, including the stock market. Thus, the household is more likely to allocate risky financial assets. If the head of household is unhealthy, the household will monetize a portion of its assets for medical expenses, which may cause it to withdraw from the equity market.

According to Fig. 13, overall, the overall coverage rate of financial products held by mid-high net worth households is significantly higher than that of non mid-high net worth households, regardless of the health status of the head of the household. Specifically, when the head of household is healthy, there is a 25.86 percentage point difference between the coverage rate of financial products held by mid-high net worth households and non mid-high net worth households. When the head of household is in fair health, there is a 21.84 percentage point difference between the coverage rate of financial products held by mid-high net worth households and non mid-high net worth households and when the head of household is not healthy, there is a 26.17 percentage point difference between the coverage rate of financial products held by mid-high net worth households and non mid-high net worth households. When the head of the household is unhealthy, there is a difference of 26.17 percentage points

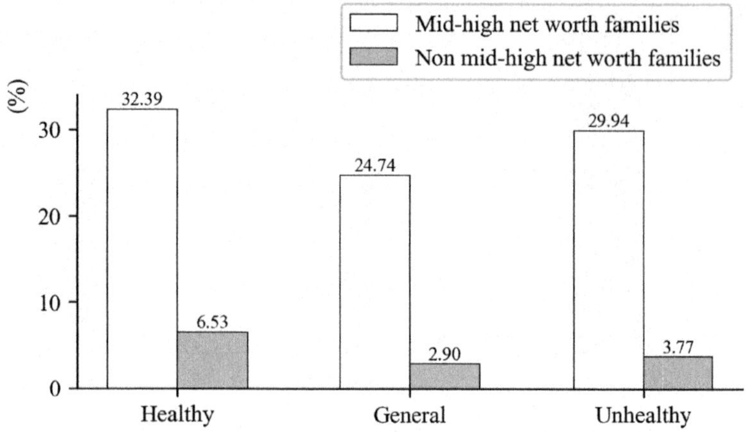


**Fig. 13** Coverage of financial product holdings (health status of household head) for mid-high net worth households and non-middle-net-worth households

between the coverage rate of financial products held by mid-high net worth households and non-high-net-worth households. In summary, the difference in coverage rates between households with different economic conditions is significant, especially when the head of the household is unhealthy, and the difference in coverage rates of financial products held by mid-high net worth households and non mid-high net worth households is the largest.

It is grouped according to the marital status of the household head and calculates the coverage of financial products held by the full sample of households. The results are summarized in Fig. 14.

According to Fig. 14, the coverage rate of financial products held by households is highest when the head of household is unmarried. Some households prepare for

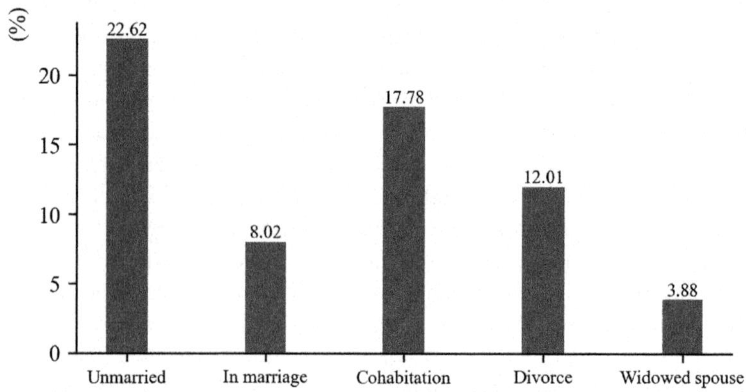


**Fig. 14** Coverage of financial products held by the full sample of households (marital status of household head)

marriage and adopt aggressive investment strategies, investing in the stock market and other channels to increase household wealth as soon as possible. In addition, being unmarried, the head of the household is more likely to be risk-averse and, therefore, more likely to hold financial products [8]. The coverage of financial products held by households was lowest when the head of household was widowed.

As shown in Fig. 15, in general, the coverage rate of financial products held by mid-high net worth households is significantly higher than that of non mid-high net worth households, regardless of the marital status of the household head. Specifically, the coverage rate of financial products held by households with unmarried heads was 29.95 percentage points higher than that of non-HNW households. The coverage rate of financial products held by households with married heads was 24.81 percentage points higher than that of non-HNW households. The coverage rate of financial products held by households with cohabiting heads was 25 percentage points higher than that of non-HNW households and the coverage rate of financial products held by households with divorced heads was 25 percentage points higher than that of non-HNW households. The coverage rate of financial products held by households with divorced heads is 31.49 percentage points higher than that of non-HNW households, and the coverage rate of financial products held by households with widowed heads is 30.25 percentage points higher than that of non-HNW households. In summary, the gap between the coverage rate of financial products held by mid-high net worth households and non mid-high net worth households is largest when the head of the household is divorced, and the gap between the coverage rate of financial products held by mid-high net worth households and non mid-high net worth households is smallest when the head of household is married.

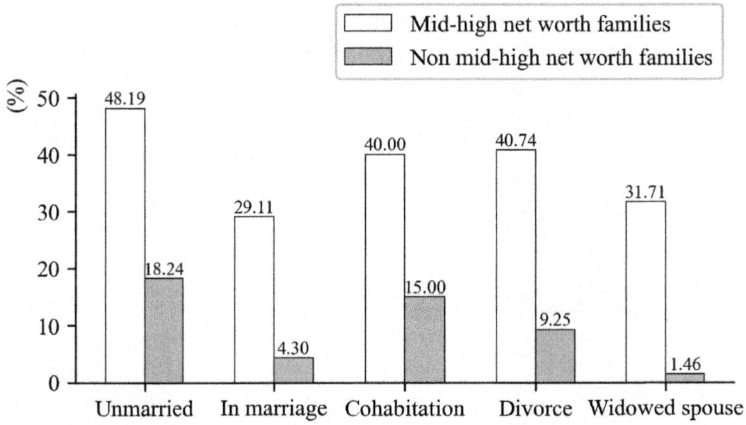


**Fig. 15** Coverage of financial products held by mid-high net worth households and non mid-high net worth households (marital status of household head)

# 2 Analysis of the Total Price of Financial Products Held by Households

The value of household financial products reflects the intensity of the allocation of risky financial assets. From the current development trend of China's financial investment and finance industry as a whole, family-based financial investment and finance activities are becoming increasingly frequent, and the amount of family financial investment and finance is increasing, which not only has many benefits for the preservation and appreciation of family assets but also has an important positive sign for the Chinese market economy's and capital market's operation. This book analyzes the value of financial products held by mid-high net worth families by calculating the average value of the total value of financial products held by families.

## 2.1 *Family Level*

It is grouped according to the nature of the community and calculates the total value of financial products held by the full sample of households, and the results are summarized in Fig. 16.

According to Fig. 16, the total price of financial products held by households whose community structure is a neighborhood council is ¥112,500 higher than that of households whose community structure is a village council, and the difference between them is significant.

According to Fig. 17, in general, the total price of financial products held by mid-high net worth households is significantly higher than that of non mid-high net worth households for both neighborhood and village committees. Specifically, the total value of financial products held by mid-high net worth households, whose

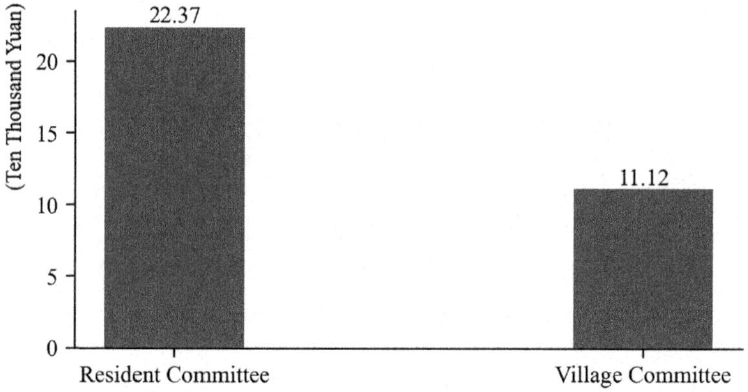


**Fig. 16** Total value of financial product holdings (community-based) for the full sample of households

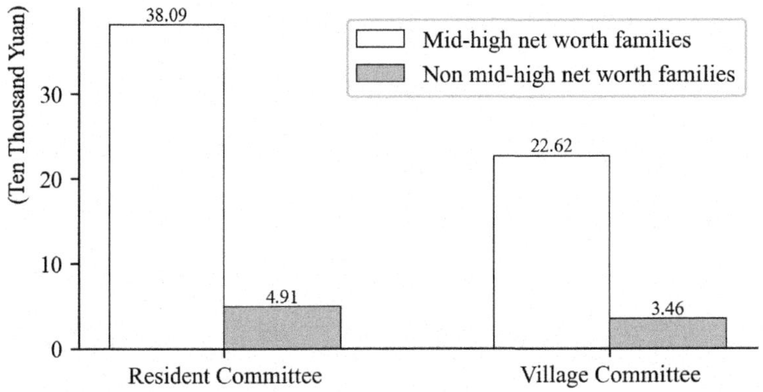


**Fig. 17** Total value of financial product holdings (community-based nature) for mid-high net worth households and non mid-high net worth households

community nature is a neighborhood committee, is ¥331,800 higher than that of non mid-high net worth households. The total value of financial products held by mid-high net worth households whose community nature is a village committee is ¥191,600 higher than that of non mid-high net worth households.

It groups households according to their size and calculates the total value of financial products held by the full sample of households, and the results are summarized in Fig. 18.

According to Fig. 18, when the household size is 4–6 people, the total price of financial products held by the household is the highest, reaching 226,800 yuan. When the household size is 10 people and above, the total price of financial products held by the household is the lowest, only 110,000 yuan.

According to Fig. 19, overall, regardless of household size, the total price of financial products held by mid-high net worth households is significantly higher than that held by non mid-high net worth households. Specifically, when the household

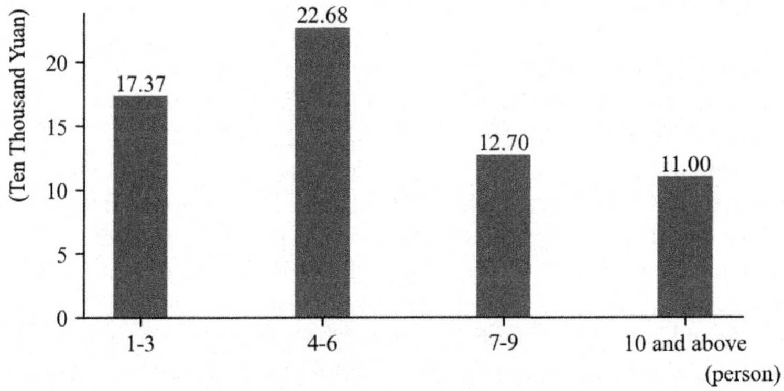


**Fig. 18** Total value of financial product holdings (household size) for the full sample of households

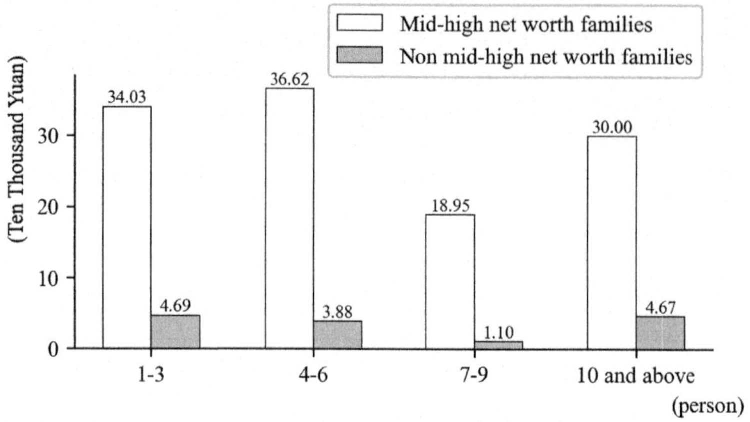


**Fig. 19** Total value of financial product holdings (household size) for mid-high net worth households and non-middle-net-worth households

size is one to three persons, the total value of financial products held by mid-high net worth households is 293,400 yuan higher than that held by non mid-high net worth households. When the household size is four to six persons, the total value of financial products held by mid-high net worth households is 327,400 yuan higher than that held by non mid-high net worth households and when the household size is seven to nine persons, the total value of financial products held by mid-high net worth households is 178,500 yuan higher than that held by non mid-high net worth households when the family size is 10 or more. The total price of financial products held by mid-high net worth households is ¥253,300 higher than that held by non mid-high net worth households. In summary, the difference between the total prices of financial products held by mid-high net worth households and non mid-high net worth households is more obvious.

It is grouped according to urban and rural divisions and calculates the total value of financial product holdings for the full sample of households. The results are summarized in Fig. 20.

According to Fig. 20, the difference between the total price of financial products held by urban households and rural households is 148,000 yuan, and the total price of financial products held by urban households is significantly higher than that of rural households, and the difference is very significant.

According to Fig. 21, the total price of financial products held by mid-high net worth households is significantly higher than those held by non mid-high net worth households in urban and rural areas. Specifically, the difference between the total price of financial products held by urban and non-MHP households was ¥335,600. The difference between the total price of financial products held by rural MHP households and non-MHP households is ¥152,100. In urban areas, the total price of financial products held by mid-high net worth households reached RMB 386,100, while in rural areas, it was RMB 181,900.

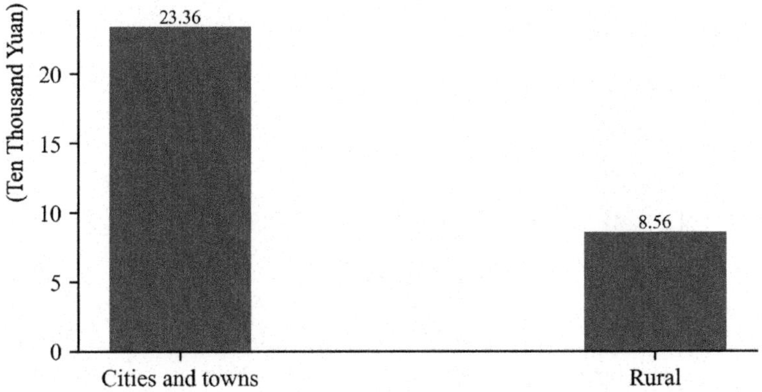


**Fig. 20** Total value of financial product holdings for the full sample of households (urban and rural divisions)

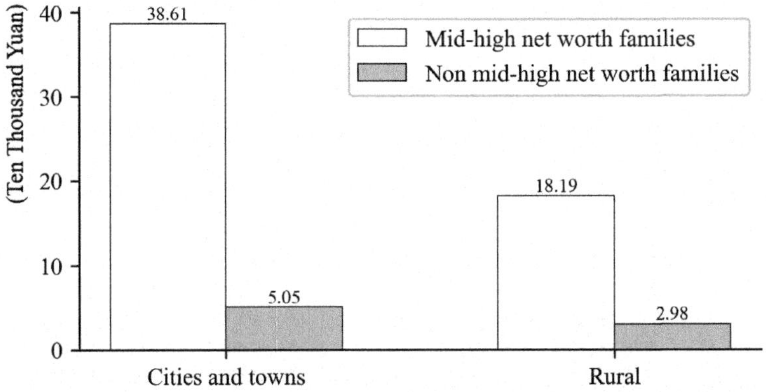


**Fig. 21** Total value of financial product holdings of mid-high net worth households and non mid-high net worth households (urban and rural divisions)

It is grouped according to city type and calculates the total value of financial product holdings for the full sample of households, and the results are summarized in Fig. 22.

According to Fig. 22, the total price of financial products held by households in tier 1 cities is the highest at 408,200 yuan. In comparison, the total price of financial products held by households in tier 2 and tier 3 cities is relatively low, close to RMB 170,000. The total price of financial products held by households in other cities was the lowest at 117,400 yuan.

According to Fig. 23, the total price of financial products held by mid-high net worth households was significantly higher than that of non mid-high net worth households in both cities. The difference between the total price of financial products held by mid-high net worth households and non mid-high net worth households in tier

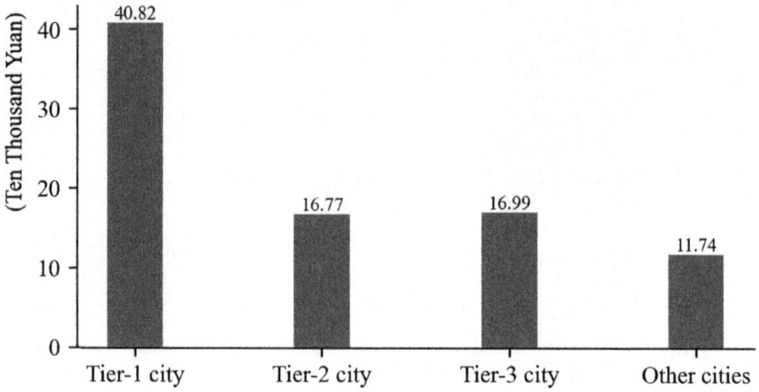


**Fig. 22** Total value of financial product holdings for the full sample of households (city type)

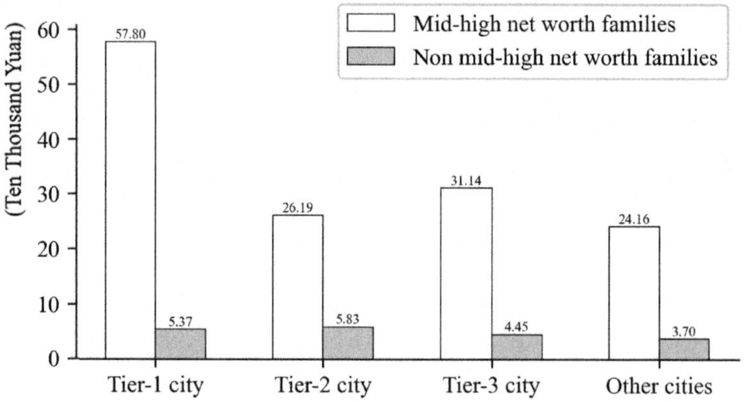


**Fig. 23** Total price of financial product holdings of mid-high net worth households and non mid-high net worth households (city type)

1 cities is RMB 524,300. The difference between the total price of financial products held by mid-high net worth households and non mid-high net worth households in tier 2 cities is RMB 203,600. The difference between the total price of financial products held by mid-high net worth households and non mid-high net worth households in tier 3 cities is RMB 266,900. The difference between the total price of financial products held by mid-high net worth households and non mid-high net worth households in other cities is RMB 204,600. The difference between the total prices of financial products held by HNW and non-HNW households in other cities was RMB 204,600.

## 2.2 *Head of Household Level*

It calculates the total value of financial products held by the full sample of households by grouping them according to the education level of the household head, and the results are summarized in Fig. 24.

According to Fig. 24, the total value of the financial products held by households tends to increase in a stepwise manner as the education level of the household head increases. The more educated the household head, the more knowledgeable he/she is about financial investment, the better he/she can manage risk, and the more likely he/she is to invest more money in financial products [9].

According to Fig. 25, in general, the total value of financial products held by mid-high net worth households is significantly higher than that of non mid-high net worth households regardless of the education level of the household head. Specifically, the difference between the total value of financial products held by mid-high net worth households and non mid-high net worth households is ¥153,100 when the education level of the household head is illiterate/semi-literate, ¥223,900 when the education level of the household head is primary, ¥266,900 when the education level of the household head is secondary education, and ¥266,900 when the total value of financial products is held by mid-high net worth households and non mid-high net worth households. When the education level of the head of household is secondary education, the difference between the total price of financial products held by mid-high net worth households and non mid-high net worth households is 266,900 yuan. When the education level of the head of household is higher education, the difference between the total price of financial products held by mid-high net worth households and non mid-high net worth households is 422,300 yuan. In summary, the difference between the total price of financial products held by mid-high net worth households and non mid-high net worth households gradually increases with an increase in the education level of the household head.

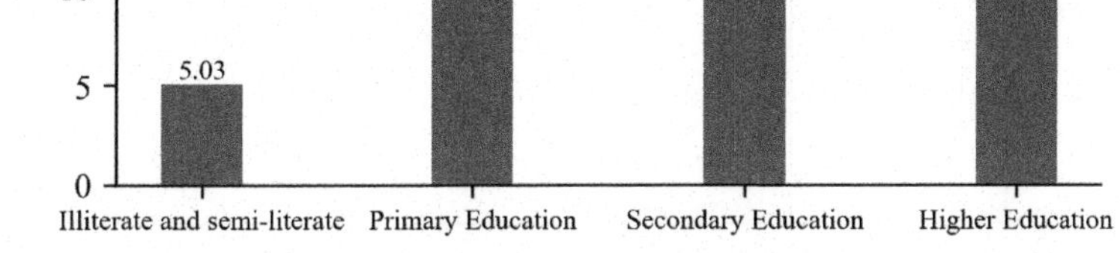


**Fig. 24** Total value of financial products held by the full sample of households (education level of household head)

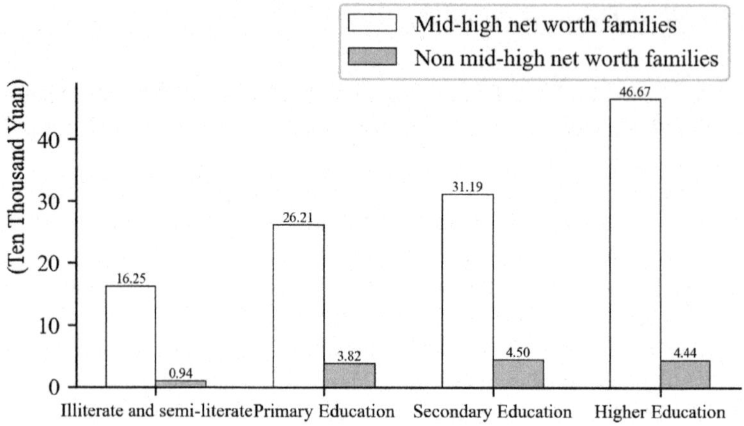


**Fig. 25** Total value of financial product holdings (education level of household head) for mid-high net worth households and non mid-high net worth households

It is grouped according to the gender of the household head and calculates the total value of financial products held by mid-high net worth households and non mid-high net worth households, and the results are summarized in Fig. 26.

According to Fig. 26, in general, the total value of financial products held by both mid-high net worth households and non mid-high net worth households is higher when the household head is male than when the household head is female. Regardless of whether the household head is male or female, the total value of financial products held by mid-high net worth households is significantly higher than that of non mid-high net worth households. Specifically, the difference between the total value of financial products held by mid-high net worth households and non mid-high net

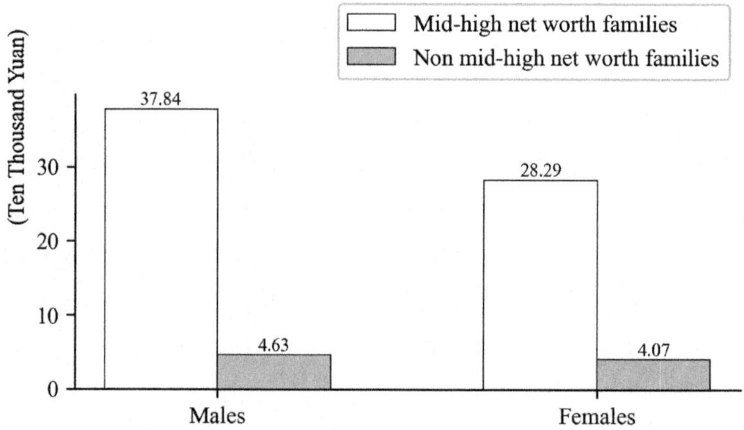


**Fig. 26** Total value of financial product holdings of mid-high net worth households and non mid-high net worth households (gender of household head)

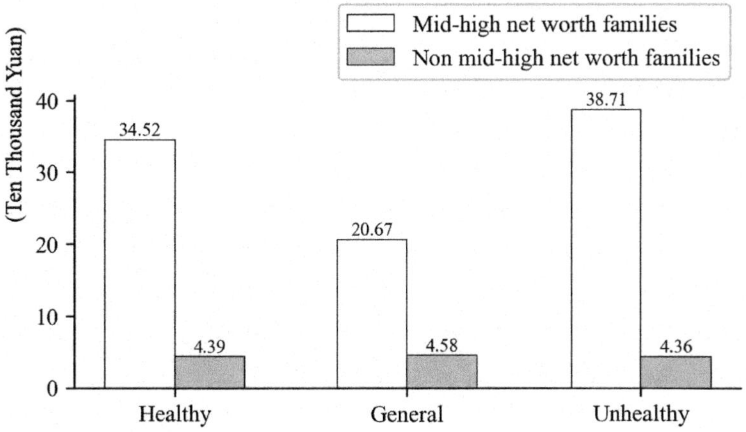


**Fig. 27** Total value of financial product holdings (health status of household head) for mid-high net worth households and non-middle-net-worth households

worth households is RMB 332,100 when the head of the household is male and RMB 242,200 when the head of the household is female. In summary, the difference between the total price of financial products held by mid-high net worth households and non mid-high net worth households is larger when the head of the household is male.

It calculates the total value of financial product holdings for mid-high net worth households and non mid-high net worth households by grouping them according to the health status of the household head, and the results are summarized in Fig. 27.

According to Fig. 27, overall, the total value of financial products held by mid-high net worth households is significantly higher than that of non mid-high net worth households, regardless of the health status of the head of the household. Specifically, when the head of household is healthy, the difference between the total value of financial products held by mid-high net worth households and non mid-high net worth households is ¥301,300. When the head of household is in fair health, the difference between the total value of financial products held by mid-high net worth households and non mid-high net worth households is ¥160,900. When the head of household is unhealthy, the difference between the total value of financial products held by mid-high net worth households and non mid-high net worth households is ¥343,500. In summary, the difference between the total price of financial products held by mid-high net worth households and non mid-high net worth households is significant. It calculates the total value of financial products held by mid-high net worth households and non mid-high net worth households by grouping them according to the marital status of the household head, and the results are summarized in Fig. 28.

According to Fig. 28, overall, regardless of the marital status of the head of household, the total value of financial products held by mid-high net worth households is significantly higher than that of non mid-high net worth households. Specifically, the

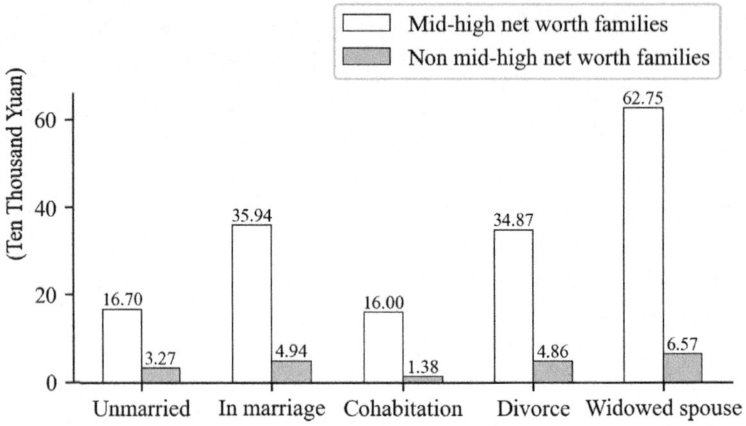


**Fig. 28** Total value of financial product holdings (marital status of household head) for mid-high net worth households and non-middle-net-worth households

total value of financial products held by MHP households with unmarried status is ¥134,300 higher than that of non-MHP households, the total value of financial products held by MHP households with married status is ¥310,000 higher than that of non-MHP households, the total value of financial products held by MHP households with cohabiting status is ¥146,200 higher than that of non-MHP households, and the total value of financial products held by MHP households with divorced status is the total value of financial products held by the mid-high net worth households with divorced heads is ¥300,100 higher than that of the non mid-high net worth households. The total value of financial products held by the mid-high net worth households with widowed heads is ¥561,800 higher than that of the non mid-high net worth households. In summary, the difference between the total value of financial products held by mid-high net worth households and non mid-high net worth households is the largest when the household head is widowed. The difference between the total value of financial products held by mid-high net worth households and non mid-high net worth households is the smallest when the household head is unmarried.

## 3 Analysis of the Proportion of Risky Financial Assets to Total Household Financial Assets

For mid-high net worth families, the purpose of good asset allocation is to ensure the steady growth of family assets as much as possible, and thus achieve the preservation and appreciation of family assets [10]. The study of "asset allocation" originated in the 1950s. Harry Markowitz's 1952 article "Portfolio Selection" laid the foundation of the Modern Portfolio Theory [11]. Later, the capital asset pricing model proposed by William F. Sharpe took the asset allocation theory a big step forward and became an important basis for decision-making in asset valuation, capital cost budgeting, and resource allocation [12]. In economic terms, "asset allocation" refers to the process of selecting and proportioning different asset classes in a portfolio to maximize the return on investment while controlling risk [13]. The asset allocation theory's main purpose is to balance risk and protect investment returns by helping investors create diversified asset classes [14]. With the development and growth of capital markets, the asset allocation theory has been empirically tested and has become an important body of knowledge to guide investors in making sound investment decisions.

With the continuous development of financial markets and rising income levels, options available to mid-high net worth households in the investment arena are becoming increasingly diverse. The rise of family finance theory has provided an important theory for the optimal asset allocation of mid-high net worth households [15]. The allocation of household financial assets is inextricably linked to uncertainty factors affecting household income and background risks, which also show significant variability depending on the country and region in which they are located [16]. Mid-high net worth households in China can choose either bank deposits with low risk or stocks, funds, and bonds with some risk, and of course, they can also transform their household financial assets into investment properties by investing in properties. For mid-high net worth families, in the short term, their financial assets decrease. However, because housing prices are generally rising, once investment property is sold, the financial assets held by the household will grow rapidly. Therefore, there is often a flow of funds between housing and stock markets in China. In terms of specific operations, mid-high net worth households adopt different investment strategies to optimize the allocation of their financial asset holdings within the risk they can bear.

Household financial assets generally refer to bonds and ownership assets held by households, characterized by the circulation of funds or money and credit relationships, including cash, bank deposits, stocks, funds, bonds, financial products, lending money, savings insurance, life insurance, housing fund balances, and other financial assets. Household financial assets can be divided into two categories. The first category is risk-free financial assets, which have zero standard deviation of expected returns and are therefore held without any risk or with very little risk. The other category is risky financial assets, which can earn future returns. However, such future returns are uncertain and may lose money due to changes in the market. Therefore, holding such financial assets involves a certain degree of risk. Therefore, the allocation of financial assets is first and foremost between risky and risk-free financial assets.

For mid-high net worth families, how to make a reasonable allocation between risk-free financial assets and risky financial assets is a key issue in family financial asset allocation. As risk and return are often proportional in the financial investment field, the allocation weight of risky financial assets for mid-high net worth families will have a direct impact on the future appreciation of family assets. Holding risky financial assets may lead to depreciation or even loss. In contrast, if risk-free financial assets are held, there is no risk of devaluation or loss, so the family's financial assets can be effectively preserved, but the ability to increase their value may be poor. For mid-high net worth families, the allocation of these two types of financial assets directly determines the preservation and appreciation of family financial assets. In addition, the allocation of mid-high net worth households to risk-free and risky financial assets reflects their degree of risk appetite.

## *3.1 Family Level*

Based on the 2020 CFPS data, the allocation weights of mid-high net worth households to the above two categories of financial assets were calculated. Risk-free financial assets include cash and bank deposits, whereas risky financial assets include stocks, funds, and bonds. The allocation weights of these two types of financial assets reflect the financial asset allocation structure of mid-high net worth households. For mid-high net worth households, the decision-making process of the above two types of financial asset allocation is generally divided into two steps: the first step is to assess the household's risk resistance, risk appetite level, and expected future returns and the second step is to determine the weight of holding the above two types of financial assets. This book calculates the proportion of risky financial assets to total household financial assets for the full sample of households based on the nature of the community, and the results are summarized in Fig. 29.

According to Fig. 29, the share of risky financial assets in total household financial assets is 10.6 percentage points higher in the community nature of neighborhood councils than in the community nature of village councils. In neighborhood councils, the share of risky financial assets in total household financial assets reached 34.52%, while in village councils, the share was 23.92%.

According to Fig. 30, in general, the proportion of risky financial assets to total household financial assets is generally higher for mid-high net worth households than

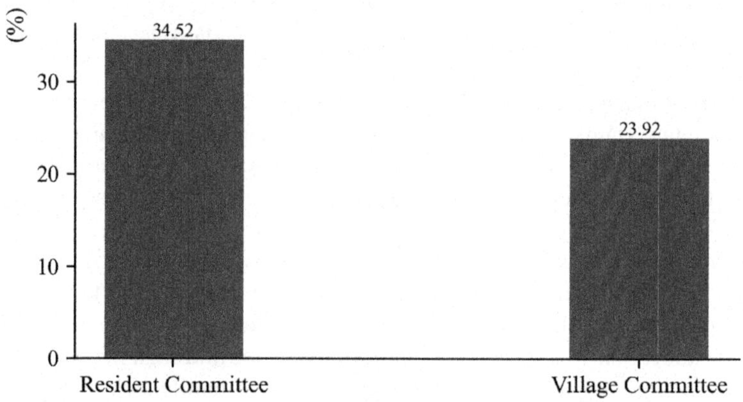


**Fig. 29** Share of risky financial assets in total household financial assets (community-based nature) for the full sample of households

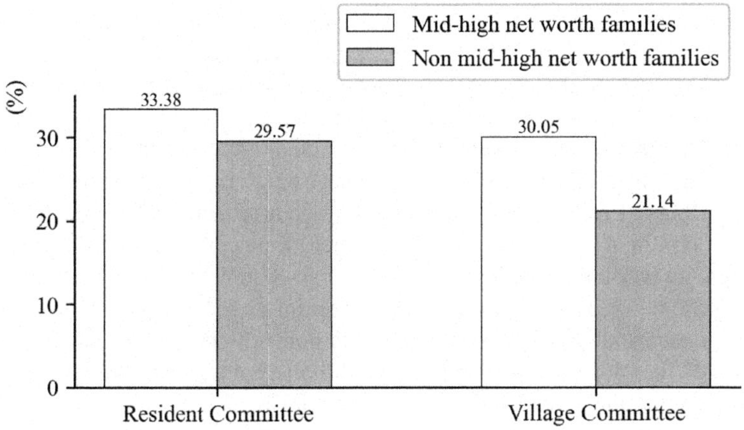


**Fig. 30** Risky financial asssets as a share of total household financial assets for mid-high net worth households and non mid-high net worth Households (community-based nature)

for non mid-high net worth households. Specifically, the proportion of risky financial assets to total household financial assets is 3.81 percentage points higher for mid-high net worth households whose community structure is a neighborhood committee than for non mid-high net worth households. The proportion of risky financial assets to total household financial assets is 8.91 percentage points higher for mid-high net worth households whose community structure is a village committee than for non mid-high net worth households. As can be seen, the gap is even larger among village committees.

It calculates the share of risky financial assets in total household financial assets for the full sample of households based on household size groupings, and the results are summarized in Fig. 31.

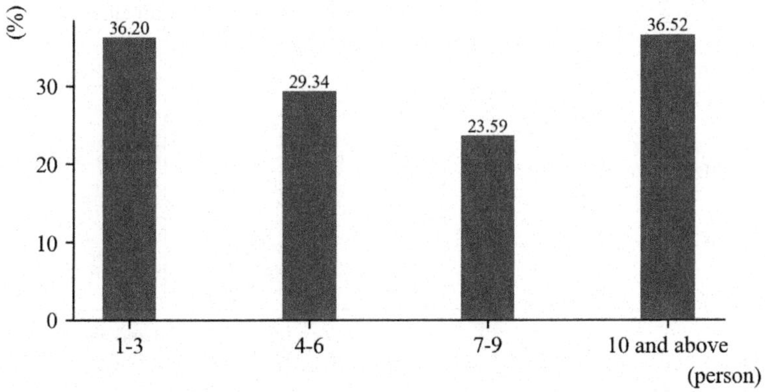


**Fig. 31** Share of risky financial assets in total household financial assets (household size) for the full sample of households

According to Fig. 31, the proportion of risky household financial assets to total household financial assets is highest when the household size is 10 and above, and lowest when the household size is 7 to 9 people. As the sample of households with 10 or more people is relatively small, this is for reference only. Excluding households with ten or more members, the overall proportion of risky household financial assets to total household financial assets shows a negative relationship with household size.

According to Fig. 32, when the household size is less than 10 people, the proportion of risky financial assets to total household financial assets is higher for both mid-high net worth households than for non mid-high net worth households. When the household size is 1–3 persons, the proportion of risky financial assets to total household financial assets is 3.46 percentage points higher for mid-high net worth households than for non mid-high net worth households, when the household size is 4–6 persons, the proportion of risky financial assets to total household financial assets is 5.89 percentage points higher for mid-high net worth households than for non mid-high net worth households, when the household size is 7–9 persons, the proportion of risky financial assets to total household financial assets is 5.89 percentage points higher for mid-high net worth households than for non mid-high net worth households. The proportion of risky financial assets in the total financial assets of households is 19.81 percentage points higher than that of non mid-high net worth households, when the household size is 10 or more, the proportion of risky financial assets in the total financial assets of non mid-high net worth households is 5.36 percentage points higher than that of mid-high net worth households.

It calculates the share of risky financial assets in total household financial assets for the full sample of households based on urban and rural divisions, and the results are summarized in Fig. 33.

According to Fig. 33, the ratio of risky household financial assets to total household financial assets is 6.92 percentage points higher in urban areas than in rural areas.

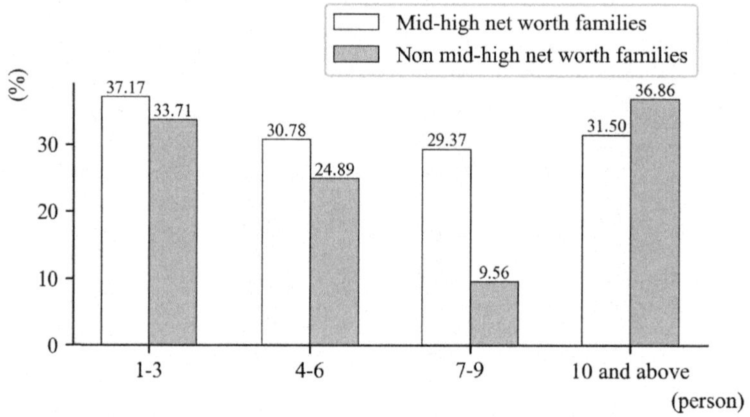


**Fig. 32** Share of risky financial assets in total household financial assets (household size) for mid-high net worth households and non mid-high net worth households

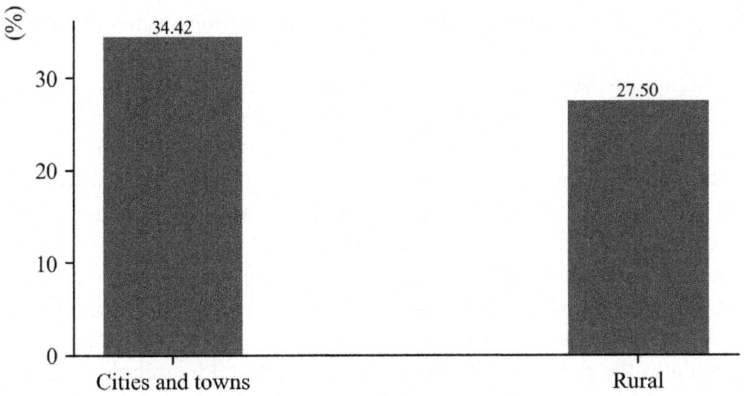


**Fig. 33** Share of risky financial assets in total household financial assets for the full sample of households (urban–rural divisions)

According to Fig. 34, the share of risky financial assets in total household financial assets is higher for mid-high net worth households than for non mid-high net worth households in both urban and rural areas. However, there are urban–rural differences in the gaps between the two. There is a difference of 4.89 percentage points between the proportion of risky financial assets to total household financial assets of urban mid-high net worth households and non mid-high net worth households and a difference of 1.54 percentage points between the proportion of risky financial assets to total household financial assets of rural and non mid-high net worth households. Therefore, in rural areas, the difference is even smaller.

Compared to rural mid-high net worth households, urban mid-high net worth households have a pronounced risk appetite and allocate more of their household

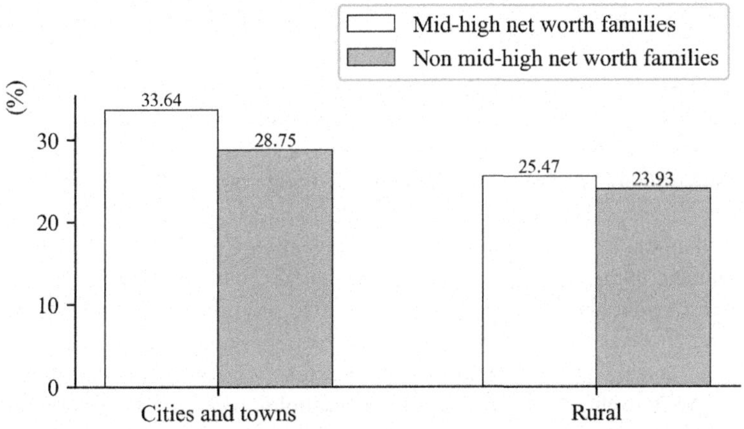


**Fig. 34** Share of risky financial assets in total household financial assets for mid-high net worth Households and non mid-high net worth Households (by urban and rural areas)

assets to risky financial assets. There were several reasons for this observation. For example, household asset allocation is constrained by household disposable income, which is generally lower in rural households than in towns [17]. Another example is that towns and cities have more complete financial mechanisms, high coverage of financial institution outlets, more stock exchanges, high-quality financial services, and relatively high financial accessibility, whereas rural areas are relatively underdeveloped in these aspects. This difference in external conditions is one reason for the difference in risky financial asset allocation between urban and rural mid-high net worth households [18]. In addition, urban residents are more educated and have more financial knowledge than rural residents, and their financial knowledge is generally higher, which has a positive effect on their participation in risky financial assets [19].

It calculates the share of risky financial assets in total household financial assets for the full sample of households based on city type, and the results are summarized in Fig. 35. According to Fig. 35, the proportion of risky household financial assets to total household financial assets is highest in tier 1 cities and lowest in tier 2 cities. A distinctive feature is that the allocation ratio of risky financial assets among HNW households in tier 1 cities is significantly higher than that in other cities. The proportion of risky financial assets to the total financial assets of HNW households in tier 1 cities was 36.18%. This result is consistent with the findings of previous studies. The 2021 China Private Wealth Report, jointly published by the China Merchants Bank and Bain and Company, defines individual holdings of stocks, funds, and bonds as capital market products. According to the report, after 2016, the ratio of capital market products to cash and deposits was almost 2:3, that is, the share of risky financial assets was approximately 40% (China Merchants Bank, Bain and Company, 2021). In addition, the Allianz Global Wealth Report 2020, published by Allianz Germany, shows that in 2019, Chinese household financial assets, such as insurance and pensions, only accounted for a very small part of the household portfolio, and Chinese household financial assets were still dominated by securities investments such as stocks, funds, bonds, and other asset management products and deposits, with stocks, funds, bonds, and other assets, and the proportion of asset management products such as stocks, funds, and bonds was 40.9% [3].

Since first-tier cities are the gathering place of mid-high net worth households, these mid-high net worth households generally hold more investable assets. Therefore, they have relatively stronger risk resistance and are more likely to increase their investment and allocation in risky financial assets. In addition, the capital market in first-tier cities is active, financial institutions are strong, the capital market is large, and the channels for household financial investment are more complete, all of which are conducive to the investment and allocation of risky financial assets for mid-high net worth households. From the perspective of family financial knowledge, first-tier cities tend to invest more in promoting and popularizing financial knowledge for the public, and this popularization is more extensive. As the financial knowledge acquired by household members grows, households have a more positive mindset toward participating in financial markets and tend to make riskier asset allocations in the asset allocation process [20]. This phenomenon is more common among HNW

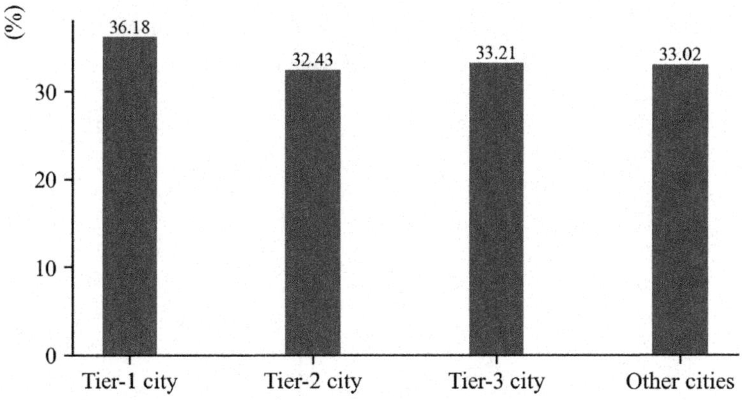


**Fig. 35** Share of risky financial assets in total household financial assets for the full sample of households (city type)

households in first-tier cities, where the financial knowledge possessed by HNW households is relatively rich and more comprehensive.

According to Fig. 36, in general, the proportion of risky financial assets to total household financial assets is generally higher for mid-high net worth households than for non mid-high net worth households, regardless of city type. Specifically, there is a difference of 4.05 percentage points between the proportion of risky financial assets to total household financial assets of HNW and non-HNW households in tier 1 cities, a difference of 3.96 percentage points between the proportion of risky financial assets and total household financial assets of HNW and non-HNW households in tier 2 cities, and a difference of 7.3 percentage points between the proportion of risky financial assets to total household financial assets of HNW and non-HNW households in tier 3 cities. There is a difference of 7.3 percentage points between the proportion of risky financial assets of HNW households in third-tier cities and non-HNW households and a difference of 2.97 percentage points between the proportion of risky financial assets of HNW households in other cities and non-HNW households.

## 3.2 *Head of Household Level*

It calculates the share of risky financial assets in total household financial assets for the full sample of households based on the education level of the household head, and the results are summarized in Fig. 37.

According to Fig. 37, the proportion of risky household financial assets to total household financial assets is lowest when the household head's education level is illiterate/semi-literate and highest when the household head's education level is secondary education.

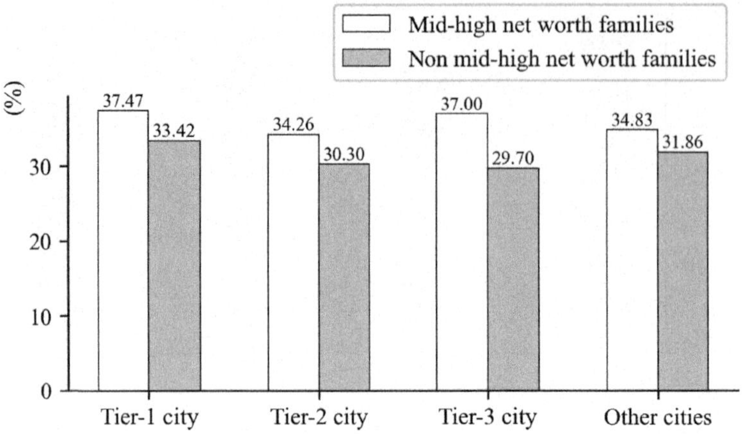


**Fig. 36** Risky financial assets as a share of total household financial assets for mid-high net worth households and non mid-high net worth households (city type)

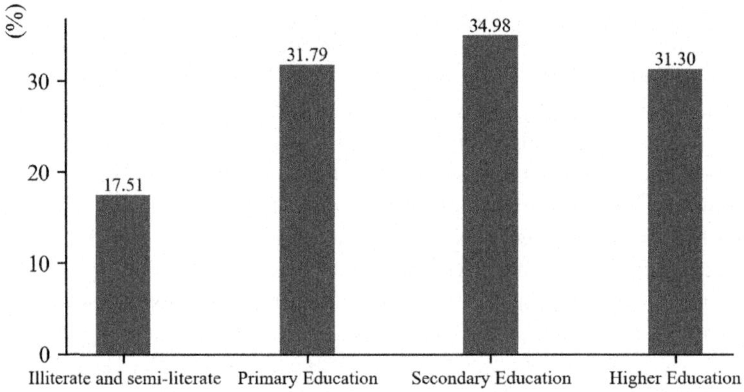


**Fig. 37** Risky financial assets as a share of total household financial assets for the full sample of households (education level of household head)

According to Fig. 38, when the education level of the household head is illiterate or semi-literate, there is a 17 percentage point difference in the proportion of risky financial assets to total household financial assets between med-high net worth households and non med-high net worth households. When the education level of the head of household is secondary, the difference between the proportion of risky financial assets to the total household financial assets of mid-high net worth households and non mid-high net worth households is 3.58 percentage points. When the education level of the head of household is tertiary, the difference between the proportion of risky financial assets to the total household financial assets of mid-high net worth households and non mid-high net worth households is 2.98 percentage points.

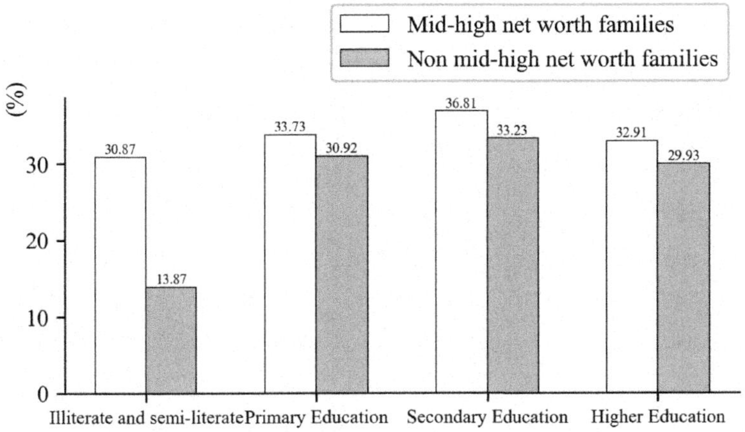


**Fig. 38** Risky financial assets as a share of total household financial assets for mid-high net worth households and non mid-high net worth households (education level of household head)

It calculates the share of risky financial assets in total household financial assets for the full sample of households based on the gender of the household head, and the results are summarized in Fig. 39.

According to Fig. 39, the share of risky household financial assets in total household financial assets is higher when the household head is male. However, this is not significantly different from the case in which the household's head is female.

According to Fig. 40, there is a 4.89 percentage point difference in the share of risky financial assets in total household financial assets between mid-high net worth households and non mid-high net worth households when the head of the household is male and a two percentage point difference when the head of the household is

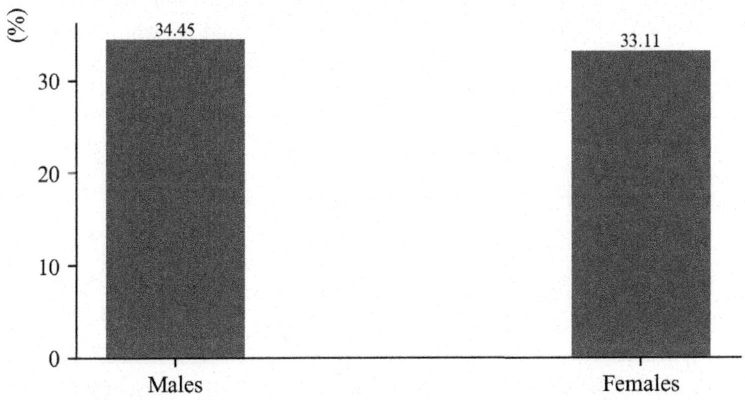


**Fig. 39** Share of risky financial assets in total household financial assets for the full sample of households (gender of household head)

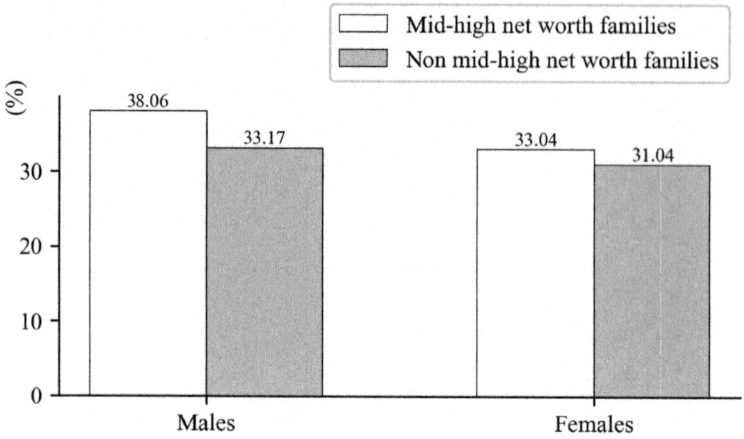


**Fig. 40** Risky financial assets as a share of total household financial assets for mid-high net worth households and non mid-high net worth households (gender of household head)

female. In summary, the difference between the two is greater when the head of the household is male.

It calculates the proportion of risky financial assets to total household financial assets for mid-high net worth households and non-mid-high net worth households based on the health status of the household head, and the results are summarized in Fig. 41.

According to Fig. 41, when the head of household is healthy, there is a 5.01 percentage point difference in the proportion of risky financial assets to total household financial assets between mid-high net worth households and non mid-high

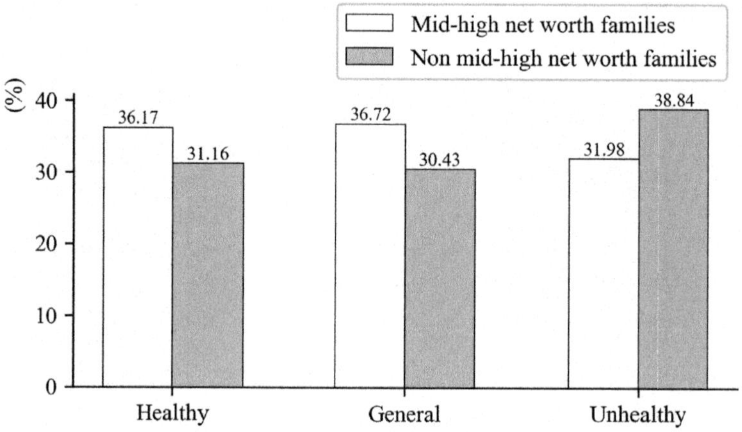


**Fig. 41** Risky financial assets as a share of total household financial assets for Mid-high net worth households and non mid-high net worth households (head of household health status)

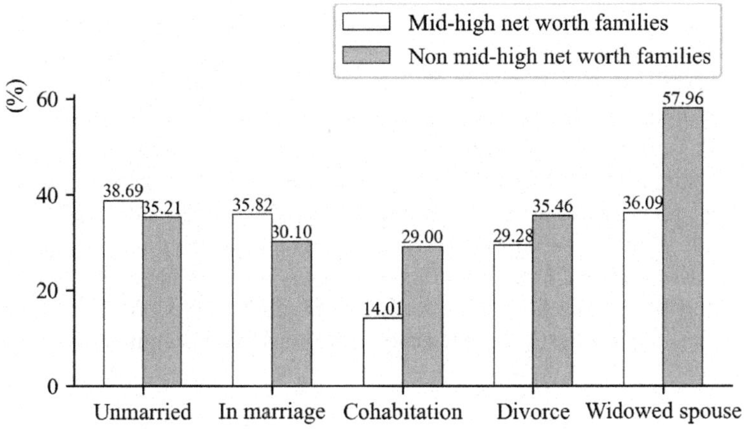


**Fig. 42** Share of risky financial assets in total household financial assets for mid-high net worth households and non-mid-high net worth households (marital status of household head)

net worth households; when the head of household is in fair health, there is a 6.29 percentage point difference in the proportion of risky financial assets to total household financial assets between mid-high net worth households and non mid-high net worth households. When the head of household is unhealthy, there is a 6.86 percentage point difference in the proportion of risky financial assets to total household financial assets between non mid-high net worth households and mid-high net worth households. When the head of the household is unhealthy, there is a 6.86 percentage point difference in the proportion of risky financial assets to total household financial assets between non-high- and medium-net-worth households.

It calculates the proportion of risky financial assets to total household financial assets for mid-high net worth households and non mid-high net worth households based on the marital status of the household head, and the results are summarized in Fig. 42.

According to Fig. 42, the proportion of risky financial assets to total household financial assets is 3.48 percentage points higher for households headed by unmarried households than for non mid-high net worth households. The proportion of risky financial assets to total household financial assets is 5.72 percentage points higher for households headed by married households than for non mid-high net worth households. Then, the proportion of risky financial assets to total household financial assets is 14.99 percentage points higher for non mid-high net worth households headed by cohabiting households than for Mid-high net worth households. Finally, the proportion of risky financial assets to total household financial assets is 14.99 percentage points higher for non mid-high net worth households headed by divorced households. The proportion of risky financial assets to total household financial assets is 14.99 percentage points higher than that of medium-high net-worth households. The proportion of risky financial assets to total household financial assets of non mid-high net worth households headed by divorced persons is 6.18 percentage points higher than that of mid-high net worth households and the proportion of risky financial assets to total household financial assets of non mid-high net worth households headed by widowed persons is 21.87 percentage points higher than that of mid-high net worth households. The proportion of risky financial assets to total household financial assets was 21.87 percentage points higher for households with widowed heads. In summary, the difference in the proportion of risky financial assets to total household financial assets is the largest between non-high and middle-net-worth households when the head of the household is widowed, and the proportion of risky financial assets to total household financial assets is much higher for non-high and middle-net-worth households than for high and middle-net-worth households. The difference is the smallest when the head of the household is unmarried.

# 4 Total Annual Earnings Analysis of Household Financial Investment

An important purpose for households holding financial products is to preserve and appreciate their wealth. The profitability of household financial investments is analyzed by examining the annual profitability of financial investments in the CFPS household sample in 2020. The specific indicator is the total annual profitability of household financial investments, that is, the total profitability of households holding financial products with certain risks, such as stocks, funds, treasury bonds, trust products, and foreign exchange products. Profits from risk-free financial products such as deposits are not included here.

## *4.1 Family Level*

It calculates the total annual earnings of financial investments for the full sample of households based on the nature of the community. The results are summarized in Fig. 43.

According to Fig. 43, the total annual profit of household financial investment is ¥112,068.4, which is significantly higher for community nature as neighborhood committees than for community nature as village committees.

According to Fig. 44, overall, the total annual profit of financial investment of mid-high net worth households is significantly higher than that of non mid-high net worth households. The total annual profit of financial investment of mid-high net worth households whose community nature is a neighborhood committee is higher than that of non mid-high net worth households by ¥331,847.93. The total annual surplus of financial investment of mid-high net worth households whose community nature is a village committee is higher than that of non mid-high net worth households by ¥191,400.29. The difference between the two was evident.

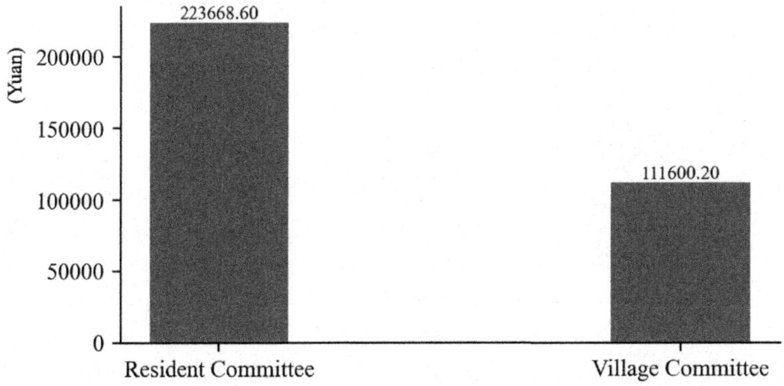


**Fig. 43** Total annual earnings of financial investments for the full sample of households (community-based in nature)

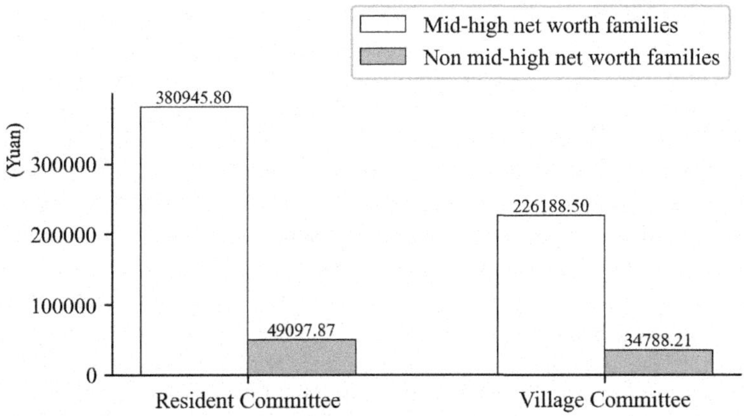


**Fig. 44** Total annual earnings from financial investments for mid-high net worth households and non mid-high net worth households (community-based)

It calculates the total annual profitability of financial investments for the full sample of households based on household size, and the results are summarized in Fig. 45. According to Fig. 45, the total annual profitability of household financial investment is the highest when the household size is 4–6 persons. When the household size is 10 persons and above, the total annual profitability of household financial investment is lower. Household size can affect the annual profitability of household financial investments.

According to Fig. 46, overall, the total annual profitability of financial investment is significantly higher for mid-high net worth households than for non mid-high net worth households, regardless of household size. Specifically, when the household size is 1–3 persons, the total annual profitability of financial investment is ¥293,291.59

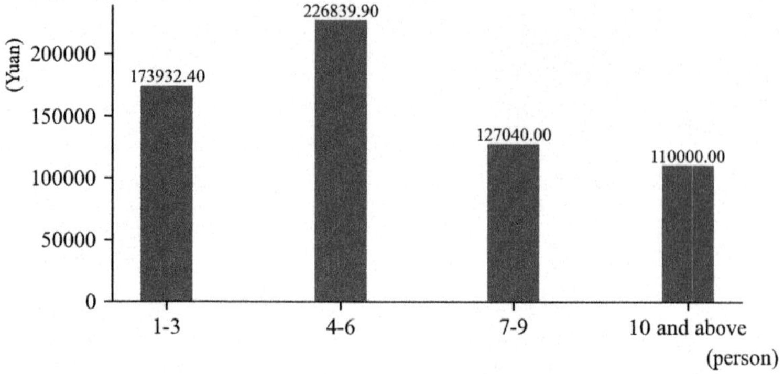


**Fig. 45** Total annual earnings of financial investments for the full sample of households (household size)

higher for mid-high net worth households than for non mid-high net worth households; when the household size is 4–6 persons, the total annual surplus of financial investment is ¥327,350.42 higher for mid-high net worth households than for non mid-high net worth households; when the household size is 7–9 persons, the total annual surplus of financial investment is ¥178,567.07 higher for mid-high net worth households than for non mid-high net worth households; and when the household size is 10 persons or more, the total annual surplus of financial investment is The total annual surplus of financial investment of mid-high net worth households is ¥178,567.07 higher than that of non mid-high net worth households when the household size is 10 persons or more, and the total annual surplus of financial investment of mid-high net worth households is ¥253,333.33 higher than that of non mid-high net worth households. In summary, the difference between the total annual financial investment surplus of mid-high net worth households and non mid-high net worth households is more obvious.

It calculates the total annual profitability of financial investments for the full sample of households based on urban and rural divisions; the results are summarized in Fig. 47.

According to Fig. 47, there is a significant difference of ¥147,367.75 between the total annual profit from financial investment in urban households and rural areas. The financial market is more active in urban areas and urban households have more choices in terms of financial investment and investment in more money. Thus, the total annual profit is higher.

According to Fig. 48, the total annual profit from the financial investment of mid-high net worth households is significantly higher than that of non mid-high net worth households in both urban and rural areas. In urban areas, the total annual profit of financial investment of mid-high net worth households is as high as RMB 386,131,600, while that of non mid-high net worth households is only RMB 50,535,130, and the difference between the total annual profit of financial investment of urban mid-high net worth households and non mid-high net worth households is

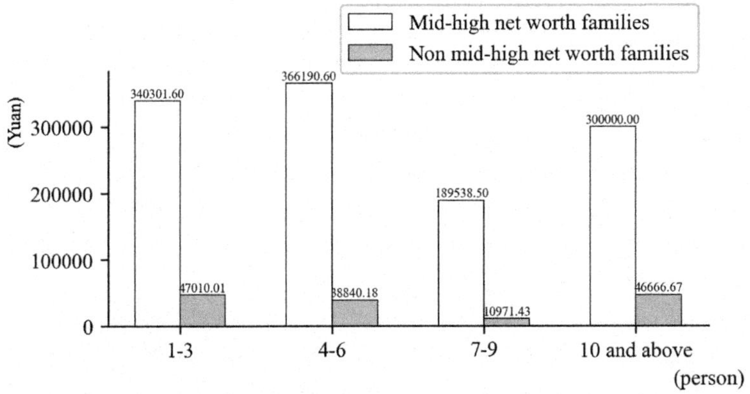


**Fig. 46** Total annual earnings from financial investments for mid-high net worth households and non mid-high net worth households (household size)

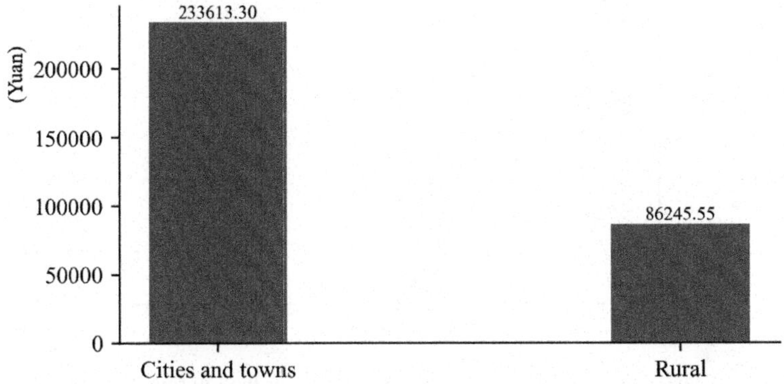


**Fig. 47** Total annual earnings of financial investments for the full sample of households (Uurban and rural divisions)

RMB 335,596.47. In rural areas, the difference between the total annual profit of financial investment of mid-high net worth households and non mid-high net worth households is, there is a difference of ¥151,733.32 between the total annual earnings of financial investment of mid-high net worth households and non mid-high net worth households.

It calculates the total annual profitability of financial investments for the full sample of households based on city type. The results are summarized in Fig. 49.

According to Fig. 49, the total annual profit of household financial investment in tier 1 cities is the highest at over 400,000 yuan. The total annual profit of household financial investment in all other cities is lower. The total annual profit from household financial investment in tier 2 and tier 3 cities is approximately 170,000 yuan, whereas it is even lower in other cities (approximately 120, 000 yuan).

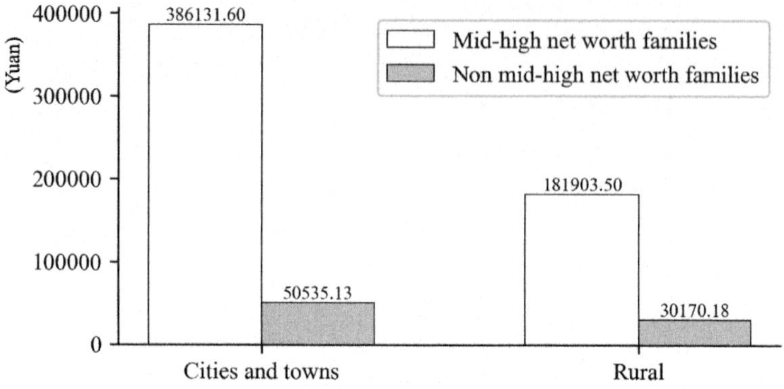


**Fig. 48** Total annual earnings from financial investments for mid-high net worth households and non mid-high net worth households (urban and rural divisions)

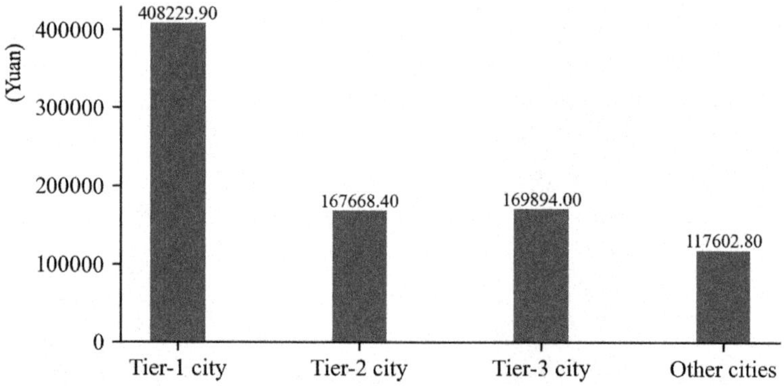


**Fig. 49** Total annual profitability of financial investments for the full sample of households (city type)

According to Fig. 50, overall, the total annual profit of financial investment of mid-high net worth households is significantly higher than that of non mid-high net worth households, regardless of city type. Specifically, the difference in total annual financial investment earnings between high-net-worth and non-high-net-worth households in tier 1 cities is RMB 524,315.75, the difference in total annual financial investment earnings between high-net-worth and non-high-net-worth households in tier 2 cities is RMB 203,597.34, the difference in total annual financial investment earnings between high-net-worth and non-high-net-worth households in tier 3 cities is RMB 266,902.78, and the difference in total annual financial investment earnings between high-net-worth and non-high-net-worth households in other cities The difference between the total annual profit of financial investment of high-net-worth families and non mid-high net worth families in other cities is RMB 204,531.65.

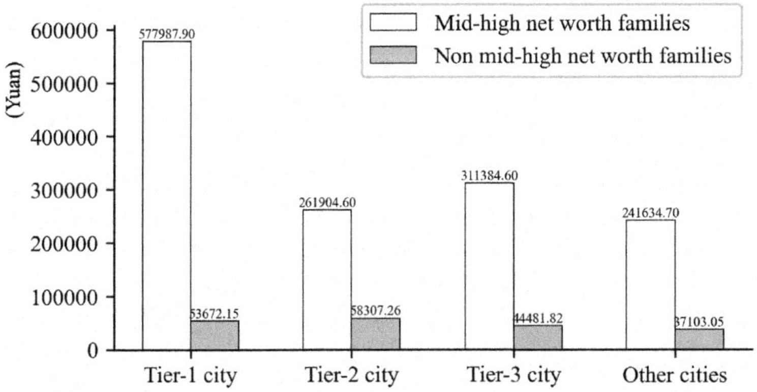


**Fig. 50** Total annual earnings from financial investments for mid-high net worth households and non mid-high net worth households (city type)

## *4.2 Head of Household Level*

At the household head level, education and gender are important factors influencing household financial investment [21]. This book calculates the total annual earnings of financial investment for the full sample of households based on the education level of the household head, and the results are summarized in Fig. 51.

According to Fig. 51, as the education level of the household head increases, the total annual profit of household financial investment also tends to increase in a stepwise manner, and the total annual profit of household financial investment is significantly lower than that of the other groups of households when the education level of the household head is illiterate/semi-literate. The higher the education level of the household head, the more comprehensive the financial investment knowledge,

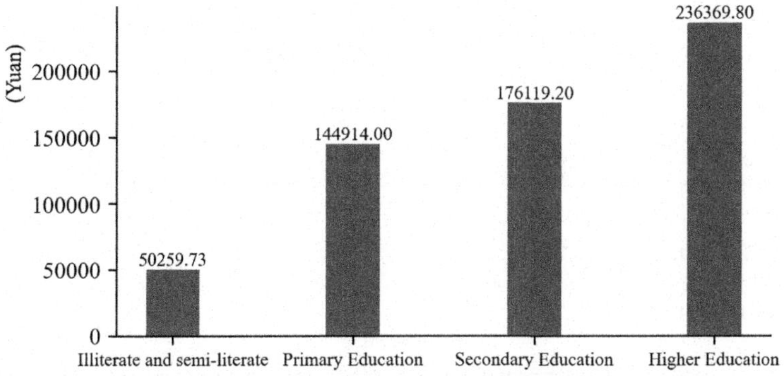


**Fig. 51** Total annual earnings of financial investments for the full sample of households (education of household head)

and the more likely the household head is to obtain significant investment returns in the financial market.

According to Fig. 52, overall, the total annual financial investment earnings of mid-high net worth households are significantly higher than those of non mid-high net worth households, regardless of the education level of the household head. Specifically, when the education level of the household head is illiterate/semi-literate, there is a difference of ¥153,054.91 between the total annual profitability of financial investments of mid-high net worth households and non mid-high net worth households; when the education level of the household head is primary education, there is a difference of ¥222,604.1 between the total annual profitability of financial investments of mid-high net worth households and non mid-high net worth households; and when the education level of the household head is secondary education, the total annual profitability of financial investments of mid-high net worth households and non mid-high net worth households is significantly higher than that of non mid-high net worth households. When the education level of the household head is secondary education, the difference between the total annual profit of financial investment of mid-high net worth households and non mid-high net worth households is ¥266,907.52; when the education level of the household head is higher education, the difference between the total annual profit of financial investment of mid-high net worth households and non mid-high net worth households is ¥422,281.63. In summary, the difference between the total annual financial investment earnings of medium-high and non-medium-high net-worth households gradually increases as the education level of the household head increases.

It calculates the total annual profitability of financial investments for the full sample of households based on the gender of the household head, and the results are summarized in Fig. 53.

According to Fig. 53, the total annual profit from household financial investment is higher when the household head is male, reaching ¥206,900. When the gender of the

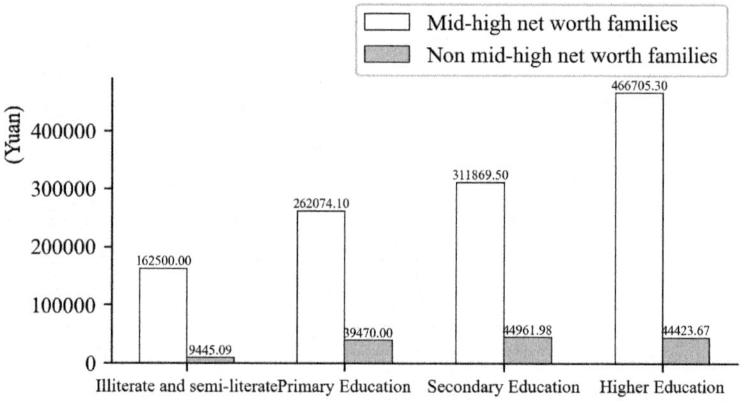


**Fig. 52** Total annual earnings from financial investments of mid-high net worth households and non mid-high net worth households (education level of household head)

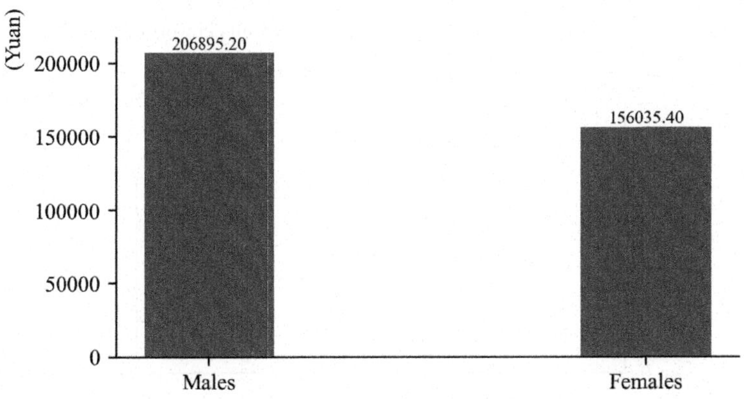


**Fig. 53** Total annual earnings of financial investments of the full sample of households (gender of household head)

household head is female, the total annual profit of household financial investment is lower, less than ¥160,000. In financial investments, men are likely to take more risks, and investment risks are proportional to investment returns. Women's risk-averse cognitive characteristics make men's market participation probability significantly higher than that of women [22].

According to Fig. 54, overall, the total annual earnings of financial investments are significantly higher for mid-high net worth households than for non mid-high net worth households regardless of whether the head of the household is male or female. Specifically, there is a difference of ¥332,186.26 between the total annual financial investment earnings of the mid-high net worth households and non mid-high net worth households when the head of the household is male and a difference of ¥242,068.64 between the mid-high net worth households and non mid-high net worth households when the head of the household is female. In summary, the difference between the total annual financial investment earnings of mid-high net worth households and non mid-high net worth households is larger when the head of the household is male.

## 5 Factors Influencing Household Financial Asset Allocation

The data used were from household and individual questionnaires from the 2020 CFPS questionnaire. This study focuses on households' financial asset allocation behaviors and decisions. Household participation in financial markets and financial asset allocation have been an area of focus for academics and an area of importance for governments [23, 24]. Research on the factors influencing household participation in financial markets and making financial asset allocations has received increasing attention from scholars at home and abroad [25, 26]. A household's decision to

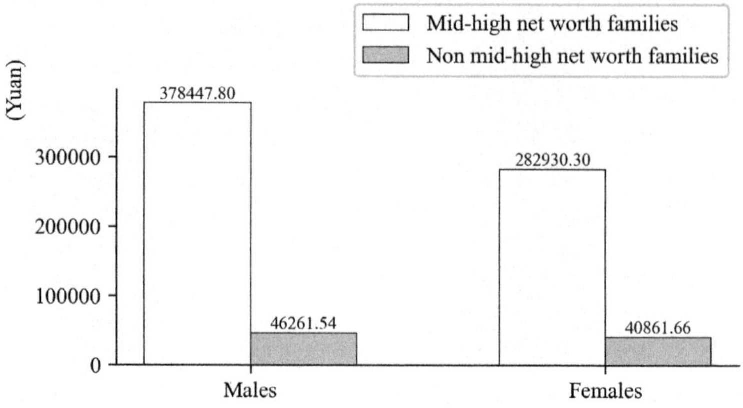


**Fig. 54** Total annual earnings from financial investments of mid-high net worth households and non mid-high net worth households (gender of household head)

participate in financial market investments is an important component of household financing and household asset allocation decisions. Based on a household micro perspective, this book further explores and examines the factors influencing household participation in financial markets and allocates financial assets from both the household and the head-of-household perspectives.

The empirical analysis in this section was conducted at two levels. The first level is a regression analysis of the weight of household participation in financial markets and risky financial asset allocation to explore the impact of household and head-of-household level factors on household financial asset allocation. The second level is built on the first level. The second level performs grouped regression analysis on household income, urban-rural heterogeneity, and urban class to explore whether there are differences in the factors influencing household financial asset allocation, that is, to conduct a heterogeneity analysis.

## *5.1 Data, Variables and Models*

1. *Key variables*

The first explanatory variable here is household financial market participation, which is operationally defined based on the question "Does your household currently hold financial products, such as stocks, funds, government bonds, trust products, foreign exchange, etc." in the CFPS household questionnaire. If the answer to this question is yes, household financial market participation is defined as 1, that is, the household participates in the financial market to buy and trade financial products. If the answer to this question is no, household financial market participation is defined as 0, that is, the household does not participate in the financial market to buy and sell financial products. The second explanatory variable is the share of risky household financial assets, which is the share of risky household financial assets in total household financial assets. The household's total financial assets are the sum of its risk-free and risky financial assets. Risk-free household financial assets include cash and bank deposits.

The core explanatory variables are mid-high net worth households (dummy variables) and household investable assets. The former consisted of values 0 and 1. The former is a mid-high net worth household, whereas the latter is a non mid-high net worth household.

The remaining control variables include household-level and head-of-household-level control variables, with household-level control variables including household entrepreneurial decisions, household property investment decisions, household size, household income, bank loans, loans from friends and relatives and private individuals, human fees, and education and training fees, and head-of-household-level control variables including gender, age, years of education, marital status, health status, self-confidence level, and whether to access the Internet.

2. *Descriptive statistics*

During data processing, this chapter eliminated samples with missing and incorrect values in the variables and finally obtained 6318 valid samples. The definition and descriptive statistics for these variables are shown in Table 1.

3. *Model setting*

This chapter examines the impact of mid-high net worth households and household investable assets on household financial asset allocation, as modeled below:

$$Financialmp = \alpha_0 + \alpha_1 \times MHW + \alpha_2 \times ln(FIA) + \alpha_3 \times X + u \tag{1}$$

$$Prfa = \beta_0 + \beta_1 \times MHW + \beta_2 \times ln(FIA) + \beta_3 \times X + u \tag{2}$$

where $Financialmp$ denotes household financial market participation, a variable consisting of 0 and 1. 0 indicates that the household does not participate in financial markets, whereas 1 indicates that the household participates in financial markets. $Prfa$ is the share of risky household financial assets in total household financial assets. $MHW$ and $FIA$ denote mid-high net worth households (dummy variables) and household investable assets, respectively. $X$ is a set of control variables containing both household-level and head-of-household-level control variables and u is the error term.

**Table 1** Definition of variables and descriptive statistics

| Variable | Definition | Mean | S.D | Min | Max |
|---|---|---|---|---|---|
| Financial market participation | Holding financial products (stocks, funds, treasury bonds, trust products, foreign exchange products, etc.) is 1, otherwise it is 0 | 0.144 | 0.351 | 0 | 1 |
| Share of risky financial assets | Risky financial assets held by households as a share of total household financial assets (%) | 5.741 | 17.711 | 0 | 100 |
| Entrepreneurship of the family | Number of self-employed or private enterprises | 0.115 | 0.363 | 0 | 5 |
| Investment properties | Number of properties other than current housing | 0.286 | 0.596 | 0 | 7 |
| Mid-high net worth families | 1 for middle and high net worth households, 0 for the rest | 0.187 | 0.39 | 0 | 1 |
| Household investable assets | Log value of household investable assets | 10.895 | 2.218 | 2.398 | 17.371 |
| Household size | Number of family members | 3.523 | 1.836 | 1 | 15 |
| Household income | Logarithmic value of household income | 87,542.41 | 99,861.971 | 0 | 1,500,000 |
| Bank loans | If the household has a bank loan, the variable takes the value of 1, otherwise it is 0 | 10.881 | 1.232 | 0 | 14.221 |
| Private loans from friends and family | If there is a family or private loan, the value is 1, otherwise it is 0 | 0.094 | 0.291 | 0 | 1 |
| Favor expenses | Last year's household spending on favors | 0.084 | 0.277 | 0 | 1 |
| Education and training fees | Spending on family education training last year | 3896.632 | 6048.707 | 0 | 100,000 |

(continued)

**Table 1** (continued)

| Variable | Definition | Mean | S.D | Min | Max |
|---|---|---|---|---|---|
| Gender | If the gender is male, the variable takes the value of 1, otherwise it is 0 | 4900.475 | 10,655.689 | 0 | 150,000 |
| Age | Age of the individual, in years | 0.57 | 0.495 | 0 | 1 |
| Year of education | Number of years of education received | 47.773 | 14.697 | 18 | 95 |
| Marriage | If the marital status is married, the variable takes the value of 1, otherwise 0 | 8.768 | 5.1 | 0 | 24 |
| Health | Health rating with a maximum of 5 and a minimum of 1 | 0.811 | 0.391 | 0 | 1 |
| Self-confidence | Self-confidence rating, highest 5, lowest 1 | 2.964 | 1.132 | 1 | 5 |
| Access to the Internet | Internet access is 1, otherwise it is 0 | 4.131 | 0.902 | 1 | 5 |

## 5.2 *Impact Analysis of Household Financial Market Participation*

Table 2 presents the regression results for the impact of mid-high net worth households on households' financial market participation. Column (1) considers only the explanatory variables of mid-high net worth households (dummy variable), column (2) adds household-level control variables, and column (3) adds household-head-level variables to the household-level control variables. On this basis, corresponding to columns (1)–(3), province-fixed effects are added to columns (4)–(6). The results show that the regression coefficients for mid-high net worth households are significantly positive in all models. As shown in column (6), after accounting for both household-level control variables and head-of-household-level control variables, as well as province-fixed effects, mid-high net worth households increased their financial market participation by 0.199 compared to non mid-high net worth households, that is, increasing household financial market participation by nearly 20 percentage points. This suggests that mid-high net worth households are more motivated to participate in financial markets and have greater demand for financial products.

**Table 2** Regression results of the impact of mid-high net worth households on household financial market participation

| | Financial market participation | | | | | |
|---|---|---|---|---|---|---|
| | (1) | (2) | (3) | (4) | (5) | (6) |
| Mid-high net worth families | 0.291*** | 0.239*** | 0.217*** | 0.254*** | 0.221*** | 0.199*** |
| | (19.80) | (12.43) | (11.56) | (17.24) | (11.51) | (10.60) |
| Investment properties | | −0.014 | −0.016 | | −0.011 | −0.012 |
| | | (−1.22) | (−1.37) | | (−0.94) | (−1.10) |
| Entrepreneurship of the family | | −0.023 | −0.028** | | −0.019 | −0.024* |
| | | (−1.54) | (−2.00) | | (−1.33) | (−1.74) |
| Household size | | −0.033*** | −0.023*** | | −0.029*** | −0.021*** |
| | | (−14.49) | (−10.23) | | (−12.23) | (−8.69) |
| Household income | | 0.059*** | 0.040*** | | 0.051*** | 0.032*** |
| | | (10.84) | (9.02) | | (9.91) | (7.64) |
| Bank Loans | | 0.046*** | 0.026 | | 0.052*** | 0.031** |
| | | (2.85) | (1.64) | | (3.27) | (2.01) |
| Private loans from friends and family | | −0.028** | −0.028** | | −0.025* | −0.025* |
| | | (−2.18) | (−2.21) | | (−1.95) | (−1.96) |
| Favor expenses | | 0.000 | 0.000 | | −0.000 | 0.000 |
| | | (0.24) | (0.69) | | (−0.20) | (0.10) |
| Education and training fees | | 0.001*** | 0.001*** | | 0.001*** | 0.001*** |
| | | (5.57) | (4.76) | | (5.05) | (4.16) |
| Gender | | | 0.006 | | | 0.007 |
| | | | (0.68) | | | (0.84) |

(continued)

**Table 2** (continued)

| | Financial market participation | | | | | |
|---|---|---|---|---|---|---|
| | (1) | (2) | (3) | (4) | (5) | (6) |
| Age | | | −0.001*** | | | −0.002*** |
| | | | (−3.39) | | | (−4.30) |
| Year of education | | | 0.010*** | | | 0.010*** |
| | | | (10.21) | | | (9.91) |
| Marriage | | | −0.048*** | | | −0.044*** |
| | | | (−4.00) | | | (−3.68) |
| Health | | | 0.005 | | | 0.004 |
| | | | (1.38) | | | (1.09) |
| Self-confidence | | | −0.010** | | | −0.007 |
| | | | (−2.29) | | | (−1.56) |
| Access to the Internet | | | 0.040*** | | | 0.039*** |
| | | | (4.93) | | | (4.78) |
| Fixed effects of provinces | No | No | No | Yes | Yes | Yes |
| Constant | 0.090*** | −0.431*** | −0.249*** | 0.169*** | −0.350*** | −0.198*** |
| | (22.47) | (−7.96) | (−4.80) | (3.08) | (-4.71) | (−2.78) |
| Observations | 6,318 | 6,318 | 6,318 | 6,318 | 6,318 | 6,318 |
| R-squared | 0.104 | 0.170 | 0.208 | 0.142 | 0.188 | 0.227 |

*Note* * $p < 0.1$, ** $p < 0.05$, *** $p < 0.01$

Table 3 presents the regression results for the effect of household investable assets on household financial market participation. In all the models, the regression coefficients of household investable assets are significantly positive. This indicates that an increase in household investable assets promotes greater household participation in financial markets and optimal allocation of household financial assets through investment in financial products. The results in column (6) show that after considering both household-level control variables and head-of-household-level control variables, as well as province-fixed effects, each 1% increase in household investable assets increases the probability of household participation in financial markets by 3.6 percentage points.

The results for the relevant control variables indicate that household- and head-of-household-level variables do not have the same impact on household participation in financial markets. The effect of household property investment decisions on household financial market participation is not significant. Household investments in the stock and housing markets are often considered to have mutually exclusive effects. However, the findings of this book suggest no significant relationship between them. Households' entrepreneurial decisions may negatively affect their participation in financial markets. The greater the number of household entrepreneurs, the less energy households must invest in financial markets and the less likely they are to participate in financial markets. The effect of household size on household participation in the financial markets is negative and significant. The effects of household income and bank loans on household participation in financial markets are positive and significant. However, the effects of family, friends, private loans, and human fees on household participation in financial markets are insignificant. In addition, education and training fees show a significant positive relationship with household financial market participation.

At the household head level, the gender of the household head does not significantly affect participation in financial markets. The age of the household head affects the demand for household participation in financial markets. The older the household head, the lower the demand for household participation in financial markets. The more years of education the household head has, the greater the demand for household participation in financial markets, and the greater the likelihood that the household will invest in financial markets. The marital status of the household head is also an important factor that influences household participation in financial markets. The marital status of the household head, level of self-confidence, and availability of internet access have significant effects on household participation in financial markets. However, the effect of the health status of the household head is insignificant.

Based on the household income level of the household head, the sample was divided into two groups, with higher and lower household income levels, and grouped for regression. The results are summarized in Table 4. Columns (1) and (2) in Table 4 show the regression results based on income heterogeneity. The results show that mid-high net worth households (dummy variables) have a significant positive effect on financial market participation for both households with higher and lower income levels. However, the intensity of the effect on the latter is greater than that on the former.

**Table 3** Regression results of the effect of household investable assets on household financial market participation

| | Financial Market Participation | | | | | |
|---|---|---|---|---|---|---|
| | (1) | (2) | (3) | (4) | (5) | (6) |
| Household investable assets | 0.057*** | 0.045*** | 0.04*** | 0.050*** | 0.043*** | 0.036*** |
| | (28.18) | (17.09) | (15.68) | (24.59) | (16.22) | (14.26) |
| Investment properties | | 0.001 | 0.002 | | 0.003 | 0.005 |
| | | (0.10) | (0.22) | | (0.29) | (0.47) |
| Entrepreneurship of the family | | −0.025* | −0.028** | | −0.022 | −0.024* |
| | | (−1.78) | (−2.11) | | (−1.57) | (−1.83) |
| Household size | | −0.032*** | −0.023*** | | −0.030*** | −0.022*** |
| | | (−14.57) | (−10.22) | | (−12.71) | (−9.01) |
| Household income | | 0.041*** | 0.028*** | | 0.035*** | 0.021*** |
| | | (8.55) | (6.94) | | (7.78) | (5.57) |
| Bank Loans | | 0.061*** | 0.039** | | 0.064*** | 0.042*** |
| | | (3.83) | (2.53) | | (4.05) | (2.72) |
| Private loans from friends and family | | 0.006 | −0.000 | | 0.005 | −0.001 |
| | | (0.48) | (−0.02) | | (0.38) | (-0.08) |
| Favor expenses | | −0.000 | 0.000 | | −0.000 | −0.000 |
| | | (−0.09) | (0.45) | | (−0.53) | (−0.13) |
| Education and training fees | | 0.001*** | 0.001*** | | 0.001*** | 0.001*** |
| | | (5.35) | (4.68) | | (4.92) | (4.15) |
| Gender | | | 0.002 | | | 0.003 |
| | | | (0.28) | | | (0.35) |

(continued)

**Table 3** (continued)

| | Financial Market Participation | | | | | |
|---|---|---|---|---|---|---|
| | (1) | (2) | (3) | (4) | (5) | (6) |
| Age | | | $-0.001^{***}$ | | | $-0.002^{***}$ |
| | | | (−3.66) | | | (−4.38) |
| Year of education | | | $0.009^{***}$ | | | $0.009^{***}$ |
| | | | (9.34) | | | (9.22) |
| Marriage | | | $-0.055^{***}$ | | | $-0.049^{***}$ |
| | | | (−4.55) | | | (−4.05) |
| Health | | | $0.006^{*}$ | | | 0.005 |
| | | | (1.81) | | | (1.51) |
| Self-confidence | | | $-0.012^{***}$ | | | $-0.008^{*}$ |
| | | | (−2.81) | | | (−1.95) |
| Access to the Internet | | | $0.030^{***}$ | | | $0.031^{***}$ |
| | | | (3.67) | | | (3.75) |
| Fixed effects of provinces | No | No | No | Yes | Yes | Yes |
| Constant | $-0.475^{***}$ | $-0.701^{***}$ | $-0.482^{***}$ | $-0.345^{***}$ | $-0.611^{***}$ | $-0.422^{***}$ |
| | (−24.14) | (−16.06) | (−9.90) | (−6.10) | (−9.07) | (−6.05) |
| Observations | 6,318 | 6,318 | 6,318 | 6,318 | 6,318 | 6,318 |
| R-squared | 0.129 | 0.174 | 0.208 | 0.157 | 0.192 | 0.226 |

*Note* $^{*}$ $p < 0.1$, $^{**}$ $p < 0.05$, $^{***}$ $p < 0.01$

**Table 4** Regression results of the impact of mid-high net worth households on household financial market participation (income and rural-urban heterogeneity)

| | Financial market participation | | | |
|---|---|---|---|---|
| | (1) | (2) | (3) | (4) |
| Income heterogeneity | High income | Low income | | |
| Urban-rural heterogeneity | | | Urban | Rural |
| Mid-high net worth families | 0.154*** | 0.165*** | 0.201*** | 1.991*** |
| | (6.94) | (4.26) | (8.72) | (2.79) |
| Household-level control variables | Yes | Yes | Yes | Yes |
| Control variables at household head level | Yes | Yes | Yes | Yes |
| Fixed effects of provinces | Yes | Yes | Yes | Yes |
| Constant | −1.415*** | 0.046 | −0.341*** | −4.295** |
| | (−6.90) | (0.71) | (−3.50) | (−2.31) |
| Observations | 3,393 | 2,925 | 3,674 | 2,644 |
| R-squared | 0.211 | 0.123 | 0.222 | 0.149 |

*Note* * $p < 0.1$, ** $p < 0.05$, *** $p < 0.01$

The sample was divided into two groups, urban and rural, and grouped into regressions based on household location. Columns (3) and (4) of Table 4 show the regression results based on urban-rural heterogeneity. The results show that mid-high net worth households (dummy variables) have a significant positive effect on households' financial market participants in both urban and rural areas. However, the effect is significantly larger for rural households than for urban households.

Based on the location of the households in the sample, the urban sample was further divided into four groups: first-tier cities, second-tier cities, third-tier cities, and fourth-tier cities, and the regressions were conducted in groups. The results are summarized in Table 5. The results show that the effect of mid-high net worth households (dummy variable) on household financial market participation in tier 3 cities is not significant, whereas the effect on household financial market participation in the remaining tier cities is significantly positive. According to the regression coefficients, the impact on household financial market participation is largest in tier 1 cities, followed by tier 2 cities and tier 4 and below cities.

Based on the household income level of the household head, the sample was divided into two groups, with higher and lower household income levels, and grouped for regression. The results are summarized in Table 6. Columns (1) and (2) of Table 6 present the regression results based on income heterogeneity. The results show that the effect of household investable assets on financial market participation is significantly positive for households with both higher and lower income levels. However, the effect is greater for the former.

The sample was divided into two groups, urban and rural, and grouped into regressions based on household location. Columns (3)–(4) of Table 6 show the regression results based on urban-rural heterogeneity. The results show that the effect of

**Table 5** Regression results of the impact of mid-high net worth households on household financial market participation (urban heterogeneity)

| | Financial market participation | | | |
|---|---|---|---|---|
| | (1) | (2) | (3) | (4) |
| Urban heterogeneity | First-tier cities | Second-tier cities | Third-tier cities | Fourth-tier cities and below |
| Mid-high net worth families | $0.247^{***}$ | $0.209^{***}$ | 0.105 | $0.175^{***}$ |
| | (4.60) | (3.97) | (1.11) | (5.62) |
| Household-level control variables | Yes | Yes | Yes | Yes |
| Control variables at household head level | Yes | Yes | Yes | Yes |
| Fixed effects of provinces | Yes | Yes | Yes | Yes |
| Constant | $-0.958^{***}$ | $-0.501^{**}$ | −0.030 | −0.043 |
| | (−3.45) | (−2.43) | (−0.10) | (−0.33) |
| Observations | 510 | 722 | 310 | 2,132 |
| R-squared | 0.327 | 0.230 | 0.253 | 0.179 |

*Note* $^{*}$ $p < 0.1$, $^{**}$ $p < 0.05$, $^{***}$ $p < 0.01$

**Table 6** Regression results for the effect of household investable assets on household financial market participation (income and urban-rural heterogeneity)

| | Financial market participation | | | |
|---|---|---|---|---|
| | (1) | (2) | (3) | (4) |
| Income heterogeneity | High income | Low income | | |
| Urban-rural heterogeneity | | | Urban | Rural |
| Investable assets | $0.060^{***}$ | $0.012^{***}$ | $0.053^{***}$ | $0.015^{***}$ |
| | (12.72) | (5.09) | (13.78) | (5.88) |
| Household-level control variables | Yes | Yes | Yes | Yes |
| Control variables at household head level | Yes | Yes | Yes | Yes |
| Fixed effects of provinces | Yes | Yes | Yes | Yes |
| Constant | $-1.655^{***}$ | −0.029 | $-0.663^{***}$ | −0.066 |
| | (−8.28) | (−0.46) | (−7.11) | (−0.56) |
| Observations | 3,393 | 2,925 | 3,674 | 2,644 |
| R-squared | 0.229 | 0.113 | 0.234 | 0.112 |

*Note* $^{*}$ $p < 0.1$, $^{**}$ $p < 0.05$, $^{***}$ $p < 0.01$

**Table 7** Regression results for the effect of household investable assets on household financial market participation (urban heterogeneity)

| | Financial market participation | | | |
|---|---|---|---|---|
| | (1) | (2) | (3) | (4) |
| Urban heterogeneity | First-tier cities | Second-tier cities | Third-tier cities | Fourth-tier cities and below |
| Investable assets | 0.064*** | 0.066*** | 0.064*** | 0.044*** |
| | (5.20) | (6.14) | (4.35) | (9.71) |
| Household-level control variables | Yes | Yes | Yes | Yes |
| Control variables at household head level | Yes | Yes | Yes | Yes |
| Fixed effects of provinces | Yes | Yes | Yes | Yes |
| Constant | −1.285*** | −0.989*** | −0.418 | −0.320** |
| | (−5.23) | (−5.01) | (−1.41) | (−2.45) |
| Observations | 510 | 722 | 310 | 2,132 |
| R-squared | 0.324 | 0.245 | 0.291 | 0.192 |

*Note* * $p < 0.1$, ** $p < 0.05$, *** $p < 0.01$

investable household assets on financial market participation is significantly positive for both urban and rural households. However, this effect is stronger for urban households.

Based on the location of the households in the sample, the urban sample was further divided into four groups: first-tier cities, second-tier cities, third-tier cities, and fourth-tier cities, and the regressions were conducted in groups. The results are summarized in Table 7. The results show that the effect of investable household assets on household financial market participation is significantly positive across different classes of cities. This finding indicates that the impact of investable household assets on household financial market participation is positive and catalytic for households in different cities. Based on the magnitude of the regression coefficients, the impact of household investable assets on household financial market participation in tier 1, 2, and 3 cities is roughly equivalent, whereas the impact on household financial market participation in tier 4 and lower cities is slightly smaller.

## 5.3 *Impact Analysis of the Proportion of Risky Financial Assets of Households*

Table 8 show the regression results for the effect of mid-high net worth households on the share of risky financial assets. In all six models, the regression coefficients for

**Table 8** Regression results of the effect of mid-high net worth households on the share of risky financial assets of households

| | Share of risky financial assets | | | | | |
|---|---|---|---|---|---|---|
| | (1) | (2) | (3) | (4) | (5) | (6) |
| Mid-high net worth families | 12.639*** | 9.501*** | 8.593*** | 10.964*** | 8.588*** | 7.7*** |
| | (15.64) | (9.28) | (8.47) | (13.77) | (8.49) | (7.67) |
| Investment properties | | 0.583 | 0.536 | | 0.759 | 0.702 |
| | | (0.84) | (0.78) | | (1.11) | (1.04) |
| Entrepreneurship of the family | | −0.913 | −1.080 | | −0.643 | −0.815 |
| | | (−1.25) | (−1.51) | | (−0.88) | (−1.14) |
| Household size | | −1.536*** | −1.137*** | | −1.404*** | −1.048*** |
| | | (−12.70) | (−9.49) | | (−10.76) | (−8.11) |
| Household income | | 2.330*** | 1.646*** | | 1.975*** | 1.263*** |
| | | (8.47) | (6.41) | | (7.43) | (5.12) |
| Bank Loans | | 2.527*** | 1.914** | | 2.834*** | 2.144** |
| | | (2.73) | (2.11) | | (3.09) | (2.38) |
| Private loans from friends and family | | −0.715 | −0.608 | | −0.616 | −0.521 |
| | | (-0.99) | (-0.86) | | (−0.86) | (−0.73) |
| Favor expenses | | 0.000 | 0.000 | | 0.000 | 0.000 |
| | | (0.71) | (0.98) | | (0.26) | (0.44) |
| Education and training fees | | 0.001*** | 0.001** | | 0.001** | 0.001* |
| | | (2.80) | (2.36) | | (2.37) | (1.90) |
| Gender | | | 0.651 | | | 0.691 |
| | | | (1.54) | | | (1.62) |
| Age | | | −0.008 | | | −0.026 |
| | | | (−0.42) | | | (−1.33) |
| Year of education | | | 0.390*** | | | 0.382*** |
| | | | (7.81) | | | (7.60) |
| Marriage | | | −2.168*** | | | −1.964*** |
| | | | (−3.51) | | | (−3.19) |
| Health | | | 0.321* | | | 0.264 |
| | | | (1.76) | | | (1.45) |
| Self-confidence | | | −0.285 | | | −0.135 |
| | | | (−1.25) | | | (−0.60) |
| Access to the Internet | | | 2.042*** | | | 1.939*** |
| | | | (4.73) | | | (4.43) |

(continued)

**Table 8** (continued)

| | Share of risky financial assets | | | | | |
|---|---|---|---|---|---|---|
| | (1) | (2) | (3) | (4) | (5) | (6) |
| Fixed effects of provinces | No | No | No | Yes | Yes | Yes |
| Constant | 3.379*** | −16.754*** | −13.299*** | 5.388** | −14.372*** | −11.675*** |
| | (17.63) | (−6.11) | (−4.52) | (2.19) | (−3.93) | (−3.09) |
| Observations | 6,318 | 6,318 | 6,318 | 6,318 | 6,318 | 6,318 |
| Pseudo R-squared | 0.077 | 0.123 | 0.145 | 0.107 | 0.139 | 0.161 |

*Note* * $p < 0.1$, ** $p < 0.05$, *** $p < 0.01$

households with medium and high-net-worth (dummy variables) were significantly positive. This indicates that mid-high net worth households allocate more to risky financial assets and have a stronger risk appetite than non mid-high net worth households. The results in column (6) show that after considering both household-level control variables and head-of-household-level control variables, as well as province-fixed effects, mid-high net worth households increase their share of risky financial assets by 7.7 percentage points compared with non mid-high net worth households, demonstrating the positive effect of mid-high net worth households on increasing the share of risky financial asset allocation.

Table 9 show the regression results for the effect of household investable assets on the share of risky household financial assets. In all six models, the regression coefficients of household investable assets were significantly positive. This indicates that the more investable the assets of households, the more risky their financial assets are allocated and the higher the share of risky financial assets in the total financial assets of households. The results in column (6) show that after considering household-level control variables, head-of-household-level control variables, and province-fixed effects, every 1% increase in household investable assets increases the share of risky household financial assets in total household financial assets by 1.149 percentage points. The regression results reflect the significant positive effect of household investable assets on the share of risky household financial assets.

Household property investment decisions, household income, bank loans, and education and training expenses are significantly and positively related to the share of risky household financial assets. Household size has a significant negative effect on the share of risky household financial assets. Household entrepreneurial decisions, loans from friends and relatives, private loans, and human fees do not significantly affect the share of risky household financial assets. In terms of the control variables at the household head level, the effects of the household head's gender, age, and self-confidence on the share of risky household financial assets are insignificant, while years of education, health status, and Internet access are significantly and positively related to the share of risky household financial assets. Additionally, households with heads of marital status are more conservative in their allocation of risky financial assets than those with heads of other marital statuses.

**Table 9** Regression results of the effect of household investable assets on the share of household risky financial assets

| | Share of risky financial assets | | | | | |
|---|---|---|---|---|---|---|
| | (1) | (2) | (3) | (4) | (5) | (6) |
| Household investable assets | 2.306*** | 1.584*** | 1.328*** | 1.980*** | 1.424*** | 1.149*** |
| | (19.54) | (10.79) | (9.28) | (16.90) | (9.89) | (8.09) |
| Investment properties | | 1.593** | 1.656*** | | 1.697*** | 1.779*** |
| | | (2.56) | (2.69) | | (2.77) | (2.93) |
| Entrepreneurship of the family | | −0.933 | −1.039 | | −0.668 | −0.774 |
| | | (−1.32) | (−1.49) | | (−0.94) | (−1.10) |
| Household size | | −1.533*** | −1.132*** | | −1.434*** | −1.071*** |
| | | (−12.75) | (−9.48) | | (−11.05) | (−8.29) |
| Household income | | 1.791*** | 1.293*** | | 1.512*** | 0.979*** |
| | | (6.46) | (5.04) | | (5.69) | (3.97) |
| Bank loans | | 3.017*** | 2.339** | | 3.201*** | 2.457*** |
| | | (3.26) | (2.57) | | (3.49) | (2.72) |
| Private loans from friends and family | | 0.429 | 0.271 | | 0.335 | 0.181 |
| | | (0.59) | (0.38) | | (0.46) | (0.25) |
| Favor expenses | | 0.000 | 0.000 | | 0.000 | 0.000 |
| | | (0.58) | (0.92) | | (0.12) | (0.38) |
| Education and training fees | | 0.001*** | 0.001** | | 0.001** | 0.001** |
| | | (2.78) | (2.40) | | (2.38) | (1.96) |
| Gender | | | 0.548 | | | 0.565 |
| | | | (1.29) | | | (1.32) |
| Age | | | −0.010 | | | −0.026 |
| | | | (−0.51) | | | (−1.31) |
| Year of education | | | 0.365*** | | | 0.366*** |
| | | | (7.33) | | | (7.27) |
| Marriage | | | −2.387*** | | | −2.096*** |
| | | | (−3.85) | | | (−3.39) |
| Health | | | 0.375** | | | 0.313* |
| | | | (2.05) | | | (1.71) |
| Self-confidence | | | −0.369 | | | −0.194 |

(continued)

**Table 9** (continued)

| | Share of risky financial assets | | | | | |
|---|---|---|---|---|---|---|
| | (1) | (2) | (3) | (4) | (5) | (6) |
| | | | (−1.61) | | | (−0.85) |
| Access to the Internet | | | 1.764*** | | | 1.734*** |
| | | | (4.09) | | | (3.97) |
| Fixed effects of provinces | No | No | No | Yes | Yes | Yes |
| Constant | −19.378*** | −26.778*** | −21.856*** | −14.557*** | −23.557*** | −19.365*** |
| | (−16.53) | (−10.97) | (−7.56) | (−5.31) | (−6.82) | (−5.13) |
| Observations | 6,318 | 6,318 | 6,318 | 6,318 | 6,318 | 6,318 |
| R-squared | 0.083 | 0.120 | 0.139 | 0.108 | 0.136 | 0.156 |

*Note* * $p < 0.1$, ** $p < 0.05$, *** $p < 0.01$

Based on the household income level of the household head, the sample was divided into two groups, with higher and lower household income levels, and grouped for regression. The results are summarized in Table 10. Columns (1) and (2) of Table 10 present the regression results based on income heterogeneity. The results show that the effect of mid-high net worth households (dummy variable) on the share of risky financial assets for households with both higher and lower income levels is significantly positive, but to a greater extent for the former than for the latter.

**Table 10** Regression results of the effect of mid-high net worth households on the share of risky financial assets of households (income and urban-rural heterogeneity)

| | Share of risky financial assets | | | |
|---|---|---|---|---|
| | (1) | (2) | (3) | (4) |
| Income heterogeneity | High income | Low income | | |
| Urban-rural heterogeneity | | | Urban | Rural |
| Mid-high net worth families | 5.791*** | 4.881*** | 7.940*** | 5.169*** |
| | (1.221) | (1.646) | (1.264) | (1.387) |
| Household-level control variables | Yes | Yes | Yes | Yes |
| Control variables at household head level | Yes | Yes | Yes | Yes |
| Fixed effects of provinces | Yes | Yes | Yes | Yes |
| Constant | −71.12*** | 1.816 | −19.00*** | 4.828 |
| | (11.71) | (3.524) | (5.404) | (9.032) |
| Observations | 3,393 | 2,925 | 3,674 | 2,644 |
| R-squared | 0.158 | 0.080 | 0.159 | 0.080 |

*Note* * $p < 0.1$, ** $p < 0.05$, *** $p < 0.01$

The sample was divided into two groups, urban and rural, and grouped into regressions based on household location. Columns (3) and (4) of Table 10 show the regression results based on urban-rural heterogeneity. The results show that the effect of mid-high net worth households (dummy variable) on the share of risky financial assets of households in both urban and rural areas is significantly positive. However, the effect is significantly larger for urban households than for rural households.

Based on the location of the households in the sample, the urban sample was further divided into four groups: first-tier cities, second-tier cities, third-tier cities, and fourth-tier cities, and the regressions were conducted in groups. The results are summarized in Table 11. The results show that the effect of mid-high net worth households (dummy variable) on the share of risky financial assets of households in tier 3 cities is not significant, while the effect on the share of risky financial assets of households in the remaining ranked cities is significantly positive. According to the magnitude of the regression coefficients, the effect of mid-high net worth households (dummy variable) on the share of risky household financial assets in tier 1 cities is the largest, followed by tier 2 cities, and then tier 4 cities and below.

Based on the household income level of the household head, the sample was divided into two groups, with higher and lower household income levels, and grouped for regression. The results are summarized in Table 12. Columns (1) and (2) of Table 12 present the regression results based on income heterogeneity. The results show that the effect of household investable assets on the share of risky financial

**Table 11** Regression results of the effect of mid-high net worth households on the share of risky financial assets of households (urban heterogeneity)

| | Share of risky financial assets | | | |
|---|---|---|---|---|
| | (1) | (2) | (3) | (4) |
| Urban heterogeneity | First-tier cities | Second-tier cities | Third-tier cities | Fourth-tier cities and below |
| Mid-high net worth families | $11.028^{***}$ | $8.722^{***}$ | 1.159 | $7.254^{***}$ |
| | (3.37) | (3.20) | (0.29) | (4.36) |
| Household-level control variables | Yes | Yes | Yes | Yes |
| Control variables at household head level | Yes | Yes | Yes | Yes |
| Fixed effects of provinces | Yes | Yes | Yes | Yes |
| Constant | $-59.255^{***}$ | $-18.364^{*}$ | 17.875 | −7.947 |
| | (−3.30) | (−1.86) | (0.87) | (−1.36) |
| Observations | 510 | 722 | 310 | 2,132 |
| R-squared | 0.219 | 0.179 | 0.273 | 0.140 |

*Note* $^{*}$ $p < 0.1$, $^{**}$ $p < 0.05$, $^{***}$ $p < 0.01$

**Table 12** Regression results of the effect of household investable assets on the share of household risky financial assets (income and urban-rural heterogeneity)

| | Share of risky financial assets | | | |
|---|---|---|---|---|
| | (1) | (2) | (3) | (4) |
| Income heterogeneity | High income | Low income | | |
| Urban-rural heterogeneity | | | Urban | Rural |
| Investable assets | $1.873^{***}$ | $0.270^{**}$ | $1.821^{***}$ | $0.358^{***}$ |
| | (0.270) | (0.122) | (0.227) | (0.123) |
| Household-level control variables | Yes | Yes | Yes | Yes |
| Control variables at household head level | Yes | Yes | Yes | Yes |
| Fixed effects of provinces | Yes | Yes | Yes | Yes |
| Constant | $-80.39^{***}$ | 0.0713 | $-30.69^{***}$ | 1.660 |
| | (11.45) | (3.596) | (5.219) | (9.031) |
| Observations | 3,393 | 2,925 | 3,674 | 2,644 |
| R-squared | 0.163 | 0.075 | 0.161 | 0.072 |

*Note* $^{*}$ $p < 0.1$, $^{**}$ $p < 0.05$, $^{***}$ $p < 0.01$

assets for both higher and lower household income levels is significantly positive. However, the effect is significantly higher for the former than the latter.

The sample was divided into two groups, urban and rural, and grouped into regressions based on household location. Columns (3) and (4) of Table 12 show the regression results based on urban-rural heterogeneity. The results show that the effect of household investable assets on the share of risky financial assets is significantly positive for both urban and rural households. However, this effect is greater for urban households.

Based on the location of the households in the sample, the urban sample was further divided into four groups: first-tier cities, second-tier cities, third-tier cities, and fourth-tier cities, and the regressions were conducted in groups. The results are summarized in Table 13. The results show that the effect of investable household assets on the share of risky household financial assets is significantly positive in all cities. According to the regression coefficients, household investable assets have the largest effect on the share of risky financial assets in tier 3 cities, followed by tier 1 and tier 2 cities, and the smallest effect on tier 4 and below cities.

## 6 Summary of This Chapter

Financial asset allocation, an important part of family wealth management, plays an important role in preserving and appreciating family wealth. In recent years, with the continuous growth of China's economy, the accumulation of household financial assets has accelerated and household demand for financial products has increased.

**Table 13** Regression results of the effect of household investable assets on the share of household risky financial assets (urban heterogeneity)

| | Share of risky financial assets | | | |
|---|---|---|---|---|
| | (1) | (2) | (3) | (4) |
| Urban heterogeneity | First-tier cities | Second-tier cities | Third-tier cities | Fourth-tier cities and below |
| Investable assets | 2.346*** | 2.317*** | 2.582*** | 1.422*** |
| | (3.01) | (4.05) | (2.90) | (5.43) |
| Household-level control variables | Yes | Yes | Yes | Yes |
| Control variables at household head level | Yes | Yes | Yes | Yes |
| Fixed effects of provinces | Yes | Yes | Yes | Yes |
| Constant | −72.874*** | −36.723*** | 4.451 | −17.590*** |
| | (−4.29) | (−3.52) | (0.25) | (−2.89) |
| Observations | 510 | 722 | 310 | 2,132 |
| R-squared | 0.211 | 0.183 | 0.298 | 0.140 |

*Note* * $p < 0.1$, ** $p < 0.05$, *** $p < 0.01$

Under such circumstances, studying household financial asset allocations is of great theoretical value and practical significance. Based on CFPS data for 2020, the main findings of this study are as follows:

Overall, the coverage rate of financial products among mid-high net worth households is significantly higher than that of non mid-high net worth households on both neighborhood and village councils. In neighborhood committees, the coverage rate of financial products held by mid-high net worth households was 42.92%. In neighborhood committees, the coverage rate of financial products held by mid-high net worth households is 30.47 percentage points higher than that of non mid-high net worth households. In village committees, the coverage rate of financial products held by mid-high net worth households is 13.09 percentage points higher than that of non mid-high net worth households.

Second, the coverage rate of the financial products held by households tends to decline in a stepwise manner as the city rank declines. The coverage rate of financial products held by households in first-tier cities reaches 32.24%, that is, approximately 1/3 of households hold financial products. The coverage rate of financial products held by households in second-tier cities dropped to 20.39%, that is, i.e. about 1/5 of households held financial products. The coverage rate of households holding financial products in third-tier cities is 14.19%, whereas that of households holding financial products in other cities is only 5.7%. The coverage rate of financial products held by mid-high net worth households is significantly higher than that of non mid-high net worth households, regardless of the city tier.

Third, the total price of financial products held by mid-high net worth households was significantly higher than that held by non mid-high net worth households in both urban and rural areas. Specifically, the difference between the total price of financial products held by urban and non-MHP households was RMB 335,600 and the difference between the total price of financial products held by rural MHP households and non-MHP households was RMB 152,100. In urban areas, the total price of financial products held by mid-high net worth households reached RMB 386,100, while in rural areas, it was RMB 181,900.

Fourth, the total price of financial products held by households in first-tier cities was the highest at 408,200 yuan. In comparison, the total price of financial products held by households in second-and third-tier cities is relatively low, close to 170,000 yuan. The total price of financial products held by households in other cities was the lowest at 117,400 yuan. Regardless of city type, the total price of financial products held by mid-high net worth households was significantly higher than that of non mid-high net worth households.

Fifth, the proportion of risky financial assets to total household financial assets is higher for mid-high net worth households than for non mid-high net worth households in both urban and rural areas. However, there are urban-rural differences in the gaps between the two. There is a difference of 4.89 percentage points between the proportion of risky financial assets to total household financial assets of urban HNW households and non-HNW households and a difference of 1.54 percentage points between the proportion of risky financial assets to total household financial assets of rural and non-HNW households. Notably, in rural areas, the difference is even smaller.

Sixth, regardless of the city type, the proportion of risky financial assets to total household financial assets is higher for mid-high net worth households than for non mid-high net worth households. Specifically, there is a difference of 4.05 percentage points between the proportion of risky financial assets to total household financial assets of HNW and non-HNW households in tier 1 cities, a difference of 3.96 percentage points between the proportion of risky financial assets to total household financial assets of HNW and non-HNW households in tier 2 cities, a difference of 7.3 percentage points between the proportion of risky financial assets to total household financial assets of HNW and non-HNW households in tier 3 cities, and a 7.3 percentage difference in the proportion of risky financial assets to total household financial assets of HNW and non-HNW households in other cities. There is a difference of 7.3 percentage points between the proportion of risky financial assets of HNW households in third-tier cities and non-HNW households and a difference of 2.97 percentage points between the proportion of risky financial assets of HNW households in other cities and non-HNW households.

Seventh, the total annual profit of financial investment of mid-high net worth households is significantly higher than that of non mid-high net worth households. The total annual profit of financial investment of middle and high net-worth households whose community nature is neighborhood committee is higher than that of non-middle and high net-worth households by ¥331,847.93, the total annual surplus of financial investment of middle and high net-worth households whose community nature is village committee is higher than that of non mid-high net worth households by ¥191,400.29.

Overall, the total annual financial investment earnings of mid-high net worth households are significantly higher than those of non mid-high net worth households, regardless of city type. Specifically, the difference in total annual financial investment earnings between high-net-worth households and non-high net-worth households in tier 1 cities is RMB 524,315.75, the difference in total annual financial investment earnings between high-net-worth households and non-high net-worth households in tier 2 cities is RMB 203,597.34, the difference in total annual financial investment earnings between high-net-worth households and non-high-net-worth households in tier 3 cities is RMB 266,902.78, and the difference in total annual financial investment earnings between The difference between the total annual profit of financial investment of high-net-worth families and non mid-high net worth families in other cities is RMB 204,531.65.

Ninth, financial market participation and the share of risky financial assets are significantly higher for mid-high net worth households than for non mid-high net worth households. Moreover, a positive relationship exists among household investable assets, household financial market participation, and the proportion of risky household financial assets.

## References


1. Wang, Y., Liu, D.: Household financial asset allocation: a literature review. Academia 191–200 (2021)
2. Tan, T., Sun, M., Li, H.: A study of rural households' financial asset allocation status–based on research data from Nanjing, Jiangsu Province. Rural Econ. Technol. **33**, 193–196 (2022)
3. Allianz. Allianz Global Wealth Report 2020. Allianz Research (2020)
4. Zhang, C.: Differential analysis of the current situation of financial asset allocation of urban and rural residents in China-based on China Household Financial Survey (CHFS) data Rural Econ. Technol. **32**, 117–119 (2021)
5. Lu, Y., Yin, J.: A study on the influence of household head's education level on household risky financial asset selection. J. Nanjing Audit Univ. **18**, 70–80 (2021)
6. Black, S.E., Devereux, P.J., Lundborg, P., Majlesi, K.: Learning to take risks? The effect of education on risk-taking in financial markets. Rev. Finan. **22**, 951–975 (2018)
7. Guiso, L., Sapienza, P., Zingales, L.: The role of social capital in financial development. Am. Econ. Rev. **94**, 526–556 (2004)
8. Fu, Y., Zhang, J., Guo, R.: Dynamic asset allocation of funds based on matching strategies. J. Syst. Manag.Manag. **26**, 879–887 (2017)
9. Min, S.: An empirical analysis of financial literacy affecting household Internet financial participation. Financ. Perspect. J. **3**, 26–36 (2022)
10. Chen, J.: Asset allocation solutions for high net worth families. Money Manag. **365**, 70–71 (2020)
11. Markowitz, H.M.: Portfolio selection. J. Financ.Financ. **7**, 77–91 (1952)
12. Sharpe, W.F.: Capital asset prices: a theory of market equilibrium under conditions of risk. J. Financ.Financ. **19**, 425–442 (1964)
13. Rios, L.M., Sahinidis, N.V.: Portfolio optimization for wealth-dependent risk preferences. Ann. Oper. Res.Oper. Res. **177**, 63–90 (2010)

14. Smimou, K., Bector, C.R., Jacoby, G.: Portfolio selection subject to experts' judgments. Int. Rev. Financ. Anal.Financ. Anal. **17**, 1036–1054 (2009)
15. Campbell, J.Y.: Household finance. Sch. Artic. **61**, 1553–1604 (2006)
16. Arrondel, L., Bartiloro, L., Fessler, P., Lindner, P., Mathä, T.Y., Rampazzi, C., Savignac, F., Schmidt, T., Schürz, M., Vermeulen, P.: How do households allocate their assets? Stylized facts from the Eurosystem household finance and consumption survey. Int. J. Cent. Bank. **12**, 129–220 (2016)
17. Yerkenbai, S.: Analysis of financial asset allocation and influencing factors of urban and rural households in China. J. Shanghai Second. Tech. Univ. **37**, 129–136 (2020)
18. Guo, D., Lei, L.: Analysis of the difference in risky asset allocation between urban and rural residents in Nanjing. Anhui Agric. Sci. 45, 212–214+227 (2017)
19. Liu, J.: A study on the impact of financial knowledge on risk preference from the perspective of urban-rural differences. Wealth Times **12**, 26–27 (2020)
20. Hu, Y.: The impact of financial literacy, investment ability on household financial market participation and asset allocation in China. China Market **1**, 13–18 (2019)
21. Wang, C., Yao, L., Chai, S.: The impact of age structure on household asset allocation and its regional differences. Int. Financ. Stud. **2**, 76–86 (2017)
22. Xiao, Z., Zhang, X.: A study of the impact of institutional and human capital on household financial market participation—survey data from Chinese private entrepreneurs. Econ. Res. **47**, 91–104 (2012)
23. Tin, J.: Household demand for financial assets: a life-cycle analysis. Q. Rev. Econ. Financ. **38**, 875–897 (1998)
24. Tomita, Y.: Does legal origin affect shareholding ratio on household financial assets?: Evidence from cross-country comparison. J. Househ. Econ. **48**, 33–48 (2018)
25. Li, C.: China's household balance sheet: accounting issues, wealth accumulation, and risk diagnosis. China Econ. Rev. **51**, 97–112 (2018)
26. Wang, W., Sang, L.: A study on the mechanism of social health insurance's influence on household financial asset allocation. J. Cap. Univ. Econ. Bus. **22**, 21–34 (2019)

# Chapter 4
# Non-financial Asset Management for Mid-High Net Worth Families

**Abstract** This chapter analyzes the allocation of household non-financial assets. This study includes the individual business situation and allocation of business assets, property investment situation, and allocation of consumer durables. On this basis, this chapter explores the factors that influence households' entrepreneurial and property investment decisions. The results show that the proportion of mid-high net worth households that are self-employed is 18.15% in towns and 21.52% in villages, which is significantly higher than that of non mid-high net worth households; mid-high net worth households make more entrepreneurial decisions than non mid-high net worth households, and household investable assets promote household entrepreneurship. Similarly, mid-high net worth households have more investment properties than non mid-high net worth households, and, household investable assets promote household asset allocation in investment properties.

Non-financial Assets (NFA) are an important part of household assets and play an important role in the maintenance and development of households. A family's investment in and allocation of non-financial assets is an important part of family wealth management, which directly affects the development trends and future value of family wealth. For mid-high net worth families, the allocation of non-financial assets is directly related to the inheritance of family wealth. Additionally, a family's non-financial asset allocation affects its allocation of financial assets. For example, a household's property allocation has a significant impact on its financial asset allocation [1, 2]. Therefore, mid-high net worth households need to plan their investment and allocation to non-financial assets in terms of household assets in general and then achieve the overall preservation and appreciation of household wealth.

In terms of development trend, in general, the value of non-financial property of households in China shows a continuous growth trend [3]. Data from the survey on assets and liabilities of urban households conducted by the survey and statistics department of the People's Bank of China on more than 30,000 urban households in 30 provinces (autonomous regions and municipalities directly under the central government) in mid- to late October 2019 show that physical household assets account for 79.6% of total household assets, while the proportion of financial



J. Gu, *Wealth Management Report for Mid-High Net Worth Families*, Spatial Demography and Population Governance, https://doi.org/10.1007/978-981-97-0387-6_4

assets is only 20.4% [4]. Data from the China Household Finance Survey Report (2014) show that in 2013, the proportion of non-financial assets of households in China was as high as 91.9% of household assets [5]. This means, on average, 90% of the total household assets in China are non-financial assets; the proportion of household non-financial assets to household assets in OECD countries generally does not exceed 70% [6]. It can be seen that compared with some developed countries in the West, the allocation ratio of households in China to non-financial assets is higher. So, how do mid-high net worth households allocate their non-financial assets? What are the characteristics? What is the future development trend? These questions are worth studying and exploring, and the relevant research has important theoretical value and practical significance for predicting the asset allocation trends of the mid-high net worth individuals.

## 1 Related Concepts

Generally, household assets include property, bonds, and other assets owned by households, which can be measured in monetary terms. Household assets were divided into two categories: financial and non-financial. Financial assets include bank deposits, bonds, stocks, investment funds, retirement funds, life insurance and various types of managed assets. In the previous chapter, the allocation of financial assets of mid-high net worth worth families was studied in depth. This chapter examines the allocation of non-financial assets of mid-high net worth worth families. As the name implies, assets other than financial assets in a household can be called non-financial assets. Generally, household non-financial assets include owner-occupied homes, non-owner-occupied homes, business assets, automobiles, consumer durables, gold, silver, jewelry, antiques, and artwork. It can be seen that non-financial assets are mainly physical assets with high value. Of course, these physical assets have the function of value preservation and appreciation and often have investment value, which is an important reflection of household wealth. Additionally, when required, these physical assets can be liquidated to transform them into financial assets.

The definition of household non-financial assets tends to vary across studies. This chapter uses the definition of household non-financial assets proposed by Gan et al. [7]–non-financial assets include assets such as agricultural or industrial and commercial production and business tools, property and land, vehicles, and durable goods [7]. This definition is consistent with the definition and caliber of relevant international survey projects, which are in line with international norms [8]. For example, a similar definition is used by the OECD Wealth Distribution Database [9]. This section extends this definition.

To define mid-high net worth households, this chapter extends the previous definition that mid-high net worth households have investable assets of USD 450,000 and above. In the 2020 CFPS data, non-financial assets involving households were mainly self-employed and private facilities, properties, and agricultural (agriculture, forestry, animal husbandry, and fishery) production tools. This section relies on household data from the CFPS and examines the non-financial asset allocation of mid-high net worth households based on the above definition. This chapter attempts to provide a panoramic portrayal and description of the allocation of mid-high net worth households to non-financial assets, explain the patterns and trends in the allocation process, and provide a reference for optimizing household non-financial asset allocation.

## 2 Operating Assets

To develop the family economy and preserve and increase the value of family wealth, families often accumulate assets by self-employment, such as family businesses, when they are in a position to do so. Self-employment generally refers to a form of business in which the means of production are owned by the individual, based on individual labor, and the income from labor belongs to the individual worker. In terms of business methods, there are two forms of self-employment and individual partnerships. Both self-employment and micro and small enterprises are important channels for households to become rich [10]. This chapter uses CFPS data to specifically analyze the situation of self-employment in households.

### *2.1 Family for Self-Employment*

However, not all households are suitable for self-employment. For households that are self-employed, physical inputs such as production equipment and other business assets needed to run the business are an important part of the household's non-financial assets. The proportion of self-employed households reflects their allocation of business assets.

There are often urban–rural differences when households engage in self-employment. This book calculates the proportion of urban and rural households engaged in self-employment, as summarized in Fig. 1.

According to Fig. 1, the overall difference between the proportions of urban and rural households engaged in self-employment was 5.45% points. The proportion of self-employment among urban households reached 11.8%, whereas that among rural households was only 6.35%.

According to Fig. 2, the proportion of mid-high net worth households that are self-employed is lower in towns than in villages; for non mid-high net worth households, the proportion is higher in towns. There is a difference of 8.16% points between the proportion of mid-high net worth households in towns and non mid-high net worth households who are self-employed. A larger difference of 16.39% points exists between the proportion of mid-high net worth households in villages and non mid-high net worth households who are self-employed. Some studies have shown that rural residents are 2.18 times more likely to choose entrepreneurship than urban

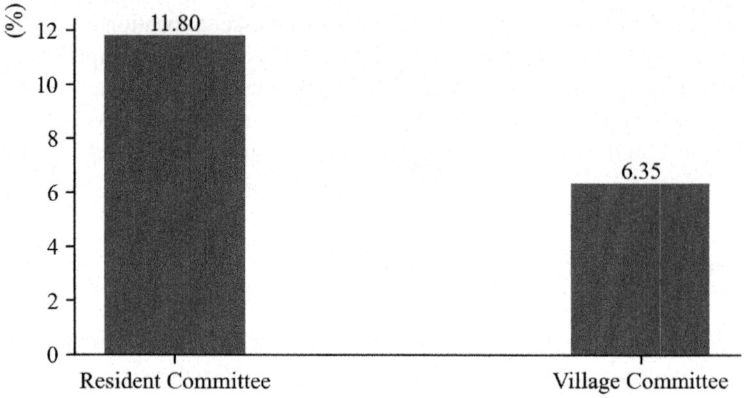


**Fig. 1** Proportion of self-employment among households in the whole sample (urban and rural types)

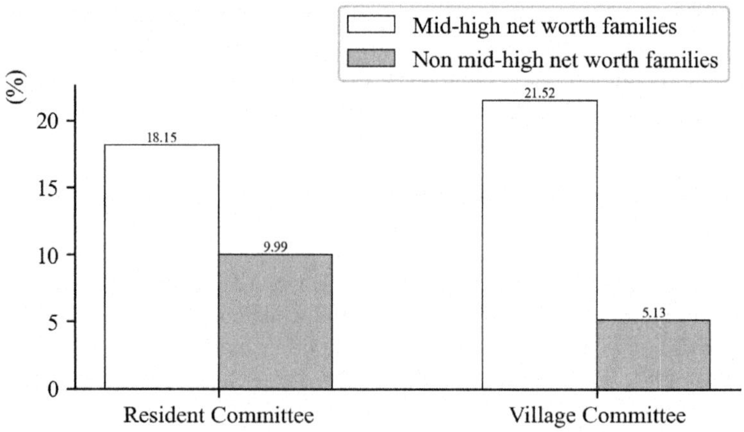


**Fig. 2** Proportion of mid-high net worth households and non mid-high net worth households engaged in self-employment (urban and rural types)

residents [11]. However, this conclusion is premised on and holds true for mid-high net worth households. Mid-high net worth households in rural areas have relatively substantial investable assets, and investment in self-employment in rural areas is lower than in towns; therefore, they are more likely to allocate household assets and achieve household wealth preservation and appreciation through self-employment.

Household self-employment varies depending on the city where the household is located. This book calculates the proportion of self-employment among different types of urban households; the results are summarized in Fig. 3.

According to Fig. 3, the proportion of self-employed households in Tier 2 and Tier 3 cities was significantly higher than in Tier 1 and other cities. One possible reason for the lowest proportion of self-employed households in Tier 1 cities is

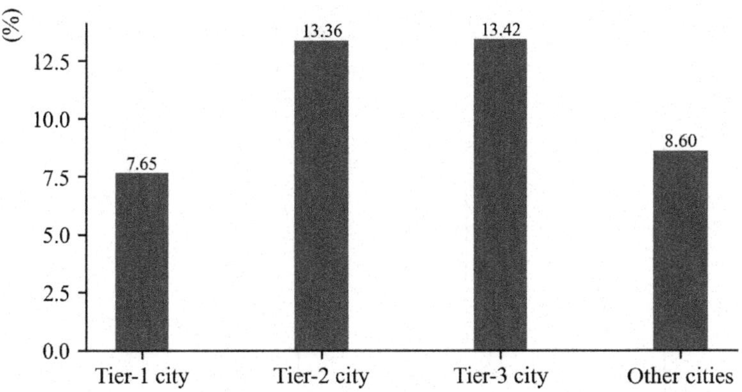


**Fig. 3** Proportion of households in the full sample that are self-employed (urban type)

that the cost of self-employment in Tier 1 cities is higher, and competition is more intense. The proportion of self-employed households in second- and third-tier cities is higher because these cities are more suitable for the survival and development of self-employment in terms of both rent costs and market competition.

According to Fig. 4, the gap between the proportion of mid-high net worth households and non mid-high net worth households who are self-employed is very clear; the proportion of mid-high net worth households who are self-employed is highest in Tier 3 cities. The proportion of self-employed non mid-high net worth households was the highest in Tier 2 cities. There was a 5.92% point difference between the proportion of mid-high net worth households in first-tier cities and the proportion of non mid-high net worth households who were self-employed; a 6.58% point difference between the two in second-tier cities; a 14.85% point difference between the two in third-tier cities; and a 13.25% point difference between the two in other cities.

This research here calculates the proportion of households in the full sample that are self-employed based on the education level of the household head; the results are summarized in Figs. 5.

As shown in Figs. 5, the overall proportion of households engaged in self-employment is gradually increasing as the education level of the household head increases. The relationship between education level and self-employment is positive [12]. For example, an important subject in the current Internet self-employment, in the "Netflix economy" is entrepreneurs who have received higher education [13]. The higher the education level of the household head, the more likely they are to encourage family members to adopt multiple methods of self-employment and entrepreneurship, including the Internet.

As shown in Fig. 6, the proportion of mid-high net worth self-employed households is significantly higher than that of non mid-high net worth households. When the education level of the household head is illiterate/semiliterate, there is a 10.63% point difference between the proportion of medium–high net worth households and non-medium–high net worth households who are self-employed; when the education

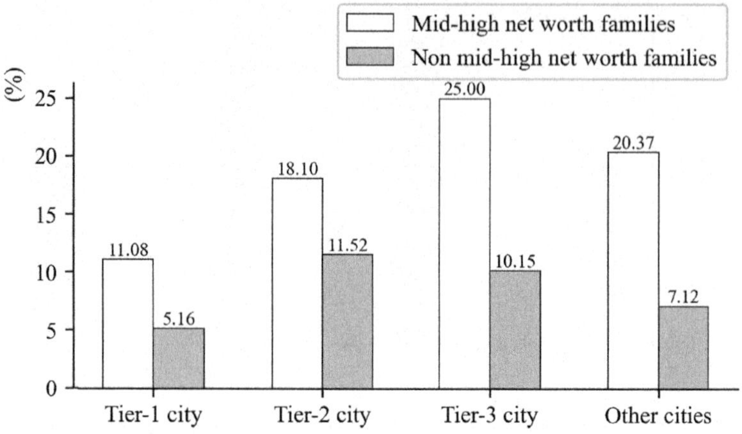


**Fig. 4** Proportion of mid-high net worth households and non mid-high net worth households engaged in self-employment (city type)

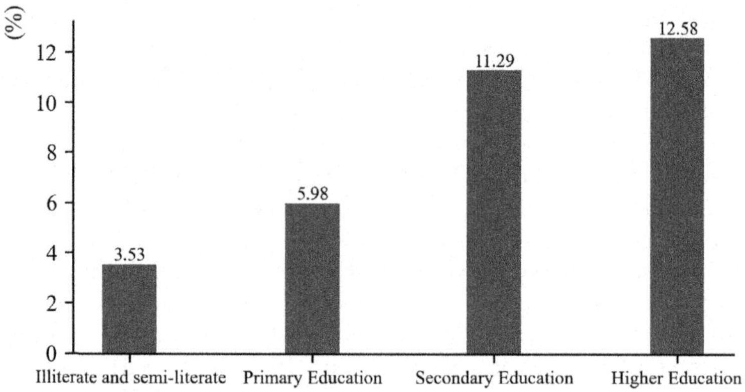


**Fig. 5** Proportion of households in the full sample that are self-employed (education level of household head)

level of the household head is primary education, there is a 10.53% point difference; when the education level of the household head is secondary education, there is a 9.07% point difference; and when the education level of the household head is higher education, there is an 8.81% point difference. The difference between these two values is 8.81% points.

Marital status can affect self-employment. This book calculates the proportion of households engaging in self-employment based on the marital status of the household head, and the results are summarized in Fig. 7.

According to Fig. 7, the proportion of households engaged in self-employment is highest when the head of the household is married and lowest when the head of the household is cohabiting. Family stability is the foundation of businesses.

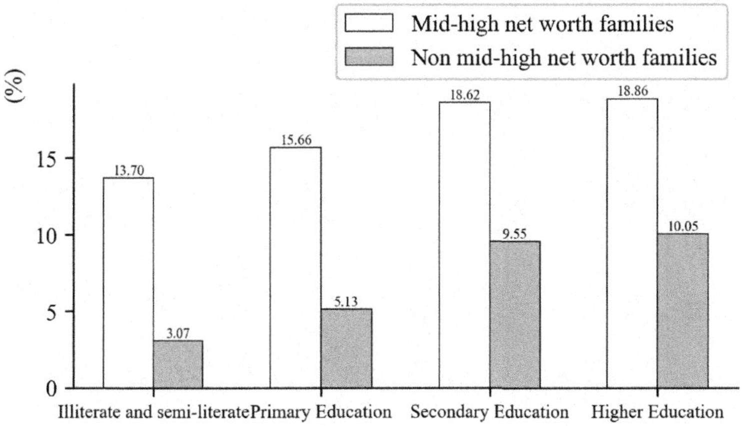


**Fig. 6** Proportion of mid-high net worth households and non mid-high net worth households engaged in self-employment (education level of household head)

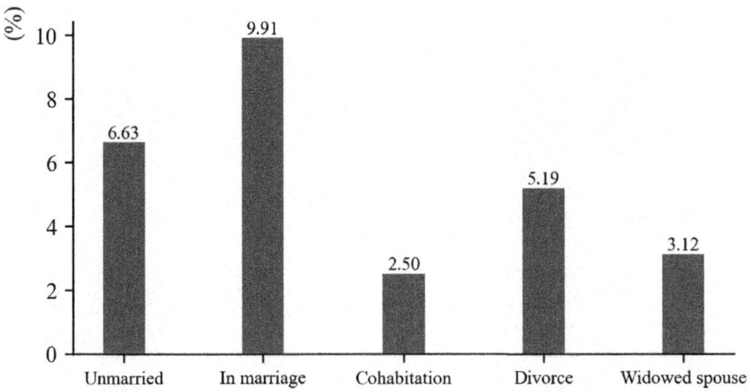


**Fig. 7** Proportion of households in the full sample that are self-employed (marital status of household head)

Marriage can significantly promote joint family entrepreneurial behavior through a "resource expansion mechanism" [14]. Cohabitation is a state of uncertainty with more uncertainty about the future; therefore, the probability of self-employment is lower. This illustrates the rationale of "family harmony."

According to Fig. 8, when the head of the household is married, the proportion of mid-high net worth households who are self-employed is significantly higher than that of non mid-high net worth households. A similar situation occurs when the household head is unmarried or divorced. When the head of the household is unmarried, there is a difference of 4.96% points between the proportion of mid-high net worth households who are self-employed and those of non mid-high net worth households. When the head of household is married, there is a difference of 11.72%

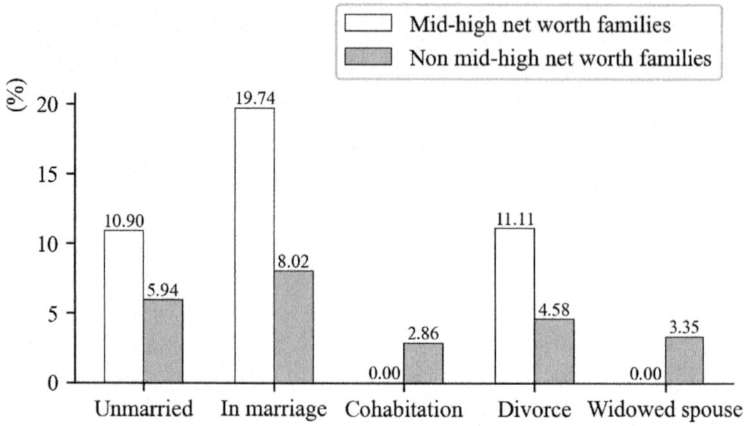


**Fig. 8** Proportion of mid-high net worth households and non mid-high net worth households engaged in self-employment (marital status of household head)

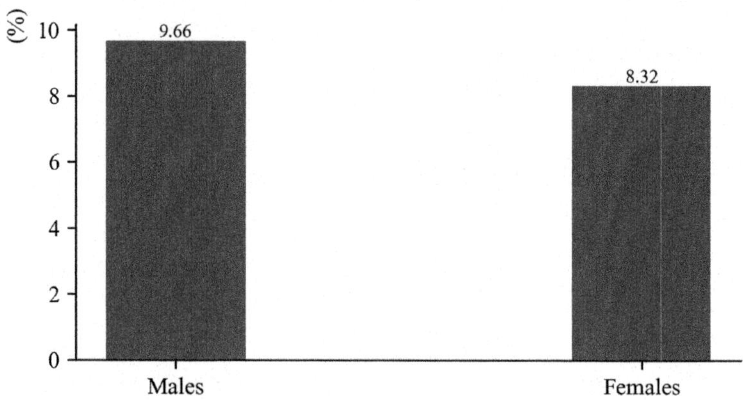


**Fig. 9** Proportion of households in the full sample that are self-employed (gender of household head)

points; when the head of household is cohabiting, there is a difference of 2.86% points; when the head of household is divorced, there is a difference of 6.53% points; when the head of household is widowed, there is a difference of 3.35% points. The difference between the two values is 3.35% points. Among them, the mid-high net worth households did not engage in self-employment when the head of the household was cohabiting or widowed.

This research here calculates the proportion of households in the full sample that are self-employed based on the gender of the household head, and the results are summarized in Fig. 9.

According to Fig. 9, the proportion of households engaged in self-employment is slightly higher when the household head is male than when it is female. Self-employment requires a certain amount of risk, and men are more likely to be willing to take risks than women. Therefore, households headed by men are more likely to start and run their own businesses than households headed by women.

According to Fig. 10, regardless of whether the head of household is male or female, the proportion of medium–high net worth households that are self-employed is significantly higher than that of non-medium–high net worth households. When the head of household is male, there is a difference of 11.88% points between the proportion of medium–high net worth households and non-medium–high net worth households who are self-employed; when the head of household is female, there is a difference of 9.34% points between the proportion of medium–high net worth households and non-medium–high net worth households who are self-employed. The difference in the proportion of self-employment between mid-high net worth households and non mid-high net worth households was significant.

Self-employment requires practitioners to be in a good physical condition. This book calculates the proportion of self-employment among the full sample of households based on the health status of the household head; the results are summarized in Fig. 11.

As shown in Fig. 11, as the health status of household heads declined, the proportion of households engaging in self-employment also tended to decline. This finding is consistent with the findings of previous studies [12]. On the one hand, with poor health status, the household head does not have the ability or energy to engage in self-employment. On the other hand, the funds in the household will be used to improve personal health, such as paying for the corresponding medical expenses and spending money on medications, so it is difficult to have additional funds for self-employment.

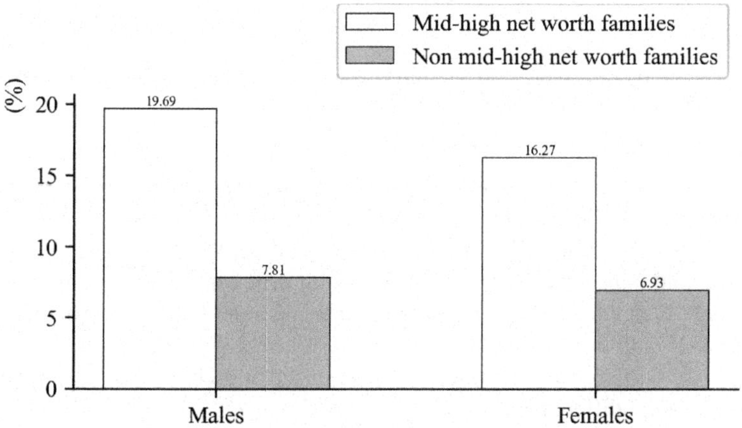


**Fig. 10** Proportion of mid-high net worth households and non mid-high net worth households engaged in self-employment (gender of household head)

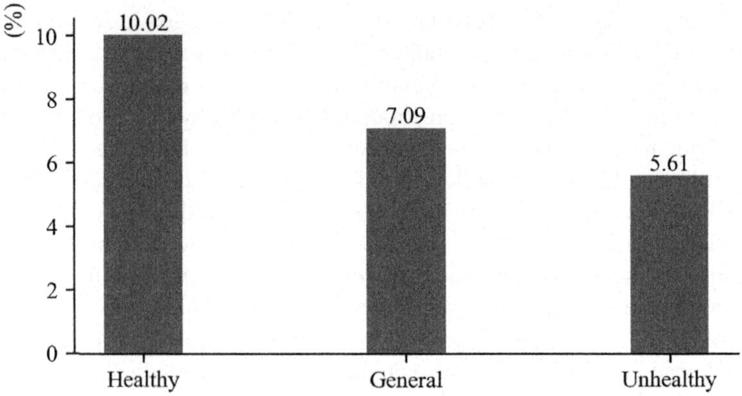


**Fig. 11** Proportion of households in the full sample that are self-employed (health status of household head)

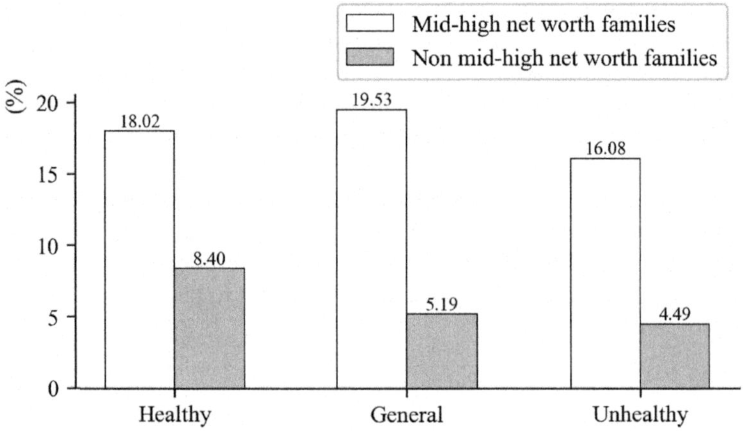


**Fig. 12** Proportion of mid-high net worth households and non mid-high net worth households engaged in self-employment (health status of household head)

According to Fig. 12, regardless of the health status of the head of household, the proportion of mid-high net worth households who are self-employed is significantly higher than that of non mid-high net worth households. When the head of the household is healthy, there is a 9.62% point difference between the proportion of medium–high net worth households and non-medium–high net worth households who are self-employed; when the head of the household is in fair health, there is a 14.34% point difference, and when the head of the household is unhealthy, there is an 11.59% point difference.

## 2.2 *Number of Households Engaged in Self-Employment Activities*

The number of self-employment activities conducted by households can vary from one household to another. This book further analyses the variability in the number of self-employment activities carried out by households in different contexts.

According to Fig. 13, overall, there was only a small difference of 0.01 items between the number of self-employment activities conducted by urban and rural households. Overall, there was no significant difference between the two groups. It can be said that there are no urban–rural differences in this regard.

According to Fig. 14, overall, more mid-high net worth households engage in self-employment activities than non mid-high net worth households. However, the difference in the number of self-employment activities conducted by mid-high net worth households and non mid-high net worth households is not significant. Compared with Fig. 13, the difference in the number of self-employment activities conducted by mid-high net worth households and non mid-high net worth households is significantly larger than the difference between urban and rural areas. It can be seen that the difference in household economic conditions is greater than the urban–rural difference in the number of self-employment activities conducted by households.

According to Fig. 15, the overall number of households conducting self-employment activities in Tier 1 and 3 cities will be higher, while the number of households conducting self-employment activities in Tier 2 and other cities will be lower. However, the difference in the number of self-employment activities conducted in different types of cities was not significant.

As shown in Fig. 16, in all cities except Tier 1, the number of self-employment activities conducted by mid-high net worth households is higher than that of non mid-high net worth households. In Tier 2 cities, the former has 0.17 items more than

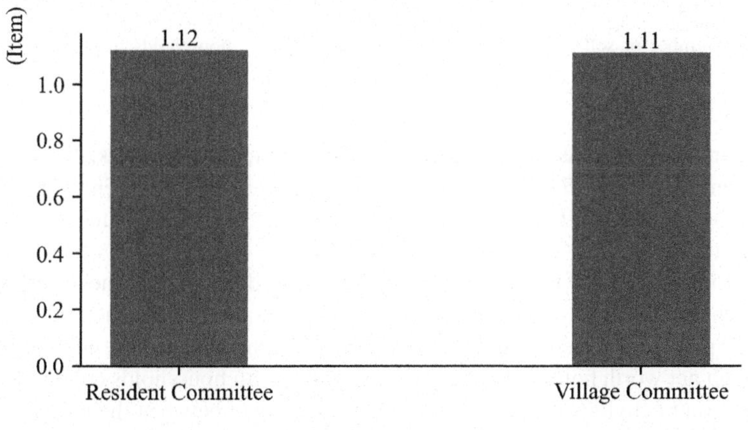


**Fig. 13** Number of self-employment activities carried out by households in the whole sample (urban and rural types)

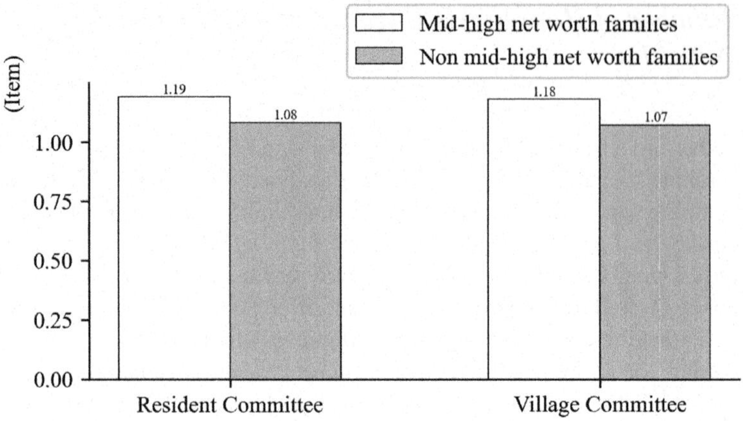


**Fig. 14** Number of mid-high net worth households and non mid-high net worth households engaged in self-employment activities (urban and rural types)

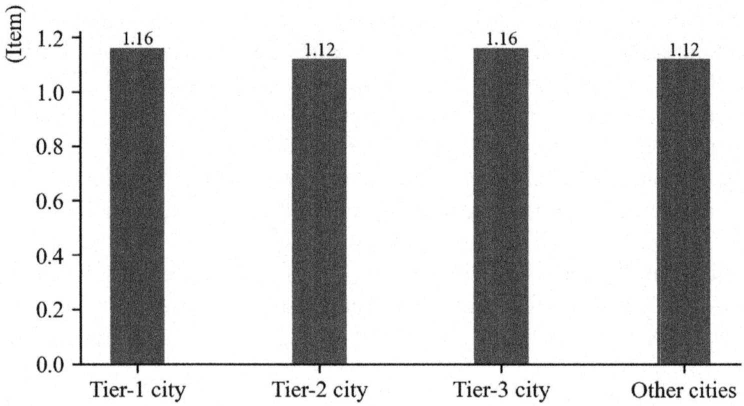


**Fig. 15** Number of self-employment activities carried out by households in the whole sample (urban type)

the latter, which indicates a certain gap between them; in Tier 3 cities, the former has 0.03 items more than the latter, which indicates a small gap between them; in other cities, the former has 0.12 items more than the latter, which indicates a certain gap between them.

The opposite is true in Tier 1 cities, where non-middle and high-net-worth households engage in more self-employment activities than mid-high net worth households. Specifically, there is a difference of 0.03 items between the number of non mid-high net worth households and mid-high net worth households conducting self-employment activities in Tier 1 cities. There was a gap between the two, but it was relatively small.

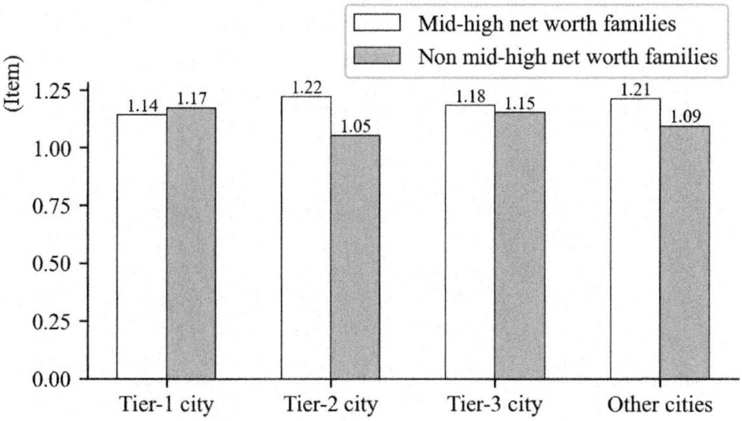


**Fig. 16** Number of mid-high net worth households and non mid-high net worth households engaging in self-employment activities (city type)

As shown in Fig. 17, overall, the number of self-employment activities conducted when the household head is in cohabitation status is the highest, one reason being that the sample in cohabitation status is relatively small. Although the number of self-employment activities conducted during cohabitation was relatively high, they were generally smaller and less stable. This was intrinsically related to the instability of cohabitation. Additionally, the smallest number of self-employment activities was observed when the household head was widowed.

According to Fig. 18, in terms of unmarried, married, and divorced status, the number of self-employment activities conducted by mid-high net worth households is higher than that of non mid-high net worth households. When the head of household is unmarried, the difference in the number of self-employment activities between the

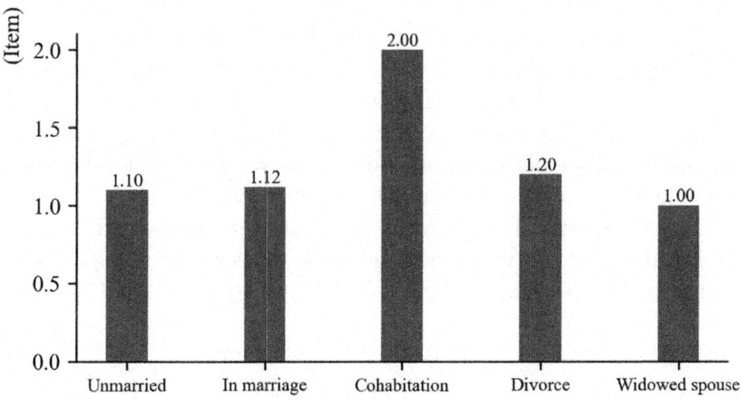


**Fig. 17** Number of self-employment activities carried out by the full sample of households (marital status of household head)

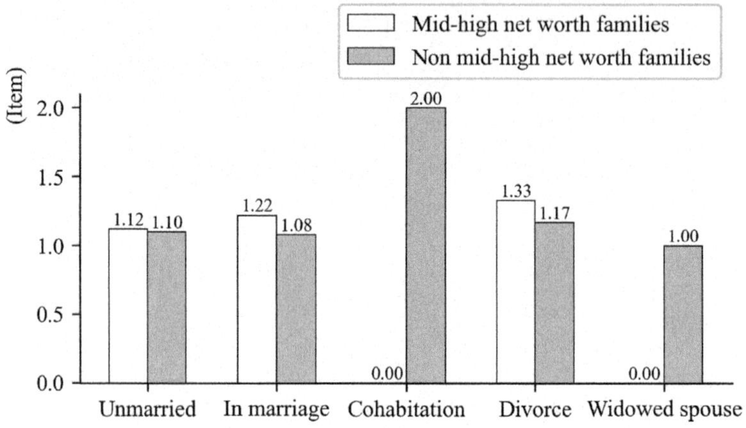


**Fig. 18** Number of mid-high net worth households and non mid-high net worth households engaging in self-employment activities (marital status of household head)

mid-high net worth households and non mid-high net worth households is 0.02. When the head of household is married, the difference in the number of self-employment activities between the two types of households is 0.14; when the head of household is cohabiting, the difference is 2; when the head of household is divorced, the difference is 0.16; when the head of household is widowed, the difference is 1. The situation of cohabitation and widowhood was unique, and the sample size was relatively small. Therefore, the data presented here are only for reference purposes.

According to Fig. 19, overall, the number of households engaging in self-employment activities tends to increase as the educational level of the household head increases. Households whose heads have higher education have more self-employment activities than other types of households, whereas households whose heads have illiterate/semi-literate education have fewer self-employment activities than other types of households.

According to Fig. 20, in general, the number of self-employment activities is generally higher in mid-high net worth households than in non mid-high net worth households, regardless of the education level of the household head. The difference in the number of self-employment activities between medium–high net worth households and non-medium–high net worth households was 0.06 items when the head of the household was illiterate/semi-literate; 0.1 items when the head of the household had primary education; 0.1 items when the head of the household had secondary education; and 0.37 items when the head of the household had higher education, which was a small difference.

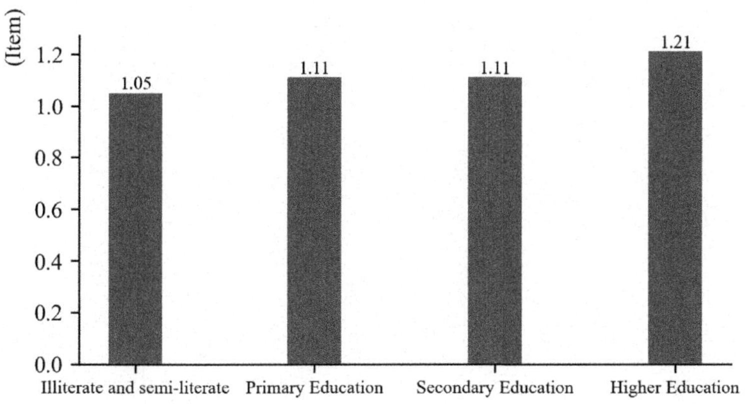


**Fig. 19** Number of self-employment activities carried out by households in the whole sample (educational level of the head of household)

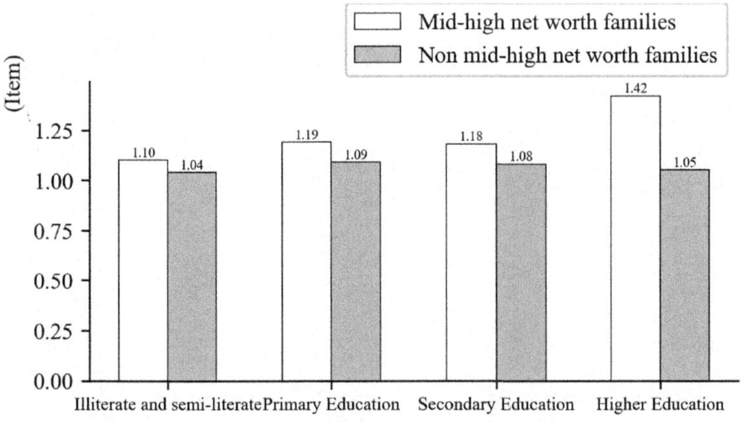


**Fig. 20** Number of mid-high net worth households and non mid-high net worth households engaged in self-employment activities (education level of household head)

According to Fig. 21, regardless of whether the household head is male or female, the number of self-employment activities conducted by medium–high net worth households is higher than that conducted by non-medium–high net worth households. When the head of the household is male, there is a difference of 0.12 items between the number of self-employment activities carried out by medium–high net worth households and non-medium–high net worth households; when the head of the household is female, there is a difference of 0.17 items between the number of self-employment activities carried out by medium–high net worth households and non-medium–high net worth households.

According to Fig. 22, the difference in the number of self-employment activities between mid-high net worth households and non mid-high net worth households is

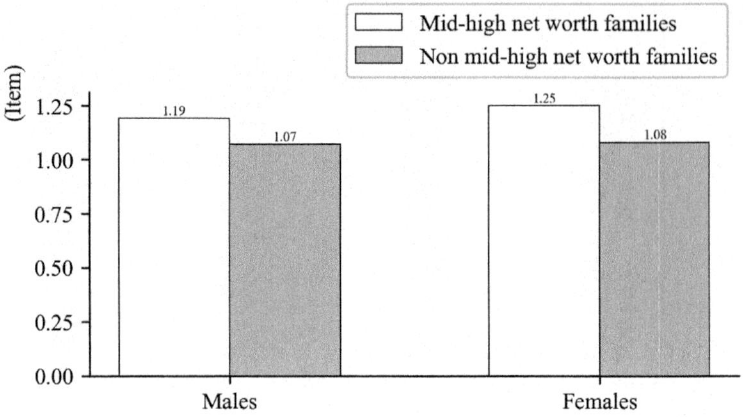


**Fig. 21** Number of mid-high net worth households and non mid-high net worth households engaging in self-employment activities (gender of household head)

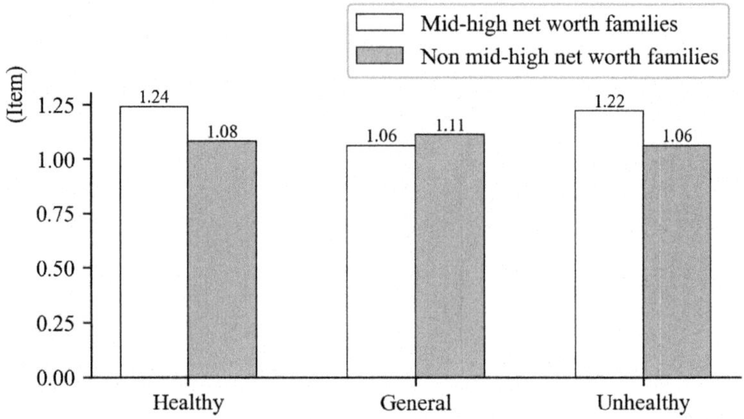


**Fig. 22** Number of mid-high net worth households and non mid-high net worth households engaging in self-employment activities (Health Status of Household Head)

0.16 when the head of the household was healthy, 0.05 when the head of the household is in average health, and 0.16 when the head of the household is unhealthy. Except for the average health status of the household head, the number of self-employment activities conducted by mid-high net worth worth households is slightly higher than that of non mid-high net worth households under all other health conditions of the household head.

## 2.3 *Total Assets of Self-Employment*

The sum of the assets from individual business activities in which the household is involved is the household's total individual business assets. This reflects the household's allocation of business assets and is an important factor influencing the future direction of household wealth. This book presents an analysis of this indicator.

According to Fig. 23, the difference between the total individual business assets of urban medium–high net worth households and non-medium–high net worth households is RMB 491,300; the difference between the total individual business assets of rural medium–high net worth households and non-medium–high net worth households is RMB 213,900, which is a very obvious difference. In addition, there is a large difference between the total individual business assets of urban medium–high net worth households and non-medium–high net worth households, and rural medium–high net worth households and non-medium–high net worth households, respectively.

According to Fig. 24, the difference in total self-employed assets between medium–high-net-worth households and non-medium–high-net-worth households in Tier 1 cities is RMB 2,428,700; the difference in total self-employed assets between medium–high-net-worth households and non-medium–high-net-worth households in Tier 2 cities is RMB 142,600; the difference in total self-employed assets between medium–high-net-worth households and non-medium–high-net-worth households in Tier 3 cities is RMB 104,600; and the difference between the two in other cities is RMB 203,600. The difference between the total self-employed assets of medium–high-net-worth households and non-medium–high-net-worth households in Tier 1 cities was the most obvious.

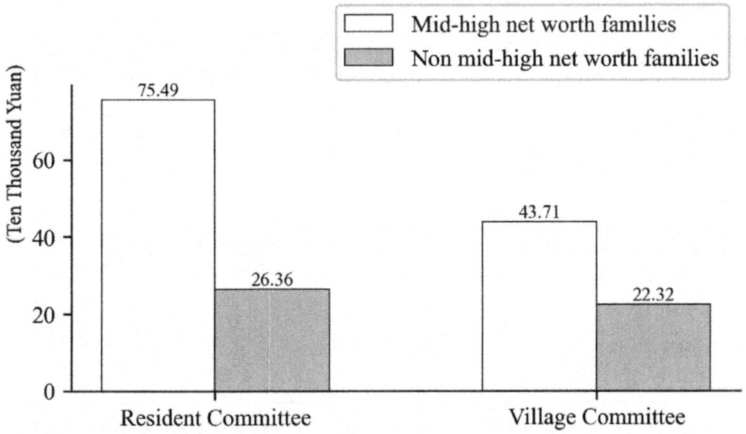


**Fig. 23** Total self-employed assets of mid-high net worth households and non mid-high net worth households (by urban and rural areas)

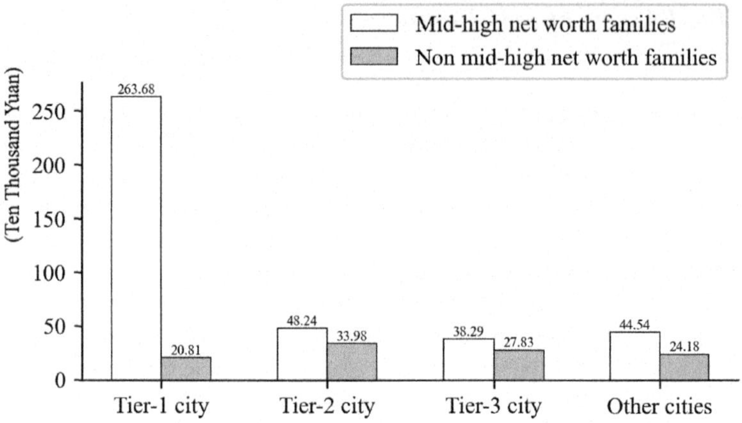


**Fig. 24** Total self-employed assets of mid-high net worth households and non mid-high net worth households (city type)

According to Fig. 25, the difference between the total self-employed assets of middle- and non-medium–high net worth households and non mid-high net worth households is ¥ 727,100 when the education level of the household head is illiterate/ semi-literate; ¥ 128,300 when the education level of the household head is primary education; ¥ 315,900 when the education level of the household head is secondary education; and ¥ 866,200 when the education level of the household head is higher education. The difference is 866,200 yuan. In summary, the difference between the total self-employed assets of mid-high net worth households and non mid-high net worth households is largest when the household head has completed higher education.

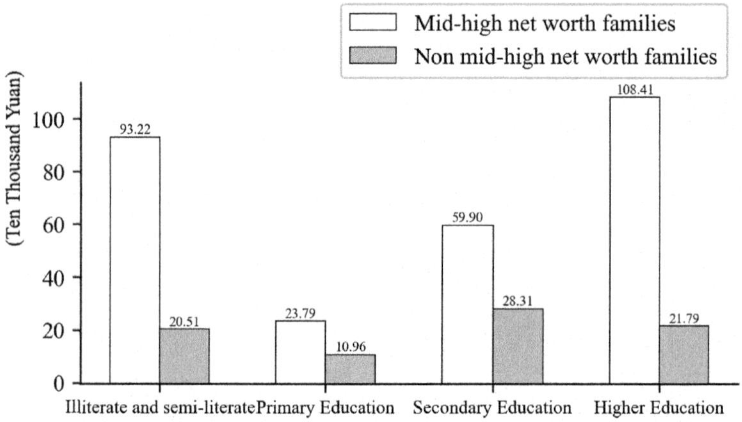


**Fig. 25** Total self-employed assets of mid-high net worth households and non mid-high net worth households (education level of household head)

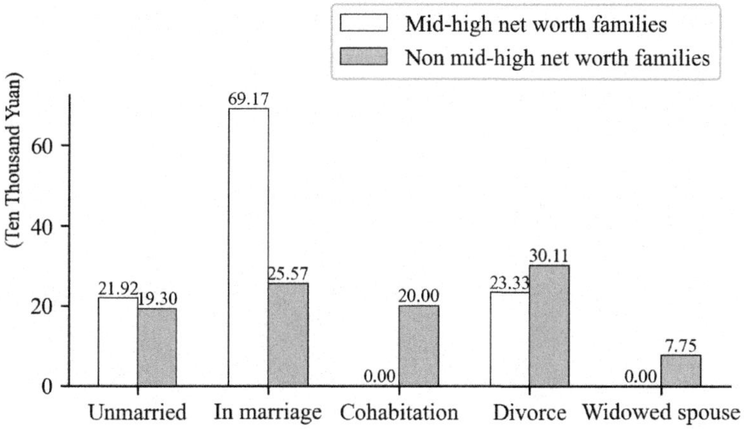


**Fig. 26** Total assets in self-employed businesses of mid-high net worth households and non-middle and high-net-worth households (marital status of household head)

According to Fig. 26, the difference between the total self-employed assets of mid-high net worth households and non mid-high net worth households is ¥ 26,200 when the household head is unmarried; ¥ 436,000 when the household head is married, ¥ 200,000 when the household head is cohabiting; ¥ 67,800 when the household head is divorced, and ¥ 77,500 when the household head is widowed. The difference is ¥ 77,500 when the head of the household was widowed. In summary, when the head of household is married, the difference between the total self-employed assets of mid-high net worth households and those of non mid-high net worth households is the largest.

According to Fig. 27, the difference in total self-employed assets between medium–high net worth households and non-medium–high net worth households is ¥ 455,200 when the head of the household is healthy, ¥ 399,500 when the head of the household is in fair health, and ¥ 0.37 million when the head of the household is unhealthy. Except when the head of the household is unhealthy, the difference between the total self-employed assets of mid-high net worth households and those of non mid-high net worth households is significant.

## 3 Real Estate Situation

In China's household asset allocation, property is a very important part and occupies a significant share of household assets. A study based on data from the "Survey on Economic Conditions and Attitudes of Chinese Urban Residents," conducted by the National Bureau of Statistics in July–August 2009 showed that at that time, the value of property accounted for 74.6% of the total financial assets of Chinese households [1]. However, for U.S. households, this figure is only 42% [15]. It is worth noting

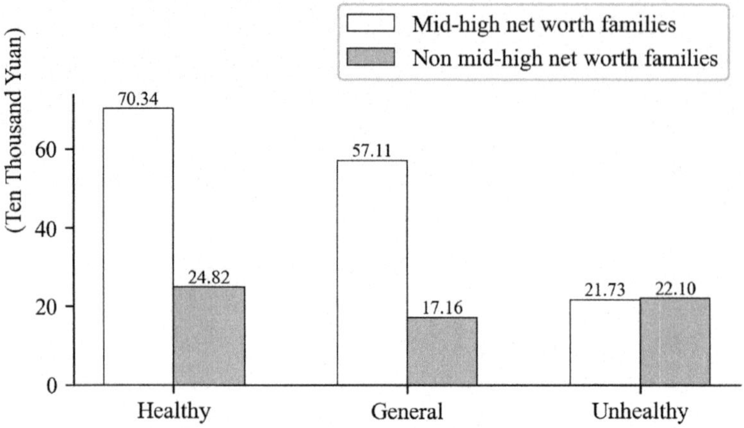


**Fig. 27** Total assets of individual businesses for mid-high net worth households and non mid-high net worth households (health status of household head)

that the value of property is included in the calculation of household financial assets after monetizing it in the above literature. Property is an important physical asset for households and is often classified as a household non-financial asset. Household investment properties are those held by households to earn rent, realize capital appreciation (the difference between the purchase and sale of real estate), or both. The need for investment in property varies according to household type. Investment-preferring households mainly demand investment properties, whereas savings-preferring households demand residential properties [16]. In general, mid-high net worth households tend to belong to investment-preferring households and are therefore more likely to invest household assets in purchasing investment properties.

### *3.1 Household Ownership Rate of Second and Above Properties*

Second, properties owned by households are often considered investment properties. When households with multiple properties predict that housing prices will increase significantly in the future, they will reduce their holdings of risky financial assets and switch to property investments [17]. It is evident that, even if they already own multiple properties, these households will not hesitate to pull out from the stock market, debt market, and funds to invest in the housing market when they see that there is still much room for housing prices to rise. To further understand households' purchases of investment properties, this book analyzes households' ownership of second and more properties.

Different estimates exist for the rates of second and higher property ownership among Chinese households. In 2015, the Financial Product Search Platform

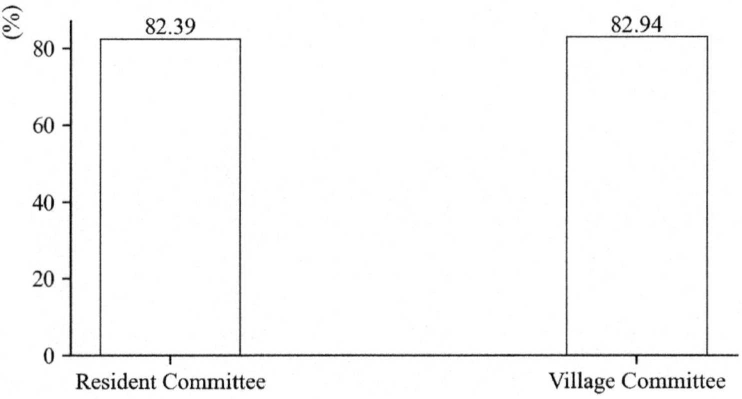


**Fig. 28** Second and higher property ownership rate of mid-high net worth households (urban and rural types)

Yinrate.com released the Report on Financial Capability of Chinese Residents, which showed that the percentage of households with second homes in China reached 40.07% [18]. However, the sample of this report was not sufficiently representative. One study used data from the 2017 China Household Financial Survey to estimate the rate of second and higher property ownership among Chinese households to be 31% [19]. However, the sample of this survey is more skewed toward urban areas, and there are fewer samples from rural areas where households own a second or more properties. Therefore, the data may have been highly biased.

According to Fig. 28, the second and higher property ownership rate of urban HNW households is 82.39% and that of rural households is 82.94%.

According to Fig. 29, overall, as the urban class decreases, the rate of household ownership of second and more properties decreases. This trend is the opposite of that in housing prices. Generally, the higher the city rank, the higher the average house price. Tier 1 cities have the highest house prices; however, the proportion of households owning second and more properties is also highest in Tier 1 cities.

According to Fig. 30, the second and above property ownership rates of HNW households in Tier 1 cities were 74.68 and 82.52% in Tier 2 cities, 86.61% in Tier 3 cities, and 85.62% in other cities.

According to Fig. 31, overall, the household ownership rate of secondary and higher properties gradually increased as the education level of the household head increased. In general, educational attainment is positively correlated with income. The higher the education level, the higher the household income, and the greater the demand for investment properties. In addition, the higher the education level, the stronger the awareness of property investment and risk tolerance and the more likely they are to invest in property.

According to Fig. 32, the second and higher home ownership rate of mid-high net worth households is 86.30% when the education level of the household head is illiterate/semiliterate, 84.94% when the education level of the household head

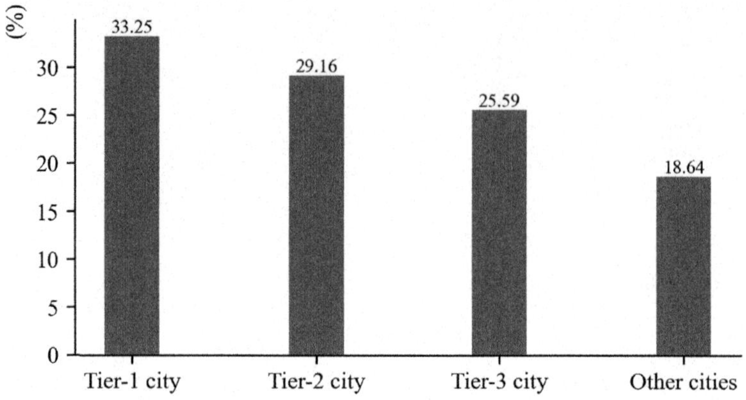


**Fig. 29** Second and higher property ownership rate for the full sample (city type)

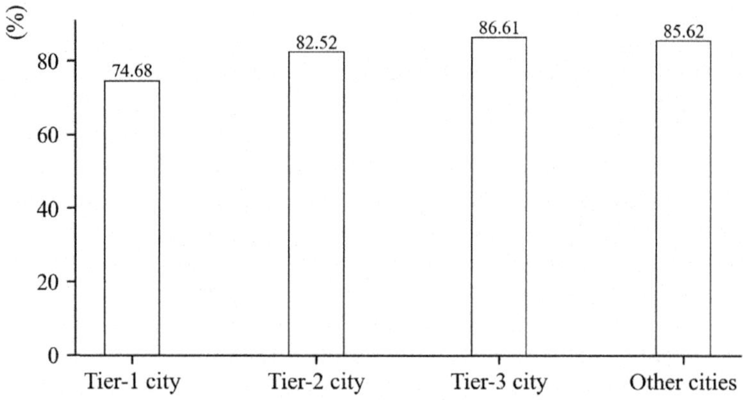


**Fig. 30** Second and higher property ownership rate of mid-high net worth households (city type)

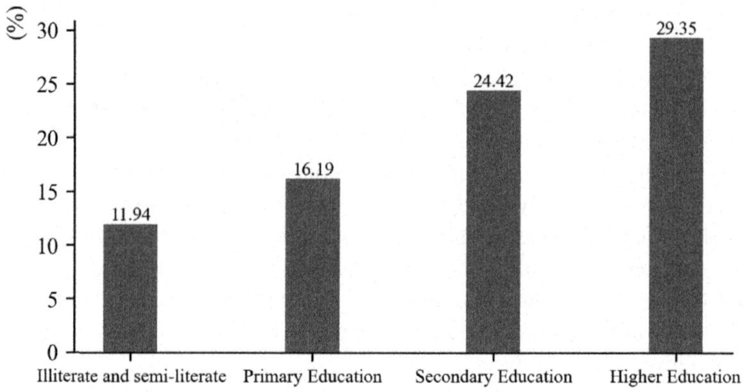


**Fig. 31** Second and higher property ownership rate for the full sample (education level of household head)

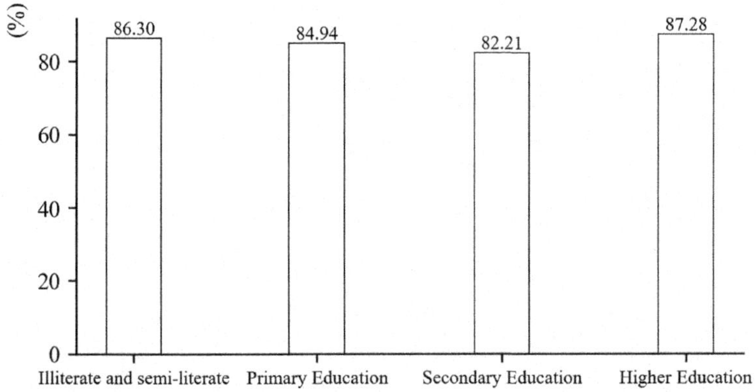


**Fig. 32** Second and higher property ownership rate of mid-high net worth households (education level of household head)

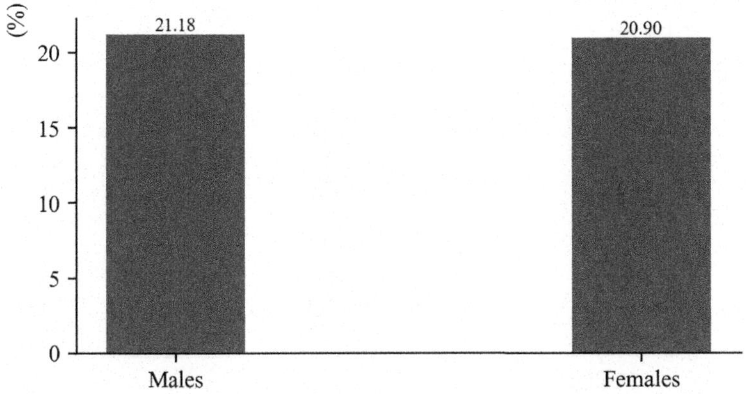


**Fig. 33** Second and higher property ownership rate for the full sample (gender of household head)

is primary education, 82.21% when the education level of the household head is secondary education, and 87.28% when the education level of the household head is higher education.

According to Fig. 33, the household ownership rate of the second and more properties is lower when the household head is female than when it is male.

According to Fig. 34, when the head of household is male, the second and higher property ownership rate of mid-high net worth households is 83.79%; when the head of household is female, it is 83.03%.

According to Fig. 35, as the health status of the head of household declines, the rate of household ownership of second and more properties also tends to decline.

According to Fig. 36, when the head of the household is healthy, the second and higher property ownership rate of mid-high net worth households is 84.33%; when

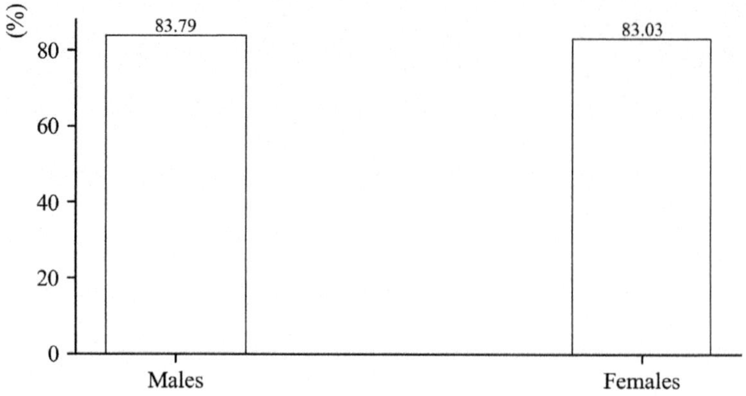


**Fig. 34** Second and higher property ownership rate of mid-high net worth households (gender of household head)

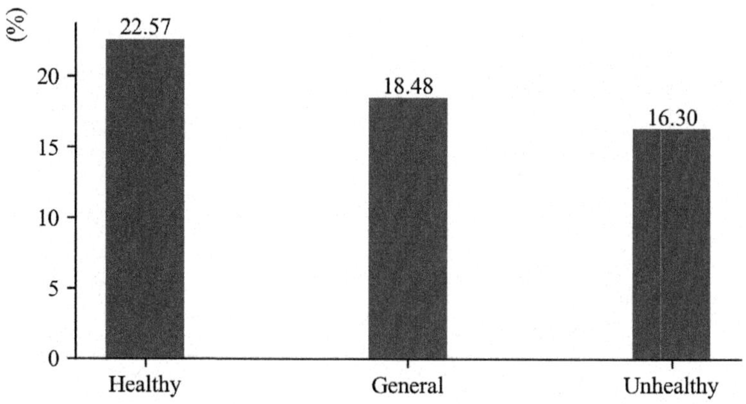


**Fig. 35** Second and more property ownership rate (household head health status) for the full sample

the head of the household is in fair health, it is 79.88%; and when the head of the household is unhealthy, it is 79.72%.

## 3.2 *Number of Second and More Properties in the Family*

The strong investment demand for housing is an important reason for the continuous increase in housing prices [20]. This is reflected mainly in the increasing trend in the number of investment properties held by a growing number of households. The average number of second and higher properties owned by households was calculated to explore the basic characteristics of household investment properties.

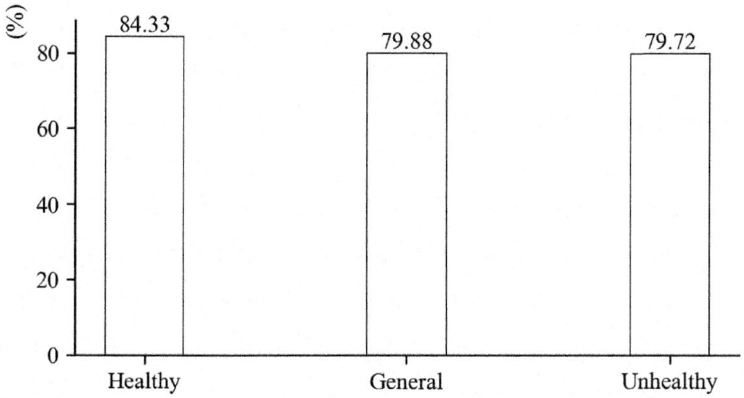


**Fig. 36** Second and higher property ownership rate of mid-high net worth households (health status of household head)

According to Fig. 37, the difference in the number of second and above properties between urban mid-high net worth households and non mid-high net worth households is 0.32. The difference in the number of second and above properties between rural mid-high net worth households and non mid-high net worth households is 0.18. The number of investment properties owned by mid-high net worth households was significantly higher than that owned by non mid-high net worth households.

According to Fig. 38, the difference in the number of second and above properties between mid-high net worth households in first-tier cities and non mid-high net worth households was 0.46; the difference between the two in second-tier cities was 0.36; the difference between the two in third-tier cities was 0.38; and the difference between the two in other cities was 0.22. It can be seen that, in general, the higher the

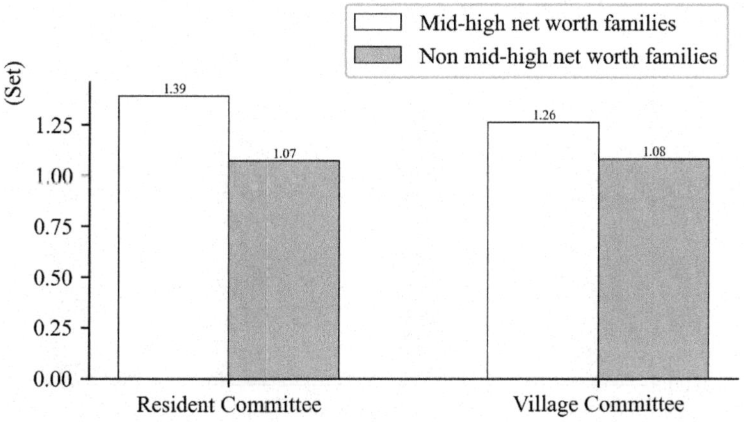


**Fig. 37** Number of second and higher properties for mid-high net worth households and non mid-high net worth households (urban and rural types)

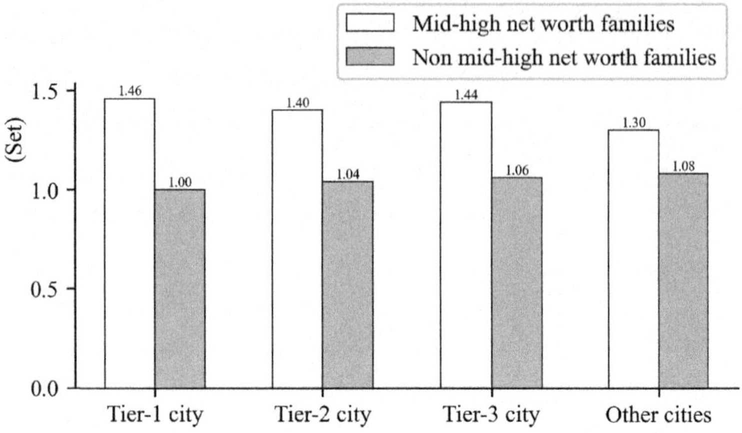


**Fig. 38** Number of second and higher properties for mid-high net worth households and non mid-high net worth households (city type)

city rank, the greater the difference in the number of investment properties owned by the two types of households.

According to Fig. 39, overall, the number of households with second and higher properties gradually increases as the education level of the household head increases. It can be seen that the more educated the household head is, the more likely the household is to allocate household assets to investment properties to achieve household wealth appreciation through the appreciation of house prices.

According to Fig. 40, the difference in the number of second and higher properties between mid-high net worth households and non mid-high net worth households is 0.15 when the education level of the household head is illiterate/semi-literate, 0.19 when the education level of the household head is primary education, 0.27 when the

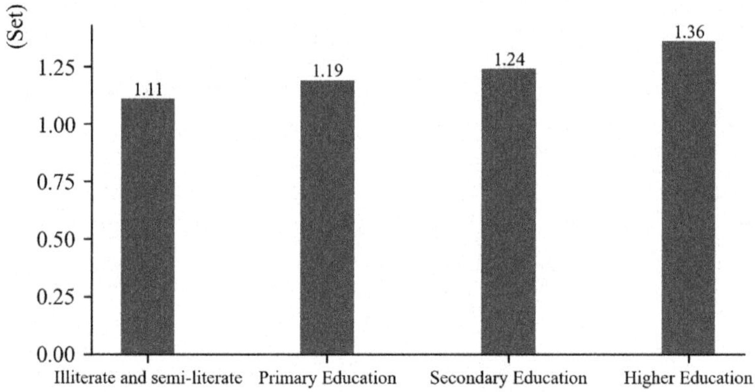


**Fig. 39** Number of second and higher properties in the full sample (education level of household head)

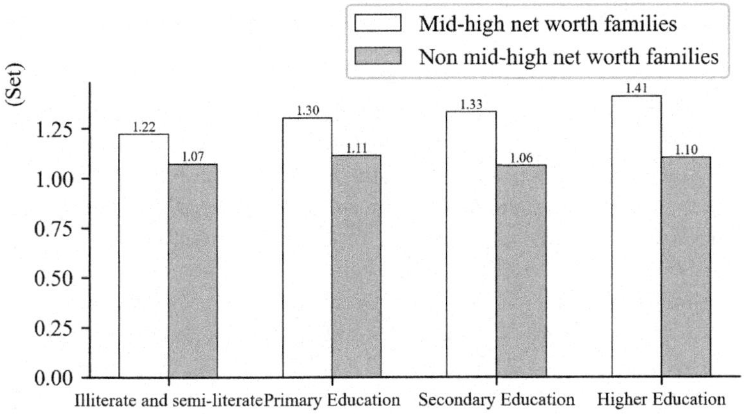


**Fig. 40** Number of second and higher properties for mid-high net worth households and non mid-high net worth households (education level of household head)

education level of the household head is secondary education, and 0.31 when the education level of the household head is higher education.

According to Fig. 41, the difference in the number of second and higher properties between mid-high net worth households and non mid-high net worth households is 0.26 when the head of the household is male, and 0.25 when the head of the household is female.

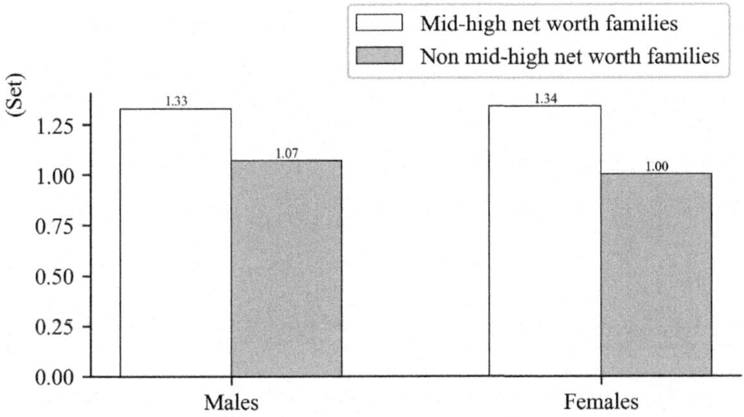


**Fig. 41** Number of second and higher properties for mid-high net worth households and non mid-high net worth households (gender of household head)

## 3.3 Value of the Second and Higher Family Properties

The value of an investment property owned by a household is the sum of the product of the number of investment properties and their market value. This is an important indicator of a household's property investment. Here is the analysis of the indicator.

As shown in Fig. 42, there is a significant difference in the value of the second and higher properties between urban and rural HNW households, with a difference of ¥ 954,600 between the two.

According to Fig. 43, the value of the second and above properties of HNW households in Tier 1 cities is RMB 3,960,500, higher than other types of cities; the value is RMB 1,556,500, RMB 1,240,200 and RMB 1,110,300 in Tier 2 cities, Tier 3 cities and other cities respectively.

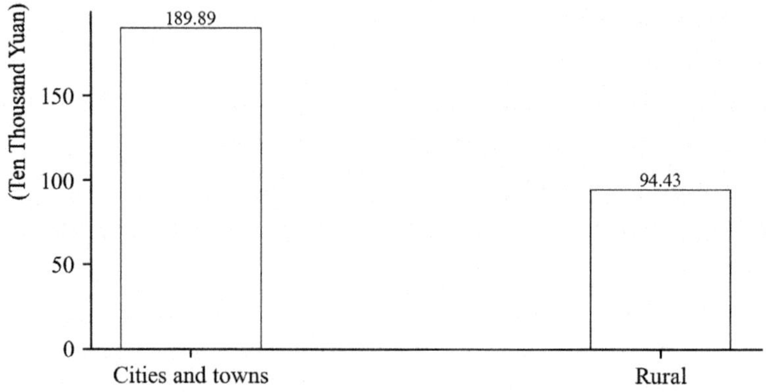


**Fig. 42** Value of second and higher properties for mid-high net worth households (urban and rural types)

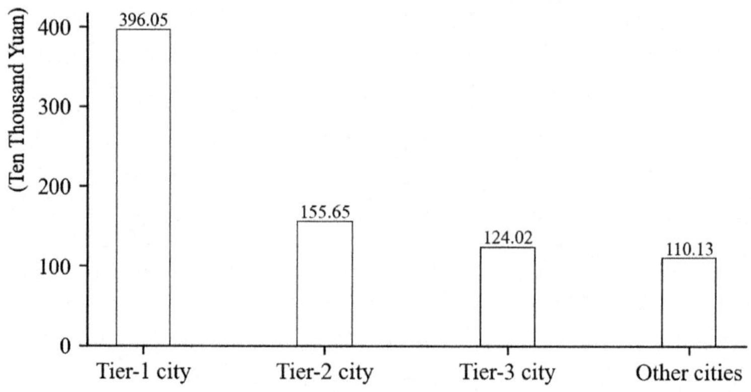


**Fig. 43** Value of second and more properties for mid-high net worth households (city type)

According to Fig. 44, the value of the second and higher properties for mid-high net worth households is ¥ 1.28 million when the household head's education level is illiterate/semi-literate, ¥ 1.0889 million when the household head's education level is primary, ¥1.5956 million when the household head's education level is secondary, and ¥1.1783 million when the household head's education level is tertiary.

According to Fig. 45, when the head of the household is male, the value of the second property and above for mid-high net worth households is ¥1,564,200; when the head of household is female, it is ¥1,526,400.

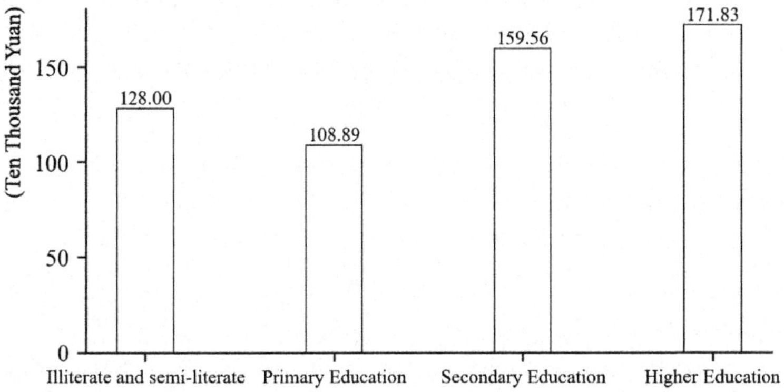


**Fig. 44** Value of second and higher properties for mid-high net worth households (education level of household head)

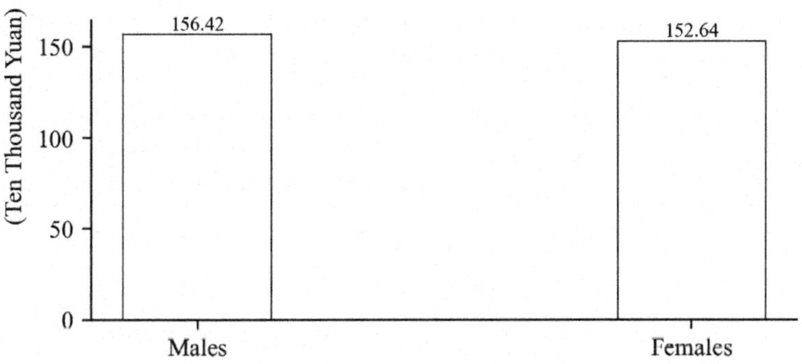


**Fig. 45** Value of second and higher properties for mid-high net worth households (gender of household head)

## 3.4 Share of Property Value in Total Household Assets

The proportion of property values to total household assets is a common indicator of a household's asset allocation to property. The Financial Capability of Chinese Residents Report published by Yinrate.com shows that 52.07% of Chinese households have property value accounting for more than half of the total household assets, and 16.19% of households have this proportion of 80% or more. Moreover, 31.99% of Chinese households use property as a means of investment [18]. Therefore, the share of property value in total household assets among Chinese households is relatively high.

According to Fig. 46, there is a 16.97% point difference in the value of all properties as a share of total assets between mid-high net worth households in towns and cities and a 7.1 % point difference in rural areas. Among mid-high net worth households, the value of all properties as a share of total assets was slightly higher in urban households than in rural households; among non mid-high net worth households, the value of all properties was higher in rural households.

According to Fig. 47, there is a 29.58% point difference in the proportion of total assets between the value of all properties of mid-high net worth households and non mid-high net worth households in Tier 1 cities, a 21.31% point difference in Tier 2 cities, a 15.87% point difference in Tier 3 cities, and a 12.87% point difference in other cities. The difference between the values of all properties of mid-high net worth households and non mid-high net worth households as a proportion of total assets also increases gradually as the city level rises, and the difference between the two is more obvious.

According to Fig. 48, there is a 7.77% point difference in the value of all properties as a share of total assets between mid-high net worth households and non mid-high

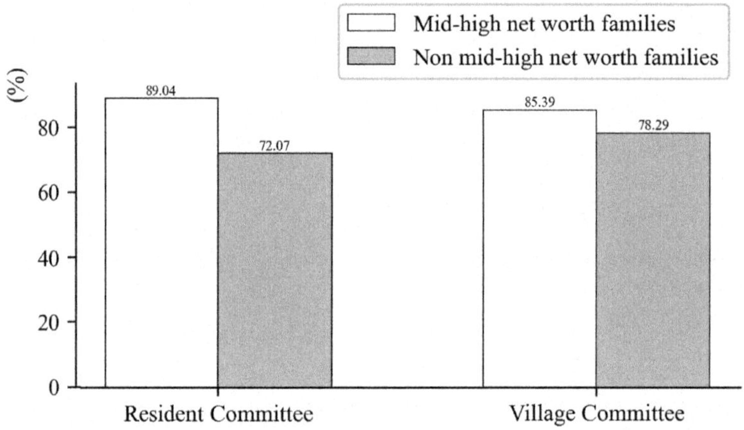


**Fig. 46** Value of all properties as a share of total assets for mid-high net worth households and non mid-high net worth households (urban and rural zones)

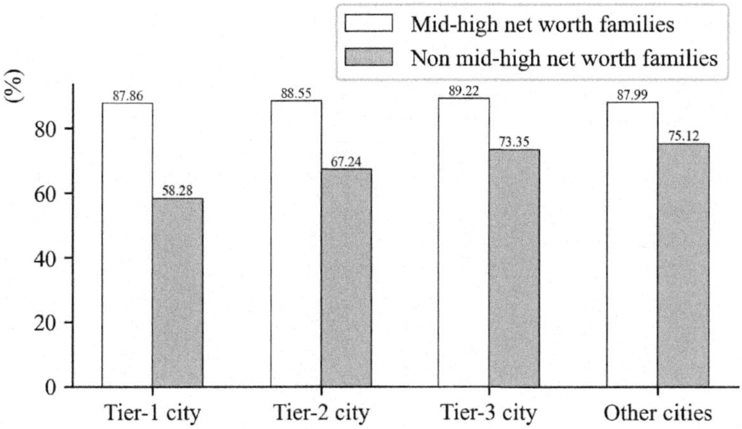


**Fig. 47** Value of all properties as a share of total assets for mid-high net worth households and non mid-high net worth households (city type)

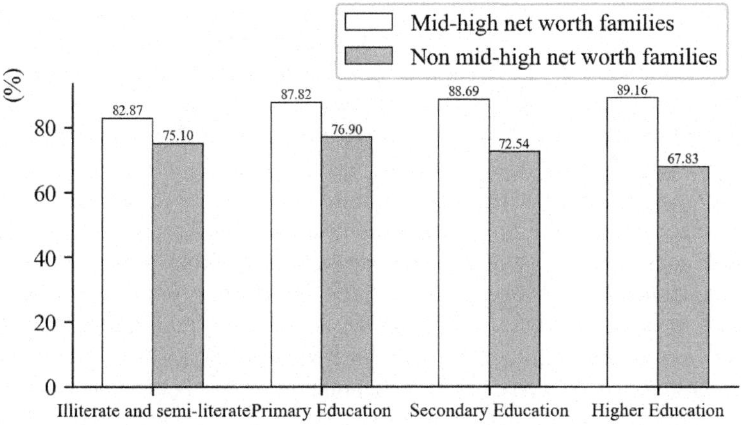


**Fig. 48** Value of all properties as a share of total assets for mid-high net worth households and non mid-high net worth households (education level of household head)

net worth households when the education level of the household head is illiterate/semi-literate; a 10.83% point difference when the education level of the household head is primary education; a 16.15% point difference when the education level of the household head is secondary education; and a 21.33% point difference when the education level of the household head. The difference between the two is 21.33% points when the education level of the household head is higher education. As the education level of the household head increases, the difference between the value of all properties as a percentage of total assets between mid-high net worth households and non mid-high net worth households also gradually increases.

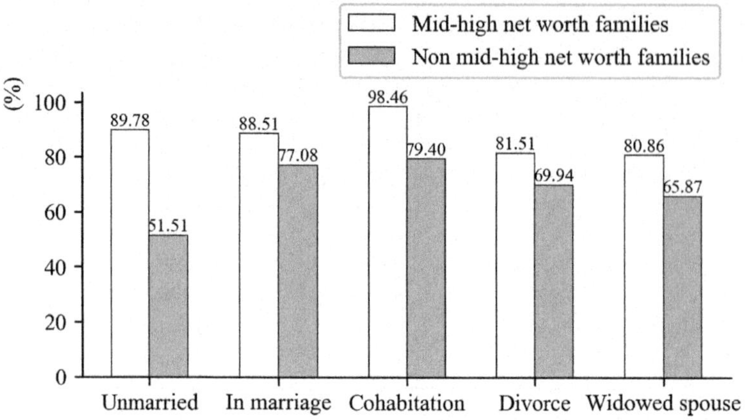


**Fig. 49** Value of all properties as a share of total assets for mid-high net worth households and non mid-high net worth households (marital status of household head)

According to Fig. 49, there is a 38.27% point difference in the value of all properties as a share of total assets between mid-high net worth households when the household head is unmarried, 11.43% points when the household head is married, 19.06% points when the household head is cohabiting, 11.87% points when the household head is divorced, and 14.99% points when the household head is widowed. When the head of household was widowed, the difference between the two was 14.99% points. In summary, when the head of a household is unmarried, the difference between the value of all properties as a percentage of total assets is the largest between mid-high net worth households and non mid-high net worth households.

As shown in Fig. 50, when the head of the household is male, there is a 14.31% point difference in the value of all properties as a share of total assets between mid-high net worth households and non mid-high net worth households; when the head of household is female, there is a 15.29% point difference between the two.

## 4 Consumer Durables

Household durables are generally defined as consumer goods owned by households that have long service lives and can be used multiple times. As consumer durables are purchased less frequently, consumers' purchase behaviors and decisions are more deliberate, and they are an important part of household assets. Common consumer durables for households include household appliances, furniture, cars, and other items. For households, consumer durables such as homes, cars, jewelry, and other luxury items have attributes that indicate social status [21, 22]. Therefore, consumer durables are a non-negligible part of household non-financial asset allocation.

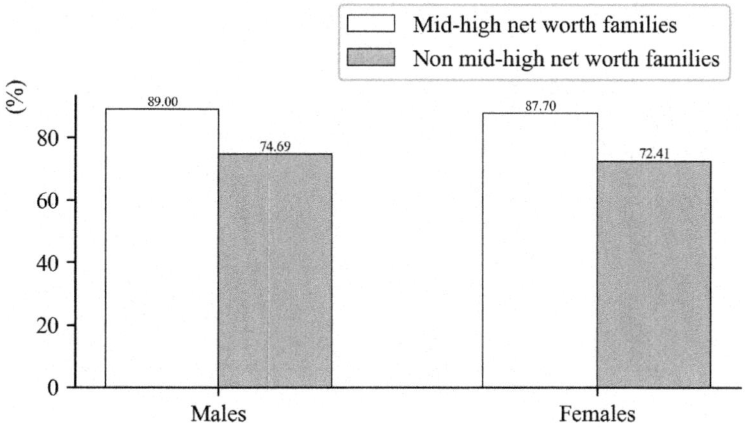


**Fig. 50** Value of all properties as a share of total assets for mid-high net worth households and non mid-high net worth households (gender of household head)

According to Fig. 51, overall, the number of consumer durables was significantly higher for urban households than for rural households. For urban households, the more frequent the social interactions, the stronger the incentive to acquire higher social status, and the greater the likelihood of borrowing to purchase consumer durables [23]. Specifically, there is a significant difference of ¥119,712.8 in the amount of consumer durables between urban mid-high net worth households and non mid-high net worth households; and a significant difference of ¥87,255.33 in the amount of consumer durables between rural mid-high net worth households and non mid-high net worth households. In addition, there is a large difference in the number of consumer durables between urban and rural mid-high net worth households; this phenomenon also appears in non mid-high net worth households.

According to Fig. 52, in general, the number of household durables tended to decrease as the city rank decreased. Specifically, the difference in the amount of consumer durables between HNW and non mid-high net worth households in first-tier cities is ¥135,602.45; in second-tier cities, the difference is ¥117,017.93; in third-tier cities, the difference is ¥85,541.17; and in other cities, the difference is ¥88,517.01. Different types of residents have different psychological thresholds of income, which have a greater impact on the demand for consumer durables [24].

According to Fig. 53, overall, households headed by males spend significantly more on consumer durables than households headed by females do. Females are generally more selective and cautious when it comes to purchasing consumer durables. In addition to being controlled by their own purchase intentions, women's purchase behavior is closely related to service guarantees, the brand image of consumer durables, marketing orientation, and purchase evaluations [25]. Specifically, when the head of the household is male, there is a difference of ¥112,554.48 in the amount of consumer durables between mid-high net worth households and non mid-high net worth households; when the head of the household is female, the

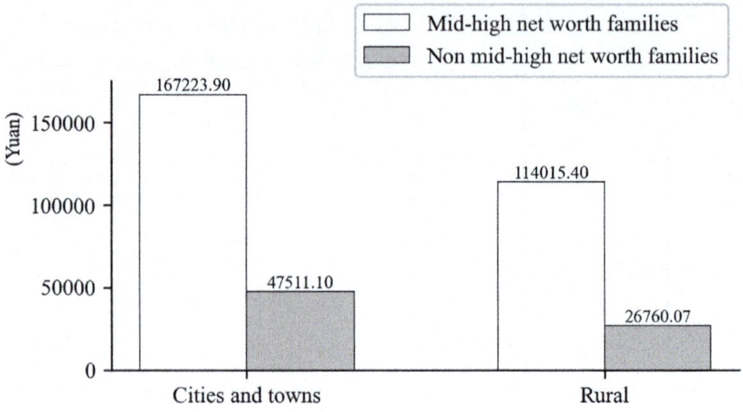


**Fig. 51** Number of consumer durables for mid-high net worth households and non mid-high net worth households (urban and rural divisions)

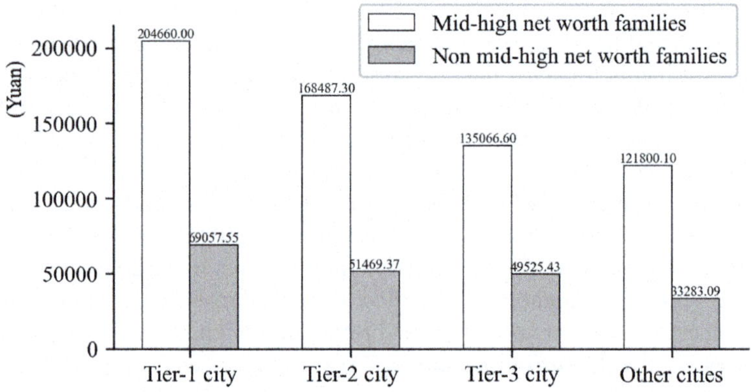


**Fig. 52** Number of consumer durables for mid-high net worth households and non mid-high net worth households (city type)

difference between the two is ¥95,104.78. The difference between the two situations is significant.

According to Fig. 54, in general, the higher the education level of the household head, the higher the number of household durables. Specifically, the difference in the amount of consumer durables between mid-high net worth households and non mid-high net worth households is ¥77,176.93 when the household head's education is illiterate/semi-literate, ¥77,182.75 when the household head's education is primary, ¥97,359.24 when the household head's education is secondary, and ¥109,835.62 when the household head's education is tertiary. 109,835.62 Yuan. In summary, as the education level of the household head increases, the difference in the amount of consumer durables between mid-high net worth households and non mid-high net worth households gradually increases.

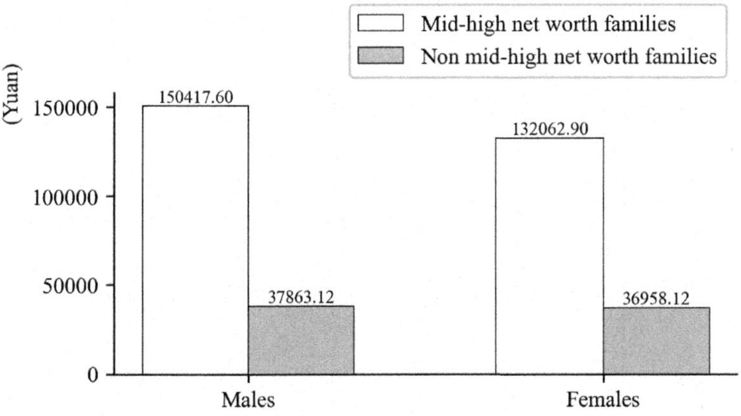


**Fig. 53** Number of consumer durables for mid-high net worth households and non mid-high net worth households (gender of household head)

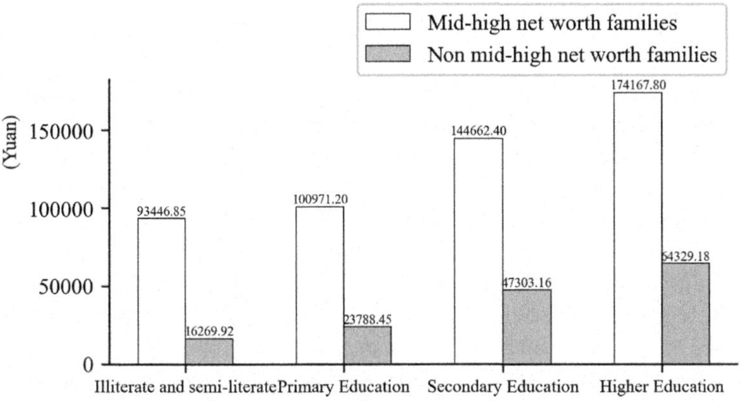


**Fig. 54** Number of consumer durables for mid-high net worth households and non mid-high net worth households (education level of household head)

According to Fig. 55, the difference in the amount of consumer durables between mid-high net worth households and non mid-high net worth households is ¥78,642.02 when the household head is unmarried, ¥109,468.09 when the household head is married, ¥45,427.14 when the household head is cohabiting, ¥73,311.03 when the household head is divorced, and ¥69,317.59 when the household head is widowed. The difference between the two is ¥69,317.59 when the household head is widowed. In summary, when the head of the household is married, the difference in the number of consumer durables between mid-high net worth households and non mid-high net worth households is the largest.

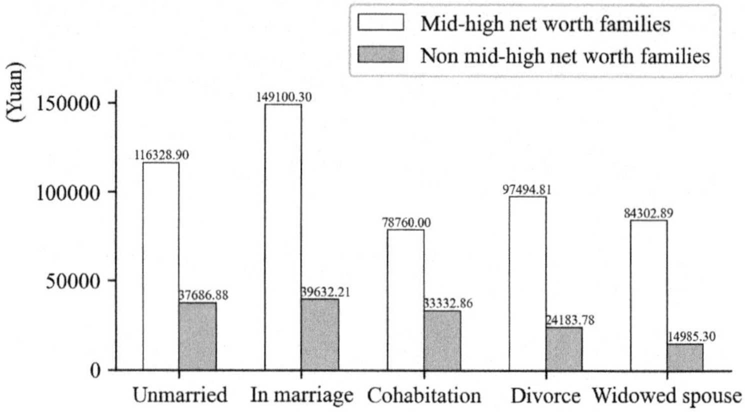


**Fig. 55** Number of consumer durables for mid-high net worth households and non mid-high net worth households (marital status of household head)

# 5 Analysis of Influencing Factors

The data used were mainly obtained from the household questionnaire and the individual questionnaire in the 2020 CFPS questionnaire. The study focused on business assets and investment properties. Business assets are related to household entrepreneurial decisions; therefore, household entrepreneurial decisions are used here as a primary object of study. Investment properties are second and more properties. Considering the cooperative and risk-sharing nature behind the explanatory variables—household entrepreneurial decision and property investment decision, which are household decisions rather than individual decisions, the dependent variable is positioned here at the household level in the selection of the dependent variable, that is, using the explanatory variables defined in the CFPS household questionnaire.

## *5.1 Data, Variables and Models*

1. *Key variables*

Explanatory variable 1 is household entrepreneurial decisions, based on question 1 of the CFPS household questionnaire—"In the past 12 months, did any member of your household engage in self-employment or start a private business?" and question 2—"In the past 12 months, how many members of your household were engaged in self-employment or have started a private business?" The variables were defined. If the answer to one of the questions was "no," the household entrepreneurial decision was defined as zero. If the answer to one of the questions was "yes," the household entrepreneurial decision is defined as the number of responses to Question 2.

Explanatory variable 2 is the household property investment decision, based on question R1 of the CFPS household questionnaire—"Do you or any other member of your household own any property other than your current home?" and question R101—"How many other properties do you or other household members own?" The variables were defined. If the answer to question R1 is "no," the household property investment decision is defined as zero. If the answer to question R1 was "yes," the household property investment decision was defined as the number of answers to question R101.

The core explanatory variables are mid-high net worth households (dummy variables) and household investable assets. The former consisted of values 0 and 1—1 if household investable assets are greater than or equal to ¥450,000, and 0 if household investable assets are less than ¥450,000.

The remaining control variables included household-level and head-of-household-level control variables. Household-level control variables included household size, household income, bank loans, friends and relatives, and private loans, and head-of-household-level control variables included gender, age, years of education, marital status, health status, and self-confidence.

2. *Descriptive statistics*

During the data processing, this chapter eliminated samples with missing and incorrect values in the variables and finally obtained 9089 valid samples. The definition and descriptive statistics of the variables are shown in Table 1.

3. *Model setting*

This chapter examines the impact of mid-high net worth households and household investable assets on household entrepreneurial decisions and household property investment decisions, as modeled below:

$$Entrepre = \alpha_0 + \alpha_1 \times M\,H\,W + \alpha_2 \times ln(FIA) + \alpha_3 \times X + u$$

$$House = \beta_0 + \beta_1 \times MHW + \beta_2 \times ln(FIA) + \beta_3 \times X + u$$

where *Entrepre* denotes the number of self-employment activities performed by the household; *House* denotes the number of properties owned by the household other than the current home; *MHW* and *FIA* denote mid-high net worth households (dummy variables) and household investable assets, respectively; $X$ is a set of control variables containing both household-level and head-of-household-level controls; and $u$ is the error term.

**Table 1** Definition of variables and descriptive statistics

| Variable | Definition | Mean | S.D | Min | Max |
|---|---|---|---|---|---|
| Entrepreneurship of the family | Number of self-employed or private enterprises | 0.102 | 0.347 | 0 | 6 |
| Investment properties | Number of properties other than current housing | 0.261 | 0.567 | 0 | 7 |
| Mid-high net worth families | 1 for middle and high net worth households, 0 for the rest | 0.155 | 0.362 | 0 | 1 |
| Household investable assets | Log value of household investable assets | 8.671 | 4.892 | 0 | 17.371 |
| Household size | Number of family members | 3.574 | 1.901 | 1 | 15 |
| Household income | Logarithmic value of household income | 10.705 | 1.429 | 0 | 14.286 |
| Bank loans | If the household has a bank loan, the variable takes the value of 1, otherwise it is 0 | 0.105 | 0.306 | 0 | 1 |
| Private loans from friends and family | If there is a family or private loan, the value is 1, otherwise it is 0 | 0.113 | 0.316 | 0 | 1 |
| Gender | If the gender is male, the variable takes the value of 1, otherwise it is 0 | 0.562 | 0.496 | 0 | 1 |
| Age | Age of the individual, in years | 48.922 | 14.626 | 18 | 95 |
| Year of education | Number of years of education received | 8.221 | 5.084 | 0 | 24 |
| Marriage | If the marital status is married, the variable takes the value of 1, otherwise 0 | 0.816 | 0.388 | 0 | 1 |
| Health | Health rating with a maximum of 5 and a minimum of 1 | 3.002 | 1.176 | 1 | 5 |
| Self-confidence | Self-confidence rating, highest 5, lowest 1 | 4.132 | 0.936 | 1 | 5 |

## 5.2 Empirical Analysis

1. *Impact of mid-high net worth households on household entrepreneurial decisions*

Table 2 presents the regression results for the effects of mid-high net worth households on households' entrepreneurial decisions. Column (1) considers only the core explanatory variable of medium–high-net-worth households (dummy variable), columns (2) to (4) add household-level control variables, and columns (5) to (7) add household head-level control variables to the household-level control variables. The results show that after considering both household- and head-of-household-level control variables, mid-high net worth households increase their household entrepreneurial decisions by 0.121 units compared to non mid-high net worth households, indicating that mid-high net worth households have a significant positive effect on increasing the number of household ventures and changing household entrepreneurial decisions.

In addition, household size, household income, bank loans, and loans from friends, relatives and private individuals, all have a significant positive contribution to household entrepreneurial decisions. Age has a significant negative effect on household entrepreneurial decisions. Marital status has a significant positive effect on household entrepreneurial decisions. However, gender, years of education, health status, and self-confidence level have insignificant effects on household entrepreneurial decisions.

2. *The impact of household investable assets on household entrepreneurial decisions*

Table 3 presents the regression results for the impact of household investable assets on household entrepreneurial decisions. Column (1) considers only the core explanatory variable of household investable assets, columns (2)—(4) add household-level control variables, and columns (5) to (7) add head-of-household-level control variables to the household-level control variables. The results show that each 1% increase in household investable assets is associated with a 0.007 unit increase in household entrepreneurial decision-making when both household- and head-of-household-level control variables are considered. Although the estimates of the explanatory variables decrease with the inclusion of control variables, the regression results reflect a significant positive effect of household investable assets on household entrepreneurial decisions.

The results of the relevant control variables indicate that household- and head-of-household-level variables also have a more significant effect on household entrepreneurial decisions. From the household-level control variables, household size is significantly and positively related to household entrepreneurial decision, with larger households having a higher likelihood of starting a business and a higher number of self-employment activities; household income also significantly promotes household entrepreneurial decision, as high income is good at easing the financing problem in the entrepreneurial process as well as reducing the constraints

**Table 2** Regression results of the impact of mid-high net worth households on household entrepreneurial decisions

| | Entrepreneurship | | | | | | |
|---|---|---|---|---|---|---|---|
| | (1) | (2) | (3) | (4) | (5) | (6) | (7) |
| Mid-high net worth families | 0.146*** | 0.139*** | 0.120*** | 0.123*** | 0.122*** | 0.121*** | 0.121*** |
| | (0.015) | (0.015) | (0.016) | (0.016) | (0.016) | (0.017) | (0.017) |
| Household size | | 0.02*** | 0.0175*** | 0.016*** | 0.016*** | 0.016*** | 0.014*** |
| | | (0.002) | (0.002) | (0.002) | (0.002) | (0.003) | (0.003) |
| Household income | | | 0.017*** | 0.016*** | 0.012*** | 0.012** | 0.012** |
| | | | (0.005) | (0.005) | (0.005) | (0.005) | (0.005) |
| Bank loans | | | | 0.089*** | 0.08*** | 0.08*** | 0.08*** |
| | | | | (0.016) | (0.016) | (0.016) | (0.016) |
| Private loans from friends and family | | | | 0.052*** | 0.048*** | 0.048*** | 0.05*** |
| | | | | (0.014) | (0.014) | (0.014) | (0.013) |
| Gender | | | | | 0.011 | 0.011 | 0.011 |
| | | | | | (0.007) | (0.007) | (0.007) |
| Age | | | | | −0.0013*** | −0.001*** | −0.001*** |
| | | | | | (0.0002) | (0.0002) | (0.0003) |
| Year of education | | | | | | 0.0003 | 0.0004 |
| | | | | | | (0.001) | (0.001) |
| Marriage | | | | | | | 0.017* |
| | | | | | | | (0.010) |
| Health | | | | | | | −0.003 |
| | | | | | | | (0.003) |
| Self-confidence | | | | | | | 0.005 |

(continued)

**Table 2** (continued)

| | Entrepreneurship | | | | | | |
|---|---|---|---|---|---|---|---|
| | (1) | (2) | (3) | (4) | (5) | (6) | (7) |
| | | | | | | | (0.004) |
| Constant | 0.08*** | 0.011 | −0.155*** | −0.154*** | −0.06 | −0.061 | −0.074 |
| | (0.003) | (0.007) | (0.047) | (0.047) | (0.055) | (0.053) | (0.058) |
| Observations | 9,089 | 9,089 | 9,089 | 9,089 | 9,089 | 9,089 | 9,089 |
| R-squared | 0.023 | 0.035 | 0.039 | 0.048 | 0.051 | 0.051 | 0.052 |

*Note* * $p < 0.1$, ** $p < 0.05$, *** $p < 0.01$

**Table 3** Regression results of the effect of household investable assets on household entrepreneurial decisions

| | Entrepreneurship | | | | | | |
|---|---|---|---|---|---|---|---|
| | (1) | (2) | (3) | (4) | (5) | (6) | (7) |
| Investable assets | 0.009*** | 0.009*** | 0.007*** | 0.008*** | 0.007*** | 0.007*** | 0.007*** |
| | (0.001) | (0.001) | (0.001) | (0.001) | (0.001) | (0.001) | (0.001) |
| Household size | | 0.02*** | 0.018*** | 0.016*** | 0.016*** | 0.016*** | 0.015*** |
| | | (0.002) | (0.002) | (0.002) | (0.002) | (0.002) | (0.00268) |
| Household income | | | 0.017*** | 0.015*** | 0.013*** | 0.012** | 0.012** |
| | | | (0.005) | (0.005) | (0.005) | (0.005) | (0.005) |
| Bank loans | | | | 0.095*** | 0.086*** | 0.086*** | 0.086*** |
| | | | | (0.017) | (0.017) | (0.017) | (0.017) |
| Private loans from friends and family | | | | 0.062*** | 0.057*** | 0.058*** | 0.059*** |
| | | | | (0.014) | (0.014) | (0.014) | (0.014) |
| Gender | | | | | 0.009 | 0.009 | 0.009 |
| | | | | | (0.007) | (0.007) | (0.007) |
| Age | | | | | −0.001*** | −0.001*** | −0.001*** |
| | | | | | (0.0002) | (0.0002) | (0.0003) |
| Year of education | | | | | | 0.001 | 0.001 |
| | | | | | | (0.001) | (0.001) |
| Marriage | | | | | | | 0.017* |
| | | | | | | | (0.01) |
| Health | | | | | | | −0.002 |
| | | | | | | | (0.003) |
| Self-confidence | | | | | | | 0.005 |
| | | | | | | | (0.004) |
| Constant | 0.026*** | −0.044*** | −0.205*** | −0.202*** | −0.118** | −0.121** | −0.137** |
| | (0.006) | (0.009) | (0.046) | (0.046) | (0.054) | (0.052) | (0.056) |
| Observations | 9,089 | 9,089 | 9,089 | 9,089 | 9,089 | 9,089 | 9,089 |
| R-squared | 0.016 | 0.028 | 0.032 | 0.043 | 0.046 | 0.046 | 0.046 |

*Note* * $p < 0.1$, ** $p < 0.05$, *** $p < 0.01$

and limitations on fundraising; bank loans, friends and relatives, and private loans all promote household Bank loans, family and friends, and private loans all contribute to household entrepreneurial decisions, reflecting the fact that financial support from borrowing can also ease financial constraints. Regarding the control variables at the household head level, gender has a non-significant effect on household entrepreneurial decisions, age has a highly significant negative effect, and marital status has a more significant facilitative effect on household entrepreneurial decisions. In addition, the effects of years of education, health status, and self-confidence on household entrepreneurial decisions were not significant.

3. *Impact of mid-high net worth households on household property investment decisions*

Tables 4 show the regression results for the impact of mid-high net worth households on household property investment decisions. Column (1) considers only the core explanatory variable of medium–high-net-worth households (dummy variable), columns (2)–(4) include household-level control variables, and columns (5)– (7) include head-of-household-level control variables in addition to household-level control variables. The results show that, after considering both household- and head-of-household-level control variables, the number of household property investment decisions increased by 1.007 units for mid-high net worth households compared to non mid-high net worth households, significantly demonstrating the positive effect of mid-high net worth households on enhancing household second homes and increasing property investment decisions.

It is worth noting that after the inclusion of mid-high net worth households (dummy variables), none of the head-of-household level control variables have significant effects on household property investment decisions. In addition, the effect of bank loans on household property investment decisions is also insignificant.

4. *The impact of household investable assets on household property investment decisions*

Tables 5 show the regression results for the impact of household investable assets on household property investment decisions. Column (1) considers only the explanatory variable of household investable assets, columns (2) to (4) add household-level control variables, and columns (5) to (7) add head-of-household-level control variables to the household-level control variables. The results show that after considering both household-level and head-of-household-level control variables, each 1% increase in household investable assets increases the number of properties other than the current home of the household by 0.049 units. The regression results reflect the significant positive effect of household investable assets on property investments and the number of secondary homes.

The regression results for the relevant control variables indicate that household- and head-of-household-level variables also have a more significant effect on household property investment decisions. In terms of household-level control variables, household size is significantly and positively related to household property investment decisions. On the one hand, the larger the household size, the greater the hard demand for housing quantity; on the other hand, the larger the household size, the more likely it is to take advantage of the policy to purchase property to diversify its investment. Household income also contributes significantly to household property investment decisions, as higher-income groups have more funds to support real estate

**Table 4** Regression results of the influence of mid-high net worth households on household property investment decisions

| | Real estate investment | | | | | | |
|---|---|---|---|---|---|---|---|
| | (1) | (2) | (3) | (4) | (5) | (6) | (7) |
| Mid-high net worth families | 1.026*** | 1.019*** | 1.004*** | 1.007*** | 1.007*** | 1.007*** | 1.007*** |
| | (0.021) | (0.021) | (0.021) | (0.021) | (0.021) | (0.021) | (0.021) |
| Household size | | 0.02*** | 0.018*** | 0.017*** | 0.017*** | 0.017*** | 0.018*** |
| | | (0.003) | (0.003) | (0.003) | (0.003) | (0.003) | (0.003) |
| Household income | | | 0.013*** | 0.012*** | 0.012*** | 0.012*** | 0.012*** |
| | | | (0.003) | (0.003) | (0.003) | (0.004) | (0.004) |
| Bank loans | | | | 0.025 | 0.024 | 0.024 | 0.024 |
| | | | | (0.016) | (0.016) | (0.016) | (0.016) |
| Private loans from friends and family | | | | 0.044*** | 0.043*** | 0.043*** | 0.044*** |
| | | | | (0.015) | (0.015) | (0.015) | (0.015) |
| Gender | | | | | 0.003 | 0.003 | 0.003 |
| | | | | | (0.009) | (0.009) | (0.009) |
| Age | | | | | −0.0003 | −0.0003 | −0.0002 |
| | | | | | (0.0003) | (0.0003) | (0.0003) |
| Year of education | | | | | | −0.0001 | −0.0001 |
| | | | | | | (0.001) | (0.001) |
| Marriage | | | | | | | −0.012 |
| | | | | | | | (0.013) |
| Health | | | | | | | 0.001 |
| | | | | | | | (0.004) |
| Self-confidence | | | | | | | 0.006 |
| | | | | | | | (0.005) |
| Constant | 0.103*** | 0.034*** | −0.092*** | −0.096*** | −0.077* | −0.077* | −0.104** |
| | (0.004) | (0.009) | (0.033) | (0.033) | (0.04) | (0.04) | (0.046) |
| Observations | 9,089 | 9,089 | 9,089 | 9,089 | 9,089 | 9,089 | 9,089 |
| R-squared | 0.429 | 0.433 | 0.434 | 0.435 | 0.435 | 0.435 | 0.435 |

*Note* * $p < 0.1$, ** $p < 0.05$, *** $p < 0.01$

**Table 5** Regression results of the effect of household investable assets on household property investment decisions

| | Real estate investment | | | | | | |
|---|---|---|---|---|---|---|---|
| | (1) | (2) | (3) | (4) | (5) | (6) | (7) |
| Investable assets | 0.052*** | 0.051*** | 0.048*** | 0.049*** | 0.05*** | 0.049*** | 0.049*** |
| | (0.001) | (0.001) | (0.001) | (0.001) | (0.001) | (0.001) | (0.001) |
| Household size | | 0.026*** | 0.022*** | 0.02*** | 0.021*** | 0.022*** | 0.023*** |
| | | (0.003) | (0.003) | (0.003) | (0.003) | (0.003) | (0.004) |
| Household income | | | 0.029*** | 0.028*** | 0.029*** | 0.025*** | 0.026*** |
| | | | (0.005) | (0.005) | (0.005) | (0.005) | (0.005) |
| Bank loans | | | | 0.06*** | 0.065*** | 0.064*** | 0.065*** |
| | | | | (0.019) | (0.019) | (0.019) | (0.019) |
| Private loans from friends and family | | | | 0.09*** | 0.093*** | 0.098*** | 0.097*** |
| | | | | (0.016) | (0.016) | (0.016) | (0.016) |
| Gender | | | | | −0.013 | −0.015 | −0.014 |
| | | | | | (0.01) | (0.01) | (0.01) |
| Age | | | | | 0.001 | 0.001*** | 0.001** |
| | | | | | (0.0003) | (0.0003) | (0.0004) |
| Year of education | | | | | | 0.005*** | 0.005*** |
| | | | | | | (0.001) | (0.001) |
| Marriage | | | | | | | −0.011 |
| | | | | | | | (0.015) |
| Health | | | | | | | 0.008* |
| | | | | | | | (0.005) |
| Self-confidence | | | | | | | 0.007 |

(continued)

**Table 5** (continued)

| | Real estate investment | | | | | | |
|---|---|---|---|---|---|---|---|
| | (1) | (2) | (3) | (4) | (5) | (6) | (7) |
| | | | | | | | (0.006) |
| Constant | −0.188*** | −0.277*** | −0.549*** | −0.552*** | −0.589*** | −0.612*** | −0.660*** |
| | (0.006) | (0.013) | (0.049) | (0.048) | (0.057) | (0.055) | (0.062) |
| Observations | 9,089 | 9,089 | 9,089 | 9,089 | 9,089 | 9,089 | 9,089 |
| R-squared | 0.200 | 0.207 | 0.212 | 0.216 | 0.216 | 0.217 | 0.218 |

*Note* * $p < 0.1$, ** $p < 0.05$, *** $p < 0.01$

investments, which are principal-demanding investments. Bank loans, friends, relatives, and private loans have a more significant impact on household property investment decisions. Age and years of education have a highly significant positive effect on the head of household-level control variables. Health status has a very weak effect on household property investment decisions. Gender, marital status, and self-confidence have insignificant effects on household property investment decisions.

## 5.3 Heterogeneity Analysis

Based on the household income level of the household head, the sample was divided into two groups, with higher and lower household income levels, and grouped into regressions. Columns (1)–(2) of Table 6 show the regression results based on income heterogeneity. The results show that mid-high net worth households (dummy variable) have a significant positive effect on the entrepreneurial decision of households with lower income levels, while the effect on the entrepreneurial decision of households with higher income levels is not significant; the positive effect of household investable assets on the entrepreneurial decision of households with higher income levels is more significant than that of households with lower income levels. This finding indicates that the entrepreneurial decisions of household heads with lower income levels are significantly influenced by the type of household and the positive effect of household investable assets.

**Table 6** Regression results of the impact of mid-high net worth households and household investable assets on household entrepreneurial decisions (income and urban–rural heterogeneity)

| | Entrepreneurship | | | |
|---|---|---|---|---|
| | (1) | (2) | (3) | (4) |
| Income heterogeneity | High income | Low income | | |
| Urban-rural heterogeneity | | | Urban | Rural |
| Mid-high net worth families | 0.031 | 0.138*** | 0.073*** | 0.147*** |
| | (0.019) | (0.04) | (0.019) | (0.034) |
| Investable assets | 0.004*** | 0.003*** | 0.006*** | 0.003*** |
| | (0.002) | (0.001) | (0.001) | (0.001) |
| Household-level control variables | Yes | Yes | Yes | Yes |
| Control variables at household head level | Yes | Yes | Yes | Yes |
| Constant | −1.481*** | 0.09 | 0.011 | −0.137** |
| | (0.198) | (0.064) | (0.096) | (0.068) |
| Observations | 4,366 | 4,723 | 4,890 | 4,103 |
| R-squared | 0.072 | 0.042 | 0.055 | 0.062 |

*Note* * $p < 0.1$, ** $p < 0.05$, *** $p < 0.01$

The sample was divided into two groups, urban and rural, and grouped into regressions based on household location. Columns (3) and (4) of Table 6 show the regression results based on urban–rural heterogeneity. The results show that mid-high net worth households have more significant and positive impacts on rural households' entrepreneurial decisions. Household investable assets have a significantly positive impact on urban households' entrepreneurial decisions.

Based on the household income level of the household head, the sample was divided into two groups, with higher and lower household income levels, and grouped into regressions. Columns (1)–(2) of Table 7 show the regression results based on income heterogeneity. The results show that mid-high net worth households (dummy variables) have a greater positive impact on property investment decisions in low-income households than in high-income households. Household investable assets have a somewhat larger positive impact on property investment decisions for high-income households than for low-income households, although they are quite close.

The sample was divided into two groups, urban and rural, and grouped into regressions based on household location. Columns (3)–(4) of Table 7 show the regression results based on urban–rural heterogeneity. The results show that the positive effects of mid-high net worth households (dummy variable) on urban and rural households are relatively similar and significant. The impact on urban households is slightly larger. The positive impacts of household investable assets on urban and rural households were similar and significant.

**Table 7** Regression results of the impact of mid-high net worth households and household investable assets on household property investment decisions (income and urban–rural heterogeneity)

| | Real estate investment | | | |
|---|---|---|---|---|
| | (1) | (2) | (3) | (4) |
| Income heterogeneity | High income | Low income | | |
| Urban-rural heterogeneity | | | Urban | Rural |
| Mid-high net worth families | 0.844*** | 0.960*** | 0.911*** | 0.824*** |
| | (0.023) | (0.057) | (0.026) | (0.035) |
| Investable assets | 0.028*** | 0.02*** | 0.024*** | 0.022*** |
| | (0.001) | (0.001) | (0.001) | (0.001) |
| Household-level control variables | Yes | Yes | Yes | Yes |
| Control variables at household head level | Yes | Yes | Yes | Yes |
| Constant | −0.696*** | −0.078* | −0.044 | −0.218*** |
| | (0.246) | (0.0441) | (0.077) | (0.049) |
| Observations | 4,366 | 4,723 | 4,890 | 4,103 |
| R-squared | 0.455 | 0.336 | 0.472 | 0.402 |

*Note* * $p < 0.1$, ** $p < 0.05$, *** $p < 0.01$

# 6 Summary

This chapter analyzes the allocation of household non-financial assets. This study includes the individual business situation and allocation of business assets, property investment situation, and allocation of consumer durables. On this basis, this chapter explores the factors that influence households' entrepreneurial and property investment decisions. The main conclusions of this study are as follows:

First, the proportion of mid-high net worth households that are self-employed is 18.15% in towns and 21.52% in villages, which is significantly higher than that of non mid-high net worth households. In terms of cities, the proportion of mid-high net worth households who are self-employed is the highest in Tier 3 cities at 25%, compared with 11.08% in Tier 1 cities.

Second, in terms of total self-employed assets, the difference between the total self-employed assets of urban mid-high net worth households and non mid-high net worth households is 491,300 yuan; the difference between the total self-employed assets of rural mid-high net worth households and non mid-high net worth households is 213,900 yuan, which is a very obvious difference.

Third, in terms of the second and higher property ownership rate, the rate of household second and higher property ownership gradually decreases as the urban class decreases, and overall, the rate of household second and higher property ownership gradually increases as the education level of the household head increases.

Fourth, in terms of the value of second and higher properties owned by mid-high net worth households, there was a difference of ¥954,600 between the value of second and higher properties in towns and villages.

Fifth, in terms of the ratio of property value to total household assets, there is a difference of 16.97% points between the ratio of all property value to total assets for mid-high net worth households in urban areas and non mid-high net worth households. In rural areas, there is a difference of 7.1% points between the two. Among mid-high net worth households, the ratio of all property values to total assets is slightly higher in urban households than in rural households, while among non mid-high net worth households, the ratio of all property values to total assets is higher in rural households.

Sixth, overall, the number of consumer durables in urban households was significantly higher than that in rural households. Specifically, there is a difference of ¥119,712.8 in the amount of consumer durables between urban medium–high-net-worth households and non-medium–high-net-worth households; and a difference of ¥87,255.33 in the number of consumer durables between rural medium–high-net-worth households and non-medium–high-net-worth households, which is very obvious.

Seventh, mid-high net worth households make more entrepreneurial decisions than non mid-high net worth households, and household investable assets promote household entrepreneurship. Similarly, mid-high net worth households have more investment properties than non mid-high net worth households, and, household investable assets promote household asset allocation in investment properties.

## References


1. Wu, W., Shen, T., Jiang, T.: Does real estate squeeze out risky financial assets from household allocation? –Empirical analysis based on microsurvey data. Sci. Decis. Making **11**, 52–69 (2014)
2. Duan, Z.: A study on the impact of homeownership on household financial asset allocation–an empirical analysis based on heckman sample selection model. Price Theory Pract. 100–104 (2021)
3. Wei, H., Zhong, Z.: A study of non-financial property gap of chinese households (1989–2011)–a regression decomposition based on micro data. Econ. Rev. **203**, 106–134 (2017)
4. Anonymous.: Survey on Household Assets and Liabilities of Chinese Urban Residents, p. 5. Shanghai Business (2020)
5. Gan, L., Yin, Z., Tan, J.: China Household Finance Survey Report 2014. Southwest University of Finance and Economics Press, Sichuang, China (2015)
6. Jantti, M., Sierminska, E.: Survey estimates of wealth holdings in OECD countries: evidence on the level and distribution across selected. WIDER Working Paper Series, 27–42 (2007)
7. Gan, L., Yin, Z., Jia, N., Xu, S., Ma, S.: Analysis of household asset status and housing needs in China. Finan. Stud. 1–14 (2013)
8. Bricker, J., Kennickell, A.B., Moore, K.B., Sabelhaus, J.: Changes in U.S. family finances from, 2004 To 2007: evidence from the survey of consumer finances. Federal Reserve Bull. **100**, 1–80 (2009)
9. Balestra, C., Tonkin, R.: Inequalities in household wealth across OECD countries: evidence from the OECD Wealth Distribution Database. OECD Statistics Working Papers, No. 88 (2018)
10. Miao, H., Qin, P.: Doing a good job in tracking small and micro enterprises and self-employed households. China Statist. 46–47 (2018)
11. Qu, Z., Guo, S.: Household registration and entrepreneurship: a study of differences in self-employment between urban and rural residents–evidence from CGSS2008. China Econ. 72–86 (2017)
12. Li, S., Long, H.: A study on the mechanisms of the impact of digital economy on farmers' entrepreneurship: an empirical analysis based on the china household tracking survey (CFPS). J. Yunnan Agric. Univ. (Soc. Sci.) **16**, 1–10 (2022)
13. Tang, S., Wang, K.: The composition of netflix subjects and the perfection of ideology. China Mark. 131–132 (2018)
14. Chen, X.: Family first, then career: does "family" affect "career"? –an empirical analysis of marital influence on men's entrepreneurial behavior in China. Popul. Dev. **26**, 118–128 (2020)
15. Guiso, L., Sodini, P.: Household finance: an emerging field. In: Constantinides, G.M., Harris, M., Stulz, R.M., (eds.) Handbook of the Economics of Finance, vol. 2, pp. 1397–1532. Elsevier (2013)
16. Hou, W., Tian, X.: Local debt spending, investment property demand and macroeconomic volatility. Stat. Decis. Mak. **37**, 128–133 (2021)
17. Xu, S.: A study of house price expectations and Chinese households' risky financial asset allocation. J. Sun Yat-sen Univ. Soc. Sci. Edn. **61**, 168–178 (2021)
18. Bankrate.: China Residents' Financial Capability Report. Bankrate, Beijing (2015)
19. Yi, C., Fan, Z., Wang, Y., Li, Y.: income inequality, multiple suite purchase decisions, and household leverage in urban China. J. Central Univ. Finance Econ. 93–104 (2022)
20. Cheng, Z., Li, C., Leng, Y.: The impact of property tax on housing investment demand. Modern Enterprise 139–140 (2020)
21. Kuhn, P., Kooreman, P., Soetevent, A., Kapteyn, A.: The effects of lottery prizes on winners and their neighbors: evidence from the dutch postcode lottery. Am. Econ. Rev. **101**, 2226–2247 (2011)
22. Solnick, S.J., Hemenway, D., Review, A.E., Duflo, E.: Are positional concerns stronger in some domains than in others? Am. Econ. Rev. **95**, 147–151 (2005)
23. Ren, G., Wang, J., Li, R.: A study of status seeking and urban households' borrowing behavior in purchasing consumer durables. J. Central Univ. Finance Econ. 79–90 (2020)

24. Yin, T.: An empirical analysis of consumption models of durable goods for urban residents in China. Consum. Econ. **34**, 82–90 (2018)
25. Zhang, N.: Behavioral analysis of consumer durables in the female market. Mall Modern. 18–19 (2017)

# Chapter 5
# Commercial Insurance Allocation for Mid-High Net Worth Families

**Abstract** This chapter analyzes the allocation of commercial insurance for mid-high net worth households. The results show that households in urban areas have greater commercial insurance coverage than those in rural areas; the higher the educational level of the heads of mid-high net worth families and non mid-high net worth families, the higher the commercial insurance coverage rate of the family; the average amount of per capita expenditure on commercial insurance for both mid-high net worth households and non mid-high net worth households decreases as the number of household members increases; mid-high net worth households invest more money in commercial insurance allocation and demand more commercial insurance coverage. For every 1% increase in household investable assets, household commercial insurance spending will increase by about 48 yuan. Mid-high net worth households increased their commercial insurance participation by 0.409 units compared with non mid-high net worth households.

Commercial insurance refers to insurance products and services operated through insurance contracts for profit and includes property insurance, life insurance, and health insurance. Specialized insurance companies operate and provide commercial insurance. It is an essential supplement to social insurance with significant potential for development. For families, commercial insurance is important for the family protection system, family wealth management, and asset allocation. For example, a recent study showed that the proportion of commercial insurance in China's household asset allocation has remained at 13% [1]. In other words, the proportion of commercial insurance in household asset allocation exceeds 10%. Commercial insurance is popular among mid-high net worth families. Some data show that 95% of China's mid-high net worth population chooses to purchase commercial life insurance [2], indicating that only 5% of mid-high net worth individuals did not purchase commercial life insurance. These data are only for the high net worth population; in the case of mid-high net worth populations, the situation may differ, and the commercial insurance coverage rate should not be high. Corresponding studies must be conducted in specific situations.

 
J. Gu, *Wealth Management Report for Mid-High Net Worth Families*, Spatial Demography and Population Governance, https://doi.org/10.1007/978-981-97-0387-6_5

# 1 A Commercial Insurance Development in China

Since its reform and opening up, China has actively promoted the development of commercial insurance and issued a series of policies, laws, and regulations to provide institutional protection for the healthy development of commercial insurance. In 1983, the State Council issued the Regulations of the People's Republic of China on Property Insurance Contracts. The Provisional Regulations on the Administration of Insurance Enterprises were issued in 1985. In 1995, the Insurance Law of the People's Republic of China and several other laws and regulations were promulgated, marking a new period of legal construction in China's insurance industry [3]. With the improvement of various systems, the commercial insurance industry has developed rapidly, and the insurance products it provides have diversified to better meet the needs of the public for insurance protection.

After joining the WTO, China has continuously enhanced the opening up of the insurance industry to the outside world, and some international insurance companies have entered the Chinese market, which, while intensifying competition in the insurance industry, has also promoted the full convergence of China's insurance market with the international insurance market. The entry of foreign insurance companies brings more advanced international insurance technology and business management concepts, which play a significant role in promoting the restructuring, industrial upgrading, and improvement of the business management capacity of China's commercial insurance industry [4]. While competing with foreign insurance companies, China's insurance companies are becoming more robust, and the commercial insurance industry is showing vigorous development [5]. In China, commercial insurance has become an important supplement to social insurance. According to data published by the China Banking and Insurance Regulatory Commission (CBIRC), the original premium income of China's insurance industry from 2012 to 2021 is summarized in Fig. 1.

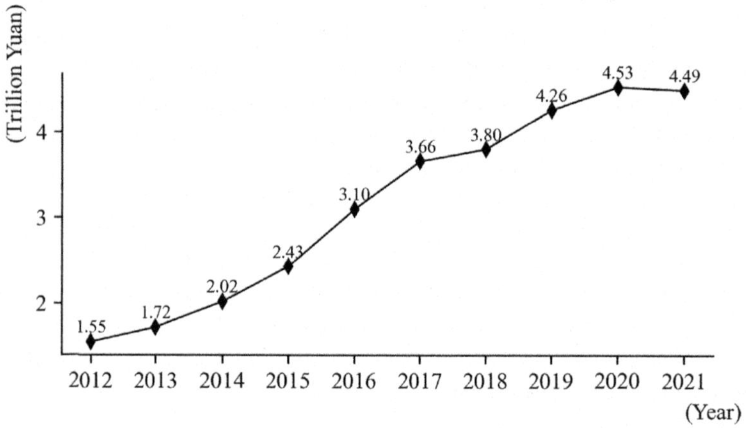


**Fig. 1** Original premium income of China's insurance industry from 2012 to 2021

Figure 1 shows that regarding original premium income, China's insurance industry will show a stable development trend from 2012 to 2021. in 2021, the original premium income of China's insurance industry was 4.49 trillion yuan, a slight decrease of 0.88% year-on-year. This small drop in the original premium income was inseparable from the impact of the New Crest Pneumonia epidemic [6]. The Newcastle pneumonia epidemic resulted in the inability of insurers to conduct offline marketing businesses, and premium income was affected to some extent. However, compared to the insurance industry's original premium income of only 1.55 trillion yuan in 2012, the insurance industry's original premium income of 4.49 trillion yuan in 2021 can be considered significant progress. Commercial insurance has become an indispensable promoter and stabilizer of China's economic and social development, providing personalized and differentiated protection to thousands of households.

China's commercial insurance industry has achieved significant development but has greater scope for future development with many development opportunities. In 2021, China's insurance depth (premium income/GDP) and density (premium income/total population) were 3.9% and ¥3,180/person, respectively [7]. In 2019, the world average insurance density was ¥818/person, China's insurance density was ¥430/person, the world average insurance depth was 7.23%, and China's insurance depth was 4.3% [8]. The two have slightly different calibers in their estimation of insurance depth; however, in general, there is still a gap between the development level of China's insurance industry and that of the world. Although China's commercial insurance system has developed rapidly in recent years, there have been many constraints. The proportion of commercial insurance in the residents' overall social security remains relatively low. The types and products of commercial insurance are still relatively singular, and the problem of homogeneous competition is relatively prominent. Seeking a new model suitable for the development of commercial insurance, meeting the diversified insurance protection needs of residents better, and making operations more efficient are problems that need to be resolved for the development of commercial insurance.

Household demand for commercial insurance can be influenced by many factors [9]. A household's allocation to commercial insurance is not yet the same as an individual's allocation. Each commercial insurance policy has only one insured person, but it is not enough for a family to have adequate insurance coverage for just one person; it is also necessary to cover all family members as much as possible. However, suppose each family member buys accident insurance, medical insurance, critical illness insurance, and other commercial insurance. In that case, the family will need to spend a considerable premium every year, putting financial pressure on the family. Each family's situation is different, and there are different things to consider when allocating business insurance. However, understanding the family's protection needs is critical to better allocate insurance to a family. Business insurance should be configured according to a family's situation and the need for protection.

Data from a survey conducted in 2017 showed that although approximately 70% of respondents believed that the basic health insurance program in China could meet their needs, more than 40% were willing to purchase commercial health insurance the following year [10]. As the standard of living increases, the demand for commercial insurance also increases. Mid-high net worth families with better financial conditions were more inclined to purchase middle and high level commercial insurance. Although the premium for this type of commercial insurance is higher, it provides a larger coverage area and better protection. On the supply side, some insurance companies have launched mid-to-high-end insurance products for mid-high net worth families, and adults can take two children into the policy for free, which is a relatively strong attraction for mid-high net worth families. At the family level, because families have different situations and economic conditions, their need for commercial insurance will also be different. This objectively causes families to differ in their choice of commercial insurance. For the government, insurance companies should be encouraged to develop commercial insurance products with universal benefits for low-income families through policy guidance and other means so that more low- and middle-income families can afford commercial insurance and thus play a more significant role in the overall social security system.

Next, this chapter analyzes household commercial insurance coverage, household commercial insurance expenditure, and per capita household commercial insurance expenditure based on CFPS data for 2020 to present a panoramic view of the allocation of households to commercial insurance in China. This chapter reveals the current situation, characteristics, and problems of household commercial insurance and puts forward suggestions for improving the allocation of household commercial insurance. This chapter can help insurance companies grasp the current situation of Chinese families' demand for commercial insurance and its characteristics to help develop corresponding insurance products. Moreover, this chapter can a) provide insight into the allocation of commercial insurance for families, b) provide a reference for the asset security and appreciation of mid-high net worth families, and c) provide a reference for the government to formulate relevant policies.

## 2 Household Commercial Insurance Coverage

The household commercial insurance coverage rate is equal to the number of households covered by commercial insurance divided by the total number of households, which is a common indicator for measuring the prevalence of commercial insurance among households and household commercial insurance participation [11]. For example, a study based on survey data from 2017 showed that the commercial household insurance coverage rate was 21.6% [12]. Another study based on survey data from 2010 showed that household commercial insurance coverage rates in urban and county cities were 47.5% and 32.9%, respectively [13]. It can be seen that there are relatively large differences in the estimated household commercial insurance coverage rates based on different survey data. There are multiple reasons for these differences, such as the representativeness of the sample and the definition of households. Therefore, specific analyses are required for specific problems.

## 2.1 Community and Family

1. *Nature of community*

Community is the grassroots of a society [14]. In rural areas, this is mainly due to village committees. In urban areas, this is primarily the neighborhood committee. Therefore, community nature often distinguishes between urban and rural areas [15]. This book analyzes the commercial insurance coverage of a full sample of households based on the nature of the community. The results are summarized in Fig. 2.

According to Fig. 2, for those on neighborhood councils, household commercial insurance coverage rates are significantly higher than those on village councils. In other words, households in urban areas have higher commercial insurance coverage than those in rural areas. In urban areas, the household commercial insurance coverage rate is nearly 50%; almost half of the urban households have purchased commercial insurance. However, the commercial household insurance coverage rate in rural areas is relatively low (approximately 30%). There are several possible reasons for this discrepancy. From a demand-level perspective, the factors influencing urban and rural households to purchase commercial insurance differ [16]. At the supply level, there are often urban–rural differences in commercial insurance pricing [17]. The Survey Report on Rural Health Protection published by the Center for Insurance and Economic Development Research of the Chinese Academy of Social Sciences shows that the percentage of rural residents who have commercial insurance in China is less than 20% [18]. This study calculates individual commercial insurance coverage rates. Several people may come from the same household. For example, according to data from the seventh national census, the average household size in China in 2020 was 2.62 people. Therefore, households' commercial insurance coverage rates are generally higher than their individual counterparts. Therefore, a household commercial insurance coverage rate of 31.79%, or the household

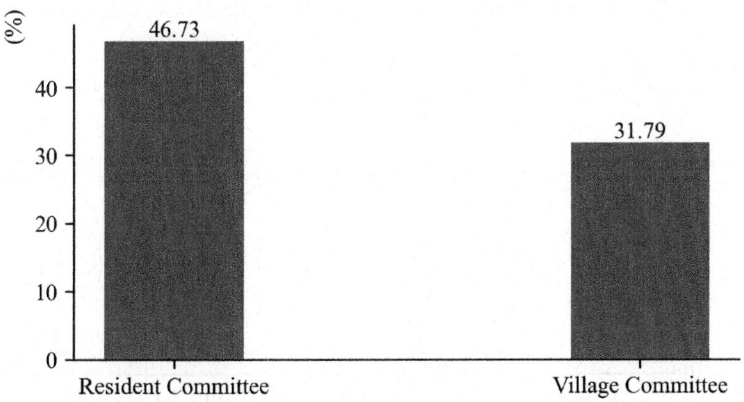


**Fig. 2** Commercial insurance coverage for the full sample of households (community-based in nature)

commercial insurance participation rate obtained from the calculation in this chapter for village committees, is more reasonable. Moreover, this coverage rate is close to the results obtained from a previous study in which the rural household commercial insurance coverage rate was 32.9% [13]. The urban household commercial insurance coverage rate was 46.73%, close to the coverage rate of 47.5% in the present study.

According to Fig. 3, for the mid-high net worth households, the gap between the commercial insurance coverage ratio of the neighborhood committee and village committee population is small, and the difference between the two is only 4.04 percentage points; there is a gap between the household commercial insurance coverage ratio of the neighborhood committee and village committee population, and the difference between the two is 11.46 percentage points. In summary, family economic status has a significant impact on willingness to purchase commercial insurance, and there is no significant urban–rural gap in the insurance coverage ratio of mid-high net worth families, while there is a certain urban–rural gap in the insurance coverage ratio of non mid-high net worth families. It is not difficult to find that there is no urban–rural gap in the purchase of commercial insurance for mid-high net worth households. In urban and rural areas, the coverage rate of commercial insurance for mid-high net worth families is approximately 65%. In other words, for mid-high net worth families, the participation in family commercial insurance is roughly comparable in urban and rural areas, and the gap is not large.

2. *Family size*

Household size is one-factor affecting household participation in commercial insurance. It has been shown that household size significantly and positively affects the likelihood of household participation in commercial insurance [19]. The larger the household, the greater the likelihood of purchasing commercial insurance. This is the linear hypothesis. This book groups households according to size to verify whether

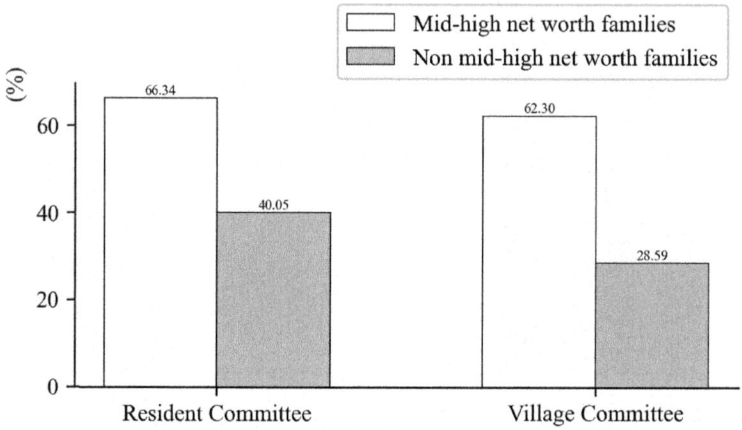


**Fig. 3** Commercial insurance coverage rates of mid-high net worth households and non mid-high net worth households (community-based)

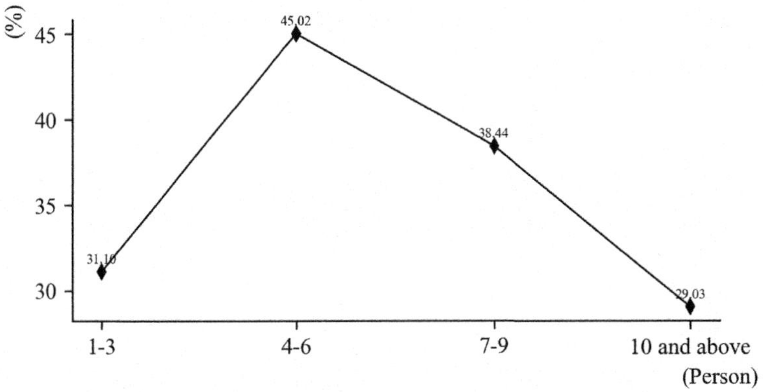


**Fig. 4** Commercial insurance coverage rate (household size) for the full sample of households

this linear relationship exists. It calculates the commercial insurance coverage rate for the total sample of households. The results are summarized in Fig. 4.

According to Fig. 4, as household size increases, the household commercial insurance coverage rate shows a trend of increasing and then decreasing. The highest commercial insurance coverage rate is for households with four to six people and the lowest for households with ten or more people. Household size affects the purchase of commercial insurance. However, this effect is not necessarily linear and is often nonlinear. When the household size is less than seven people, the larger the household size, the higher the likelihood of purchasing commercial insurance. However, the likelihood of purchasing commercial insurance decreases when the household exceeds this size. The decision to purchase commercial insurance is usually a result of intrafamilial negotiations. If the household is too large, it will be more expensive to negotiate within the household, and it will be more challenging to reach a consensus; therefore, the likelihood of purchasing commercial insurance will be lower. Of course, the possible effect of the sample size should also be considered here, as the number of households larger than nine was relatively small in the CFPS sample.

According to Fig. 5, the commercial insurance coverage rates of mid-high net worth households and non mid-high net worth households show a trend of first increasing and then decreasing with an increase in household size, which is the same as the overall trend. In addition, the difference between the commercial insurance coverage rates of mid-high net worth households and non mid-high net worth households was significantly larger. However, the fluctuation rate within each group was lower, indicating that the impact of household economic status on commercial insurance coverage rates is more pronounced. Within the same group, the magnitude of the change in household commercial insurance coverage was relatively small, even when household size changed. This finding suggests that household type significantly influences the effect of household size on commercial insurance purchases. Therefore, when analyzing the relationship between household size and commercial insurance coverage, it is important to adopt a comprehensive analysis perspective to avoid "seeing the trees but not the forest" due to simplistic and linear thinking.

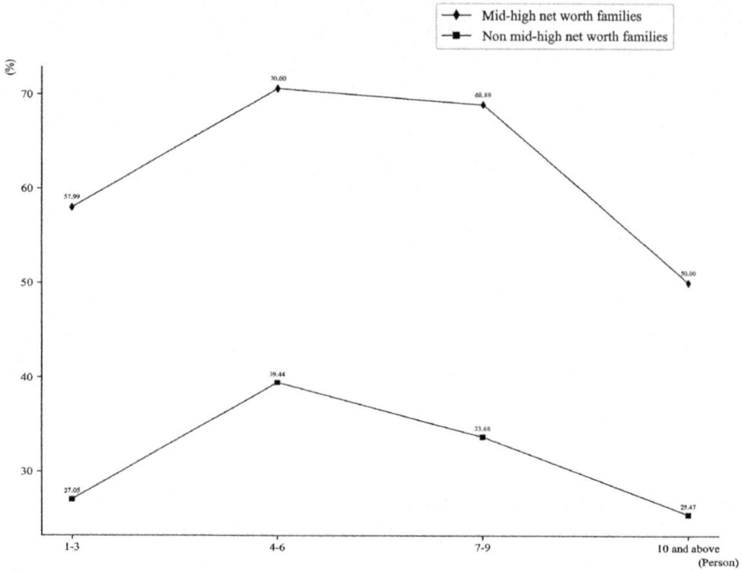


**Fig. 5** Commercial insurance coverage rates (household size) for mid-high net worth households and non mid-high net worth households

## 2.2 *Characteristics of the Head of Household*

1. *Education level of the head of household*

Although the purchase of commercial insurance by a family is generally a joint decision of the entire family, the role and influence of the head of the household cannot be ignored [16]. Traditionally, the head of a household is the head of the family, the head of a household in the household register, and generally, the first household member in the household register. However, with rapid changes in the social structure and the shrinking size of households, the concept of the head of the household has been subtly adjusted. Here, the household financial head is considered the head of the household because their opinion often plays an important, if not decisive, role in the household's decision to purchase commercial insurance. The results are summarized in Fig. 6. This book calculates the commercial insurance coverage of a total sample of households by grouping them according to the education level of the household head.

As shown in Fig. 6, overall, the higher the education level of the household head, the higher the household commercial insurance coverage rate. The difference between the commercial insurance coverage rate of households whose heads have higher education and those who are illiterate or semiliterate is the largest (40.04%). In other words, the higher the education level of the household head, the higher the probability that the household will purchase commercial insurance. This is consistent with the findings of a previous study [20]. The higher the education level of the

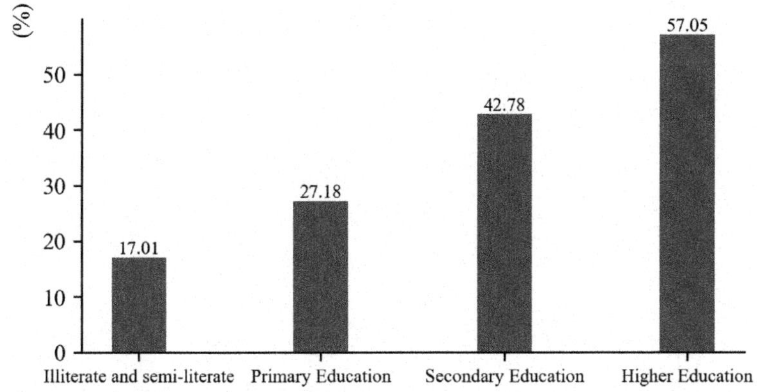


**Fig. 6** Commercial insurance coverage rate for the full sample of households (education level of household head)

household head, the higher the awareness of risk prevention, and therefore, the more likely it is that the household will promote the purchase of commercial insurance. In addition, in household asset allocation, the more educated the household head is, the more he/she generally understands the idea of asset mix in asset allocation; while allocating household wealth to riskier assets such as stocks, they will allocate to lower-risk commercial insurance for risk control reasons. In this way, the risk of the family's total assets can be controlled and made relatively safe, thus ensuring the safety of family assets and the smooth growth of wealth.

According to Fig. 7, the higher the education level of the head of the mid-high net worth household and the non-mid-high net worth household, the higher the household commercial insurance coverage rate. The differences between the two types of household commercial insurance coverage rates were 15.75 percentage points in the illiterate/semiliterate group, 24.03 percentage points in the primary education group, 29.79 percentage points in the secondary education group, and 15.67 percentage points in the higher education group. Notably, for mid-high net worth households, the commercial insurance coverage rates of households in the secondary education and higher education groups are comparable but significantly higher than those in the primary education group. This indicates that for mid-high net worth households, those households headed by those with primary education or below still have great potential and room for improvement in commercial insurance, which can become an important growth point in the future commercial insurance market and an important target group for commercial insurance companies to explore in the future.

2. *Marital status of the head of household*

The marital status of the household head is also an important factor influencing a household's purchase of commercial insurance [16]. However, the effect of marital status on participation in commercial household insurance is complex [21]. Here, the marital status of the household head is used to group the full sample of households

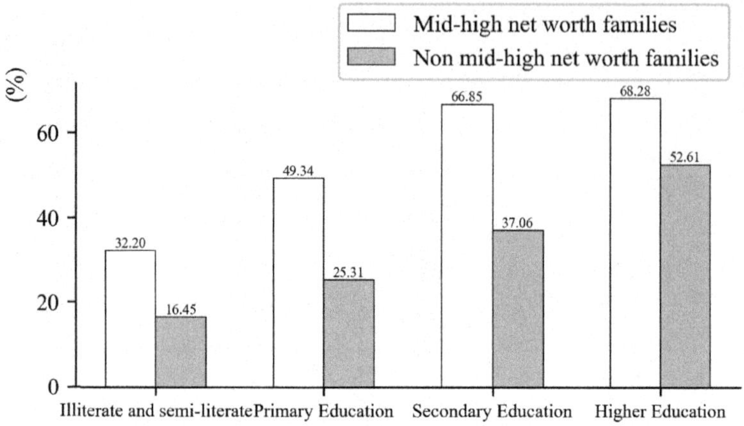


**Fig. 7** Commercial insurance coverage rates of mid-high net worth households and non mid-high net worth households (education level of household head)

to calculate the commercial insurance coverage rate, and the results are summarized in Fig. 8.

As shown in Fig. 8, households with marital heads have the highest rate of commercial insurance coverage, while those with cohabiting heads have a lower rate of commercial insurance coverage. The increased income and wealth level of married households, along with the effectiveness of the couple's joint decision-making in household wealth management and commercial insurance allocation, allows households to have more options when facing various risks and making possible responses [22]. Conversely, when cohabiting, there is a great deal of uncertainty because the future is not clear, and people are less inclined to purchase commercial insurance to reduce risk and future behavior with uncertainty.

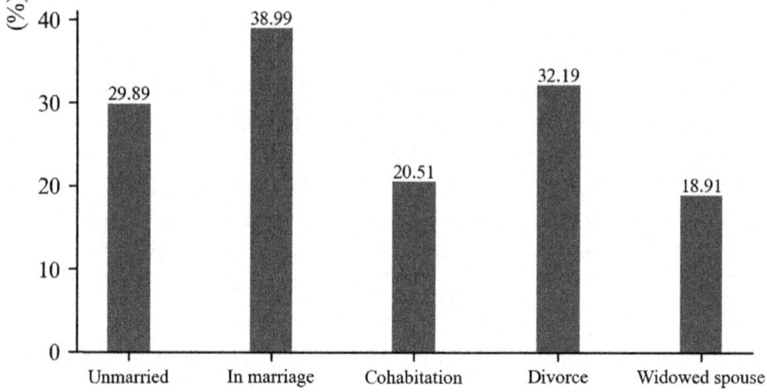


**Fig. 8** Commercial insurance coverage for the full sample of households (marital status of household head)

According to Fig. 9, there was a 28.33 percentage point difference in the commercial insurance coverage rate between the unmarried and non mid-high net worth households, a 32.99 percentage point difference between the married group, a 22.35 percentage point difference between the cohabiting group, a 17.58 percentage point difference between the divorced group, and a 17.73 percentage point difference between the widowed group. For families in the married group, economic conditions still have a greater impact on the purchase of commercial insurance, and the level of participation in commercial insurance is significantly higher for mid-high net worth families than for non mid-high net worth families.

3. *Health status of the head of household*

A household's decision to participate in commercial insurance is generally related to the head's health status. The commercial insurance coverage rate of the full sample of households was calculated based on the health status of the household head, and the results are summarized in Fig. 10.

According to Fig. 10, overall, the commercial insurance coverage rate of households in the healthy group is significantly higher than that in the other two groups, which indicates that the better the health status of the household head, the higher the commercial insurance coverage rate. It has been shown that, with other variables held constant, the probability of a household purchasing commercial insurance decreases by approximately 15 percentage points for each unit deterioration in the health status of the head of household [16]. On the insurance supply side, insurance companies charge more for life insurance or outright refuse to underwrite it for people with poor health, which also reduces, to some extent, the proportion of households with a head of household in poor health participating in commercial insurance.

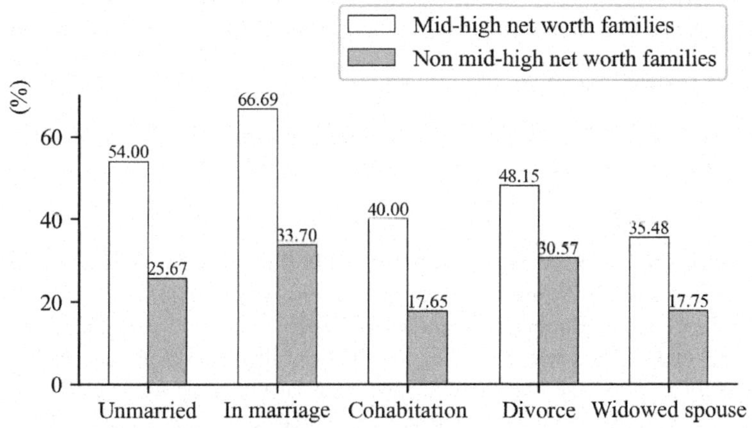


**Fig. 9** Commercial insurance coverage rates of mid-high net worth households and non mid-high net worth households (marital status of household head)

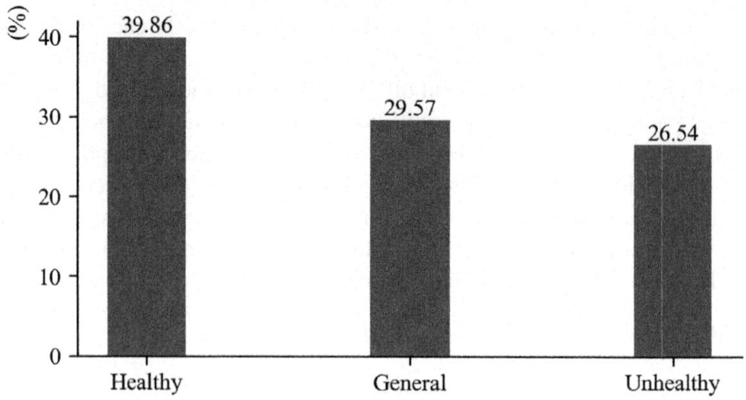


**Fig. 10** Commercial insurance coverage of the full sample of households (health status of household head)

According to Fig. 11, in mid-high net worth households, there is a difference of 8.26 percentage points between the commercial insurance coverage rates of households with healthy and average heads of households. In comparison, the difference between the commercial insurance coverage rates of households with healthy and unhealthy heads of households is 5.99 percentage points, which is a smaller difference. In the group of non-HNWI households, there is a difference of 9.55 percentage points between the commercial insurance coverage rate of households with healthy and average heads of households and a difference of 11.85 percentage points between the commercial insurance coverage rate of households with healthy and unhealthy heads of households, which is larger than that of HNWI households. In addition, the gap between the commercial insurance coverage rates of mid-high net worth households and non mid-high net worth households was obvious.

4. *Gender of the head of household*

Gender also influences the purchase of commercial insurance. The gender of the household head is grouped in this book to calculate the commercial insurance coverage rate for the full sample of households, and the results are summarized in Fig. 12.

According to Fig. 12, the overall commercial insurance coverage rate is higher for households headed by women. One of the reasons why female heads of households are more inclined to purchase commercial insurance is that women themselves lack a sense of security and seek more security and stability than men, and therefore, are more likely to purchase commercial insurance; at the same time, when insurance marketers are marketing insurance products, women are more likely to listen and be more receptive to insurance products than men [16]. However, overall, the difference in the household commercial insurance coverage rates between household heads of different genders is only 1.89 percentage points, which is small.

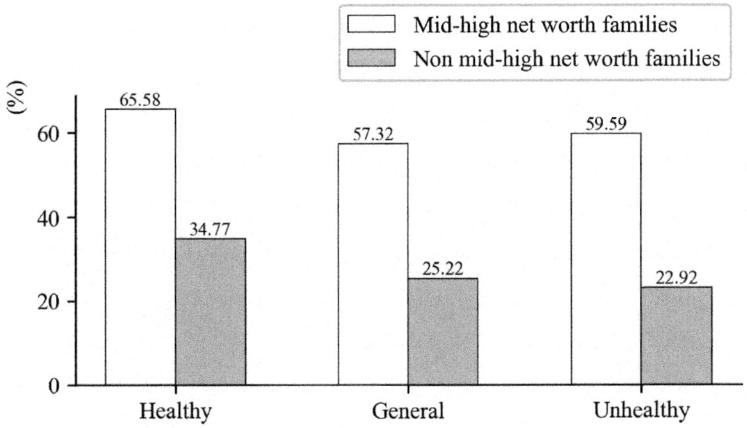


**Fig. 11** Commercial insurance coverage rates of mid-high net worth households and non mid-high net worth households (health status of household head)

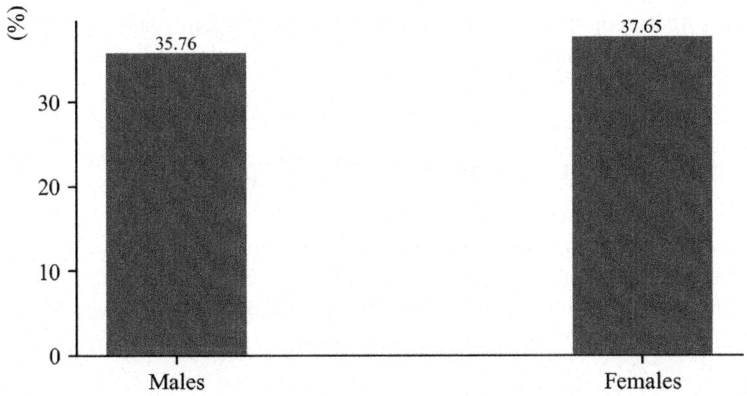


**Fig. 12** Commercial insurance coverage of the full sample of households (gender of household head)

According to Fig. 13, the commercial insurance coverage rate is higher among mid-high net worth households with male heads, whereas among non mid-high net worth households, the commercial insurance coverage rate is higher among households with female heads. The difference between the commercial insurance coverage rates of different household head genders among mid-high net worth households is 0.64 percentage points, which is a small difference. The difference between the commercial insurance coverage rates of different household head genders among non mid-high net worth households is 2.65 percentage points, which is also insignificant. However, the difference between the commercial insurance coverage rates of mid-high net worth families and non mid-high net worth families is more obvious,

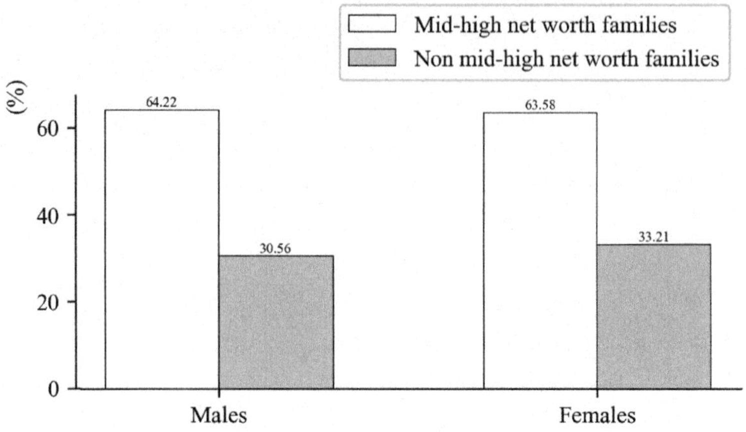


**Fig. 13** Commercial insurance coverage rates of mid-high net worth households and non mid-high net worth households (gender of household head)

indicating that economic conditions are still an important reason for purchasing family commercial insurance.

# 3 Household Commercial Insurance Expenditure

Household business insurance expenditure is an important indicator of how much households spend on business insurance. Here, the average annual household expenditure on commercial insurance for different groups of households was analyzed by calculating the average annual household premium expenditure from the CFPS data.

## 3.1 *Community and Family*

1. *Nature of community*

It calculates the average business insurance expenditure for the full sample of households by grouping them according to the nature of the community; the results are summarized in Fig. 14.

As shown in Fig. 14, the average amount of commercial insurance expenditure is significantly higher for the sample of households on neighborhood councils than for the sample of households on village councils. That is, households in urban areas spend more on commercial insurance than households in rural areas. Regarding premium expenditures, one report stated that household users currently spend ¥4,790 per year on premiums [23]. The annual premium expenditure of households obtained from this book is higher than in this report. This is mainly due to the difference in the survey

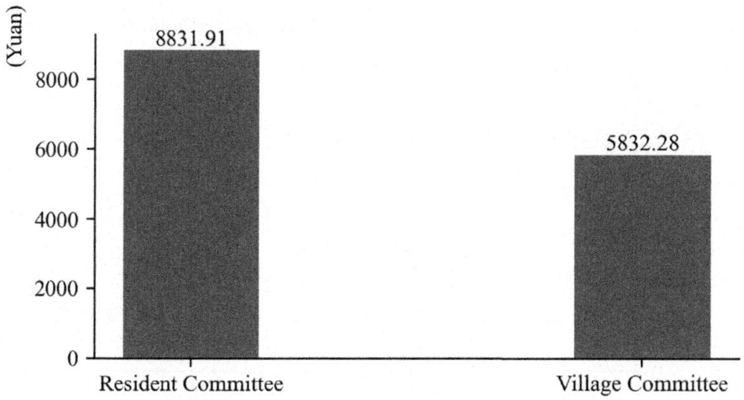


**Fig. 14** Average amount of commercial insurance expenditures for the full sample of households (community-based in nature)

sample; the Waterdrop Insurance User Research Center report surveyed household users on its Internet brokerage platform, while the CFPS survey used in this book surveyed a nationally representative sample of households.

According to Fig. 15, for the mid-high net worth households, the mean amount of household commercial insurance expenditure of the neighborhood council household sample is ¥2,679.74 higher than that of the village council household sample; among the non mid-high net worth households, the mean amount of household commercial insurance expenditure of the neighborhood council sample is ¥2,214.18 higher than that of the village council household sample. The above results indicate that the nature of the community is also one of the factors affecting the amount of household business insurance expenditures, and both the economic status gap and the urban–rural gap lead to a significant gap in business insurance expenditures.

2. *Family size*

It calculates the average amount of business insurance expenditure for the full sample of households based on household size grouping, and the results are summarized in Fig. 16.

According to Fig. 16, on the whole, the average amount of household commercial insurance expenditure shows a trend of first increasing and then decreasing when the number of household members is 1–9. In contrast, the average household commercial insurance expenditure increases significantly when the number of household members is 10 and above. For larger families, because of the large number of people in the family, the more pressure they need to protect themselves through commercial insurance, the more the family invests in it.

According to Fig. 17, the average value of business insurance expenditures of mid-high net worth households and non mid-high net worth households have different trends. The average value of business insurance expenditures of mid-high net worth households first shows a small upward trend with an increase in population and then

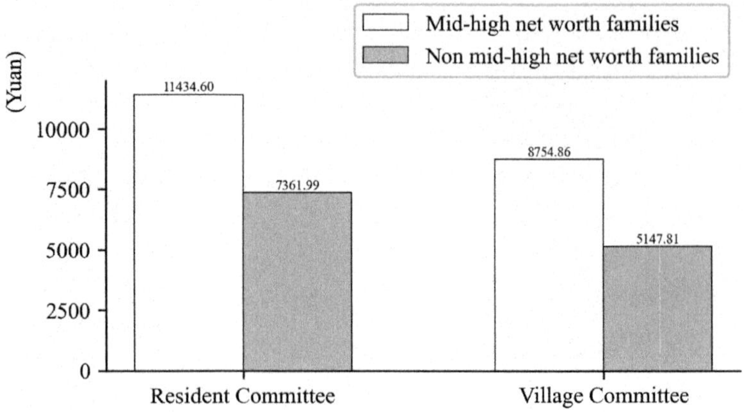


**Fig. 15** Average amount of commercial insurance expenditures of mid-high net worth households and non mid-high net worth households (community-based)

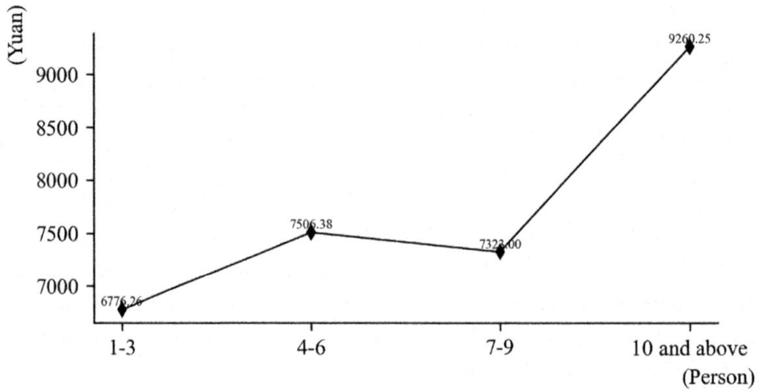


**Fig. 16** Average amount of commercial insurance expenditures for the full sample of households (household size)

a downward trend; the average value of business insurance expenditures of non mid-high net worth households shows a constant upward trend. The difference between the average amount of commercial insurance expenditure of mid-high net worth families with 1–9 members and non mid-high net worth families is larger, and the difference is smaller when there are 10 or more members.

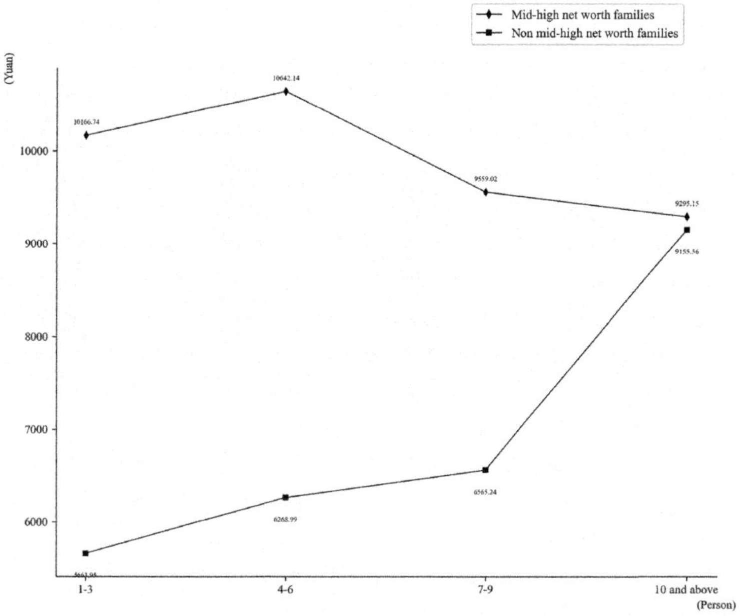


**Fig. 17** Average amount of commercial insurance expenditures of mid-high net worth households and non mid-high net worth households (household size)

## *3.2 Characteristics of the Head of Household*

1. *Education level of the head of household*

It is grouped according to the education level of the household head, and the average amount of business insurance expenditure is calculated for the entire sample of households; the results are summarized in Fig. 18.

According to Fig. 18, overall, household spending on commercial insurance increases as the education level of the household head increases. Well-educated people are more aware of the advantages of commercial insurance and are better off affording the financial cost of commercial insurance. In addition, the more educated the household head, the stronger the awareness of insurance protection, and the more willing they are to invest more in commercial insurance.

Figure 19 shows a significant difference between the average commercial insurance expenditures of mid-high net worth households and non mid-high net worth households. Looking at the amount of commercial insurance expenditures of mid-high net worth households, it can be found that the fluctuation is small. In contrast, the amount of commercial insurance expenditures of non mid-high net worth households shows a gradual increase, indicating that the education level of the heads of non mid-high net worth households significantly affects commercial insurance expenditures of households, while it does not have much impact on mid-high net worth households.

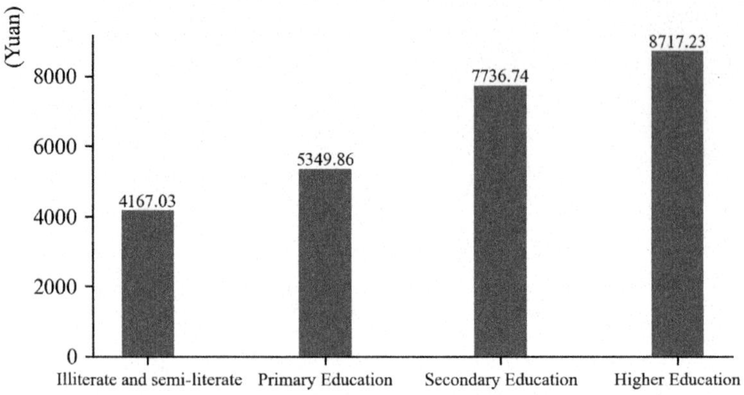


**Fig. 18** Average amount of commercial insurance expenditures for the full sample of households (education level of household head)

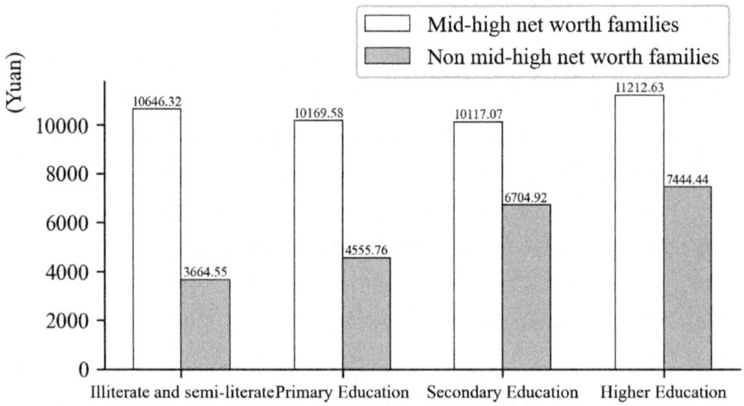


**Fig. 19** Average amount of commercial insurance expenditure of mid-high net worth households and non mid-high net worth households (education level of household head)

2. *Marital status of the head of household*

This book calculates the average amount of business insurance expenditure for the full sample of households in groups based on the marital status of the household head; the results are summarized in Fig. 20.

According to Fig. 20, the difference between the average amount of household business insurance expenditure when the household head is in the state of being married, divorced, and widowed is small, while the average amount of household business insurance expenditure when the household head is in the state of being unmarried and cohabiting has a more obvious difference with the above three states and is significantly less than the above three marital states. These results indicate that the commercial insurance expenditures of household heads are relatively high when they are married. It is worth noting that business insurance expenditure is significantly lower when the head of household cohabits. One reason is the insurance

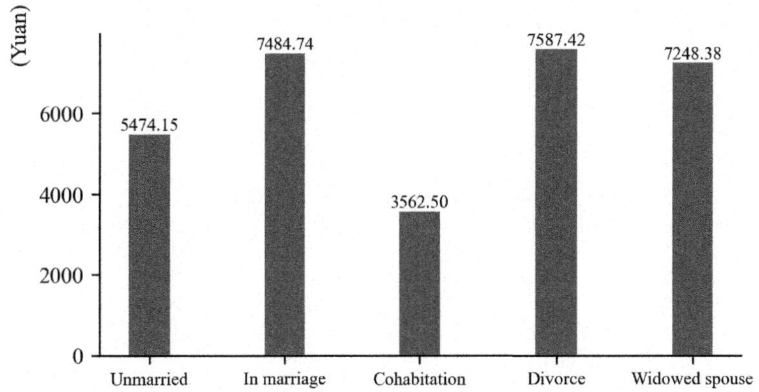


**Fig. 20** Average amount of commercial insurance expenditures for the full sample of households (marital status of household head)

benefit provisions for spouses under Insurance Law. The Marriage Law stipulates that cohabitation without marriage registration is not legal, the insured and the insured are not spouses in the legal sense and are not protected by the law, and the Insurance Law's provisions on insurance benefits between spouses do not apply [24]. Therefore, the willingness to ensure a cohabiting partner was much lower.

According to Fig. 21, the difference in the marital status of the head of the household between mid-high net worth households and non mid-high net worth households causes a difference in the mean amount of commercial insurance expenditure. Mean business insurance expenditure is significantly higher for households with divorced heads than for other groups. Except for the cohabitation group, the difference in the average business insurance expenditure between mid-high net worth households and non mid-high net worth households in the other groups is more obvious. In other words, the difference in business insurance expenditure is insignificant for mid-high net worth households and non mid-high net worth households without legal marriage relationships. With the accelerated rate of social change and changing concepts of family and marriage, the population of non-marital cohabitants is rising. It has become a phenomenon that cannot be ignored in society. In 2014, the proportion of cohabitants among those who were about to get married was more than 1/3 [25]. However, commercial insurance expenditures for the cohabiting population are generally relatively low. Encouraging the cohabiting population to purchase commercial insurance will be a breakthrough in promoting the development of commercial insurance.

3. *Health status of the head of household*

It calculates the average commercial insurance expenditure for the full sample of households based on the health status of the household head group, as summarized in Fig. 22.

According to Fig. 22, overall, the better the health status of the household head, the higher the mean value of household business insurance expenditure. The mean value of household commercial insurance expenditure in the healthy group was significantly higher than in the other two groups. On the one hand, the better the health

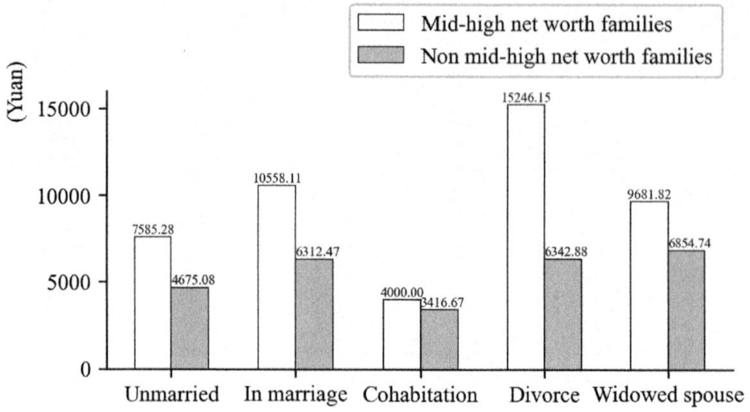


**Fig. 21** Average amount of commercial insurance expenditures of mid-high net worth households and non mid-high net worth households (marital status of household head)

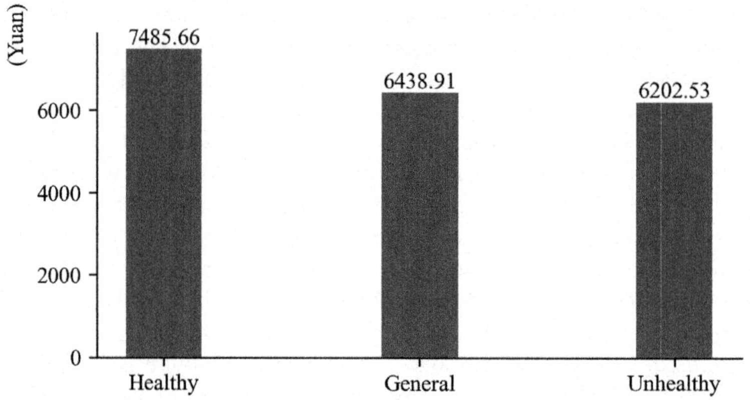


**Fig. 22** Average amount of commercial insurance expenditures for the full sample of households (health status of household head)

condition, the easier it is to buy commercial health insurance. On the other hand, healthy people are more conscious of their health protection, have higher requirements for medical conditions, the more likely they are to buy better commercial health insurance, and the higher the premiums they need to pay.

According to Fig. 23, the mean value of commercial insurance expenditures varies with the health status of the household head for both mid-high net worth households, and the healthier the household head, the higher the mean value of commercial insurance expenditures. This result is consistent with the overall trend. Among the mid-high net worth households and the non mid-high net worth households, the fluctuation in the average amount of commercial insurance expenditure in different health groups was smaller; however, the difference in the average amount of commercial

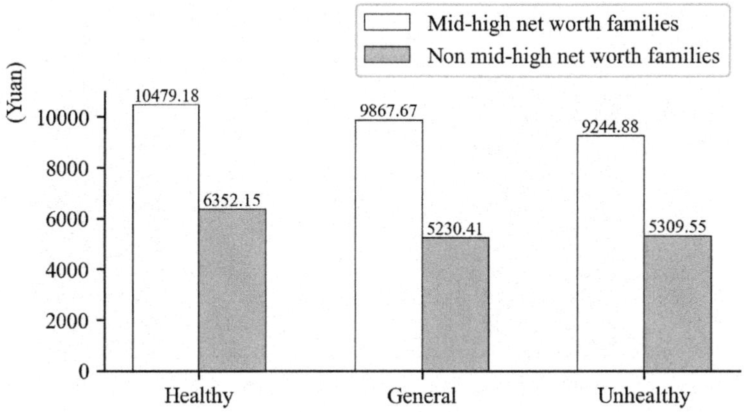


**Fig. 23** Average amount of commercial insurance expenditures of mid-high net worth households and non mid-high net worth households (health status of household head)

insurance expenditure between the mid-high net worth households and the non mid-high net-worth households was larger. For mid-high net worth families, purchasing commercial insurance is not only to protect their families but also an important tool and way of family asset allocation [26]. In other words, many mid-high net worth families no longer buy commercial insurance simply to obtain protection but take commercial insurance as an important option for family asset allocation and to accumulate wealth or diversify investment risks. Consequently, mid-high net worth households spend more on commercial insurance.

4. *Gender of the head of household*

It calculates the average business insurance expenditure for the full sample of households in groups according to the gender of the household head, as summarized in Fig. 24.

According to Fig. 24, overall, the average amount of household business insurance expenditure is higher for households headed by women, and there is no significant difference of ¥833.02 from the average amount of expenditures for households headed by men. In addition to women's higher demand for safety, there is a factor from the insurance supply perspective. Because the mortality and death risk of women of the same age are lower than men, women are cheaper than men in terms of commercial insurance, especially life insurance, and this phenomenon is more evident. However, in terms of family insurance allocation, the principle of primary to secondary insurance is generally followed, and the head of the household is the main character of the family; therefore, family insurance is first allocated to the head of the household. If the head of household is a woman, family insurance expenses are relatively higher.

According to Fig. 25, the mean amount of commercial insurance expenditure is higher among mid-high net worth households with male heads, while the mean amount of commercial insurance expenditure is higher among non mid-high net

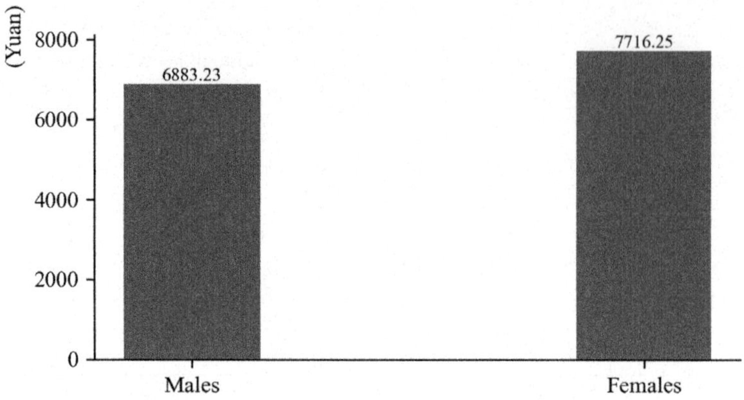


**Fig. 24** Average amount of commercial insurance expenditures for the full sample of households (gender of household head)

worth households with female heads. The difference between the mean amount of commercial insurance expenditure of different household head genders in mid-high net worth households is ¥102.69, which is a small difference; the difference between the mean amount of expenditure of different household head genders in non mid-high net worth households is ¥1326.69, which is a large difference. The above results show that the gender of the household head has a significant effect on the average amount of business insurance expenditure of non mid-high net worth households, but the effect is not significant for mid-high net worth households, while the difference between the average amount of expenditure of mid-high net worth households and non mid-high net worth households is significant. In other words, the effect of the household head's gender on the amount of business insurance expenditure is not significant in mid-high net worth households. In mid-high net worth households, commercial insurance has the function of family asset allocation; therefore, the purchase of commercial insurance is often the result of rational discussion and research by the core members of the household, and the amount of household commercial insurance expenditure is not significantly affected by the gender of the head of the household.

## 4 Per Capita Household Expenditure on Commercial Insurance

Per-capita insurance expenditure is an important indicator of the degree of insurance development. Insurance density in the insurance industry is obtained by dividing premium income by the total population, which is the per capita premium income. This measures the insurance industry's development from the perspective of premium income. For example, in 2020, the insurance density in China was only 430 USD per person [8]. That year, the average exchange rate of RMB to USD was almost ¥2900/

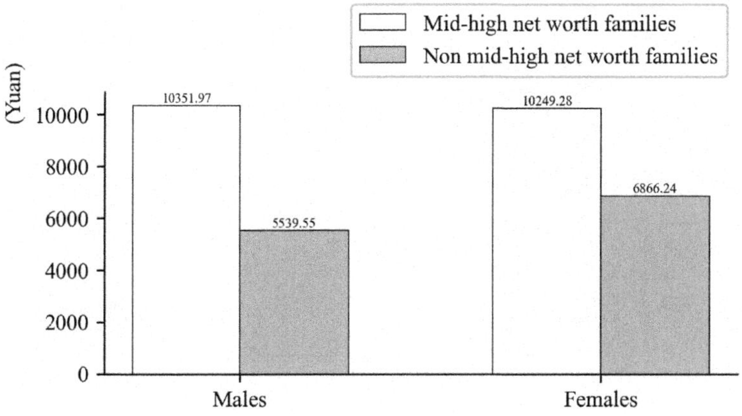


**Fig. 25** Average amount of commercial insurance expenditure of mid-high net worth households and non mid-high net worth households (gender of household head)

person. This book estimates the development of the commercial insurance industry from the perspective of household commercial insurance expenditure per capita. The per capita household commercial insurance expenditure is equal to the amount of household commercial insurance expenditure divided by the number of household members.

## *4.1 Community and Family*

1. *Nature of community*

It is grouped according to the nature of the community. The average amount of per capita expenditure on business insurance is calculated for the full sample of households, and the results are summarized in Fig. 26.

According to Fig. 26, the average per capita expenditure on commercial insurance for households on neighborhood councils was significantly higher than that on village councils. Urban households spend significantly more per capita on commercial insurance than rural households. This is expected to be the case in the future.

According to Fig. 27, for the medium–high-net-worth households, the average amount of per capita expenditure on commercial insurance is ¥1,427.95 higher for the neighborhood council household sample than for the village council household sample; for the non-medium–high-net-worth households, the average amount of per capita expenditure on commercial insurance is ¥1,161.64 higher for the neighborhood council sample than for the village council. The urban–rural gap in per capita expenditure on commercial insurance for the sample of mid-high net worth households is larger than that for the sample of non mid-high net worth households.

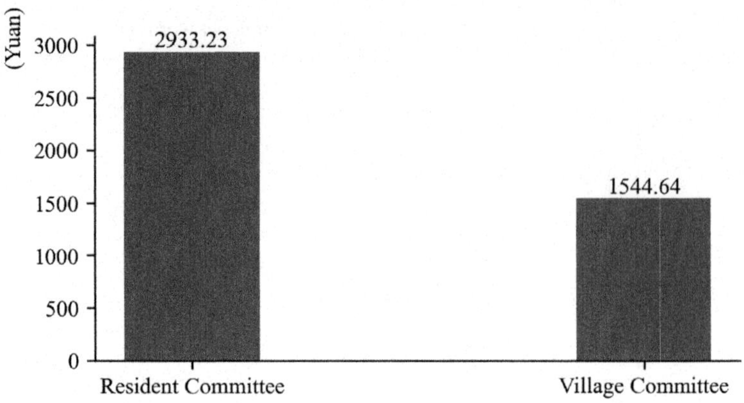


**Fig. 26** Average per capita expenditure on commercial insurance for the full sample of households (community-based in nature)

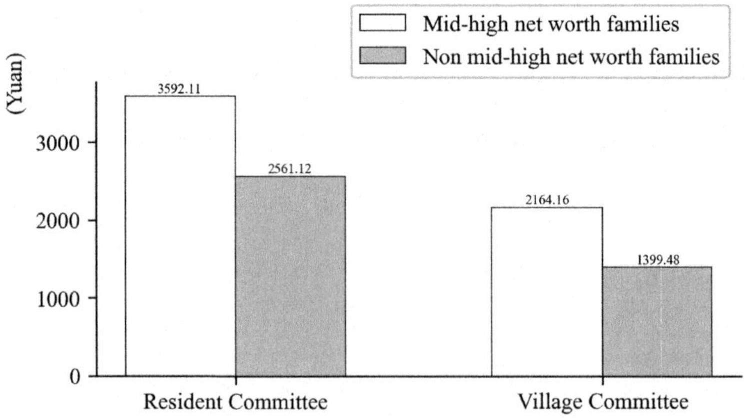


**Fig. 27** Average amount of per capita expenditure on commercial insurance for mid-high net worth households and non mid-high net worth households (community-based in nature)

2. *Family size*

It groups households according to size and calculates the average per capita expenditure on business insurance for the full sample of households. The results are summarized in Fig. 28.

According to Fig. 28, the average per capita expenditure on household business insurance decreased gradually with an increase in household size. Moreover, there is a significant difference in the average per capita expenditure on business insurance between households with six or fewer people and those with seven or more people. When the number of people is less than 7, the average amount of per capita business insurance expenditure decreases rapidly with the increase in the number of people. However, after the number of people exceeds seven, although the average per capita

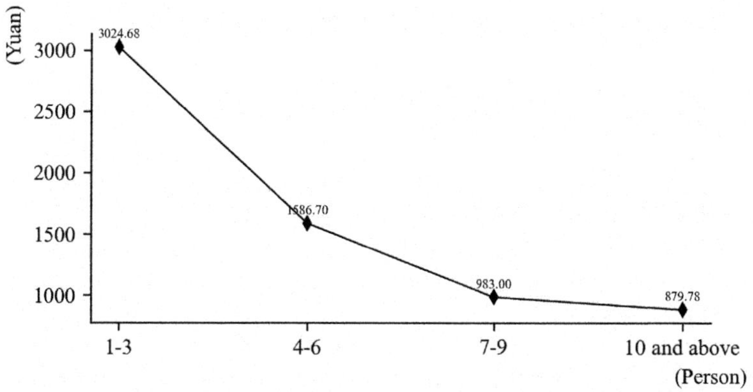


**Fig. 28** Average per capita expenditure on commercial insurance for the full sample of households (household size)

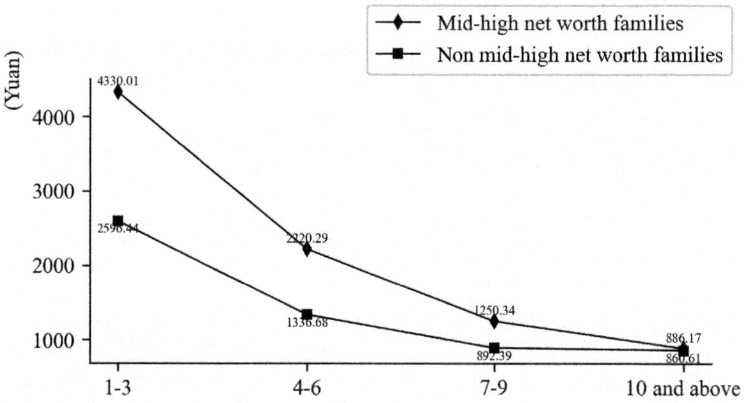


**Fig. 29** Average amount of per capita expenditure on commercial insurance for mid-high net worth households and non mid-high net worth households (household size)

household business insurance expenditure decreases with an increase in the number of people, the decrease is relatively small, and the change is very gentle.

According to Fig. 29, the average per capita expenditure on commercial insurance for both mid-high net worth households and non mid-high net worth households decreases with an increase in household size, and the difference between the two is decreasing. This may be due to the dilution effect of the household size.

## 4.2 Characteristics of the Head of Household

1. *Education level of the head of household*

It is grouped according to the education level of the household head. The average per capita expenditure on business insurance is calculated for the whole sample of households, and the results are summarized in Fig. 30.

According to Fig. 30, the mean per capita household business insurance expenditure increases with the educational level of the household head. This is consistent with previous analyses.

According to Fig. 31, the average per capita household business insurance expenditure increases with the educational level of the household head. The average per-capita expenditure was significantly higher for mid-high net worth households than for non mid-high net worth households. For the illiterate/semi-literate group, the difference between the two is 1293.7 yuan; for the primary education group, the difference is 1182.63 yuan; for the secondary education group, the difference is 974.23 yuan; and for the higher education group, the difference is 557.58 yuan. The difference between the average per capita commercial insurance expenditure of mid-high net worth households and non mid-high net worth households decreased as the education level of the household head increased.

2. *Marital status of the head of household*

It is grouped according to the marital status of the head of the household. The average amount of per capita expenditure on business insurance is calculated for the whole sample of households, and the results are summarized in Fig. 32.

According to Fig. 32, the mean per capita household business insurance expenditure when the head of the household is divorced is significantly higher than that of the other marital status groups. This is directly related to the household size. Divorced

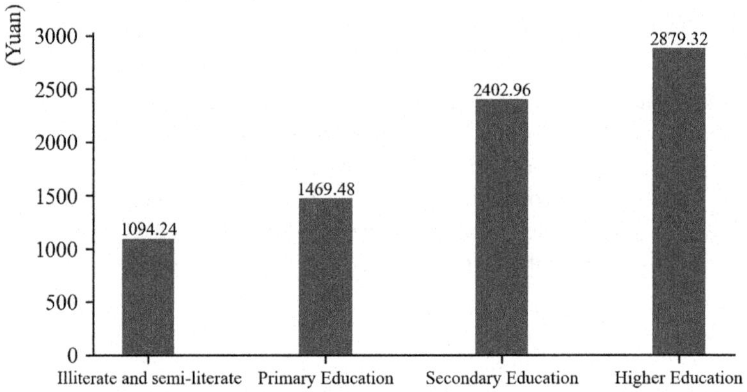


**Fig. 30** Average amount of per capita expenditure on commercial insurance for the full sample of households (education level of household head)

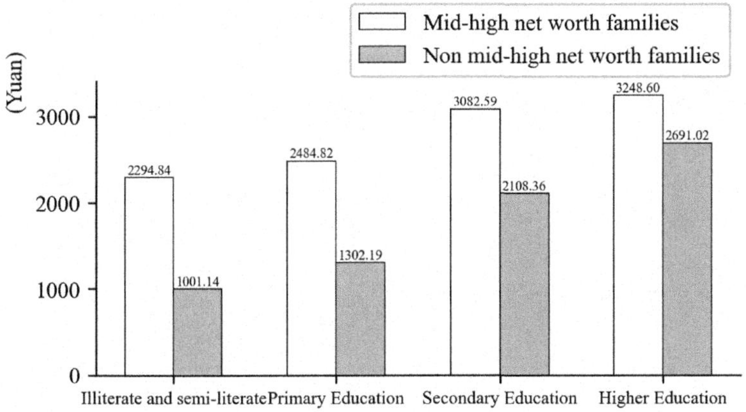


**Fig. 31** Average amount of per capita expenditure on commercial insurance for mid-high net worth households and non mid-high net worth households (education level of household head)

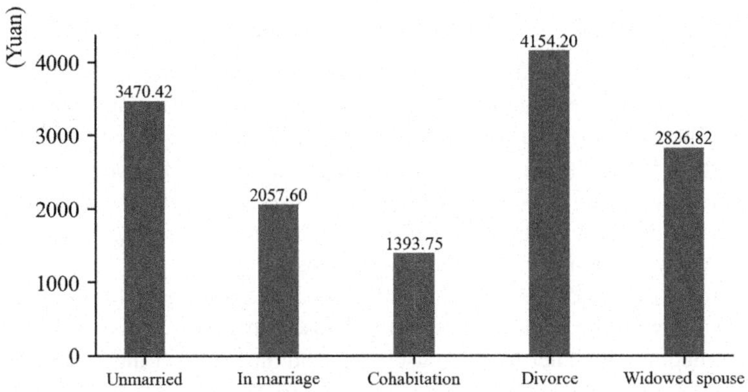


**Fig. 32** Average amount of per capita expenditure on commercial insurance for the full sample of households (marital status of the head of household)

household heads are generally single and alone, so the denominator is smaller when calculating per capita household business insurance expenditure; therefore, the calculated value will be larger. Similarly, the average per capita expenditure on business insurance for households in the married and cohabiting groups is lower because of the relatively large size of these two types of households compared with other types of households.

According to Fig. 33, the average amount of per capita business insurance expenditure of mid-high net worth households with unmarried heads is ¥1302.48 higher than that of non mid-high net worth households; the difference between the two in the married group is ¥1098.98; the difference between the two in the cohabitation group is ¥308.33; the difference between the two in the divorced group is ¥3428.96; and the difference between the two in the widowed group is ¥1852.3.

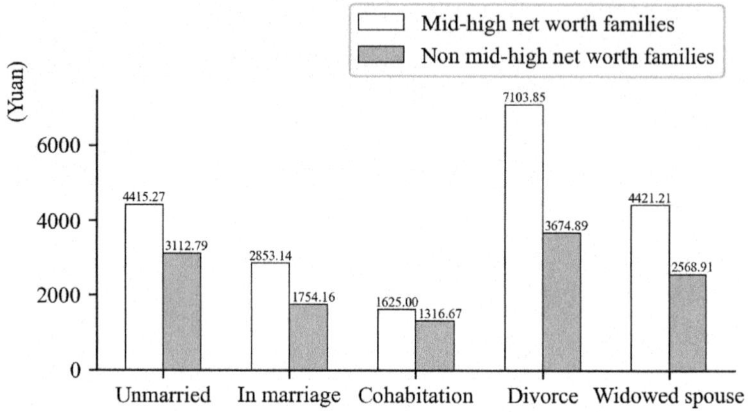


**Fig. 33** Average amount of per capita expenditure on commercial insurance for mid-high net worth households and non mid-high net worth households (marital status of household head)

3. *Health status of the head of household*

It is grouped according to the health status of the head of household, and the average amount of per capita expenditure on business insurance is calculated for the whole sample of households; the results are summarized in Fig. 34.

According to Fig. 34, overall, the better the health status of the household head, the higher the mean value of per capita household business insurance expenditure. The mean per-capita household business insurance expenditure was significantly higher in the healthy group than in the other two groups.

According to Fig. 35, the mean amount of per capita commercial insurance expenditure varies with the health status of the household head for both medium–high and non-medium–high net-worth households, and the healthier the household head,

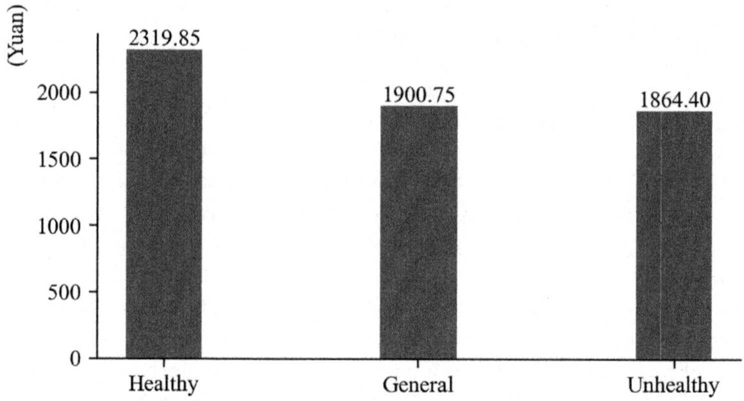


**Fig. 34** Average per capita expenditure on commercial insurance for the full sample of households (health status of household head)

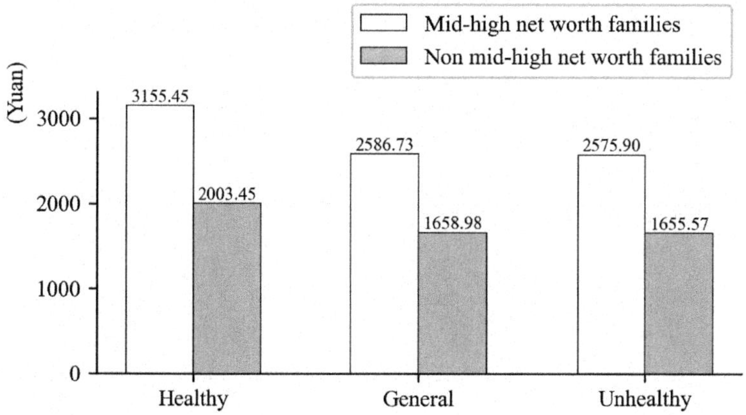


**Fig. 35** Average amount of per capita expenditure on commercial insurance (health status of household head) for mid-high net worth households and non-middle-net-worth households

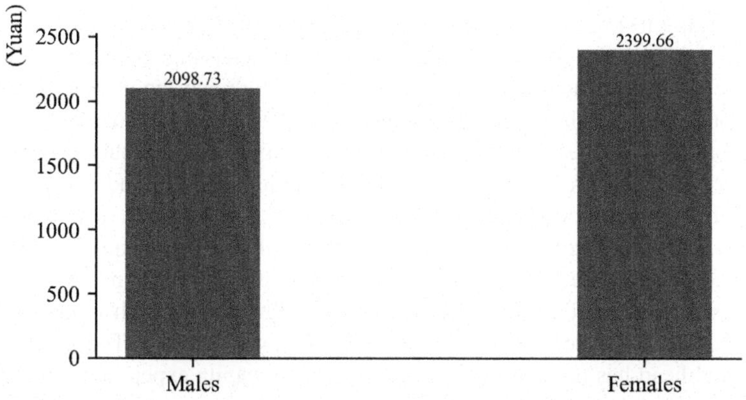


**Fig. 36** Average per capita expenditure on commercial insurance for the full sample of households (gender of household head)

the higher the mean amount of per capita expenditure. Among the medium–high and non-medium–high net-worth households, the fluctuation in the average amount of per capita expenditure on commercial insurance in different health groups was smaller; however, the difference between the average amount of per capita expenditure on commercial insurance in medium–high and non-medium–high net-worth households was larger.

4. *Gender of the head of household*

It is grouped according to the gender of the household head. The average amount of per capita expenditure on business insurance is calculated for the whole sample of households, and the results are summarized in Fig. 36.

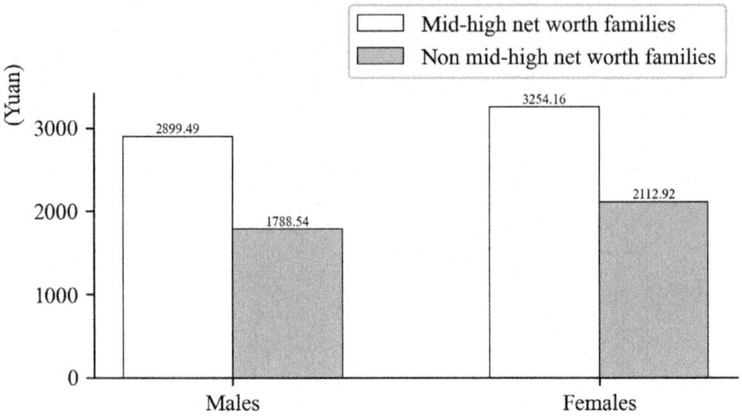


**Fig. 37** Average amount of per capita expenditure on commercial insurance for mid-high net worth households and non mid-high net worth households (gender of household head)

According to Fig. 36, overall, the average amount of per capita expenditure on commercial insurance for households headed by women is higher, and the difference between the average amount of per capita expenditure and the average amount of expenditure for households headed by men is ¥300.93, which is smaller.

According to Fig. 37, the average per capita expenditure on business insurance is lower for mid-high net worth households headed by men and higher for non mid-high net worth households headed by women. Among the mid-high net worth households, the difference in the average amount of per capita household business insurance expenditure between household heads of different genders is ¥354.67, which is a small difference; among the non mid-high net worth households, the difference between the two is ¥324.38, which is not significant. The gender of the household head has no significant effect on the per capita expenditure on business insurance of either medium–high or non-medium high-net-worth households, and the difference between the per capita expenditure on business insurance of medium high-net-worth households and non-medium high-net-worth households is significant.

## 5 Family Business Insurance Influence Factors

The data used in this chapter were mainly from the household and individual questionnaires of the 2020 CFPS. This study focuses on households' commercial insurance behavior and decisions. Household expenditure on commercial insurance and participation in commercial insurance have been the focus of academia and an important aspect of government attention [27]. Research on the factors influencing insurance demand has received increasing attention from scholars worldwide, and it has been confirmed that many factors can influence insurance demand [28, 29]. A household's decision to purchase commercial insurance is an important part of household finance, and household asset allocation decisions. As an important part of household financial asset allocation, commercial insurance generally changes with changes in household needs, household income, financial capacity, and individual characteristics of family members. It is directly related to the conditions and environment in which the household lives. At different stages of development, families face different levels of burden and have different insurance protection needs, and asset allocation is adjusted and optimized accordingly. Each family uses commercial insurance and other channels to reasonably allocate financial assets according to their specific situation to preserve and appreciate family wealth while avoiding related risks. Therefore, based on the household micro perspective, we further explore and examine the factors influencing household commercial insurance from both the household and head of household perspectives.

The empirical analysis in this section was conducted at two levels. The first level is a regression analysis of household business insurance expenditures and business insurance participation to explore the influence of household and heads of household factors on household business insurance. The second level builds on the first by conducting grouped regression analyses on household income, urban and rural classes, and urban classes to explore whether there are differences in the factors influencing household business insurance, which is known as a heterogeneity analysis.

## 5.1 Data, Variables, and Models

1. *Key variables*

The first explanatory variable here is household expenditure on commercial insurance, which is defined according to the question in the CFPS household questionnaire, "In the past 12 months, how much did your household spend on commercial insurance (e.g., commercial health insurance, auto insurance, homeowner's insurance, commercial life insurance, etc.)? The second explanatory variable was commercial insurance participation. If the answer to this question is 0, then commercial insurance participation is defined as 0; that is, the household is not involved in commercial insurance. If the answer is greater than 0, then commercial insurance participation is defined as 1; that is, the household is involved in commercial insurance.

The core explanatory variables are mid-high net worth households (dummy variables) and household investable assets. The former consisted of values 0 and 1. The former is a medium–high net-worth household, and the latter is a non-medium–high net-worth household.

The remaining control variables include household-level and head-of-household-level control variables, with household-level control variables including household entrepreneurial decisions, household property investment decisions, household size, household income, bank loans, loans from friends and relatives and private individuals, human fees, and education and training fees, and head-of-household-level control variables including gender, age, years of education, marital status, health status, self-confidence level, and whether to access the Internet.

2. *Descriptive statistics*

During data processing, samples with missing or incorrect values in the variables were eliminated, and 8775 valid samples were finally obtained. The definition and descriptive statistics for these variables are shown in Table 1.

3. *Model setting*

This chapter examines the impact of mid-high net worth households and household investable assets on household business insurance expenditure and participation, as modeled in the following settings:

**Table 1** Definition of variables and descriptive statistics

| Variable | Definition | Mean | S.D | Min | Max |
|---|---|---|---|---|---|
| Commercial insurance expenses | Amount of commercial insurance spending last year | 2669.962 | 6986.453 | 0 | 100,000 |
| Commercial insurance participation | Participation in commercial insurance is 1, otherwise it is 0 | 0.366 | 0.482 | 0 | 1 |
| Entrepreneurship of the family | Number of self-employed or private enterprises | 0.104 | 0.349 | 0 | 6 |
| Investment properties | Number of properties other than current housing | 0.261 | 0.566 | 0 | 7 |
| Mid-high net worth families | 1 for mid-high net worth households, 0 for the rest | 0.155 | 0.362 | 0 | 1 |
| Household investable assets | Log value of household investable assets | 8.686 | 4.879 | 0 | 17.371 |
| Household size | Number of family members | 3.566 | 1.89 | 1 | 15 |
| Household income | Logarithmic value of household income | 10.705 | 1.427 | 0 | 14.286 |
| Bank loans | If the household has a bank loan, the variable takes the value of 1, otherwise it is 0 | 0.105 | 0.306 | 0 | 1 |
| Private loans from friends and family | If there is a family or private loan, the value is 1, otherwise it is 0 | 0.112 | 0.316 | 0 | 1 |
| Favor expenses | Last year's household spending on favors | 3839.593 | 6008.965 | 0 | 120,000 |

(continued)

**Table 1** (continued)

| Variable | Definition | Mean | S.D | Min | Max |
|---|---|---|---|---|---|
| Education and training fees | Spending on family education training last year | 4673.67 | 10,355.027 | 0 | 152,000 |
| Gender | If the gender is male, the variable takes the value of 1, otherwise it is 0 | 0.562 | 0.496 | 0 | 1 |
| Age | Age of the individual, in years | 48.916 | 14.592 | 18 | 95 |
| Year of education | Number of years of education received | 8.255 | 5.073 | 0 | 24 |
| Marriage | If the marital status is married, the variable takes the value of 1, otherwise 0 | 0.817 | 0.386 | 0 | 1 |
| Health | Health rating with a maximum of 5 and a minimum of 1 | 3.001 | 1.174 | 1 | 5 |
| Self-confidence | Self-confidence rating, highest 5, lowest 1 | 4.134 | 0.936 | 1 | 5 |
| Access to the internet | Internet access is 1, otherwise it is 0 | 0.65 | 0.477 | 0 | 1 |

$$Insurance = \beta_0 + \beta_1 \times MHW + \beta_2 \times ln(FIA) + \beta_3 \times X + u$$

$$IP = \beta_0 + \beta_1 \times MHW + \beta_2 \times ln(FIA) + \beta_3 \times X + u$$

where *Insurance* denotes annual household commercial insurance expenditure, which is a continuous variable; *IP* denotes household participation in commercial insurance, which is a variable consisting of 0 and 1; *MHW* and *FIA* denote mid-high net worth households (dummy variables) and household investable assets, respectively; *X* is a series of control variables containing household-level and head-of-household-level control variables, *u* and is the error term. In the regression of Eq. (2), the logit regression model is used instead of the least squares regression (OLS) model because the explanatory variables are categorical.

## 5.2 Empirical Analysis

1. *Impact of mid-high net worth families on household commercial insurance spending*

Table 2 presents the regression results for the effects of mid-high net worth households on household business insurance expenditure. Column (1) considers only the explanatory variables of mid-high net worth households, column (2) adds household-level control variables, and column (3) adds household head-level control variables to the household-level control variables. On this basis, province-fixed effects are added in Columns (4)–(6), corresponding to Columns (1)–(3). The results show that all models' regression coefficients for mid-high net worth households are significantly positive. As shown in column (6), after accounting for both household-level control variables and head-of-household-level control variables, as well as province fixed effects, mid-high net worth households spend about ¥1,744 more on annual business insurance than non mid-high net worth households. This indicates that mid-high net worth households allocate and invest more money in commercial insurance and have a greater demand for commercial insurance coverage.

2. *Impact of household investable assets on household business insurance expenditure*

Table 3 presents the regression results for the effect of household investable assets on household business insurance expenditure. The regression coefficients of household investable assets are significantly positive in all the models. This indicates that increased household investable assets increases household business insurance expenditure. The results in column (6) show that after considering household-level control variables, head-of-household-level control variables, and province fixed effects, each 1% increase in household investable assets raises household business insurance expenditures by about USD 48.

The results of the relevant control variables indicate that household- and head-of-household-level variables also have a more significant effect on household entrepreneurial decisions. The more investment properties a household has, the more likely it is to increase its investment and allocation in commercial insurance because homeowners' insurance falls under the category of household property insurance. The more investment property a household owns, the more it must be protected under home property insurance. Household entrepreneurial decisions are important for households and can profoundly impact other household decisions [30]. The greater the number of household start-ups, the greater the allocation to business insurance. Household size has no significant effect on household business insurance expenditure; however, household income has a significant positive relationship with household business insurance expenditure. Bank loans have a significantly positive relationship with household business insurance expenditures, whereas the effects of friends, relatives, and private loans are significantly negative. In addition, both favorable expenses and education and training expenses have a significant positive relationship with household business insurance expenditure.

**Table 2** Regression results of the effect of mid-high net worth households on household business insurance expenditures

| | Commercial insurance expenses | | | | | |
|---|---|---|---|---|---|---|
| | (1) | (2) | (3) | (4) | (5) | (6) |
| Mid-high net worth families | 4,668.608*** (14.98) | 1,933.265*** (5.48) | 1,723.786*** (4.94) | 4,472.890*** (14.20) | 1,981.049*** (5.42) | 1,743.772*** (4.85) |
| Investment properties | | 734.383** (2.56) | 735.628** (2.56) | | 674.396** (2.32) | 681.318** (2.34) |
| Entrepreneurship of the family | | 2,266.414*** (5.87) | 2,181.051*** (5.71) | | 2,219.505*** (5.78) | 2,133.867*** (5.63) |
| Household size | | 19.412 (0.52) | 19.117 (0.45) | | 39.878 (0.99) | 32.413 (0.73) |
| Household income | | 679.936*** (10.83) | 518.741*** (8.48) | | 669.776*** (10.55) | 502.228*** (8.17) |
| Bank loans | | 1,232.929*** (4.22) | 1,025.692*** (3.52) | | 1,335.937*** (4.51) | 1,108.844*** (3.77) |
| Private loans from friends and family | | −483.840** (−2.45) | −492.166** (−2.47) | | −447.822** (−2.26) | −469.276** (−2.35) |
| Favor expenses | | 0.080*** (4.35) | 0.078*** (4.29) | | 0.078*** (4.21) | 0.075*** (4.10) |
| Education and training fees | | 0.110*** (5.94) | 0.101*** (5.38) | | 0.108*** (5.85) | 0.100*** (5.29) |
| Gender | | | −480.417*** (−3.31) | | | −430.762*** (−2.95) |
| Age | | | −21.688*** (−3.52) | | | −24.570*** (−3.88) |
| Year of education | | | 68.573*** (3.73) | | | 65.185*** (3.53) |

(continued)

**Table 2** (continued)

| | Commercial insurance expenses | | | | | |
|---|---|---|---|---|---|---|
| | (1) | (2) | (3) | (4) | (5) | (6) |
| Marriage | | | 633.088*** (3.36) | | | 620.132*** (3.26) |
| Health | | | 61.979 (1.24) | | | 67.881 (1.35) |
| Self-confidence | | | 74.761 (1.15) | | | 69.272 (1.06) |
| Access to the internet | | | 573.842*** (3.88) | | | 601.625*** (4.01) |
| Fixed effects of provinces | No | No | No | Yes | Yes | Yes |
| Constant | 1,946.926*** (29.99) | −6,300.896*** (−10.23) | −5,084.994*** (−6.89) | 1,007.681** (1.99) | −7,440.968*** (−8.46) | −6,403.620*** (−6.63) |
| Observations | 8,775 | 8,775 | 8,775 | 8,775 | 8,775 | 8,775 |
| R-squared | 0.058 | 0.150 | 0.160 | 0.069 | 0.157 | 0.167 |

*Note* * $p < 0.1$, ** $p < 0.05$, *** $p < 0.01$

**Table 3** Regression results of the effect of household investable assets on household business insurance expenditures

| | Commercial insurance expenses | | | | | |
|---|---|---|---|---|---|---|
| | (1) | (2) | (3) | (4) | (5) | (6) |
| Household investable assets | 276.727*** (17.99) | 71.779*** (4.80) | 49.992*** (3.37) | 259.873*** (16.79) | 71.526*** (4.67) | 47.536*** (3.11) |
| Investment properties | | 1,251.678*** (4.85) | 1,236.519*** (4.76) | | 1,203.045*** (4.68) | 1,189.537*** (4.59) |
| Entrepreneurship of the family | | 2,308.011*** (6.02) | 2,229.923*** (5.87) | | 2,271.596*** (5.96) | 2,190.545*** (5.81) |
| Household size | | 13.270 (0.35) | 15.639 (0.37) | | 35.930 (0.89) | 29.901 (0.67) |
| Household income | | 684.013*** (10.65) | 532.481*** (8.62) | | 669.076*** (10.33) | 511.407*** (8.25) |
| Bank loans | | 1,270.539*** (4.31) | 1,051.572*** (3.56) | | 1,372.278*** (4.60) | 1,129.041*** (3.80) |
| Private loans from friends and family | | −444.201** (−2.23) | −477.562** (−2.37) | | −408.761** (−2.04) | −457.812** (−2.27) |
| Favor expenses | | 0.086*** (4.62) | 0.083*** (4.53) | | 0.083*** (4.42) | 0.079*** (4.28) |
| Education and training fees | | 0.112*** (6.02) | 0.103*** (5.44) | | 0.110*** (5.92) | 0.101*** (5.35) |
| Gender | | | −497.820*** (−3.41) | | | −453.242*** (−3.08) |
| Age | | | −19.703*** (−3.19) | | | −22.895*** (−3.59) |
| Year of education | | | 74.108*** (4.01) | | | 71.056*** (3.81) |

(continued)

**Table 3** (continued)

| | Commercial insurance expenses | | | | | |
|---|---|---|---|---|---|---|
| | (1) | (2) | (3) | (4) | (5) | (6) |
| Marriage | | | 632.637*** (3.35) | | | 626.760*** (3.28) |
| Health | | | 68.299 (1.37) | | | 73.356 (1.45) |
| Self-confidence | | | 70.893 (1.09) | | | 69.130 (1.05) |
| Access to the internet | | | 603.288*** (4.06) | | | 630.311*** (4.19) |
| Fixed effects of provinces | No | No | No | Yes | Yes | Yes |
| Constant | 266.271** (2.51) | −6,823.618*** (−11.15) | −5,707.185*** (−7.74) | −300.698 (−0.55) | −7,783.834*** (−8.86) | −6,842.223*** (−7.05) |
| Observations | 8,775 | 8,775 | 8,775 | 8,775 | 8,775 | 8,775 |
| R-squared | 0.037 | 0.147 | 0.157 | 0.050 | 0.153 | 0.164 |

*Note* * $p < 0.1$, ** $p < 0.05$, *** $p < 0.01$

Considering the control variables at the household head level, gender significantly affects household business insurance expenditures. Female heads of household invest more in business insurance and have a greater need for business insurance than male heads. Age also affects the demand for household business insurance. The older the head of the household, the lower the need for commercial insurance. The more years of education the head of household has, the greater the need for family business insurance and the greater the family's business insurance expenses. The marital status of the household head is also an important factor affecting a family's commercial insurance expenditure. Marital status has a greater impact on household business insurance spending than the other marital statuses. Health status and self-confidence have no significant effects on commercial household insurance expenditure. Access to the Internet was significantly and positively related to commercial household insurance expenditure.

3. *Impact of mid-high net worth households on commercial insurance participation*

Table 4 presents the regression results for the effect of mid-high net worth households on commercial insurance participation. The regression coefficients for mid-high net worth households are significantly positive in all six models. This indicates that mid-high net worth households are more likely to participate in commercial insurance than non mid-high net worth households. The results in column (6) show that after accounting for both household-level control variables and head-of-household-level control variables as well as province fixed effects, mid-high net worth households increase their commercial insurance participation by 0.409 units compared to non mid-high net worth households, demonstrating a significant positive effect of mid-high net worth households on increasing the level of commercial insurance participation.

4. *Impact of household investable assets on commercial insurance participation*

Table 5 show the regression results for the effect of household investable assets on commercial insurance participation. The regression coefficients for household investable assets in all six models were significantly positive. This finding indicates that the more investable assets a household has, the more likely it is to purchase commercial insurance. The results in column (6) show that, after accounting for household-level control variables, head-of-household-level control variables, and province fixed effects, each 1% increase in household investable assets increases the probability of a household purchasing commercial insurance by 0.043 percentage points. The regression results show a significant positive effect of household investable assets on commercial insurance participation.

Regarding control variables, households that engage in entrepreneurship, own investment properties, are larger, and hold bank loans have higher expenditures on business insurance, all of which have a significant positive relationship with business insurance expenditures. However, the effects of friends, relatives, and private loans on household business insurance expenditure are insignificant. In addition, both favor expenses and education and training expenses have a significant positive relationship with household commercial insurance expenditure. At the household

**Table 4** Regression results of the effect of mid-high net worth households on commercial insurance participation

| | Commercial insurance participation | | | | | |
|---|---|---|---|---|---|---|
| | (1) | (2) | (3) | (4) | (5) | (6) |
| Mid-high net worth families | 1.365$^{***}$<br>(22.06) | 0.389$^{***}$<br>(4.19) | 0.377$^{***}$<br>(4.02) | 1.327$^{***}$<br>(20.61) | 0.449$^{***}$<br>(4.81) | 0.409$^{***}$<br>(4.32) |
| Investment properties | | 0.183$^{***}$<br>(3.22) | 0.195$^{***}$<br>(3.37) | | 0.156$^{***}$<br>(2.73) | 0.177$^{***}$<br>(3.02) |
| Entrepreneurship of the family | | 0.529$^{***}$<br>(5.77) | 0.459$^{***}$<br>(5.00) | | 0.534$^{***}$<br>(5.75) | 0.474$^{***}$<br>(5.11) |
| Household size | | 0.043$^{***}$<br>(3.19) | 0.037$^{**}$<br>(2.45) | | 0.049$^{***}$<br>(3.43) | 0.050$^{***}$<br>(3.09) |
| Household income | | 0.635$^{***}$<br>(12.30) | 0.425$^{***}$<br>(7.66) | | 0.655$^{***}$<br>(11.56) | 0.416$^{***}$<br>(7.06) |
| Bank loans | | 0.445$^{***}$<br>(5.69) | 0.278$^{***}$<br>(3.47) | | 0.474$^{***}$<br>(5.90) | 0.317$^{***}$<br>(3.86) |
| Private loans from friends and family | | 0.082<br>(1.04) | 0.027<br>(0.34) | | 0.105<br>(1.32) | 0.050<br>(0.61) |
| Favor expenses | | 0.001$^{***}$<br>(4.52) | 0.001$^{***}$<br>(5.15) | | 0.001$^{***}$<br>(4.20) | 0.001$^{***}$<br>(4.61) |
| Education and training fees | | 0.001$^{***}$<br>(5.65) | 0.001$^{***}$<br>(3.97) | | 0.001$^{***}$<br>(5.46) | 0.001$^{***}$<br>(3.67) |
| Gender | | | −0.043<br>(−0.84) | | | −0.013<br>(−0.25) |
| Age | | | −0.027$^{***}$<br>(−11.58) | | | −0.029$^{***}$<br>(−12.00) |
| Year of education | | | 0.028$^{***}$<br>(4.50) | | | 0.026$^{***}$<br>(4.19) |

(continued)

**Table 4** (continued)

| | Commercial insurance participation | | | | | |
|---|---|---|---|---|---|---|
| | (1) | (2) | (3) | (4) | (5) | (6) |
| Marriage | | | $0.743^{***}$ (8.79) | | | $0.728^{***}$ (8.53) |
| Health | | | 0.034 (1.47) | | | 0.035 (1.52) |
| Self-confidence | | | $0.067^{**}$ (2.36) | | | $0.061^{**}$ (2.11) |
| Access to the internet | | | $0.560^{***}$ (8.11) | | | $0.578^{***}$ (8.21) |
| Fixed effects of provinces | No | No | No | Yes | Yes | Yes |
| Constant | $-0.776^{***}$ (−31.05) | $-8.032^{***}$ (−14.65) | $-6.023^{***}$ (−10.00) | $-1.010^{***}$ (−4.18) | $-8.718^{***}$ (−12.82) | $-6.467^{***}$ (−9.23) |
| Observations | 8,775 | 8,775 | 8,775 | 8,774 | 8,774 | 8,774 |
| Pseudo R-squared | 0.0445 | 0.140 | 0.181 | 0.0524 | 0.146 | 0.189 |

*Note* $^{*}$ $p < 0.1$, $^{**}$ $p < 0.05$, $^{***}$ $p < 0.01$

**Table 5** Regression results for the effect of household investable assets on commercial insurance participation

| | Commercial insurance participation | | | | | |
|---|---|---|---|---|---|---|
| | (1) | (2) | (3) | (4) | (5) | (6) |
| Household investable assets | 0.120*** (20.17) | 0.049*** (7.07) | 0.042*** (6.01) | 0.117*** (19.23) | 0.052*** (7.44) | 0.043*** (6.14) |
| Investment properties | | 0.185*** (3.76) | 0.215*** (4.24) | | 0.173*** (3.50) | 0.206*** (4.02) |
| Entrepreneurship of the family | | 0.515*** (5.67) | 0.448*** (4.93) | | 0.521*** (5.68) | 0.464*** (5.07) |
| Household size | | 0.047*** (3.52) | 0.039*** (2.59) | | 0.053*** (3.71) | 0.051*** (3.18) |
| Household income | | 0.596*** (11.36) | 0.403*** (7.32) | | 0.618*** (10.74) | 0.398*** (6.79) |
| Bank loans | | 0.499*** (6.29) | 0.327*** (4.02) | | 0.526*** (6.47) | 0.363*** (4.36) |
| Private loans from friends and family | | 0.166** (2.05) | 0.097 (1.16) | | 0.190** (2.33) | 0.119 (1.42) |
| Favor expenses | | 0.001*** (4.70) | 0.001*** (5.30) | | 0.001*** (4.34) | 0.001*** (4.71) |
| Education and training fees | | 0.001*** (5.65) | 0.001*** (3.94) | | 0.001*** (5.48) | 0.001*** (3.66) |
| Gender | | | −0.054 (−1.05) | | | −0.026 (−0.49) |
| Age | | | −0.026*** (−11.40) | | | −0.028*** (−11.83) |
| Year of education | | | 0.027*** (4.36) | | | 0.026*** (4.09) |

(continued)

**Table 5** (continued)

| | Commercial insurance participation | | | | | |
|---|---|---|---|---|---|---|
| | (1) | (2) | (3) | (4) | (5) | (6) |
| Marriage | | | $0.742^{***}$<br>(8.78) | | | $0.728^{***}$<br>(8.53) |
| Health | | | 0.036<br>(1.56) | | | 0.038<br>(1.63) |
| Self-confidence | | | $0.068^{**}$<br>(2.35) | | | $0.061^{**}$<br>(2.10) |
| Access to the internet | | | $0.554^{***}$<br>(7.99) | | | $0.568^{***}$<br>(8.04) |
| Fixed effects of provinces | No | No | No | Yes | Yes | Yes |
| Constant | $-1.642^{***}$<br>(−25.99) | $-8.024^{***}$<br>(−14.99) | $-6.148^{***}$<br>(−10.60) | $-1.822^{***}$<br>(−7.51) | $-8.728^{***}$<br>(−13.04) | $-6.601^{***}$<br>(−9.69) |
| Observations | 8,775 | 8,775 | 8,775 | 8,774 | 8,774 | 8,774 |
| R-squared | 0.0496 | 0.143 | 0.183 | 0.0576 | 0.150 | 0.191 |

*Note* $^{*}$ $p < 0.1$, $^{**}$ $p < 0.05$, $^{***}$ $p < 0.01$

head level, age has a significant negative relationship with household business insurance expenditure, and years of education has a significant positive relationship with business insurance expenditure. In addition, households headed by married individuals have higher business insurance expenditures than households with other marital statuses. Confident heads of households and those with Internet access have higher household business insurance expenditures. However, the effects of the health status and sex of the household head on household business insurance expenditures were not significant.

## 5.3 Heterogeneity Analysis

1. *Heterogeneity of mid-high net worth households' expenditure on household commercial insurance*

Based on the head's income level, the sample was divided into two groups, with higher and lower household income levels, and then, grouped into regressions. Columns (1) and (2) in Table 6 show the regression results based on income heterogeneity. The results show no significant positive effect of mid-high net worth households (dummy variable) on the commercial insurance expenditure of households with higher income levels. In comparison, there is a significant effect on the commercial insurance expenditure of households with lower income levels. This indicates that for households with relatively high-income levels, the gap in commercial insurance expenditures between mid-high net worth households and between non mid-high net worth households is not significant. However, for households with relatively low-income levels, mid-high net worth households spend significantly more on commercial insurance than non mid-high net worth households.

The sample was divided into urban and rural groups and then grouped into regressions based on household location. Columns (3) and (4) of Table 6 show the regression results based on urban–rural heterogeneity. The results show that mid-high net worth households (dummy variable) have a significant positive effect on household business insurance expenditures in urban and rural areas; however, the effect is significantly larger for rural households than for urban households.

Based on the location of the households in the sample, the urban sample was further divided into four groups: first-tier cities, second-tier cities, third-tier cities, and fourth-tier cities, and the regressions were conducted in groups; the results are summarized in Table 7. The results show that the effect of mid-high net worth households (dummy variable) on household business insurance expenditure in tier 3 and above cities is insignificant. In contrast, the effect on household business insurance expenditure in tier 4 and below cities is significantly positive. This indicates no significant gap between mid-high net worth households and non mid-high net worth households regarding household business insurance expenditure in tier 3 and above

**Table 6** Regression results of the impact of mid-high net worth households on household commercial insurance expenditures (income and urban–rural heterogeneity)

| | Commercial insurance expenses | | | |
|---|---|---|---|---|
| | (1) | (2) | (3) | (4) |
| Income heterogeneity | High income | low income | | |
| Urban-rural heterogeneity | | | Urban | Rural |
| Mid-high net worth families | −30.44<br>(487.3) | 2,349***<br>(613.2) | 1,286***<br>(458.4) | 2,201***<br>(592.2) |
| Household-level control variables | Yes | Yes | Yes | Yes |
| Control variables at household head level | Yes | Yes | Yes | Yes |
| Fixed effects of provinces | Yes | Yes | Yes | Yes |
| Constant | −49,003***<br>(5,053) | −1,070**<br>(536.0) | −9,934***<br>(1,611) | −2,558**<br>(1,181) |
| Observations | 4,219 | 4,556 | 4,772 | 4,003 |
| R-squared | 0.161 | 0.095 | 0.169 | 0.143 |

*Note* * $p < 0.1$, ** $p < 0.05$, *** $p < 0.01$

**Table 7** Regression results of the impact of mid-high net worth households on household business insurance expenditures (urban heterogeneity)

| | Commercial insurance expenses | | | |
|---|---|---|---|---|
| | (1) | (2) | (3) | (4) |
| Urban heterogeneity | First-tier cities | Second-tier cities | Third-tier cities | Fourth-tier cities and below |
| Mid-high net worth families | −1,346.355<br>(−1.07) | 549.686<br>(0.56) | 1,727.555<br>(1.48) | 2,226.462***<br>(3.85) |
| Household-level control variables | Yes | Yes | Yes | Yes |
| Control variables at household head level | Yes | Yes | Yes | Yes |
| Fixed effects of provinces | Yes | Yes | Yes | Yes |
| Constant | −14,856.087**<br>(−2.25) | −9,199.454**<br>(−2.50) | −1,431.064<br>(−0.41) | −7,912.981***<br>(−4.08) |
| Observations | 584 | 906 | 391 | 2,891 |
| R-squared | 0.253 | 0.173 | 0.222 | 0.179 |

*Note* * $p < 0.1$, ** $p < 0.05$, *** $p < 0.01$

cities. However, this situation differs in cities below Tier 4, where mid-high net worth households spend significantly more on commercial insurance than non mid-high net worth households.

2. *Heterogeneity of household investable assets for household business insurance expenditures*

Based on the head's income level, the sample was divided into two groups, with higher and lower household income levels, and grouped into regressions. Columns (1)–(2) of Table 8 show the regression results based on income heterogeneity. The results show that the effect of household investable assets on the commercial insurance expenditures of households with higher income levels is not significant; however, there is a significant positive effect on the commercial insurance expenditures of households with lower income levels.

The sample was divided into two groups, urban and rural, and grouped into regressions based on household location. Columns (3) and (4) of Table 8 show the regression results based on urban–rural heterogeneity. The results show that the effect of household investable assets on commercial insurance expenditure is significantly positive for both urban and rural households; however, the effect is greater for urban households.

Based on the location of the households in the sample, the urban sample was further divided into four groups: first-tier cities, second-tier cities, third-tier cities, and fourth-tier cities, and the regressions were conducted in groups; the results are summarized in Table 9. The results show that the effect of household investable assets on household business insurance expenditure in tier 2 cities is significantly positive. In contrast, none of the effects on household business insurance expenditure in the remaining classes of cities are significant. This finding indicates that the impact of household investable assets on household business insurance expenditure differs for households in cities of different classes. Therefore, for specific questions, a specific

**Table 8** Regression results of the effect of household investable assets on household business insurance expenditures (income and urban–rural heterogeneity)

| | Commercial insurance expenses | | | |
|---|---|---|---|---|
| | (1) | (2) | (3) | (4) |
| Income heterogeneity | High income | low income | | |
| Urban–rural heterogeneity | | | Urban | Rural |
| Investable assets | 25.89<br>(32.58) | $18.55^{*}$<br>(10.96) | $57.50^{**}$<br>(24.92) | $38.72^{**}$<br>(16.19) |
| Household-level control variables | Yes | Yes | Yes | Yes |
| Control variables at household head level | Yes | Yes | Yes | Yes |
| Fixed effects of provinces | Yes | Yes | Yes | Yes |
| Constant | $-48{,}766^{***}$<br>(4,750) | $-1{,}158^{**}$<br>(536.3) | $-10{,}456^{***}$<br>(1,607) | $-2{,}889^{**}$<br>(1,167) |
| Observations | 4,219 | 4,556 | 4,772 | 4,003 |
| R-squared | 0.161 | 0.084 | 0.168 | 0.136 |

*Note* $^{*}$ $p < 0.1$, $^{**}$ $p < 0.05$, $^{***}$ $p < 0.01$

**Table 9** Regression results for the effect of household investable assets on household business insurance expenditures (urban heterogeneity)

| | Commercial insurance expenses | | | |
|---|---|---|---|---|
| | (1) | (2) | (3) | (4) |
| Urban heterogeneity | First-tier cities | Second-tier cities | Third-tier cities | Fourth-tier cities and below |
| Investable assets | −33.871<br>(−0.36) | 111.107*<br>(1.87) | 34.657<br>(0.46) | 46.962<br>(1.64) |
| Household-level control variables | Yes | Yes | Yes | Yes |
| Control variables at household head level | Yes | Yes | Yes | Yes |
| Fixed effects of provinces | Yes | Yes | Yes | Yes |
| Constant | −13,845.723**<br>(−2.19) | −9,353.343***<br>(−2.58) | −1,912.185<br>(−0.53) | −8,734.254***<br>(−4.45) |
| Observations | 584 | 906 | 391 | 2,891 |
| R-squared | 0.251 | 0.175 | 0.219 | 0.173 |

*Note* * $p < 0.1$, ** $p < 0.05$, *** $p < 0.01$

analysis should be conducted according to the different cities in which the households are located.

## 6 Summary

This chapter analyzes the allocation of commercial insurance for mid-high net worth households. The main findings are as follows.

For example, households in urban areas have greater commercial insurance coverage than those in rural areas. In urban areas, households' commercial insurance coverage rate is close to 50%; that is, almost half of urban households have purchased commercial insurance. However, the commercial insurance coverage rate of households in rural areas is relatively low (approximately 30%). There is no significant urban–rural difference in the commercial insurance coverage rate of mid-high net worth households, while there is a certain urban–rural gap in the commercial insurance coverage rate of non mid-high net worth households. The commercial insurance coverage rates of mid-high net worth households and non mid-high net worth households show a trend of first increasing and then decreasing with an increase in population size, which is the same as the overall trend.

Second, the higher the educational level of the heads of mid-high net worth families and non mid-high net worth families, the higher the commercial insurance coverage rate of the family. The better the health status of the household head, the higher the commercial insurance coverage rate. For the marital status of the head of household, the difference between the commercial insurance coverage rate of unmarried and non-high-net-worth households was 28.33 percentage points; in the married group, the difference was 32.99 percentage points; in the cohabiting group, the difference was 22.35 percentage points; in the divorced group, the difference was 17.58 percentage points; and in the widowed group, the difference was 17.73 percentage points.

Third, for the middle and high net-worth households, the mean amount of household commercial insurance expenditure for the neighborhood council household sample is ¥2,679.74, which is higher than that of the village council household sample. The mean commercial insurance expenditure of mid-high net worth households first shows a small increase and then a decreasing trend with an increase in population. For the education level of the head of household, the difference between the mean amount of commercial insurance expenditure of mid-high net worth households and the mean amount of commercial insurance expenditure of non mid-high net worth households was significant. The difference in the mean amount of household business insurance expenditure is caused by the difference in the marital status of the heads of middle/high net-worth households and non-middle/high net-worth households. The average business insurance expenditure of households with divorced heads was significantly higher than that of the other groups. Except for the cohabitation group, the difference in the average business insurance expenditure between mid-high net worth households and non-high-net-worth households was more obvious. The mean amount of business insurance expenditure is higher among mid-high net worth households headed by males, while the mean amount of business insurance expenditure is higher among non mid-high net worth households headed by females.

Fourth, for mid-high net worth households, the average per capita expenditure on commercial insurance for the sample of households in the neighborhood council is higher than that of the sample of households in the village council by ¥1,427.95. The average amount of per capita expenditure on commercial insurance for both mid-high net worth households and non mid-high net worth households decreases as the number of household members increases, and the gap between them becomes smaller. For the education level of the head of household, the average amount of per capita commercial insurance expenditure of mid-high net worth households is significantly higher than the average amount of per capita commercial insurance expenditure of non mid-high net worth households. The mean amount of per capita business insurance expenditure of the mid-high net worth households with unmarried heads is higher than that of the non mid-high net worth households by ¥1302.48; the difference between the two in the married group is ¥1098.98; the difference between the two in the cohabitation group is ¥308.33; the difference between the two in the divorce group is ¥3428.96; and the difference between the two in the widowed group is ¥1852.3. Among mid-high net worth families, the difference between the average amount of per capita household commercial insurance expenditure of heads of different genders is RMB 354.67, which is small. In contrast, the difference between the two is RMB 324.38, which is not obvious.

Fifth, mid-high net worth households spend about ¥1,744 more on annual commercial insurance than non mid-high net worth households. This indicates that mid-high net worth households invest more money in commercial insurance allocation and demand more commercial insurance coverage. For every 1% increase in household investable assets, household commercial insurance spending will increase by about ¥48. Mid-high net worth households increased their commercial insurance participation by 0.409 units compared with non mid-high net worth households, demonstrating the significant positive effect of mid-high net worth households on raising the level of commercial insurance participation. For every 1% increase in household investable assets, the probability of a household purchasing commercial insurance increased by 0.043 percentage points.

## References


1. Xu, J., Li, P.: Study on the structural characteristics and drivers of commercial insurance in Chinese household asset allocation. Insurance Res. 15–29 (2020)
2. Xia, S.: More than one million high net worth individuals in China 95% choose to buy commercial life insurance. Popular Financial Advisor, 28–29 (2016)
3. Wang, X., Wang, H.: Review and prospect of the development of China's insurance industry since the reform and opening up. J. Beijing Univ. Technol. Bus.: Soc. Sci. Edition **35**, 91–104 (2020)
4. Xu, X.: The development of China's insurance industry and further financial opening: a review and outlook on the 20th anniversary of China's WTO accession under the new opening pattern. Insurance Theory and Practice, 1–35 (2021)
5. Sun, Q., Suo, L., Zheng, W.: China's insurance industry: developments and prospects. In: Cummins, J.D., Venard, B. (eds.) Handbook of International Insurance: Between Global Dynamics and Local Contingencies, pp. 597–640. Springer, Boston, MA (2007)
6. Wang, Y., Zhang, D., Wang, X., Fu, Q.: How does COVID-19 affect China's insurance market? Emerg. Mark. Financ. Trade **56**, 2350–2362 (2020)
7. Wang, X.: China's insurance protection level still needs to be improved. Financial Times, p. 1 (2020)
8. Sigma: World Insurance: Riding Out the 2020 Pandemic Storm, pp. 1–34. Swiss Re Institute, London (2020)
9. Yin, Z., Yan, Y., Jiang, J.: Income volatility, social networks, and household demand for commercial insurance. Stud. Finance Econ. 52–61 (2021)
10. Yue, Q., Pei, G.: Survey report on demand for commercial health insurance in China. In: China's Commercial Health Insurance, Foundation (CDRF), C.D.R., Ed.; Routledge, London (2020)
11. Zeng, L., Xing, S.: A study on the impact of Internet finance on household commercial insurance participation—an empirical analysis based on CHFS. J. Wuhan Univ. Technol.: Soc. Sci. Edition **34**, 126–134 (2021)
12. Wu, A., Zheng, X.: Assortative matching and commercial insurance participation: evidence from the China household finance survey. J. Asian Econ. **80**, 101459 (2022)
13. Taikang; PKU. China Household Life Insurance Demand Study Report; Taikang Life Insurance Co., Ltd., China Center for Insurance and Social Security Research, Peking University, Beijing (2011)
14. Gu, J.: Research on community livelihood monitoring and governance: the "five development concepts" and community livelihood development index. Economic Daily Press, Beijing (2021)
15. Jin, L.: Experimental discussion on the differences between village councils and neighborhood councils. Agric. Archaeol. **3**, 297–299 (2012)

16. Fu, Y., Su, Z.: Analysis of factors influencing the purchase of commercial insurance by urban and rural households in China. J. Harbin Univ. Commerce: Soc. Sci. Edition 17–28 (2016)
17. Wang, Q.: Analysis of differential pricing strategies for urban and rural commercial insurance. Hainan Finance, 62–64 (2010)
18. CRIED: Rural Health Protection Survey Report; Center for Research on Insurance and Economic Development, Chinese Academy of Social Sciences, Beijing (2020)
19. Qiu, F.: Experimental analysis of the impact of aging on the purchase of commercial insurance by households—an empirical analysis based on CHFS2017. Western Finance Account. 65–69 (2020)
20. Yang, F.: Does entrepreneurship influence household business insurance purchase decisions?—Based on 2018 CFPS data. Bus. Econ. 180–184 (2021)
21. Wang, X., Yan, J., Jia, H., Li, Y.L.: The impact of marriage on household life insurance demand—an empirical study based on the China household finance survey (CHFS). Financ. Rev. **12**, 96–107 (2020)
22. Christiansen, C., Joensen, J.S., Rangvid, J.: Understanding the effects of marriage and divorce on financial investments: the role of background risk sharing. Econ. Inq. **53**, 431–447 (2015)
23. WDPURC: Insurance Market Segment Insights Report; Water Drop Protection User Research Center, Beijing (2021)
24. Wang, X.: Analysis of insurance interest relationship between unmarried cohabitants—a personal insurance case as an analytical perspective. J. Insurance Vocational College **27**, 76–77 (2013)
25. Yu, J., Xie, Y.: Analysis of the status of cohabitation before first marriage and the factors influencing it among Chinese residents. Population Res. 5–18 (2017)
26. Sun, A., Qi, N.: How high net worth individuals optimize asset allocation with insurance. Financ. Econ. 32–33 (2017)
27. Webb, B.L., Flitner, A.L., Trupin, J.: Commercial insurance. Commercial Insurance, New York (1996)
28. Gao, L., Guan, J., Wang, G.: Does media-based health risk communication affect commercial health insurance demand? Evidence from China. Appl. Econ. **54**, 2122–2134 (2022)
29. Sun, W., Zhao, M.: Lasso-based analysis of factors affecting business insurance. Adv. Appl. Math. **10**, 4153–4161 (2021)
30. Aldrich, H.E., Cliff, J.E.: The pervasive effects of family on entrepreneurship: toward a family embeddedness perspective. J. Bus. Ventur. **18**, 573–596 (2003)

# Chapter 6
# Allocation of Children's Commercial Health Insurance for Mid-High Net Worth Families

**Abstract** This chapter analyzes the allocation of children's commercial health insurance for mid-high net worth families. The results show that the coverage rate of children's commercial medical insurance for mid-high net worth families is significantly higher than that of non mid-high net worth families; there are some differences in the trends in the average cost of children's commercial medical insurance for mid-high net worth households and non mid-high net worth households; the average cost of children's commercial medical insurance is significantly higher for girls than for boys in mid-high net worth families, whereas the average cost for boys is higher than for girls in non mid-high net worth families; mid-high net worth households invest more money in children's commercial health insurance and have more demand for children's commercial health insurance. This also shows that mid-high net worth families can provide better insurance coverage for their children.

Commercial health insurance refers to insurance companies that pay benefits for losses caused by health reasons through sickness insurance, medical insurance and loss of income insurance for disabilities. With the increasing importance of health, commercial health insurance has developed rapidly in recent years, leading to an entire insurance industry. From 2007 to 2017, the compound annual growth rate was 27.6% [1]. Commercial health insurance has become an important force in China's healthcare reform, playing an increasingly prominent role in the multi-level medical security system. In 2020, the commercial health insurance premium income exceeded 800 billion yuan, accounting for 30% of the income from the basic medical insurance fund, and commercial health insurance payouts accounted for more than 10% of the basic medical insurance fund expenditure. In 2020, 13 departments, including the China Banking and Insurance Regulatory Commission (CBIRC), jointly issued "Opinions on Promoting the Development of Commercial Insurance in Social Services," which clearly proposed striving for the commercial health insurance market size to exceed 2 trillion yuan by 2025. Commercial health insurance has considerable space for development. The coverage rate of commercial health insurance in the United States is approximately 70% [2], whereas that in China is only up to 10% [3]. It can be seen that there is still a large gap between China's



J. Gu, *Wealth Management Report for Mid-High Net Worth Families*, Spatial Demography and Population Governance, https://doi.org/10.1007/978-981-97-0387-6_6

commercial health insurance market and the markets of developed Western countries. This indicates that the development potential of China's commercial health insurance market is significant.

With the rapid development of China's economy, many mid-high net worth individuals have gradually emerged. In general, this group of people generally pursues a better quality of life, pays attention to and values the physical and mental health of individuals and their families, has relatively high requirements for medical conditions and services, and finds it difficult to endure the difficulties, restrictions, and poor medical experiences of visiting doctors. In response to the needs of this group of people, medium and high-end commercial medical insurance products have emerged one after another in the commercial health insurance market. With the features of "high coverage, less restrictions and better services," mid-high end commercial medical insurance products have attracted more and more attention from the mid-high net worth groups and become an important part of the insurance allocation for mid-high net worth families. Mid-high net worth families generally face the problem of family wealth inheritance [4], and therefore pay particular attention to the education and health of their children. This chapter focuses on allocating children's commercial medical insurance for mid-high net worth families; that is, the allocation of commercial medical insurance for children aged 16 and below. The allocation of commercial medical insurance to this segment has generally been neglected, but its potential is significant. Providing protection for children's health from an early age is a core component of commercial insurance allocations, especially for mid-high net worth families.

## 1 Basic Information of Children's Commercial Medical Insurance

Children's commercial medical insurance, also known as children's commercial health insurance, is an insurance company that provides a certain amount of coverage for the costs of treatment, hospitalization, and surgery incurred by minor children due to illness. Children represent the future and hope of the country. It is a common wish of countries worldwide for children to grow healthy and strong. Countries around the world generally attach importance to children's health and have designed and provided affordable, multilevel, comprehensive, and higher-level medical coverage for children. Commercial insurance companies play an increasingly important role in children's healthcare systems. For example, not only are there an increasing number of health- and medical-related insurance policies for children in the commercial insurance market in Japan, but there are also some comprehensive insurance policies that integrate medical care, childcare, and education investment, equivalent to a family insurance package and are sought after by Japanese families [5]. In the United States, there are significant differences in access to healthcare among children with commercial health insurance, those without commercial health insurance, and those with Medicaid coverage for the poor [6]. Commercial health insurance participation can affect a child's healthy development. For example, children who participate in Medicaid are more likely to be overweight or obese than those who participate in commercial health insurance [7]. In the information age, Electronic Health Record (EHR) databases are often used to monitor children's commercial health insurance status, which has become an important channel for agencies to develop mechanisms to help sick children access and maintain insurance coverage interventions [8].

The emergence of commercial health insurance for children has played an important role in protecting their health and reducing the burden of healthcare on their families. For example, in the United States, 12 percent of all children enrolled in commercial health insurance plans have special healthcare needs, and nearly 40 percent have emotional or behavioral disorders. These disorders are more limiting than chronic physical illnesses, are more difficult to diagnose and treat, and can be more severely detrimental to children's quality of life and physical and mental health [9]. The emergence and development of commercial medical insurance for children is an important complement to basic medical insurance. In China, basic medical insurance for children falls within the scope of basic medical insurance for urban and rural residents, basic medical insurance for urban residents, and the new rural cooperative medical insurance. However, there are obvious regional differences in the existing basic medical insurance for children, and there are problems such as duplicate enrollment and the omission of insurance. In some regions, the basic medical insurance for children may be doubled. For example, Shanghai has established a mutual fund for the hospitalization of primary and secondary school students, infants, and children to further improve the level of medical protection for children in the city [10]. The emergence of commercial medical insurance for children can effectively complement the existing basic medical insurance for children, giving different families more options and diversifying the medical insurance system for children.

From a family perspective, children's health is vulnerable to threats owing to their relatively poor physical adaptability, weak ability to resist diseases, naturally active nature, weak ability to recognize potential dangers, and poor ability to save themselves in the event of accidents. Numerous studies have shown that children are more prone to accidental personal injuries than adults [11, 12]. Consequently, there is a growing demand for commercial medical insurance for children among families [13]. A distinctive feature of children's commercial medical insurance is that the policyholder and the insured are separate and generally not the same person. In families, the decision to purchase children's commercial medical insurance is generally made by the parents who pay the premiums are paid by parents [9]. Therefore, parents are key factors influencing children's commercial medical insurance. Parents of mid-high net worth families generally have a sense of planning ahead, not only considering the elimination of factors that threaten their children's health but also providing as good conditions as possible for their children's medical treatment in case of illness. Therefore, they are willing to buy mid- to high-end children's commercial medical insurance for their children.

However, research on children's commercial medical insurance in China is lacking [14]. Panoramic and systematic studies and portrayals of children's commercial medical insurance are insufficient. Therefore, breakthroughs in this area are urgently needed. For families, children are the continuation of the family and the heirs of family property. If a child's physical and mental health can be effectively protected, it will not only reduce the burden on the family but also allow parents to devote themselves to production and construction without distractions. In the insurance industry, there are relatively few commercial medical insurance products for children, and the market potential has not been effectively explored. Therefore, it is necessary to strengthen the research on the population and market segments to provide a basis for designing and launching attractive insurance products. Children are the future and hope of the country and the reserve of the future workforce. Therefore, ensuring the healthy growth of children is an important foundation for developing a country's economy and ensuring social stability. Thus, research in this area is significant.

## 2 Children's Commercial Medical Insurance Coverage

The children's commercial health insurance coverage rate was equal to the number of children covered by commercial health insurance in the sample divided by the total number of children in the sample. This is an important indicator of the prevalence of children's commercial health insurance and reflects the extent of insurance coverage among children.

### *2.1 Age Grouping*

The commercial health insurance coverage rates for the full sample of children were calculated based on the 2020 CFPS survey data, and the results are summarized in Fig. 1. As shown in Fig. 1, the coverage rate for young children aged 0 to 7 years is higher than that for children aged 8 to 16 years. The highest coverage rate of 23.61% was for ages 4 to 7 years, and the lowest coverage rate of 21.05% was for ages 12 to 16 years. This may indicate that parents of children born within the last few years are more willing to purchase commercial medical insurance. In recent years, parents have become more aware of the need to obtain commercial medical insurance for their children as early as possible to protect them from an early age. Overall, 20% of the families purchased commercial medical insurance for their children. This is consistent with data from a previous survey. A survey of 814 preschool children in six community health service centers in Qiaokou District, Wuhan City, showed that 24.63% of the children had commercial medical insurance [15]. This percentage is quite high compared to the 10% coverage rate of commercial medical insurance for the entire population in China. This indicates that parents were more willing to purchase commercial medical insurance for their children.

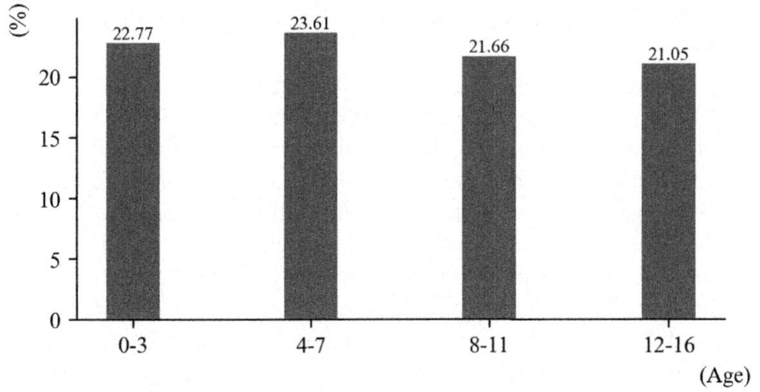


**Fig. 1** Commercial medical insurance coverage for children in the full sample (age group)

This study separately calculates the coverage rates of children's commercial medical insurance for different age groups of mid-high net worth families and non mid-high net worth families; the results are summarized in Fig. 2.

As shown in Fig. 2, the coverage rate of children's commercial medical insurance for mid-high net worth families is significantly higher than that of non mid-high net worth families, with the coverage rate of the former exceeding 30%, while the coverage rate of the latter is approximately 20%. This indicates that family financial conditions may be a key factor for parents in deciding whether to purchase commercial medical insurance for their children. Parents of mid-high net worth families are more conscious of their children's health protection and are, therefore, more likely to buy commercial medical insurance for their children from an early age. In addition, the data in Fig. 2 shows that the coverage rate of commercial medical insurance for

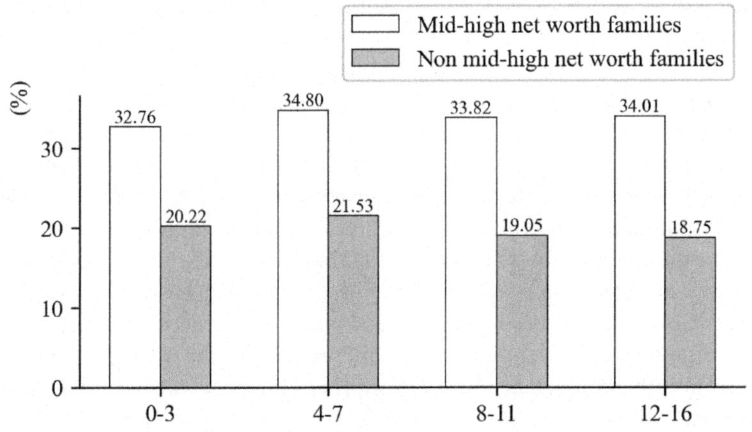


**Fig. 2** Coverage of children's commercial medical insurance for mid-high net worth households and non mid-high net worth households (age group)

children in the 0–3-year-old group was 12.54 percentage points higher than that of non mid-high net worth households; the 4–7-year-old group was 13.27 percentage points higher; the 8–11 year-old group was 14.77 percentage points higher; and the 12–16-year-old group was 15.26 percentage points higher. These results indicate that the gap in children's commercial medical insurance coverage between mid-high net worth households and between non mid-high net worth households gradually increases with age. Overall, families with children born in recent years have a strong willingness to insure, and the gap between the coverage rates of mid-high net worth families and non mid-high net worth families tends to decrease. This suggests that in recent years, parents of families other than mid-high net worth families have gradually realized the importance of purchasing commercial medical insurance for their children. This indicates the impact of a family financial situation on children's health [16].

## 2.2 *Household Grouping*

There may be significant urban–rural regional differences in the development of commercial medical insurance. Based on CFPS data, this book calculates commercial medical insurance coverage rates for children in agricultural, non-agricultural, and residential households, and the results are summarized in Fig. 3. The difference between non-agricultural and resident households is that resident households are classified as urban or township households, whereas non-agricultural households are a type of urban household, and the people concerned are mainly flexibly employed. The coverage rate of commercial medical insurance for children in agricultural households is the lowest at 19.17%; the coverage rate for non-agricultural households is 29.02%; and the coverage rate for resident households is the highest at 36.03%. The coverage rate of non-agricultural households is 9.85 percentage points higher than that of agricultural households, which indicates a significant urban–rural difference in households' willingness to purchase commercial medical insurance for children. This is consistent with the findings of a previous study [14]. A survey study based on the Pinggu area of Beijing showed that by 2005, the local children's health insurance coverage rate had risen to 54%, with comparable coverage rates for farmers' and non-farmers' children. However, 76% of insured farmers' children were enrolled in a low-premium plan that protected against only major medical events, compared to 42% of insured non-farmers' children [17]. In other words, there was little difference between children in urban and rural areas regarding basic medical insurance coverage. However, concerning commercial medical insurance coverage, rural children are significantly lower than urban children; that is, the urban–rural gap is still evident. This urban–rural gap is not only seen in Beijing but is also similar throughout the country.

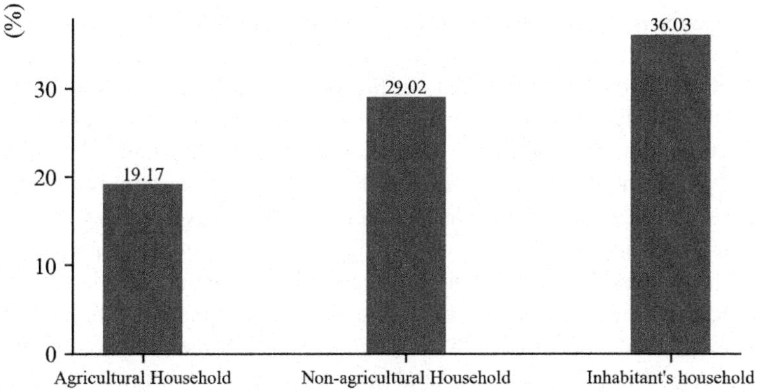


**Fig. 3** Commercial medical insurance coverage for children in the full sample (household group)

It separately calculates the coverage rates of children's commercial medical insurance for different household sizes of mid-high net worth families and non mid-high net worth families, and the results are summarized in Fig. 4.

According to Fig. 4, there is a 12.88 percentage-point-difference between the coverage rates of children's commercial medical insurance for mid-high net worth households in agricultural households and non mid-high net worth households; a 9.51 percentage-point-difference between the two in non-agricultural households; and a 7.57 percentage-point-difference between the two in residential households. The above results indicate a significant difference in the willingness to insure between mid-high net worth households and non mid-high net worth households in different household subgroups, and that people with good economic conditions are more willing to insure. The gap between the coverage rate of children's commercial medical

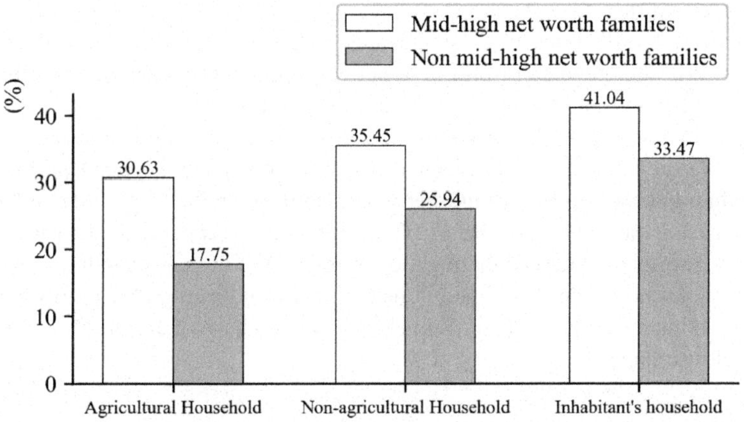


**Fig. 4** Coverage rate of children's commercial medical insurance for mid-high net worth families and non mid-high net worth families (household group)

insurance is the largest among mid-high net worth families in agricultural households and non mid-high net worth families. This may indirectly reflect the large gap in education and economic levels among the population in agricultural households, which is the smallest among the resident households after the household registration system reform, and the coverage rate is relatively higher than the other two groups. In recent years, the areas where the household registration system reform has been implemented have gradually increased, which may be a side verification that, in recent years, an increasing number of households are choosing to purchase commercial medical insurance. Previous research has also shown that smaller household size, higher income levels, at least one form of hospitalization, and living in rural areas are significantly associated with lower coverage rates of commercial medical insurance for children [18]. In other words, rural non mid-high net worth families have low commercial medical insurance coverage for children and, therefore, need to be given more attention and medical coverage.

## 2.3 Gender Grouping

As shown in Fig. 5, the commercial medical insurance coverage rate of children by gender observed in the full sample was 22.42% for males and 21.96% for females. The males' were slightly higher than the females', but there was no significant difference between the two groups. This result may indicate that parents tend to place equal importance on their sons and daughters, breaking the traditional "son preference." Overall, children's commercial health insurance coverage needs to be improved [19]. Because of the persistently low rates of children's commercial health insurance coverage for girls, there is a need to strengthen health insurance and coverage for girls to ensure that they have the same level of children's commercial health insurance coverage.

It separately calculates the coverage rates of children's commercial medical insurance for different genders of mid-high net worth households and non mid-high net worth households, and the results are summarized in Fig. 6.

As shown in Fig. 6, there is a 14.6 percentage point difference in the coverage rate of children's commercial medical insurance for males between mid-high net worth families and non mid-high net worth families and a 13.1 percentage-point-difference in the coverage rate of children's commercial medical insurance for females. However, when comparing the coverage rates of males and females in each type of household, the difference is insignificant, indicating that family financial strength remains the main factor influencing the purchase of children's commercial medical insurance.

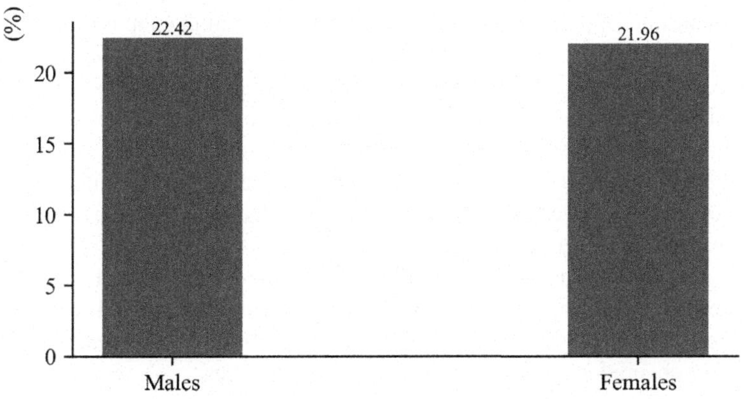


**Fig. 5** Commercial medical insurance coverage for children in the full sample (gender group)

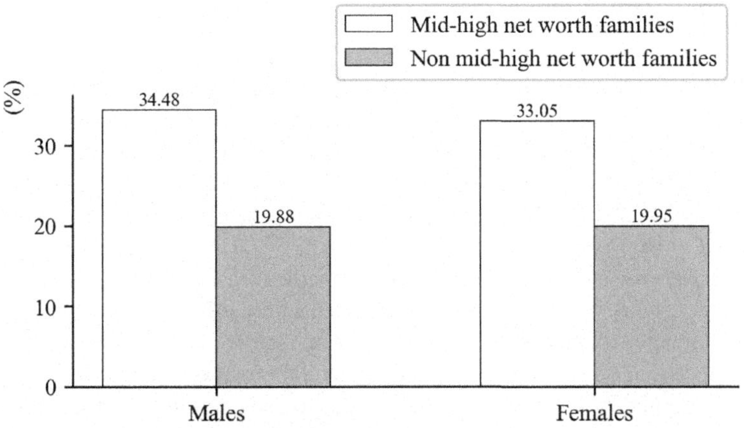


**Fig. 6** Coverage rate of children's commercial medical insurance for mid-high net worth families and non mid-high net worth families (gender group)

# 3 Situation of Children's Commercial Medical Insurance Cost

Children's medical costs are an important factor affecting commercial medical insurance expenditures. Accurate measurement is a prerequisite and basis for the optimal management of children's medical expenses and the determination of children's commercial medical insurance expenditures [20]. From the perspective of family insurance decision-making, an important indicator is the family's annual expenditure on commercial medical insurance for children, which is an integral part of family expenditure. From the current pricing of children's commercial medical insurance products, the low premiums are tens of dollars per year, and the high premiums are tens of thousands of dollars per year. As shown, the premium gap is relatively large. Different families choose to purchase their children's commercial medical insurance at different price points depending on their own financial conditions and the child's situation. The scope of children's commercial medical insurance offered by insurance companies varies. For example, some commercial insurance policies do not cover the cost of outpatient visits to doctors for children; however, some commercial insurance policies cover the cost of outpatient visits. When visiting an outpatient clinic, parents should choose a commercial insurance policy with a higher claims amount and claims for specific diseases. In addition, mid-high net worth families are better off and, therefore, choose maternal and child commercial insurance [21]. This type of commercial insurance generally covers upcoming babies. Babies can be effectively covered, even if born with congenital diseases.

## *3.1 Age Grouping*

Annual household expenditures on children's commercial health insurance are generally correlated with age. The average cost of children's commercial medical insurance for the full sample was calculated based on the 2020 CFPS data and is summarized in Fig. 7. The difference between ages 0 to 3 and 4 to 7 was insignificant, with a difference of ¥229.99 between the two age groups; the difference between ages 8 to 11 and 12 to 16 was larger, with a difference of ¥374.04 between the two age groups. The average cost of children's commercial medical insurance for ages 0 to 7 was significant. This result may be because children's immunity is relatively weak due to their young age, coupled with a low sense of self-protection, which makes medical risks higher, and therefore the cost of commercial medical insurance for children is relatively higher. A distinction must be made between children's critical illness and medical health insurances. For the former, the younger the child, the less expensive it is. However, the opposite is true for children's healthcare insurance, in which costs usually decrease with age. In other words, the younger the child, the higher the cost. Children under the age of 7 are susceptible to disease because their immune systems are not fully established. This is a high-risk group for insurance companies; therefore, the cost of commercial medical insurance for children is higher. When children grow beyond the age of 7, their immune systems are established, the risk of developing diseases is greatly reduced, and the cost of commercial medical insurance is low. This coincides with Fig. 7.

The cost of children's commercial medical insurance varies depending on the financial situation of the family. This book calculates the average cost of children's commercial medical insurance for mid-high net worth families and non mid-high net worth families separately, and the results are summarized in Fig. 8.

As shown in Fig. 8, there are some differences in the trends in the mean child commercial medical insurance costs for middle and high net worth households and non-middle and high net worth households under the age group of 0 to 7 years.

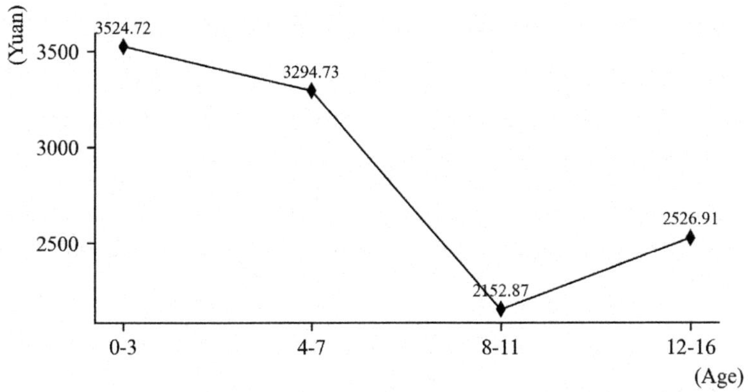


**Fig. 7** Average cost of commercial medical insurance for children in the full sample (age group)

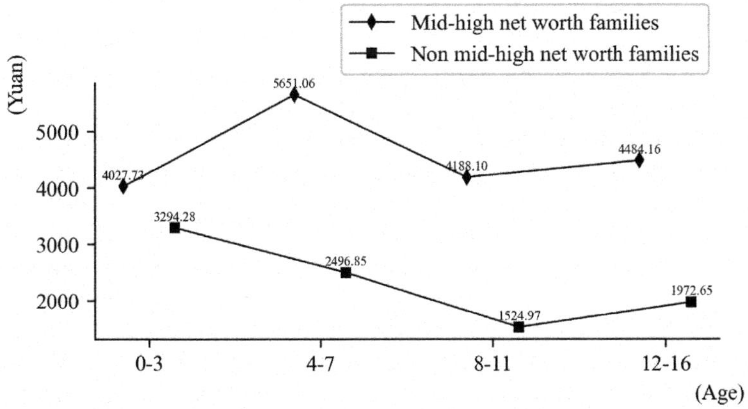


**Fig. 8** Average cost of children's commercial medical insurance for mid-high net worth families and non mid-high net worth families (age group)

First, the average cost of children's commercial medical insurance for 0 to 7 years for mid-high net worth households shows a significant increasing trend, whereas non mid-high net worth households show a decreasing trend. Second, the difference between mid-high net worth families and non mid-high net worth families is the smallest in the age group of 0 to 3 years, with a difference of ¥733.45. After the child turns 3, the gap between the average cost of children's commercial medical insurance for mid-high net worth families and non mid-high net worth families becomes larger, with a difference of ¥3,154.21 at ages 4 to 7; ¥2,663.13 at ages 8 to 11; and ¥2,511.51 at ages 12 to 16. Overall, the cost of children's commercial medical insurance is significantly higher for mid-high net worth families than for non mid-high net worth families after four years of age. This result may indicate that when the children of non mid-high net worth families grow up, they may choose commercial medical insurance categories with fewer insurance guarantee items and relatively lower costs due to their financial condition; however, mid-HNW families still choose more items for their children. In other words, mid-high net worth families have certain financial strength and hope that their children will not have to go to the general ward with a poor environment when they get sick and receive treatment, but can enter the special needs department, international department, VIP department of public hospitals or high-end private hospitals, and other wards with good conditions to receive medical treatment. Therefore, they will choose the mid-high-end children's commercial medical insurance with relatively more premiums.

## *3.2 Household Grouping*

This study separately calculates the average cost of commercial medical insurance for children in the full sample of different household types and summarizes them in Fig. 9.

Figure 9 reports the average cost of children's commercial medical insurance for different household types. Notably, agricultural households receive land compensation during rural land expropriation, and they tend to purchase commercial insurance, including children's commercial medical insurance, after losing their land security. The difference in the average cost of children's commercial medical insurance between non-agricultural households and residential households is 621.45 yuan, which is a small difference; however, the difference is larger with agricultural households, at 2084.08 yuan. The above results show the large gap between the cost of commercial medical insurance for children in urban and rural areas in China.

Figure 10 reports the average cost of children's commercial medical insurance for mid-high net worth households versus non mid-high net worth households.

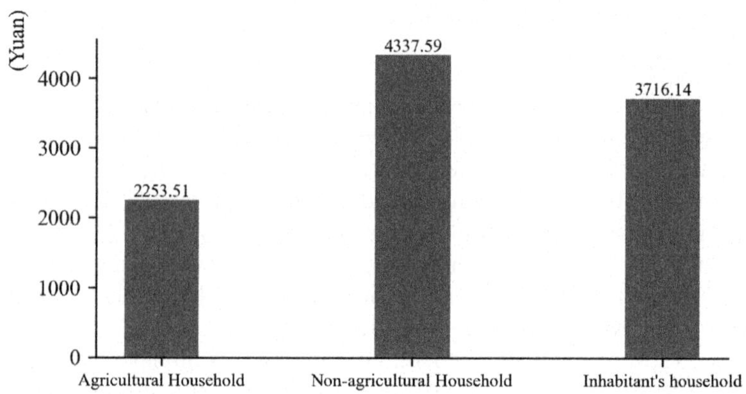


**Fig. 9** Average cost of commercial medical insurance for children in the full sample (household group)

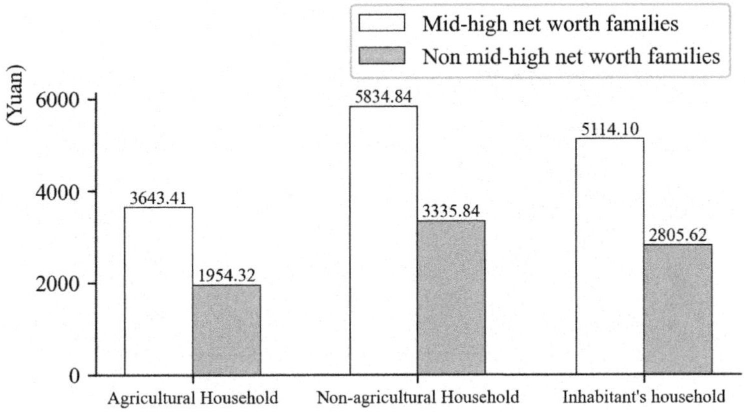


**Fig. 10** Average cost of children's commercial medical insurance for mid-high net worth families and non mid-high net worth families (household group)

The difference between the agricultural household group is ¥1,689.09, the smallest difference; the difference between the non-agricultural household group is ¥2,499, the largest difference; and the difference between the resident household group is ¥2,308.48. The above results show that there is still a large difference between the average cost of children's commercial medical insurance for mid-high net worth families and non mid-high net worth families when analyzed by household registration type. As a transitional state, non-agricultural households are, on the whole, more willing to purchase commercial medical insurance for the children in their families.

### *3.3 Gender Grouping*

The sample is grouped according to sex, and the average cost of commercial medical insurance for the full sample of children is calculated separately and summarized in Fig. 11.

Based on the results of the data analysis in Fig. 11, the difference between the average cost of children's commercial health insurance for males and females was smaller, differing by only ¥268.60. This situation differs from the demand for commercial health insurance for the entire population sample, including adults. For example, some studies have shown that men are less likely to purchase commercial health insurance than women, which may be because women are more risk-aware, risk-averse, and more likely to transfer health risk issues by taking out health insurance [22]. Because the purchase decision for children's commercial health insurance in the family is made by the parents, gender does not influence their purchase choice.

Overall, the average cost of commercial medical insurance for children was higher for males than for females. One important reason is that boys are more likely to be

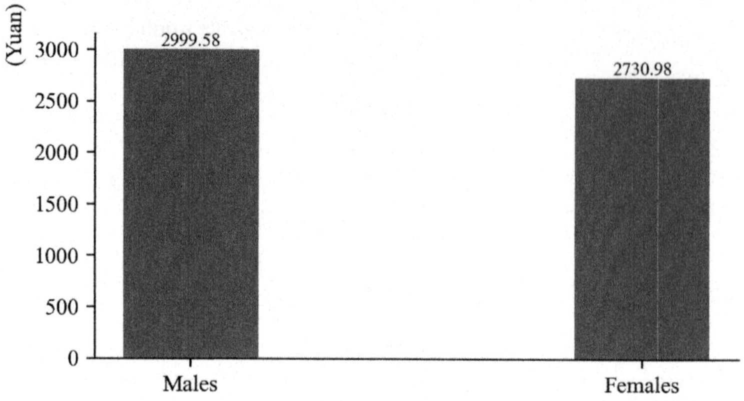


**Fig. 11** Average cost of commercial medical insurance for children in the full sample (gender group)

sick than girls. For example, studies have shown that boys are more likely than girls to experience stunting from early infancy to the age 3 [23]. Boys are more likely than girls to experience malnutrition [24]. The effect of sex hormones on immune function in boys may also make them more susceptible to infectious diseases than girls. In addition, boys are more active and adventurous by nature and engage in a wider range of activities; therefore, they are more likely to experience injuries such as trauma, fractures, and infections than girls. Consequently, families pay more for boys than for girls regarding their children's medical insurance costs.

As shown in Fig. 12, the average cost of children's commercial health insurance was significantly higher for girls than for boys in mid-high net worth households, whereas the average cost was higher for boys than for girls in non mid-high net worth households. This was a significant social phenomenon. For mid-high net worth families, the overall level of commercial health insurance coverage for children was higher. With more effective health and medical coverage for children, mid-high net worth families tend to invest more in critical illness insurance for girls. Typically, the cost of commercial critical illness insurance is higher for girls than for boys. Mid-high net worth families have sufficient financial resources to purchase better commercial critical illness insurance for girls in their families. In addition, depending on the girl's health condition and specific illnesses, mid-high net worth families will also add some special coverage involving girls and purchase the corresponding special commercial medical insurance. Therefore, the cost of commercial medical insurance for girls purchased by mid-high net worth families was higher than that for boys.

In addition, Fig. 12 also shows that the difference in the average cost of children's commercial medical insurance between mid-high net worth households and non mid-high net worth households is larger, with a difference of ¥1,526.87 in the average cost for boys; and ¥3,458.92 in the average cost for girls. This may indicate that the difference between the values placed on girls by mid-high net worth families and non mid-high net worth families is greater, with better-off families being more willing

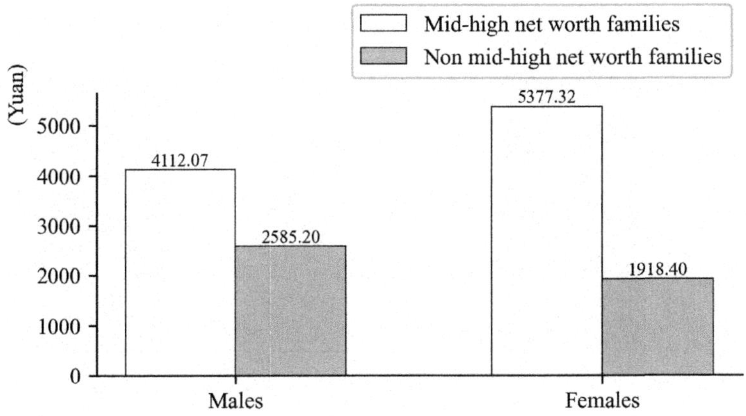


**Fig. 12** Average cost of children's commercial medical insurance for mid-high net worth families and non mid-high net worth families (gender group)

to purchase higher amounts of insurance for girls. Of course, this may not only be caused by the difference in families' economic conditions but may also be related to parents' perceptions. Therefore, this issue must also be analyzed for specific family situations and cannot be generalized.

## 4 Children's Health and Commercial Medical Insurance

The relationship between individual health and the need for commercial medical insurance is a common concern in both academia and industry [25]. An important purpose of purchasing commercial medical insurance for children is to allow them to receive better treatment for eventual recovery when they are sick and require medical treatment, which can effectively reduce the family's burden in terms of medical care. For children at home, there is generally a correlation between their health status and their parents' purchase of commercial medical insurance.

### *4.1 Sickness*

It calculates the proportion of the full sample purchasing children's commercial medical insurance in terms of whether they were sick in the past month, and the results are summarized in Fig. 13.

As shown in Fig. 13, children being sick in the past month did not significantly impact parents purchasing commercial health insurance. There is only a small difference of 3.1 percentage points between the percentage of children who had an illness

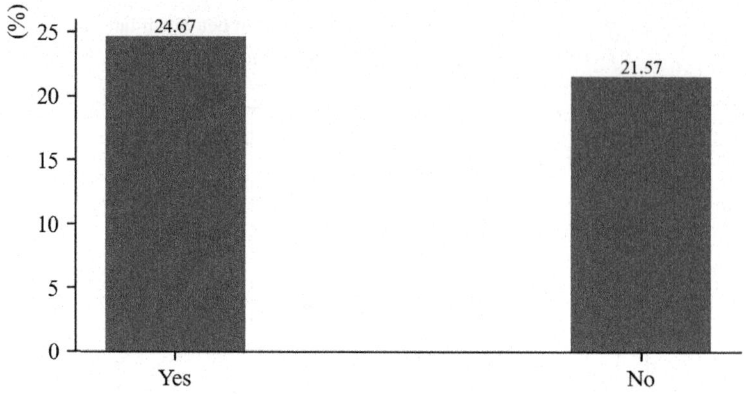


**Fig. 13** Proportion of the full sample purchasing children's commercial medical insurance (whether they were sick in the past month)

in the past month who purchased commercial health insurance and the percentage of those who did not. This may be related to both the short- and long-term shocks of sick children. The main factors influencing commercial health insurance are chronic and malignant diseases. The illnesses that children have experienced in the past month are generally more acute minor illnesses; therefore, their impact on the short-term demand for children's commercial medical insurance is not very significant. However, its impact on long-term demand for children's commercial medical insurance may be significant.

Figure 14 reports the percentage of mid-high net worth households and non mid-high net worth households that purchased children's commercial medical insurance for whether or not they were sick in the past month. In the sick group, the proportion of mid-high net worth households purchasing children's commercial medical insurance is 12.45 percentage points higher than that of non mid-high net worth households; in the group that is not sick, there is a difference of 12.42 percentage points. From these results, it is clear that economic conditions significantly influence the proportion of families purchasing children's commercial medical insurance compared to whether or not they were sick in the past month.

## 4.2 *Number of Illnesses*

An exploration of the relationship between children's health and commercial medical insurance requires further differentiation of illness frequency. Frequent illnesses in children indicate poor health or weaker immune systems. It is intuitively presumed that the more frequently children get sick, the greater the demand for children's commercial medical insurance, and the higher the insurance coverage. However, the actual situation often differs from what has been hypothesized. This book calculates

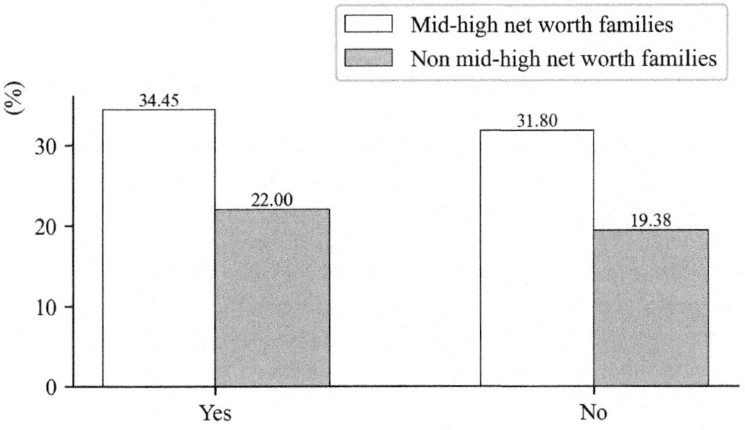


**Fig. 14** Proportion of mid-high net worth households and non mid-high net worth households purchasing children's commercial medical insurance (whether they were sick in the past month)

the proportion of the full sample purchasing children's commercial medical insurance based on the number of times they have been sick in the past month; the results are summarized in Fig. 15.

According to Fig. 15, the highest proportion of the sample with one to two illnesses in the past month purchased children's commercial medical insurance, and the lowest proportion with seven or more illnesses. In other words, the relationship between the number of times children were sick in the past month and the proportion of children purchasing commercial medical insurance was nonlinear. The reason for these results may be that the health condition of the insured is evaluated by the person in charge when purchasing commercial medical insurance. Generally, it is impossible to purchase insurance if the health condition does not meet the insurance

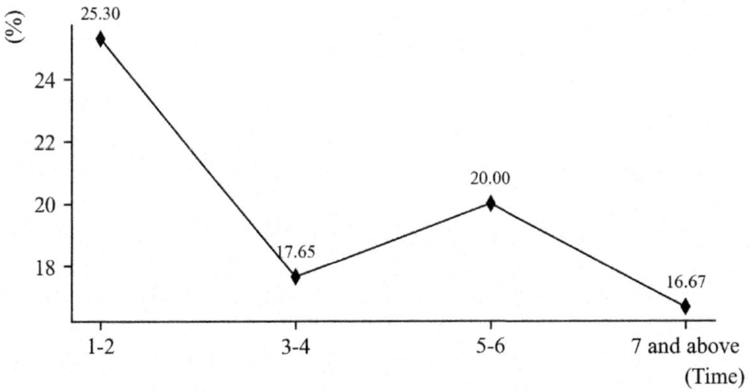


**Fig. 15** Proportion of the full sample purchasing children's commercial medical insurance (number of times they were sick in the past month)

company's standards before implementing the policy; therefore, the worse the health condition, the lower the possibility of successfully purchasing commercial medical insurance. This phenomenon should be interpreted cautiously because the appearance of such results may also be related to the sample size. For example, the sample size of children who had been sick seven or more times in the past month was relatively small. Therefore, it is important to consider the effect of a small sample size when making inferences.

As shown in Fig. 16, the difference between the proportion of children's commercial medical insurance purchased by mid-high net worth households and non mid-high net worth households was not significant when the number of illnesses in the past month was 1 to 4; however, the difference was significant when the number of illnesses was more than four. The difference between the proportions of children's commercial medical insurance purchased by mid-high net worth households and non mid-high net worth households was 100% when the number of illnesses was seven or more. These results may be explained by the fact that better-off families can afford relatively higher health insurance costs. Insurance companies also design high-cost programs for high-risk (i.e., relatively poor health) people, so the increase in the number of illnesses does not cause the proportion of mid-high net worth families to purchase children's commercial medical insurance to decrease; however, for families with average financial conditions, the high cost of commercial medical insurance can cause a certain family burden, so as the number of illnesses of children increases, their proportion of purchasing children's commercial medical insurance The proportion of children's commercial medical insurance is gradually decreasing.

Of course, there is another reason why for economically disadvantaged families, children rely mainly on basic social, medical coverage rather than commercial medical insurance, which requires a higher premium to be paid for the choice of commercial medical insurance. This reflects the importance of the basic social

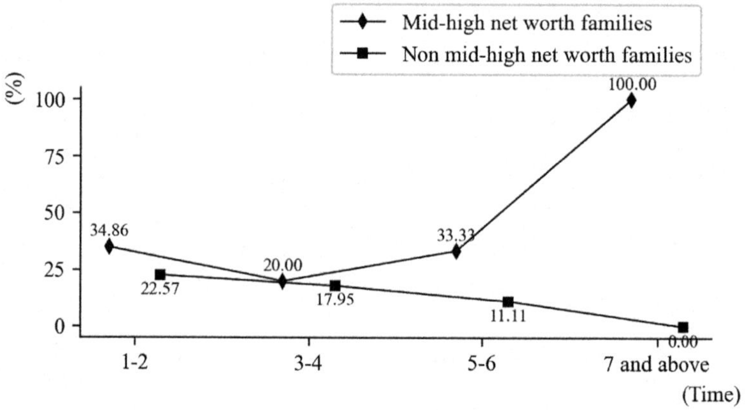


**Fig. 16** Proportion of mid-high net worth households and non mid-high net worth households purchasing children's commercial medical insurance (number of times they were sick in the past month)

medical insurance system, which is highly dependent on basic social, medical insurance for economically disadvantaged families.

## 4.3 The Number of Medical Visits Due to Illness

The number of medical visits is an important factor affecting medical expenditure. Currently, the number of medical visits per capita in China is rising rapidly, and the per capita medical expenditure has also shown a continuous rise. Data from the China Health and Health Statistical Yearbook (2020) showed that the number of resident visits reached 6.2 in 2019 (National Health and Health Commission, 2020). in 2010; this figure was 4.4. Here, the proportion of children purchasing commercial medical insurance for the full sample was calculated based on the number of visits to the doctor for illness in the past month, and the results are summarized in Fig. 17.

According to Fig. 17, among the number of medical visits in the past month due to illness, the percentage of the sample with five to six visits to purchase children's commercial medical insurance was significantly different from the other groups at 14.29%. This may be due to the so-called medical externality problem. That is, as the number of medical visits increases, basic medical knowledge acquired by people gradually increases, thus reducing the average number of medical visits for themselves and their families (Xu, 2009). The existence of this medical externality leads to the fact that children who have relatively few medical visits may not be as healthy as they should be; therefore, the families involved need to purchase commercial medical insurance for children.

According to Fig. 18, there is a significant gap between the proportion of mid-high net worth households purchasing children's commercial medical insurance and non mid-high net worth households when the number of medical visits in the past month

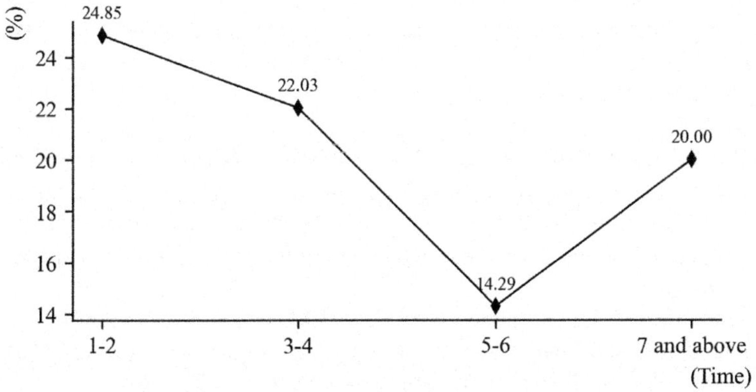


**Fig. 17** Proportion of children's commercial medical insurance purchased for the full sample (number of medical visits in the past month due to illness)

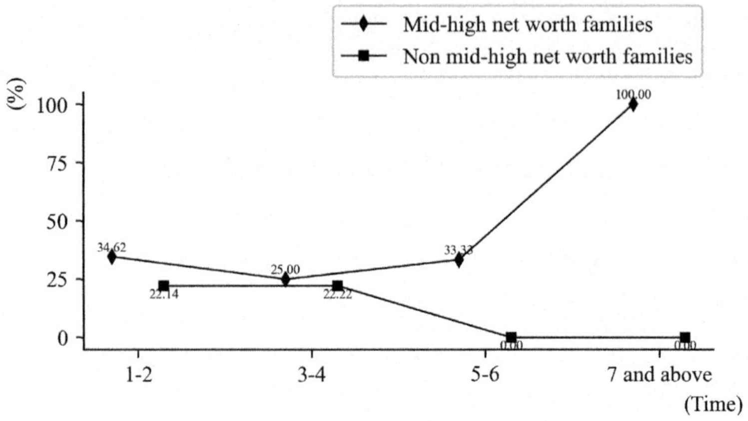


**Fig. 18** Proportion of mid-high net worth households and non mid-high net worth households purchasing children's commercial medical insurance (number of medical visits in the past month due to illness)

is greater than four. The proportion of non mid-high net worth households purchasing children's commercial medical insurance for five or more medical visits in the past month is zero, indicating that households with average economic conditions and less healthy children generally do not purchase children's commercial medical insurance. In this case, less well-off families rely mainly on basic social, medical coverage rather than commercial medical insurance.

## *4.4 Children's Injury and Illness Expenses*

The more medical visits children undergo, the more they spend in their average household. This book analyzes whether there is a difference in average child injury and illness medical expenditures by comparing families with and without children's commercial medical insurance. The average injury and illness expenditures for the full sample are shown in Fig. 19.

As shown in Fig. 19, families who purchased children's commercial medical insurance spent more on their children's injuries and illnesses. Overall, families who spend more time on children's injuries and illnesses are more likely to purchase commercial medical insurance because it reduces the pressure on the family to spend time in this area.

When analyzed in conjunction with Figs. 19 and 20, the purchase of children's commercial medical insurance impacts on injury and illness spending averages, both overall and from different household perspectives. The mean injury and illness spending was slightly higher for those who had purchased children's commercial medical insurance than those who had not.

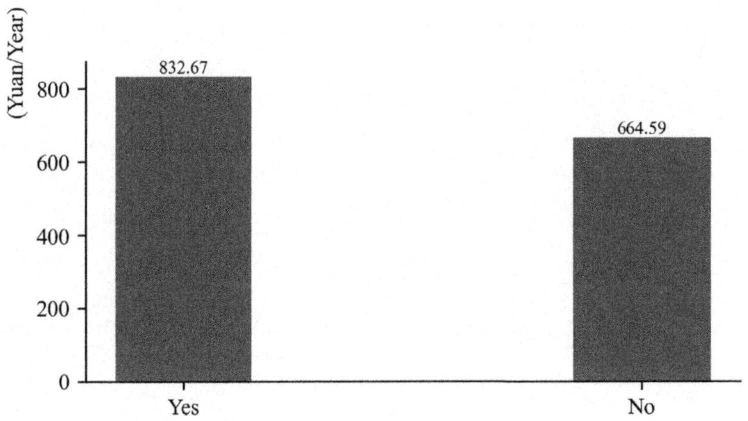


**Fig. 19** Average injury and illness costs for the full sample (with or without children's commercial medical insurance)

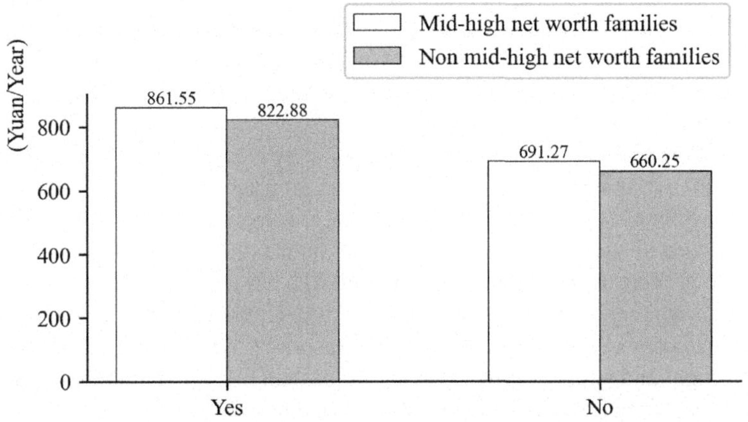


**Fig. 20** Average spending on injuries and illnesses for mid-high net worth families and non mid-high net worth families (with or without children's commercial medical insurance)

## 4.5 *Out-of-Pocket Medical Expenses*

Since medical expenditures can be influenced by many factors, it is necessary to explore the relationship between families' children's medical expenditures and children's commercial medical insurance from the perspective of out-of-pocket medical expenses, which are summarized in Fig. 21 for the full sample as a percentage of medical expenditures.

According to Fig. 21, the proportion of out-of-pocket medical costs to medical expenditures is high overall. A previous study showed that the average out-of-pocket proportion of hospitalization costs for active workers was 50.99% [26]. The

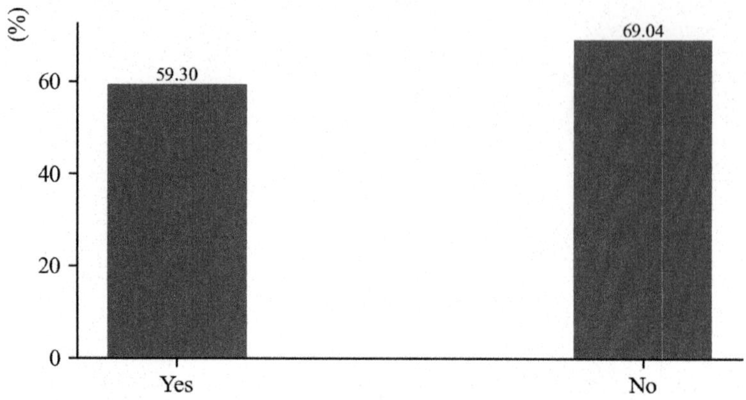


**Fig. 21** Proportion of out-of-pocket medical expenses to medical expenditures for the full sample (with or without children's commercial medical insurance)

proportion of medical out-of-pocket costs to medical expenditures without children's commercial medical insurance was 9.74 percentage points higher than that with children's commercial medical insurance. This indicates that children's commercial medical insurance can still somewhat reduce the burden of family medical expenditure.

From Fig. 22, we can see that the proportion of medical out-of-pocket expenses to medical expenditures for mid-high net worth families and non mid-high net worth families who purchase children's commercial medical insurance is lower than that for families who do not purchase children's commercial medical insurance. Among them, the proportion was higher for non mid-high net worth families. For the group that purchased children's commercial medical insurance, the proportion of out-of-pocket medical expenses to medical expenditures was 7.54 percentage points higher for non-high- and middle-net-worth households than for high- and middle-net-worth households; in the group that did not purchase children's commercial medical insurance, the proportion was 2.7 percentage points higher for non-high- and middle-net-worth households than for high- and middle-net-worth households. This further indicates that children's commercial medical insurance can reduce the burden on families in terms of children's medical care; at the same time, mid-high net worth families will choose insurance programs with higher costs and therefore pay a smaller percentage of out-of-pocket expenses.

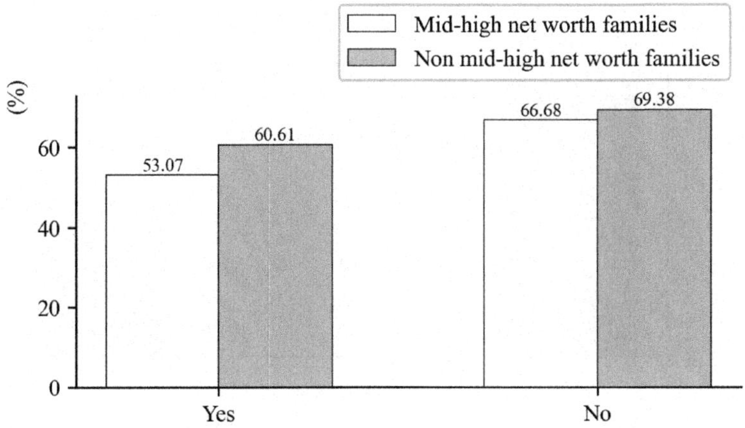


**Fig. 22** Proportion of out-of-pocket medical expenses to medical expenditures for mid-high net worth households and non mid-high net worth households (with or without children's commercial medical insurance)

# 5 Children's Education Conditions and Commercial Medical Insurance

Children's education and health are major concerns for parents. For mid-high net worth individuals, both these matters are directly related to family wealth inheritance; therefore, they are their priority concerns [27]. In terms of family decision-making, children's education and health are often interrelated, and both are related to the future and growth of children. Therefore, parents pay continuous attention to and invest in both matters, hoping to provide good conditions for their children's growth. However, with limited family income, some families with lower income levels need to make trade-offs between investment in children's education and health, and there may be a crowding-out effect on a family's investment in children's education and health.

## *5.1 Whether to Save Money for Children's Education*

According to Fig. 23, on the whole, parents choose to save their children's education while also choosing to purchase commercial medical insurance, which indicates that there is a correlation between the two. Both investments in education and commercial medical insurance guarantee the healthy growth of children. In addition, the gap shows that the percentage of families who save money for their children's education by buying children's commercial medical insurance is 22.79 percentage points higher

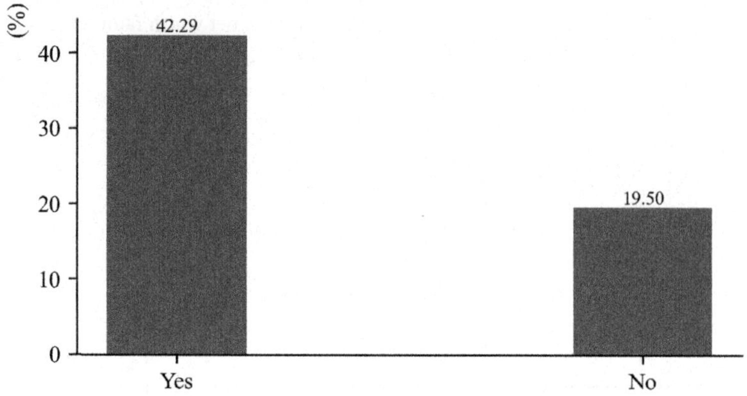


**Fig. 23** Proportion of full sample purchasing children's commercial health insurance (whether saving for children's education)

than those who do not choose to save money for their children's education, and the gap is still very obvious.

According to Fig. 24, a higher percentage of families who chose to save for their children's education purchased children's commercial medical insurance. In the group of those who save money for their children's education, the proportion of mid-high net worth households purchasing children's commercial medical insurance is 12.49 percentage points higher than that of non mid-high net worth households. In the group of those who do not save money for their children's education, the proportion of mid-high net worth households purchasing children's commercial medical insurance is higher than that of non mid-high net worth households, and the difference between the two is 11.76 percentage points. The above results further indicate that families who save money for their children's education are more likely to purchase children's commercial medical insurance and are aware of investing in their children's health and education; families with good economic conditions are more willing to take out insurance.

According to Fig. 25, families who choose to save for their children's education incur a higher average cost of purchasing children's commercial health insurance. One possible reason is that such families are willing to purchase mid- to high-end products under their children's commercial health insurance, which carries relatively higher premiums. Specifically, the average cost of purchasing children's commercial medical insurance is ¥1,396.78 higher for families who have saved for their children's education than for families who have not saved for their children's education, a large difference.

As shown in Fig. 26, the average cost of children's commercial health insurance among mid-high net worth families who save for their children's education is ¥1,740.64 higher than those who do not save for their children's education; among non-Mid-high net worth families, the difference between the two is ¥981.07, both of which are significant. The above results indicate that families who save for their

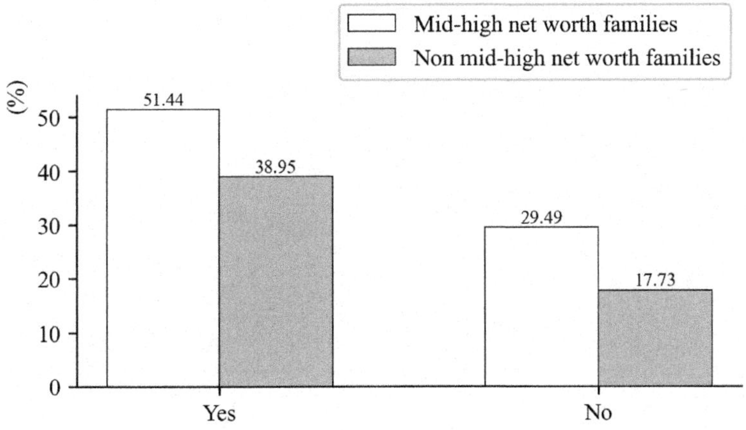


**Fig. 24** Proportion of mid-high net worth households and non mid-high net worth households purchasing children's commercial medical insurance (whether saving for children's education)

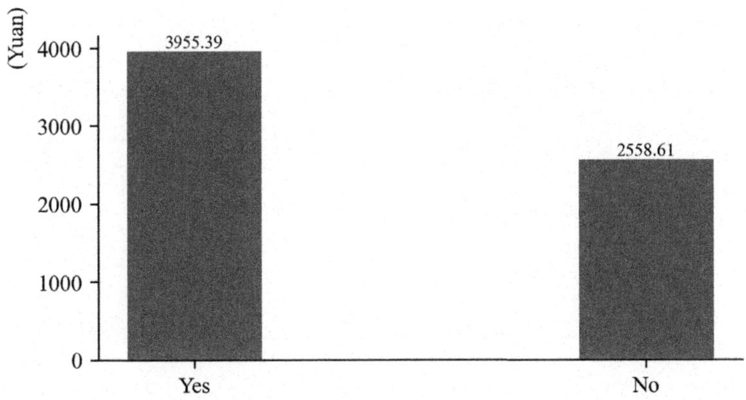


**Fig. 25** Average cost of purchasing children's commercial medical insurance for the full sample (whether saving for children's education)

children's education are likely to choose commercial medical insurance programs with higher premiums, which are higher for mid-high net worth families.

## *5.2 Amount of Money Saved for Education*

Figure 27 reports the average amount of money saved for children's education in one year for the full sample for whether or not they purchased children's commercial health insurance. The mean is higher for families who have purchased children's commercial health insurance, with a significant difference of ¥2,330.23 between

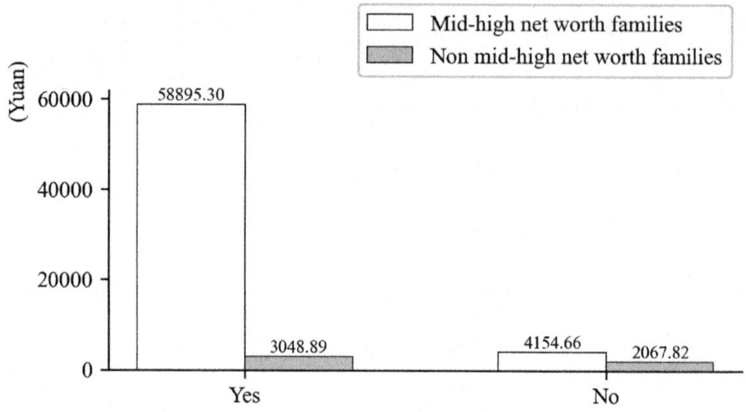


**Fig. 26** Average cost of children's commercial medical insurance purchased by mid-high net worth households and non-middle-net-worth households (whether saving for children's education)

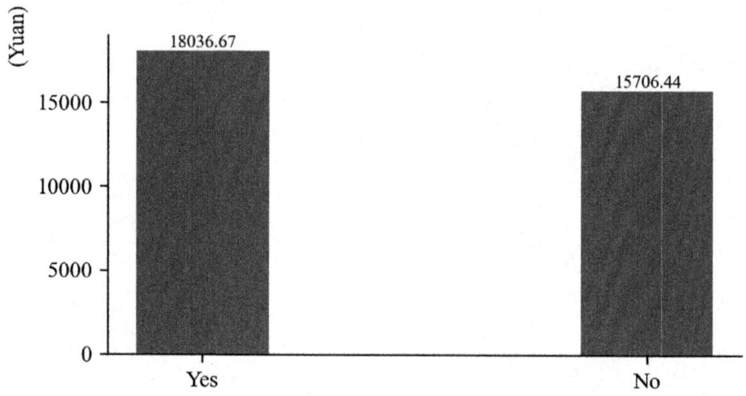


**Fig. 27** Average amount of money saved for children's education in one year for the full sample (whether or not to purchase children's commercial medical insurance)

the two. In summary, it shows a correlation between families who are conscious of investing in education spending more on their children's health insurance, and families who have commercial health insurance investment behavior also increase the value of their children's education money accumulation.

As seen in Fig. 28, the relevant data for mid-high net worth households are consistent with the conclusions of the previous analysis, indicating that the more education funds are accumulated, the more the cost of children's commercial medical insurance. However, for non mid-high net worth families, a different conclusion is obtained: for families with average economic conditions, there is a certain competitive relationship between health investment and education investment; those who choose to buy children's commercial medical insurance have relatively fewer education savings, but families who do not buy children's commercial medical insurance will invest more

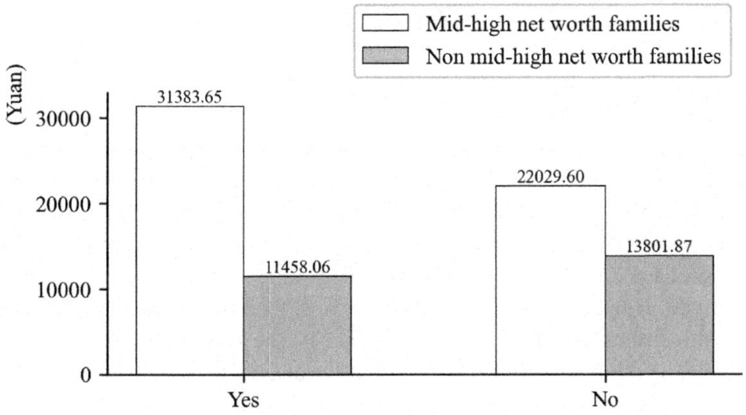


**Fig. 28** Average amount of money saved for children's education in one year by mid-high net worth families and non mid-high net worth families (with or without children's commercial medical insurance)

in their children's education, that is, there is a so-called "crowding out effect." In families with income constraints, parents are likely to spend less on their children's commercial health insurance because they want to ensure their children's education first, or they may choose to buy lower-end children's commercial health insurance with lower premiums.

## 6 Analysis of the Factors Influencing Children's Commercial Medical Insurance

The data used in this book were mainly from the household and individual questionnaires of the 2020 CFPS. This study focused on the factors influencing children's commercial health insurance. The fact that children's participation in commercial medical insurance effectively improves their health is a common concern in society. However, in China, the coverage rate of children's commercial medical insurance is not yet very high, and many families do not purchase commercial medical insurance for their children at home. Currently, there are few studies on the factors that affect families' demand for children's commercial medical insurance, and these studies are neither comprehensive nor systematic. Therefore, this section presents an empirical study and tests the factors that influence families' children's commercial medical insurance using micro-survey data to gain a more in-depth and comprehensive understanding of this issue.

## 6.1 Data, Variables, and Models

(1) *Key variables*

The explanatory variables are children's commercial health insurance expenditure and children's commercial health insurance participation. The first explanatory variable was the children's participation in commercial health insurance. Based on the question in the CFPS household questionnaire, "In the past 12 months, did your family purchase commercial health insurance for you (the child)?" The variables were defined. If the answer to this question is 0, then the definition of commercial child health insurance participation is 0, that is, the household does not purchase commercial health insurance for the child; if the answer to this question is 1, then the definition of commercial health insurance participation is 1; that is, the household is involved in commercial child health insurance. The second explanatory variable was children's commercial health insurance expenditure. Based on the question in the CFPS household questionnaire, "In the past 12 months, how much did the household spend on commercial health insurance for this child?" is used to define operationally child commercial health insurance expenditures.

The core explanatory variables are mid-high net worth households (dummy variables) and investable household assets. The remaining control variables include household-level and head-of-household-level control variables, with household-level control variables including household entrepreneurial decisions, household property investment decisions, household size, household income, bank loans, loans from friends and relatives and private individuals, human costs, education, and training costs. Head-of-household-level control variables include gender, age, years of education, marital status, health status, self-confidence level, and whether to access the Internet. In addition, the control variables include some of the children's own factors, such as whether they attend school, the number of medical visits, and out-of-pocket medical expenses. Therefore, this is a multilevel holistic analysis of the household, which helps to study the purchase and demand for commercial medical insurance for children in the household in a more comprehensively and systematically.

(2) *Descriptive statistics*

During data processing, this chapter eliminated samples with missing and incorrect values in the variables, and finally obtained 5166 valid samples. The definition and descriptive statistics for these variables are shown in Table 1.

(3) *Model setting*

This chapter examines the impact of mid-high net worth households and household investable assets on children's commercial health insurance expenditures and children's commercial health insurance participation, as modeled by the following settings:

**Table 1** Definition of variables and descriptive statistics

| Variable | Definition | Mean | S.D | Min | Max |
|---|---|---|---|---|---|
| Children's commercial medical insurance expenses | Last year's children's commercial insurance spending | 605.44 | 2787.443 | 0 | 120,000 |
| Children's commercial medical insurance participation | Purchase children's business insurance for 1, otherwise 0 | 0.22 | 0.414 | 0 | 1 |
| Mid-high net worth families | 1 for middle and high net worth households, 0 for the rest | 0.171 | 0.377 | 0 | 1 |
| Household investable assets | Log value of household investable assets | 8.991 | 4.745 | 0 | 17.371 |
| Entrepreneurship of the family | Number of self-employed or private enterprises | 0.314 | 0.611 | 0 | 7 |
| Investment properties | Number of properties other than current housing | 0.156 | 0.421 | 0 | 5 |
| Household size | Number of family members | 5.366 | 2.014 | 1 | 15 |
| Household income | Logarithmic value of household income | 10.957 | 1.286 | 0 | 14.221 |
| Bank loans | If the household has a bank loan, the variable takes the value of 1, otherwise it is 0 | 0.146 | 0.353 | 0 | 1 |
| Private loans from friends and family | If there is a family or private loan, the value is 1, otherwise it is 0 | 0.145 | 0.352 | 0 | 1 |
| Favor expenses | Last year's household spending on favors | 4232.046 | 6940.165 | 0 | 120,000 |
| Education and training fees | Spending on family education training last year | 6707.607 | 11,124.213 | 0 | 152,000 |
| Gender | If the gender is male, the variable takes the value of 1, otherwise it is 0 | 0.545 | 0.498 | 0 | 1 |
| Age | Age of the individual, in years | 43.529 | 12.128 | 19 | 83 |
| Year of education | Number of years of education received | 8.358 | 5.004 | 0 | 22 |

(continued)

**Table 1** (continued)

| Variable | Definition | Mean | S.D | Min | Max |
|---|---|---|---|---|---|
| Marriage | If the marital status is married, the variable takes the value of 1, otherwise 0 | 0.939 | 0.24 | 0 | 1 |
| Health | Health rating with a maximum of 5 and a minimum of 1 | 2.859 | 1.147 | 1 | 5 |
| Self-confidence | Self-confidence rating, highest 5, lowest 1 | 4.176 | 0.884 | 1 | 5 |
| Access to the internet | Internet access is 1, otherwise it is 0 | 0.724 | 0.447 | 0 | 1 |
| Attending school or not | 1 for attending school, 0 otherwise | 0.746 | 0.435 | 0 | 1 |
| Number of medical visits | Number of child medical visits in the past year | 1.359 | 2.501 | 0 | 36 |
| Out-of-pocket medical expenses | Amount of out-of-pocket medical expenses for the child's illness in the past year | 916.272 | 4543.951 | 0 | 120,000 |

$$Hinsurance = \alpha_0 + \alpha_1 \times MHW + \alpha_2 \times ln(FIA) + \alpha_3 \times X + u \quad (1)$$

$$HIP = \beta_0 + \beta_1 \times MHW + \beta_2 \times ln(FIA) + \beta_3 \times X + u \quad (2)$$

*Hinsurance* denotes the annual household expenditure on child commercial health insurance, which is a continuous variable; *HIP* denotes household participation in child commercial health insurance, which is a variable consisting of zeros and ones; *MHW* and *FIA* denote mid-high net worth households (dummy variables) and investable household assets, respectively; $X$ is a set of control variables containing household-level, head-of-household, and child-level control variables; and u is the error term.

In the regression of Eq. (2), the logit regression model is used instead of the least squares regression (OLS) model because the explanatory variables are categorical.

## 6.2 Empirical Analysis

1. *Impact of mid-high net worth families on children's commercial medical insurance spending*

Table 2 presents regression results for the effect of mid-high net worth households on children's commercial health insurance expenditures. Column (1) considers only the explanatory variable of mid-high net worth households (dummy variable), column (2) adds household-level control variables, and column (3) adds household head-level control variables and child-related control variables to the household-level control variables. On this basis, corresponding to columns (1) to (3), province-fixed effects are added in columns (4) to (6). The results show that the regression coefficients for mid-high net worth households are significantly positive in all models. As shown in column (6), after accounting for both household-level control variables, head-of-household-level control variables, child-related control variables, and province-fixed effects, mid-high net worth households spend about ¥417 more per year on children's commercial health insurance than non mid-high net worth households. This indicates that mid-high net worth households invest more money in children's commercial health insurance and have more demand for children's commercial health insurance. It also shows that mid-high net worth families can provide better insurance coverage for their children.

2. *The impact of investable household assets on children's commercial medical insurance expenditures*

Table 3 presents the regression results for the effect of household investable assets on children's commercial health insurance expenditure. In columns (1) and (4), the regression coefficient of investable household assets is significantly positive. However, in the remaining four columns, the regression coefficients were insignificant. This finding suggests that overall household investable assets do not directly affect children's commercial health insurance expenditure. For example, the effect of investable household assets on children's commercial health insurance expenditure is not significant when household-level control variables, head-of-household-level control variables, child-related control variables, and province-fixed effects are included.

The results for the relevant control variables show that the effects of household- and head-of-household-level variables on children's commercial health insurance expenditures vary. As shown in Table 3, the effect of household entrepreneurial decisions is insignificant, the effect of household size is significantly negative, and the effect of household income is significantly positive. Bank loans have a significantly positive relationship with household expenditure on children's commercial medical insurance, whereas the effects of family, friends, and private loans are significantly negative. In addition, the effect of human fees was not significant, while the effects of education and training fees had a significantly positive relationship with children's commercial medical insurance expenditures.

**Table 2** Regression results of the impact of mid-high net worth households on children's commercial medical insurance expenditures

| | Children's commercial health insurance expenses | | | | | |
|---|---|---|---|---|---|---|
| | (1) | (2) | (3) | (4) | (5) | (6) |
| Mid-high net worth families | 973.371*** | 456.972** | 388.344* | 852.743*** | 477.941** | 416.563** |
| | (5.53) | (2.19) | (1.87) | (5.25) | (2.26) | (1.97) |
| Investment properties | | 161.141* | 143.137 | | 127.953 | 112.567 |
| | | (1.74) | (1.54) | | (1.36) | (1.19) |
| Entrepreneurship of the family | | 161.995 | 165.941 | | 166.126 | 172.961 |
| | | (1.36) | (1.40) | | (1.36) | (1.40) |
| Household size | | −115.473*** | −104.434*** | | −95.203*** | −87.230*** |
| | | (−7.04) | (−5.74) | | (−6.31) | (−5.07) |
| Household income | | 152.111*** | 122.268*** | | 145.781*** | 120.251*** |
| | | (4.04) | (3.45) | | (3.79) | (3.36) |
| Bank loans | | 222.877 | 218.004 | | 261.765* | 252.191* |
| | | (1.61) | (1.50) | | (1.86) | (1.71) |
| Private loans from friends and family | | −137.170* | −102.329 | | −114.982* | -89.476 |
| | | (−1.89) | (−1.48) | | (−1.66) | (−1.34) |
| Favor expenses | | 0.004 | 0.004 | | 0.003 | 0.002 |
| | | (0.46) | (0.47) | | (0.34) | (0.26) |
| Education and training fees | | 0.020*** | 0.019*** | | 0.017*** | 0.016** |
| | | (3.01) | (2.78) | | (2.67) | (2.49) |
| Gender | | | −19.816 | | | 10.684 |

(continued)

**Table 2** (continued)

| | Children's commercial health insurance expenses | | | | | |
|---|---|---|---|---|---|---|
| | (1) | (2) | (3) | (4) | (5) | (6) |
| | | | (−0.28) | | | (0.15) |
| Age | | | 4.438 | | | 3.890 |
| | | | (1.02) | | | (0.88) |
| Year of education | | | 37.605*** | | | 34.225*** |
| | | | (4.84) | | | (4.47) |
| Marriage | | | −41.423 | | | −42.117 |
| | | | (−0.38) | | | (−0.37) |
| Health | | | 1.388 | | | −5.044 |
| | | | (0.04) | | | (−0.15) |
| Self-confidence | | | 52.711* | | | 43.238 |
| | | | (1.93) | | | (1.55) |
| Access to the internet | | | 28.020 | | | 33.210 |
| | | | (0.45) | | | (0.54) |
| Attending school or not | | | −80.004 | | | −74.201 |
| | | | (−0.89) | | | (−0.83) |
| Number of medical visits | | | 33.939 | | | 41.872* |
| | | | (1.41) | | | (1.70) |
| Out-of-pocket medical expenses | | | 0.003 | | | 0.001 |

(continued)

**Table 2** (continued)

| | Children's commercial health insurance expenses | | | | | |
|---|---|---|---|---|---|---|
| | (1) | (2) | (3) | (4) | (5) | (6) |
| | | | (0.45) | | | (0.25) |
| Fixed effects of provinces | No | No | No | Yes | Yes | Yes |
| Constant | 438.878*** | −757.425** | −1,160.500*** | 764.838 | −1,019.135 | −1,399.869 |
| | (14.90) | (−2.05) | (−2.78) | (1.08) | (−1.15) | (−1.53) |
| Observations | 5,166 | 5,166 | 5,166 | 5,166 | 5,166 | 5,166 |
| R-squared | 0.017 | 0.040 | 0.045 | 0.037 | 0.053 | 0.058 |

*Note* * $p < 0.1$, ** $p < 0.05$, *** $p < 0.01$

**Table 3** Regression results of the effect of investable household assets on children's commercial medical insurance expenditures

| | Children's commercial health insurance expenses | | | | | |
|---|---|---|---|---|---|---|
| | (1) | (2) | (3) | (4) | (5) | (6) |
| Household investable assets | 49.802*** | 4.092 | −2.650 | 39.275*** | 3.331 | −2.835 |
| | (4.84) | (0.38) | (−0.24) | (4.07) | (0.31) | (−0.26) |
| Investment properties | | 319.602*** | 294.290*** | | 293.472*** | 271.649*** |
| | | (3.72) | (3.48) | | (3.51) | (3.29) |
| Entrepreneurship of the family | | 180.320 | 185.934 | | 186.325 | 194.152 |
| | | (1.50) | (1.56) | | (1.52) | (1.58) |
| Household size | | −119.764*** | −107.426*** | | −99.047*** | −90.192*** |
| | | (−7.33) | (−6.17) | | (−6.62) | (-5.50) |
| Household income | | 165.522*** | 135.010*** | | 158.487*** | 132.289*** |
| | | (3.98) | (3.52) | | (3.75) | (3.43) |
| Bank loans | | 225.840* | 211.699 | | 263.595* | 245.610* |
| | | (1.70) | (1.52) | | (1.94) | (1.74) |
| Private loans from friends and family | | -165.707** | −133.601* | | −145.541** | −121.627* |
| | | (−2.14) | (−1.85) | | (−1.98) | (−1.75) |
| Favor expenses | | 0.006 | 0.005 | | 0.005 | 0.004 |
| | | (0.74) | (0.70) | | (0.57) | (0.45) |
| Education and training fees | | 0.021*** | 0.019*** | | 0.018*** | 0.017*** |
| | | (3.14) | (2.91) | | (2.81) | (2.61) |
| Gender | | | −19.828 | | | 9.598 |

(continued)

**Table 3** (continued)

| | Children's commercial health insurance expenses | | | | | |
|---|---|---|---|---|---|---|
| | (1) | (2) | (3) | (4) | (5) | (6) |
| | | | (−0.28) | | | (0.13) |
| Age | | | 4.770 | | | 4.300 |
| | | | (1.14) | | | (1.02) |
| Year of education | | | 39.775*** | | | 36.572*** |
| | | | (4.72) | | | (4.41) |
| Marriage | | | −24.726 | | | −24.165 |
| | | | (−0.22) | | | (−0.21) |
| Health | | | 2.389 | | | −4.528 |
| | | | (0.07) | | | (−0.13) |
| Self-confidence | | | 51.772* | | | 43.210 |
| | | | (1.89) | | | (1.55) |
| Access to the internet | | | 45.739 | | | 52.101 |
| | | | (0.74) | | | (0.84) |
| Attending school or not | | | −93.372 | | | −87.033 |
| | | | (−1.07) | | | (−1.01) |
| Number of medical visits | | | 33.891 | | | 41.642* |
| | | | (1.42) | | | (1.69) |
| Out-of-pocket medical expenses | | | 0.003 | | | 0.002 |

(continued)

**Table 3** (continued)

| | Children's commercial health insurance expenses | | | | | |
|---|---|---|---|---|---|---|
| | (1) | (2) | (3) | (4) | (5) | (6) |
| | | | (0.50) | | | (0.33) |
| Fixed effects of provinces | No | No | No | Yes | Yes | Yes |
| Constant | 157.688* | −902.231** | −1,300.381*** | 889.653 | −1,024.908 | −1,437.050 |
| | (1.80) | (−2.28) | (−2.99) | (1.23) | (−1.15) | (−1.56) |
| Observations | 5,166 | 5,166 | 5,166 | 5,166 | 5,166 | 5,166 |
| R-squared | 0.007 | 0.038 | 0.043 | 0.029 | 0.051 | 0.056 |

*Note* *$p < 0.1$, **$p < 0.05$, ***$p < 0.01$

Considering the control variables at the household head level, neither gender nor age significantly affected children's commercial health insurance expenditure. The more years of education the household head has, the more the children's commercial medical insurance expenditures. In addition, after controlling for province-fixed effects, the effect of the number of medical visits on children's commercial medical insurance expenditure is positive and significant.

3. *Impact of mid-high net worth families on children's commercial medical insurance participation*

Table 4 presents regression results for the effect of mid-high net worth households on children's commercial health insurance participation. In all six models, the regression coefficients for mid-high net worth households are significantly positive. This indicates that mid-high net worth households are more likely to participate in children's commercial health insurance than non mid-high net worth households; they are more likely to purchase commercial health insurance for their children in the household. The results in column (6) show that after considering both household-level control variables, head of household-level control variables, child-related control variables, and province-fixed effects, mid-high net worth households are 0.322 units more likely to participate in children's commercial health insurance than non-middle and high net worth households, demonstrating a significant positive effect of middle and high net worth households on increasing household participation in children's commercial health insurance.

4. *Impact of investable family assets on children's commercial medical insurance participation*

Table 5 presents the regression results for the effect of household investable assets on children's participation in commercial health insurance. In Columns (1) and (4), the regression coefficients of household investable assets are significantly positive. However, after introducing the control variables, the regression coefficients of this variable were not significant in either case. This suggests that overall, the effect of investable household assets on the likelihood of households purchasing children's commercial health insurance is insignificant.

In terms of control variables, households that engage in family entrepreneurship and hold bank loans are more likely to participate in children's commercial health insurance, and all these household-level factors are significantly and positively related to the purchase of children's commercial health insurance. However, the effects of family property investment decisions, family and friends, and private loans on children's participation in commercial medical insurance were insignificant. In addition, the effect of household size on children's participation in commercial medical insurance was significantly negative. The larger the family size, the more the children's participation in commercial medical insurance may be overshadowed by other matters.

Regarding household head-level control variables, sex and age were not significantly related to children's commercial health insurance participation. However, the household head's years of education had a significant positive relationship with

**Table 4** Regression results of the impact of mid-high net worth households on children's commercial medical insurance participation

| | Children's commercial health insurance participation | | | | | |
|---|---|---|---|---|---|---|
| | (1) | (2) | (3) | (4) | (5) | (6) |
| Mid-high net worth families | $0.695^{***}$ | $0.279^{**}$ | $0.257^{**}$ | $0.636^{***}$ | $0.343^{***}$ | $0.322^{***}$ |
| | (8.56) | (2.30) | (2.11) | (7.31) | (2.79) | (2.61) |
| Investment properties | | 0.032 | 0.011 | | 0.002 | −0.018 |
| | | (0.44) | (0.16) | | (0.02) | (−0.24) |
| Entrepreneurship of the family | | $0.202^{**}$ | $0.218^{***}$ | | $0.201^{**}$ | $0.214^{***}$ |
| | | (2.51) | (2.74) | | (2.47) | (2.66) |
| Household size | | $-0.103^{***}$ | $-0.093^{***}$ | | $-0.089^{***}$ | $-0.080^{***}$ |
| | | (−5.25) | (−4.45) | | (−4.33) | (−3.69) |
| Household income | | $0.302^{***}$ | $0.268^{***}$ | | $0.297^{***}$ | $0.267^{***}$ |
| | | (4.01) | (3.39) | | (3.75) | (3.26) |
| Bank loans | | $0.212^{**}$ | $0.226^{**}$ | | $0.243^{**}$ | $0.252^{***}$ |
| | | (2.23) | (2.37) | | (2.51) | (2.59) |
| Private loans from friends and family | | −0.003 | 0.022 | | 0.007 | 0.026 |
| | | (−0.03) | (0.21) | | (0.06) | (0.25) |
| Favor expenses | | −0.000 | −0.000 | | −0.000 | −0.000 |
| | | (−0.47) | (−0.37) | | (−0.61) | (−0.62) |
| Education and training fees | | $0.001^{***}$ | $0.001^{***}$ | | $0.001^{***}$ | $0.001^{**}$ |
| | | (3.12) | (2.64) | | (2.81) | (2.39) |

(continued)

**Table 4** (continued)

| | Children's commercial health insurance participation | | | | | |
|---|---|---|---|---|---|---|
| | (1) | (2) | (3) | (4) | (5) | (6) |
| Gender | | | −0.068 | | | −0.037 |
| | | | (−0.96) | | | (−0.51) |
| Age | | | 0.005 | | | 0.004 |
| | | | (1.28) | | | (1.05) |
| Year of education | | | 0.030*** | | | 0.028*** |
| | | | (3.46) | | | (3.27) |
| Marriage | | | −0.275* | | | −0.251* |
| | | | (−1.91) | | | (−1.70) |
| Health | | | 0.042 | | | 0.049 |
| | | | (1.30) | | | (1.51) |
| Self-confidence | | | 0.030 | | | 0.029 |
| | | | (0.72) | | | (0.69) |
| Access to the internet | | | 0.042 | | | 0.044 |
| | | | (0.39) | | | (0.39) |
| Attending school or not | | | 0.128 | | | 0.132 |
| | | | (1.56) | | | (1.60) |

(continued)

**Table 4** (continued)

| | Children's commercial health insurance participation | | | | | |
|---|---|---|---|---|---|---|
| | (1) | (2) | (3) | (4) | (5) | (6) |
| Number of medical visits | | | 0.028** | | | 0.034** |
| | | | (2.17) | | | (2.57) |
| Out-of-pocket medical expenses | | | −0.000 | | | −0.000 |
| | | | (−0.04) | | | (−0.37) |
| Fixed effects of provinces | No | No | No | Yes | Yes | Yes |
| Constant | −1.402*** | −4.267*** | −4.511*** | −1.457** | −4.907*** | −5.195*** |
| | (−36.51) | (−5.24) | (−5.26) | (−2.46) | (−4.43) | (−4.64) |
| Observations | 5,166 | 5,166 | 5,166 | 5,155 | 5,155 | 5,155 |
| R-squared | 0.0128 | 0.0388 | 0.0437 | 0.0310 | 0.0526 | 0.0573 |

*Note* *$p < 0.1$, **$p < 0.05$, ***$p < 0.01$

**Table 5** Regression results for the effect of investable household assets on children's commercial health insurance participation

| | Children's commercial health insurance participation | | | | | |
|---|---|---|---|---|---|---|
| | (1) | (2) | (3) | (4) | (5) | (6) |
| Household investable assets | 0.056*** | 0.017* | 0.014 | 0.049*** | 0.018* | 0.016 |
| | (6.57) | (1.68) | (1.46) | (5.63) | (1.77) | (1.56) |
| Investment properties | | 0.090 | 0.067 | | 0.079 | 0.057 |
| | | (1.40) | (1.05) | | (1.21) | (0.88) |
| Entrepreneurship of the family | | 0.201** | 0.218*** | | 0.203** | 0.217*** |
| | | (2.52) | (2.77) | | (2.51) | (2.71) |
| Household size | | −0.105*** | −0.095*** | | −0.091*** | −0.083*** |
| | | (−5.35) | (−4.58) | | (−4.44) | (−3.84) |
| Household income | | 0.303*** | 0.270*** | | 0.300*** | 0.271*** |
| | | (3.96) | (3.39) | | (3.72) | (3.27) |
| Bank loans | | 0.224** | 0.237** | | 0.253*** | 0.262*** |
| | | (2.33) | (2.45) | | (2.59) | (2.66) |
| Private loans from friends and family | | −0.003 | 0.022 | | 0.001 | 0.021 |
| | | (−0.03) | (0.22) | | (0.01) | (0.21) |
| Favor expenses | | −0.000 | −0.000 | | −0.000 | −0.000 |
| | | (−0.19) | (−0.12) | | (−0.34) | (−0.37) |
| Education and training fees | | 0.001*** | 0.001*** | | 0.001*** | 0.001** |
| | | (3.19) | (2.71) | | (2.88) | (2.47) |

(continued)

**Table 5** (continued)

| | Children's commercial health insurance participation | | | | | |
|---|---|---|---|---|---|---|
| | (1) | (2) | (3) | (4) | (5) | (6) |
| Gender | | | −0.071 | | | −0.043 |
| | | | (−1.00) | | | (−0.59) |
| Age | | | 0.005 | | | 0.005 |
| | | | (1.41) | | | (1.19) |
| Year of education | | | 0.030*** | | | 0.029*** |
| | | | (3.46) | | | (3.30) |
| Marriage | | | −0.270* | | | −0.242* |
| | | | (−1.88) | | | (−1.65) |
| Health | | | 0.043 | | | 0.051 |
| | | | (1.34) | | | (1.56) |
| Self-confidence | | | 0.029 | | | 0.029 |
| | | | (0.71) | | | (0.68) |
| Access to the internet | | | 0.045 | | | 0.046 |
| | | | (0.42) | | | (0.41) |
| Attending school or not | | | 0.125 | | | 0.128 |
| | | | (1.52) | | | (1.55) |

(continued)

**Table 5** (continued)

| | Children's commercial health insurance participation | | | | | |
|---|---|---|---|---|---|---|
| | (1) | (2) | (3) | (4) | (5) | (6) |
| Number of medical visits | | | 0.028** | | | 0.034** |
| | | | (2.13) | | | (2.53) |
| Out-of-pocket medical expenses | | | −0.000 | | | −0.000 |
| | | | (−0.01) | | | (−0.33) |
| Fixed effects of provinces | No | No | No | Yes | Yes | Yes |
| Constant | −1.783*** | −4.399*** | −4.659*** | −1.582*** | −4.973*** | −5.291*** |
| | (−20.01) | (−5.49) | (−5.51) | (−2.60) | (−4.49) | (−4.72) |
| Observations | 5,166 | 5,166 | 5,166 | 5,155 | 5,155 | 5,155 |
| R-squared | 0.0100 | 0.0384 | 0.0433 | 0.0283 | 0.0517 | 0.0565 |

*Note* *$p < 0.1$, **$p < 0.05$, ***$p < 0.01$

children's participation in commercial health insurance. Marital status negatively affected on children's participation in commercial medical insurance; however, its significance was relatively weak. In addition, health status, self-confidence level, and Internet access had non-significant effects on children's commercial health insurance participation.

In terms of child-related control variables, the number of medical visits had a significant positive effect on children's commercial health insurance participation. However, neither school attendance nor out-of-pocket medical expenses had a significant effect on children's commercial health insurance participation.

## *6.3 Heterogeneity Analysis*

The heterogeneity analysis aims to explore whether the impact is universal for mid-high net worth households and for households' investable assets. If this is not universal, then what types of households will be affected? This is an important foundation for accurate decision-making. When conducting a heterogeneity analysis, group regressions are generally conducted based on specific attributes, and the consistency of the results across independent group regression studies is checked. If consistency exists, the results of the study could be combined. However, if there is no consistency, the results of studies may differ owing to different conditions based on them. This allowed for the precise identification of the scope and conditions of applicability of the relevant findings.

1. *Heterogeneity of mid-high net worth families on children's commercial medical insurance expenditure*

The sample was divided into two groups based on the household income level of the household head and higher and lower household income levels and grouped into regressions. Columns (1) and (2) of Table 6 present the regression results based on income heterogeneity. The results show no significant positive effect of mid-high net worth households (dummy variable) on children's commercial health insurance expenditures in households with higher income levels, while there is a significant effect in households with lower income levels.

The sample was divided into two groups, urban and rural, and grouped into regressions based on the location of households in the sample. Columns (3) and (4) of Table 6 show the regression results based on urban–rural heterogeneity. The results show a positive effect of mid-high net worth households (dummy variable) on children's commercial medical insurance expenditures in both urban and rural areas; however, the effect is significant in rural areas.

**Table 6** Regression results of the impact of mid-high net worth households on children's commercial medical insurance expenditures (income and urban–rural heterogeneity)

| | Children's commercial health insurance expenses | | | |
|---|---|---|---|---|
| | (1) | (2) | (3) | (4) |
| Income heterogeneity | High income | Low income | | |
| Urban–rural heterogeneity | | | Urban | Rural |
| Mid-high net worth families | 45.722 | 938.661*** | 376.144 | 334.617** |
| | (0.20) | (3.09) | (1.12) | (2.28) |
| Household-level control variables | Yes | Yes | Yes | Yes |
| Control variables at household head level | Yes | Yes | Yes | Yes |
| Fixed effects of provinces | Yes | Yes | Yes | Yes |
| Constant | −10,040.129*** | 107.509 | -1,954.117 | −1,135.389*** |
| | (−3.57) | (0.36) | (−1.27) | (−3.27) |
| Observations | 2,900 | 2,266 | 2,542 | 2,624 |
| R-squared | 0.064 | 0.109 | 0.061 | 0.064 |

*Note* *$p < 0.1$, **$p < 0.05$, ***$p < 0.01$

Based on the location of the households in the sample, the urban sample is further divided into four groups: first-tier cities, second-tier cities, third-tier cities, and fourth-tier cities, and the regressions are conducted in groups. The results are summarized in Table 7. The results show that the effect of mid-high net worth households (dummy variable) on children's commercial medical insurance expenditures in Tiers 2, 3, and 4 and below are insignificant. This indicates insignificant gap between mid-high net worth households and non mid-high net worth households in these cities.

According to the National Bureau of Statistics' Methodology for Dividing East, West, Central, and Northeast Regions, the sample is divided into four major regions, East, Central, West, and Northeast, grouped into regressions according to the provinces and cities where they are located, and the results are summarized in Table 8. The results show that the effect of mid-high net worth households on children's commercial medical insurance expenditures is significantly positive only in the northeastern region but not in the eastern, central, and western regions.

2. *Heterogeneity of investable household assets for children's commercial medical insurance expenditures*

Based on the household income level of the household head, the sample was divided into two groups, with higher and lower household income levels, and grouped into regressions. Columns (1) and (2) of Table 9 show the regression results based on income heterogeneity. The results show that the effect of investable household assets on children's commercial health insurance expenditure for households with higher and lower income levels is insignificant.

**Table 7** Regression results of the impact of mid-high net worth households on children's commercial medical insurance expenditures (urban heterogeneity)

| | Children's commercial health insurance expenses | | | |
|---|---|---|---|---|
| | (1) | (2) | (3) | (4) |
| Urban heterogeneity | First-tier cities | Second-tier cities | Third-tier cities | Fourth-tier cities and below |
| Mid-high net worth families | −3,104.908** | 90.230 | 301.338 | 253.278 |
| | (-2.42) | (0.23) | (0.59) | (0.93) |
| Household-level control variables | Yes | Yes | Yes | Yes |
| Control variables at household head level | Yes | Yes | Yes | Yes |
| Fixed effects of provinces | Yes | Yes | Yes | Yes |
| Constant | −6,279.421 | 247.510 | 1,751.045 | −2,133.640 |
| | (−0.94) | (0.07) | (0.79) | (−1.36) |
| Observations | 182 | 416 | 219 | 1,725 |
| R-squared | 0.298 | 0.227 | 0.356 | 0.105 |

*Note* $^{*}p < 0.1$, $^{**}p < 0.05$, $^{***}p < 0.01$

**Table 8** Regression results of the impact of mid-high net worth households on children's commercial medical insurance expenditures (regional heterogeneity)

| | Children's commercial health insurance expenses | | | |
|---|---|---|---|---|
| | (1) | (2) | (3) | (4) |
| Regional heterogeneity | East | Central | West | Northeast |
| Mid-high net worth families | 22.833 | 733.010 | 237.084 | 2,398.404*** |
| | (0.10) | (1.13) | (1.62) | (2.67) |
| Household-level control variables | Yes | Yes | Yes | Yes |
| Control variables at household head level | Yes | Yes | Yes | Yes |
| Fixed effects of provinces | Yes | Yes | Yes | Yes |
| Constant | −1,538.620 | −1,490.990 | −1,315.789*** | −4,792.956 |
| | (−1.27) | (−1.58) | (−3.70) | (−0.88) |
| Observations | 1,654 | 1,407 | 1,720 | 385 |
| R-squared | 0.124 | 0.026 | 0.068 | 0.181 |

*Note* $^{*}p < 0.1$, $^{**}p < 0.05$, $^{***}p < 0.01$

**Table 9** Regression results for the effect of household investable assets on children's commercial medical insurance expenditures (income and urban–rural heterogeneity)

| | Children's commercial health insurance expenses | | | |
|---|---|---|---|---|
| | (1) | (2) | (3) | (4) |
| Income heterogeneity | High income | Low income | | |
| Urban–rural heterogeneity | | | Urban | Rural |
| Investable assets | −19.983 | −4.720 | −11.830 | −2.835 |
| | (−0.89) | (−0.76) | (−0.50) | (−0.26) |
| Household-level control variables | Yes | Yes | Yes | Yes |
| Control variables at household head level | Yes | Yes | Yes | Yes |
| Fixed effects of provinces | Yes | Yes | Yes | Yes |
| Constant | −10,261.177*** | 94.934 | −1,984.838 | −1,437.050 |
| | (−3.45) | (0.32) | (−1.29) | (−1.56) |
| Observations | 2,900 | 2,266 | 2,542 | 5,166 |
| R-squared | 0.064 | 0.089 | 0.060 | 0.056 |

*Note* *p < 0.1, **p < 0.05, ***p < 0.01

The sample was divided into two groups, urban and rural, and grouped into regressions based on the location of households in the sample. Columns (3) and (4) of Table 9 show the regression results based on urban–rural heterogeneity. The results show that the effect of investable household assets on children's commercial medical insurance expenditure is insignificant for both urban and rural households.

Based on the location of the households in the sample, the urban sample is further divided into four groups: first-tier cities, second-tier cities, third-tier cities, and fourth-tier cities, and the regressions are conducted in groups. The results are summarized in Table 10. The results show that the effect of investable household assets on children's commercial medical insurance expenditure in tier 2 cities is significantly positive, whereas none of the effects on children's commercial medical insurance expenditure in the remaining classes of cities are significant. This indicates that the impact of investable household assets on children's commercial medical insurance expenditure differs for households in different classes of cities. Therefore, when analyzing specific issues, it is important to focus on the different cities in which the household is located.

According to the National Bureau of Statistics' Methodology for Dividing East, West, Central, and Northeast Regions, the sample was divided into four major regions, namely, East, Central, West, and Northeast, according to the provinces and municipalities where they are located. The regressions were conducted in groups, and the results are summarized in Table 11. The results show that the effect of investable household assets on children's commercial medical insurance expenditure is insignificant in any of the four major regions.

**Table 10** Regression results for the effect of investable household assets on children's commercial health insurance expenditures (urban heterogeneity)

| | Children's commercial health insurance expenses | | | |
|---|---|---|---|---|
| | (1) | (2) | (3) | (4) |
| Urban heterogeneity | First-tier cities | Second-tier cities | Third-tier cities | Fourth-tier cities and below |
| Investable assets | −114.049 | 69.283* | 35.733 | −37.883 |
| | (−1.05) | (1.78) | (0.96) | (−1.25) |
| Household-level control variables | Yes | Yes | Yes | Yes |
| Control variables at household head level | Yes | Yes | Yes | Yes |
| Fixed effects of provinces | Yes | Yes | Yes | Yes |
| Constant | −3,344.094 | −211.820 | 1,551.502 | −2,027.933 |
| | (−0.47) | (−0.06) | (0.68) | (−1.31) |
| Observations | 182 | 416 | 219 | 1,725 |
| R-squared | 0.270 | 0.229 | 0.357 | 0.107 |

*Note* *$p < 0.1$, **$p < 0.05$, ***$p < 0.01$

**Table 11** Regression results for the effect of investable household assets on children's commercial health insurance expenditures (regional heterogeneity)

| | Children's commercial health insurance expenses | | | |
|---|---|---|---|---|
| | (1) | (2) | (3) | (4) |
| Regional heterogeneity | East | Central | West | Northeast |
| Investable assets | 6.091 | 13.523 | −7.131 | −58.461 |
| | (0.53) | (1.34) | (−0.76) | (−0.80) |
| Household-level control variables | Yes | Yes | Yes | Yes |
| Control variables at household head level | Yes | Yes | Yes | Yes |
| Fixed effects of provinces | Yes | Yes | Yes | Yes |
| Constant | −1,561.860 | −1,746.125 | −1,354.167*** | −5,242.465 |
| | (−1.30) | (−1.52) | (−3.84) | (−1.04) |
| Observations | 1,654 | 1,407 | 1,720 | 385 |
| R-squared | 0.124 | 0.023 | 0.067 | 0.167 |

*Note* *$p < 0.1$, **$p < 0.05$, ***$p < 0.01$

The results of the above heterogeneity analysis show that the impact of mid-high net worth families and investable family assets on children's commercial medical insurance should be analyzed specifically according to different regions, cities, and families, and cannot be generalized. In particular, when financial institutions design and develop products and services, they should make comprehensive deployment and planning according to time, place, and families, to enhance the attractiveness of products and services to different types of families.

## 7 Summary

This chapter analyzes the allocation of children's commercial health insurance for mid-high net worth families. The main conclusions are as follows:

First, the coverage rate of children's commercial medical insurance for mid-high net worth families is significantly higher than that of non mid-high net worth families, with the coverage rate of the former exceeding 30%, while that of the latter is approximately 20%, and 15.26 percentage points higher for the 12- to 16-year-old group. The difference between the coverage rates of children's commercial medical insurance for mid-high net worth households in agricultural households and non mid-high net worth households was 12.88 percentage points; for non-agricultural households, the difference was 9.51 percentage points; and for residents, the difference was 7.57 percentage points. The difference between the commercial medical insurance coverage rate for male children in mid-high net worth households and non mid-high net worth households is 14.6 percentage points; the difference between the commercial medical insurance coverage rate for female children is 13.1 percentage points.

Second, there are some differences in the trends in the average cost of children's commercial medical insurance for mid-high net worth households and non mid-high net worth households under the age group of 0 to 7 years. First, the average cost of children's commercial medical insurance for ages 0 to 7 for mid-high net worth households shows a significantly increasing trend, whereas non mid-high net worth households show a decreasing trend. Second, the difference between middle- and high-net worth families and non-middle- and high-net worth families is the smallest in the age group of 0 to 3 years, with a difference of ¥733.45. After the child turns 3, the gap between the average cost of children's commercial medical insurance for Mid-high net worth families and non mid-high net worth families becomes larger, with a difference of ¥3,154.21 at ages 4 to 7; ¥2,663.13 at ages 8 to 11; and ¥2,511.51 at ages 12 to 16. Overall, the cost of children's commercial medical insurance is significantly higher for middle- and high-net worth families than for non-middle- and high-net worth families after four years of age.

Third, the average cost of children's commercial medical insurance is significantly higher for girls than for boys in mid-high net worth families, whereas the average cost for boys is higher than for girls in non mid-high net worth families. The difference between the average cost of children's commercial medical insurance for middle- and high-net-worth families is large, with a difference of ¥1,526.87 for boys and ¥3,458.92 for girls.

Fourth, in the sickness group, the proportion of middle and high net worth households that purchase children's commercial medical insurance is 12.45 percentage points higher than that of non-middle and high net worth households. In the group with no sickness, there is a difference of 12.42 percentage points between the two. Regarding the ratio of out-of-pocket medical expenses to medical expenditures for mid-high net worth households and non mid-high net worth households, the ratio of mid-high net worth households that purchased children's commercial medical insurance and non mid-high net worth households were lower than that of households that did not purchase children's commercial medical insurance.

Fifth, the average cost of purchasing children's commercial medical insurance among mid-high net worth families who save money for their children's education is ¥1,740.64 higher than those who do not save money for their children's education; among non mid-high net worth families, the difference between the two is ¥981.07, both of which are significant. There is a correlation between families who are conscious of investing more in education spending for their children's health insurance and those who have commercial health insurance investment behaviors that increase the value of their children's education capital accumulation.

Sixth, after considering household-level control variables, head-of-household-level control variables, child-related control variables, and province-fixed effects, mid-high net worth households spend approximately ¥417 more per year on children's commercial medical insurance than non mid-high net worth households. This indicates that mid-high net worth households invest more money in children's commercial health insurance and have more demand for children's commercial health insurance. This also shows that mid-high net worth families can provide better insurance coverage for their children.

## References


1. Wu, H.: How to choose commercial medical insurance? Modern Bus. Banking, 52–54 (2019)
2. Fang, L., Jing, P.: Comparative analysis of commercial health insurance in China and the United States and the direction of health insurance development in China. Insurance Theory and Practice, 62–68 (2020)
3. Guo, X.: How commercial health insurance can be "well received and appreciated". *Xiaokang*, 44–46 (2018)

4. Zhai, W.: Chase global: Do only high net worth individuals need to do wealth transfer? Economy 80 (2019)
5. Xu, N., Gu, X., Xiang, G.: A review of China's children's health care policy. Health Econ. Res. **37**, 32–35 (2020)
6. Stacey, K., Burns, T.J., Anthony, S., Michael, D.J.: Health insurance, neighborhood income, and emergency department usage by Utah children 1996–1998. BMC Health Serv. Res. **5**, 29–29 (2005)
7. Zarrabi, M., Kumar, S., Macary, S., Honigfeld, L.: The relationship between body mass index in children and insurance type, parental eating concern, asthma, and allergies. J. Pediatr. Health Care **33**, e29–e37 (2019)
8. Hatch, B., Angier, H., Marino, M., Heintzman, J., Nelson, C., Gold, R., Vakarcs, T., DeVoe, J.: Using electronic health records to conduct children's health insurance surveillance. Pediatrics **132**, e1584–e1591 (2013)
9. Humensky, J., Ireys, H.T., Wickstrom, S., Rheault, P.: Mental Health Services for Children with Special Health Care Needs in Commercial Managed Care, 1999–2001. Mathematica Policy Research, Washington, DC (2004)
10. Dong, Y., Zhang, L., Yang, Y., Dong, W., Mo, D., Fang, Y., Qian, K., Luo, M., Li, N., Zhang, Z.: A comparative study of children's basic medical insurance systems and policies in four municipalities directly under the central government in China. J. Shanghai Jiao Tong Univ. Med. Edition **38**, 671–675 (2018)
11. Kurtz, M.P., Eswara, J.R., Vetter, J.M., Nelson, C.P., Brandes, S.B.: Blunt abdominal trauma from motor vehicle collisions from 2007 to 2011: renal injury probability and severity in children versus adults. J. Urol. **197**, 906–910 (2017)
12. Pitcairn, T.K., Edlmann, T.: Individual differences in road crossing ability in young children and adults. Br. J. Psychol. **91**, 391–410 (2000)
13. Wu, J.: How to buy children's "insurance" the most insurance? Business Week, 54–56 (2015)
14. Yang, X.: An empirical study on the influencing factors of children's commercial medical insurance in China. Modern Business Banking, 23–24 (2016)
15. Ye, S., Guo, D., Wei, W., Su, Y., Juyang, X.: Analysis of health insurance coverage of preschool children and its influencing factors in Wuhan. Chinese J. Soc. Med. **33**, 59–61 (2016)
16. Edwards, L.N., Grossman, M.: Children's Health and the Family. Adv. Health Econ. Health Serv. Res. **2**, 35–84 (1981)
17. Zhu, J.M., Zhu, Y., Liu, R.: Health insurance of rural/township schoolchildren in Pinggu, Beijing: coverage rate, determinants, disparities, and sustainability. Int. J. Equity Health **7**, 1–9 (2008)
18. Osamura, T., Kiyosawa, N., Tei, J., Kinugasa, T., Mori, K., Ito, H., Sawada, T.: An effective system of activities in local communities to prevent injuries in children: An opinion survey of public health nurses concerning injury preventing activities. J. Child Health **63**, e39157 (2004)
19. Mckenzie, H.: Children's health insurance programs: do they provide the coverage that is needed? Home Healthc. NurseHealthc. Nurse **29**, 124–125 (2011)
20. Yan, C., Zhan, H., Du, Y., Huang, C., Wu, Q., Li, L., Dong, Y., Zhou, L.: Measurement of children's healthcare costs in Hunan Province and analysis of results. Bus. Watch, 23–25 (2021)
21. Jin, M.: Maternal and child insurance: Umbrella for mothers-to-be. Popular Financ. Advisor **68** (2015)
22. Qiu, F.: An empirical investigation of factors influencing the demand for commercial health insurance in China. J. Insur. Vocat. Coll. **35**, 66–72 (2021)
23. Bork, K.A., Diallo, A.: Boys are more stunted than girls from early infancy to 3 years of age in rural senegal. J. Nutr.Nutr. **147**, 940–947 (2017)

24. Thurstans, S., Opondo, C., Seal, A., Wells, J., Khara, T., Dolan, C., Briend, A., Myatt, M., Garenne, M., Sear, R., et al.: Boys are more likely to be undernourished than girls: A systematic review and meta-analysis of sex differences in undernutrition. BMJ Glob. Health **5**, e004030 (2020)
25. Zhao, X.: The impact of health factors on the demand for commercial health insurance. Times Financ. **20**, 144–146 (2020)
26. Xia, S.: Analysis of the out-of-pocket ratio of hospitalized patients with medical insurance. China Hospital Manage., 54–56 (2005)
27. Yue, M.: Wealth inheritance and children's education of the high-end crowd. Popular Financ. Advisor, 80–81 (2011)

# Chapter 7
# Retirement and Insurance for Mid-High Net Worth Families

**Abstract** With China's rapidly growing aging population, retirement has become an important issue for economic and social development. Protecting the lives of the older adults after retirement is a family as well as a social issue. Thus, this study here analyzed the situation of families receiving retirement/pension or old-age pension and the participation of family commercial pension insurance through Chinese household tracking survey data and obtained the following main conclusions. The results show that the proportion of mid-high net worth households receiving pension or retirement benefits is somewhat higher than that of non mid-high net worth households; mid-high net worth households receive more severance/pension or old-age pension, which plays a positive role in ensuring a high quality of retirement life for older adults in mid-high net worth households.

China has the largest older adult population worldwide and is currently one of the fastest aging countries today. The results of the seventh national census show that the population aged 60 years and above in China is 264.02 million, accounting for 18.70% of the population. Among them, the population aged 65 years and above is 190.64 million, accounting for 13.50%. Compared to 2010, the proportion of the population aged 60 years and above increased by 5.44%. This proportion is expected to increase to 34% by 2050 when China's aging population reaches 487 million people, accounting for 1/4 of the global older adult population [1]. With this rapid population aging, the issue of "ageing in place" has become increasingly challenging and is an important issue of concern for the government, enterprises, society, and families. In China, family aging is the traditional method of aging. However, as the birth rate decreases and children leave home to work, family retirement is becoming increasingly vulnerable [2, 3]. In contrast, the modern social pension system, led by the government, enterprises, and commercial insurance companies, plays an increasingly important role in supporting older adults [4].

The pension insurance system is a social insurance system established by the state in accordance with relevant laws and regulations to guarantee the basic livelihood of workers after they reach the age limit set by the state to be relieved of their labor obligations or withdraw from their labor positions owing to old age and incapacity [5].

 
J. Gu, *Wealth Management Report for Mid-High Net Worth Families*, Spatial Demography and Population Governance, https://doi.org/10.1007/978-981-97-0387-6_7

The main purpose and core function of old-age insurance is to use social insurance as a means to provide the basic needs of older adults who have retired or lost their working capacity, to provide them with a stable and reliable source of livelihood, and to effectively solve the problem of "old age" [6]. Old-age insurance includes social pension, commercial pension, and other pension insurance. Social pension insurance includes six types of pension insurance: pension insurance for government agencies and institutions, pension insurance for enterprise employees, urban residents' pension insurance, unified residents' pension insurance, new rural pension insurance, and subsidies for senior citizens. Commercial pension insurance includes enterprise supplementary pension insurance, non-life commercial pension insurance, life insurance, and other types of commercial pension insurance. Additionally, China has expropriation pension insurance. Pension insurance is an important household asset [7].

## 1 Pension Insurance and Income

The development of pension insurance is closely related to the introduction of relevant national policies and the improvement of the system and people's income levels. Generally, the pension insurance system affects the labor supply behavior of older adults mainly by three factors: the setting of the normal retirement and early retirement age, the amount of pension, and the implicit tax rate for continuing to work [8]. Hence, the government has adjusted and improved the pension insurance system by introducing targeted policies to promote the positive contribution of the pension insurance system to economic and social development while ensuring that older adults have a secure life after retirement. Pension insurance development is directly related to the income level of the people. Individuals with different income levels have different pension insurance requirements. Low-income people emphasize their basic provision in old age, whereas middle- and high-income people want a relatively high-quality old-age life. The different pension insurance needs of people with different income levels make pension insurance products diverse.

### *1.1 Current Pension Insurance System*

In China, urban and rural areas adopt different social pension systems with obvious urban–rural differences, with a typical urban–rural dual structure [9]. In urban areas, it is mainly the pension insurance of government agencies and institutions with the state treasury providing the relevant pension insurance premiums. The current pension insurance system for institutions was first established in the 1950s and created in 1978. In 2011, China promulgated the guidance of the State Council on launching pilot social pension insurance for urban residents, which started the pilot work of social pension insurance in urban areas. On January 14, 2015, the State Council on instituting the decision on the reform of the pension insurance system for staff of organs and institutions was issued, deciding to reform it from October 1, 2014.

Enterprise employee pension insurance is another important type of pension insurance in urban areas. In June 1991, the State Council promulgated the decision on the reform of the pension insurance system for enterprise employees, which stipulated that enterprises with certain economic capacities and better business conditions could establish supplementary pension insurance. However, the academic community generally believes that the basic pension insurance for enterprise employees in China was formally established in 1994 [9]. Thereafter, the name was changed from "enterprise supplementary pension insurance" to "enterprise annuity" in the "Pilot Program on Improving the Urban Social Security System" by the State Council. In December 2000 and 2004, the "Trial Measures for the Management of Enterprise Annuity Funds" and "Enterprise Annuity" were promulgated. In 2004, the promulgation of the "Trial Measures for Enterprise Pension Fund Management" and "Trial Measures for Enterprise Pension" marked the full implementation of the enterprise pension system in China. After over a decade of efforts, a foundation has been established for enterprise employees' pension insurance. The data in the "Statistical Bulletin on the Development of Human Resources and Social Security in 2019" published by the Ministry of Human Resources and Social Security of China show that in 2019, the income of the basic pension insurance fund for urban employees was RMB 529.19 billion, the fund expenditure was RMB 4,922.8 billion, and the accumulated balance of the basic pension insurance fund for urban employees was RMB 5,462.3 billion. Scholars estimate that, from 2010 to 2050, the financial subsidies for basic pension insurance for urban workers discounted in 2010 were 52.3 trillion yuan, equivalent to 130% of the GDP in that year [10].

In rural areas, social pensions rely primarily on the new rural social pension insurance system. In the past, pensions in rural areas of China were dominated by traditional family pensions and clan network mutual aid pension models [11]. However, with the rapid decline in the fertility rate of the rural population and the departure of young and strong rural laborers for work, the endogenous vulnerability and unsustainability of the traditional family pension model in rural areas based on land have become increasingly obvious. The shift from the rural family pension model to the social pension model has become inevitable [12]. In 2009, the State Council's "guidance on the launching of new rural social pension insurance, the promulgation of the guiding opinions of the State Council on piloting new rural social pension insurance," marked a new stage of social pension in China's rural areas. The new rural social pension insurance system was officially implemented on October 1, 2010. The number participants increased from 33.26 million in early 2010 to 460 million by the end of 2012, basically achieving nationwide coverage of the new rural social pension insurance system [13].

## 1.2 The Impact of Income on Pension Insurance

Income is one of the important factors that have an impact on the demand for older adult services and pension insurance. Some studies have shown that the differences between mid-high income groups in how they support their parents as they age and their preferential demands and propensity activities are statistically significant [14]. Most previous studies on the need for old-age insurance focused on mid-low income groups [15, 16]. China's population has grown rapidly in recent years, and the number of mid-high net worth households has increased significantly, with a unique need for retirement-related protection. Various targeted old-age protection solutions have emerged for high-income households [17]. Some studies point out the development trend of lowering the age of mid-high income older adult groups in their retirement planning, and their acceptance of institutions has increased [18]. In the Internet era, mid-high income groups are equipped with the concept of aging in modern society, retaining traditional family and home aging methods and willing to try the combination of institutional and community aging supported by the Internet as a technology [19]. These changing trends indicate that middle- and high-income individuals have more systematic planning for retirement and higher expectations of a high-quality retirement life.

Foreign studies show that pensions, which play an important role in guaranteeing material security and well-being for most of the population, are distributed in society in a significantly unequal manner [7]. At the micro level, the coverage profiles of different income level groups in Latin American countries show that income level directly determines individual participation [20, 21]. This difference is particularly evident for commercial pension insurance. Individuals with mid-high net worth form the focus group for commercial pension insurance services [22]. Therefore, many insurance companies tailor commercial pension insurance products and services to meet the needs of this group for a high-quality retirement life. There is a lack of research on pension insurance for mid-high net worth families and related groups in China. Moreover, the exploration of personal pension management for mid-high net worth families is not systematic and in-depth [23]. To a certain extent, the research and theoretical deficiencies limit the awareness of mid-high net worth families regarding pension insurance and financial management.

To promote the construction of a multi-level and multi-pillar pension insurance system and the sustainable development of the pension insurance system, on April 21, 2022, the opinions of the general office of the State Council on promoting the development of individual pensions were released, proposing the development of individual pensions that are suitable for China's national conditions, supported by government policies, voluntarily supported by individuals, and operated by the market, to connect with basic pension insurance and corporate (occupational) annuities and to realize the supplementary function of pension insurance. The personal pension system is a supplement to the first and second pillars and a reform of the entire existing pension insurance system [24]. As optional types of personal pensions include financial products such as bank wealth management, commercial pension insurance, and public funds, they have good financial management functions. Therefore, it is more attractive to mid-high net worth households. Certainly, because this policy has only recently been introduced, its specific effect remains to be further observed and studied [25]. Low-income earners may be unable to meet their needs in old age, even with full contributions, which limits the smooth operation of the personal pension system. To encourage workers (especially low-income earners) to participate in personal pensions, incentives other than tax benefits, such as interest subsidies, should be provided.

## 2 Family Separation/Pension or Pension Coverage Rate

The concepts of severance/retirement pension and old-age pension differ. The former is part of the remuneration paid by an enterprise or institution to an employee or staff member for their services after they leave/retire in one lump sum or in several installments, while the latter is one of the most dominant social pension insurance benefits in current society. From a household perspective, both can help alleviate the problem of family retirement security. This study uses households as a unit to calculate the proportion of households receiving either a severance/retirement pension or an old-age pension-the so-called coverage ratio.

### *2.1 Family Level*

The family level calculates the coverage rate of the full sample of households receiving a severance/pension or old-age pension according to the structure of the community separately for neighborhood and village councils; the results are summarized in Fig. 1.

According to Fig. 1, the coverage rate of households receiving a retirement/pension or old-age pension is 0.09% higher for those whose community structure is a village council than for those whose community structure is a neighborhood council. The difference between the two is small. Therefore, from this indicator, there is no urban–rural gap. Additionally, the coverage rate of households receiving retirement/pension or old-age pension is approximately 38%. Currently, China has a high coverage rate of basic pensions. As the analysis here is on the receipt of a severance/pension or old-age pension, overall, the current coverage rate is much lower than the basic pension because many family members are still relatively young and have not yet reached the age of receiving a severance/pension or old-age pension.

This study calculates the coverage rate of divorce/pension or old-age pension for mid-high net worth households and non mid-high net worth households separately, and the results are summarized in Fig. 2. According to Fig. 2, the coverage rate of the mid-high net worth households receiving a severance/pension or old-age pension is

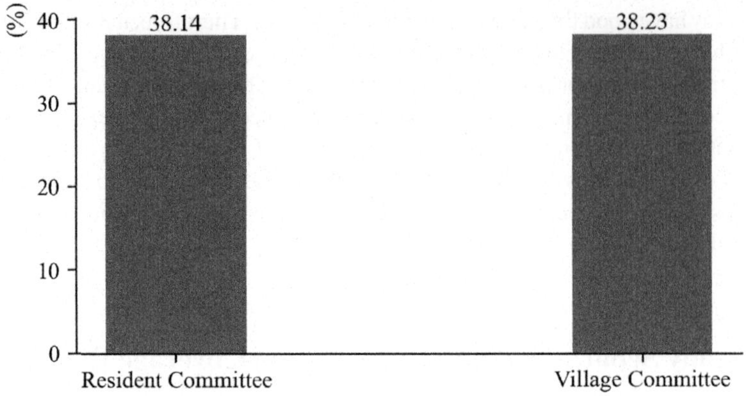


**Fig. 1** Coverage of the full sample of households receiving a severance/pension or old-age pension (community-based in structure)

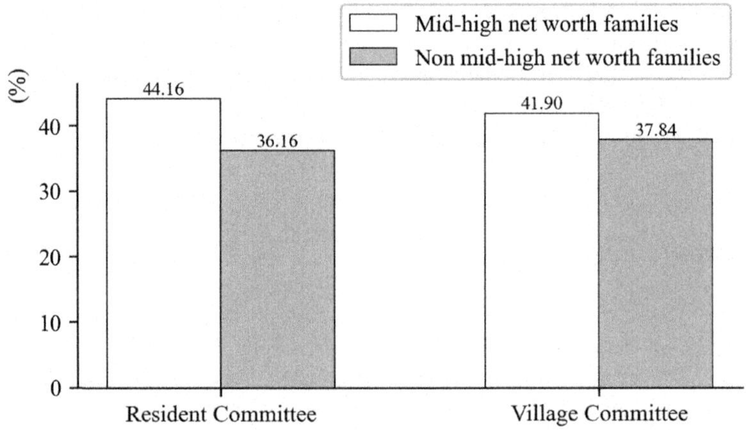


**Fig. 2** Coverage of mid-high net worth households and non mid-high net worth households receiving a severance/pension or pension (community-based in structure)

8% higher in community-based committees than in non mid-high net worth households; the difference between the two is 4.06% in village committees. In general, the coverage rate of mid-high net worth households receiving divorce/pension or old-age pension will be higher than that of non mid-high net worth households. When financial conditions allow it, mid-high net worth households may experience early retirement and receive early severance/pension payments. Additionally, some mid-high net worth family members may also receive a portion of their pension early when they emigrate abroad. These situations are more likely to occur in mid-high net worth families.

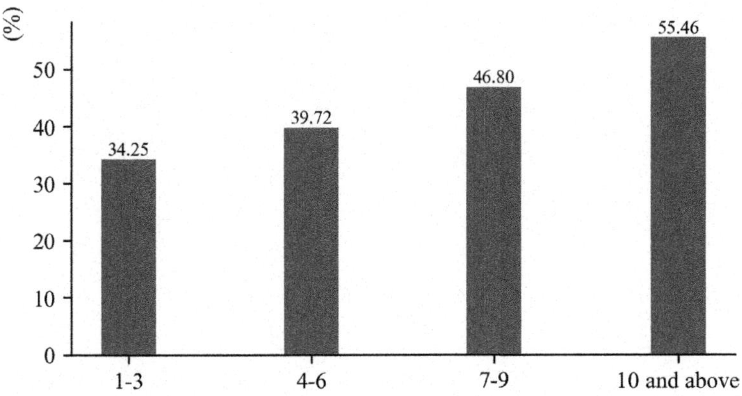


**Fig. 3** Coverage of the full sample of households receiving a severance/pension or old-age pension (household size)

It is grouped to calculate the coverage rate of households of different sizes receiving a severance/pension or old-age pension, and the results are summarized in Fig. 3.

According to Fig. 3, the coverage of household members receiving a severance/pension or old-age pension tends to increase stepwise as household size increases. This is because the larger the number of household members, the more generations the household tends to have, and the more likely it is to have older people in the household; therefore, the higher the coverage rate for receiving a severance/pension or old-age pension.

According to Fig. 4, when the household size is one to three members, the coverage rate of mid-high net worth households is 6.25% lower than that of non mid-high net worth households in terms of divorce/pension or pension coverage. When the household size is four to six members, the difference is 15.71%. When the household size is seven to nine members, the difference is 8.95%. When the household size is 10 members or more, the difference is 0.62%. Except for households with one to three members, the coverage rate of mid-high net worth households is higher than that of non mid-high net worth households. When the household size is relatively small, the coverage rate of mid-high net worth households receiving divorce/pension or pension is lower than that of non mid-high net worth households. This is because when the household size is relatively small, the mid-high net worth households are financially stronger; therefore, there is no need to draw on divorce/pension or pension.

This study calculates the coverage rate of households receiving divorces/pensions or old-age pensions according to urban and rural divisions, and the results are summarized in Fig. 5.

According to Fig. 5, there is a difference of 0.77% between the coverage rate of urban household members receiving a divorce/pension or old-age pension and rural households. This indicates that the urban–rural gap is insignificant.

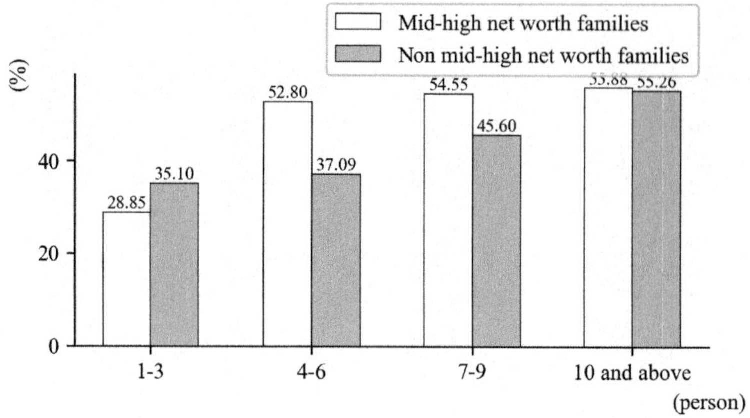


**Fig. 4** Coverage of mid-high net worth households and non mid-high net worth households receiving a divorce/pension or pension (household size)

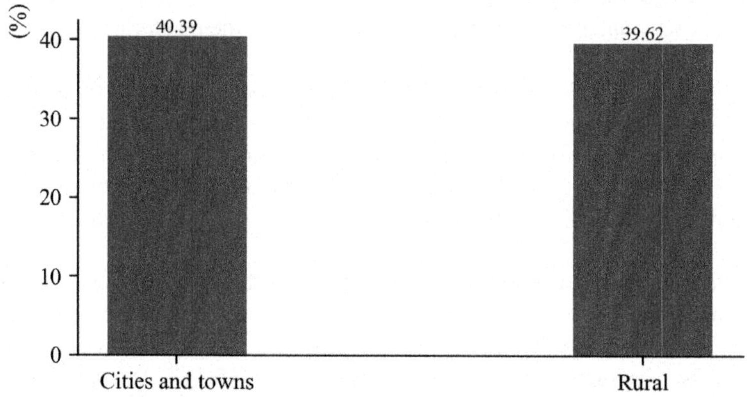


**Fig. 5** Coverage of the full sample of households receiving divorce/pension or old-age pension (urban–rural divisions)

According to Fig. 6, there is a difference of 11.11% between the coverage rates of urban mid-high net worth households and non mid-high net worth households receiving a divorce/pension or pension and a difference of 3.57% between the coverage rates of rural non mid-high net worth households and mid-high net worth households receiving a divorce/pension or pension. It is noteworthy that in rural areas, the coverage rate of mid-high net worth households receiving divorce/pension or old-age pension is lower than that of non mid-high net worth households.

This study calculates the coverage of households receiving a severance/pension or old-age pension according to urban-type subgroups. The results are summarized in Fig. 7.

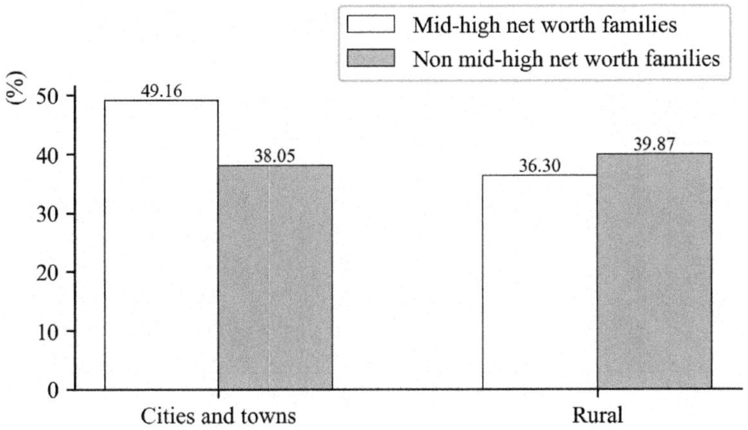


**Fig. 6** Coverage of mid-high net worth households and non mid-high net worth households receiving a severance/pension or old-age pension (in urban and rural areas)

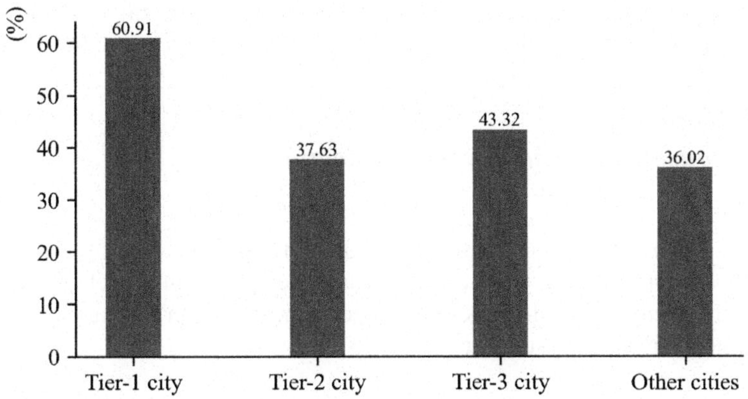


**Fig. 7** Coverage of the full sample of households receiving a severance/pension or old-age pension (urban type)

According to Fig. 7, households in tier-1 cities have the highest coverage rate of receiving a severance/pension or pension whereas households in other cities have the lowest coverage rate. It is worth noting that the coverage rate of households receiving divorces/pensions or pensions in tier-3 cities is significantly higher than that in tier-2 cities. This indicates that tier-3 cities may face a more serious pension-gap problem in the future.

According to Fig. 8, the difference between the coverage rates of mid-high net worth households and non mid-high net worth households receiving divorces/ pensions or old-age pensions is 14.25% in tier-1 cities, 4.95% in tier-2 cities, 7.2% in tier-3 cities, and 1.29% in other cities. In summary, the largest gap between the

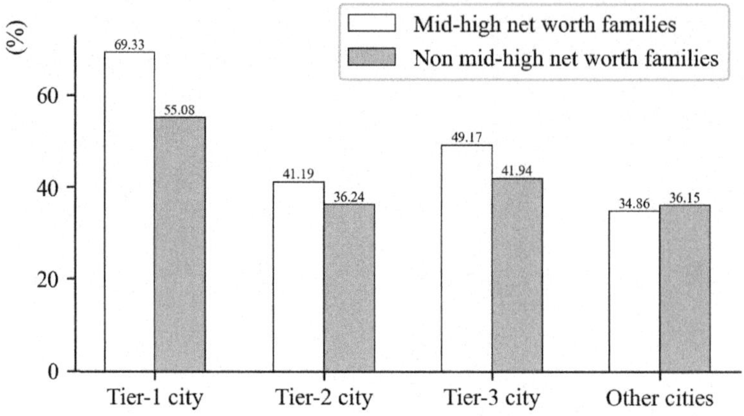


**Fig. 8** Coverage of mid-high net worth households and non mid-high net worth households receiving divorce/pension or old-age pension (city type)

coverage rate of mid-high net worth households and non-medium- and mid-high net worth households receiving divorce/pension or old-age pension is in tier-1 cities.

## *2.2 Household Head Level of Education*

The education level of the household head is an important factor that influences household decisions. This study calculates the coverage rate of households receiving a severance/pension or old-age pension based on the education level of the household head, and the results are summarized in Fig. 9.

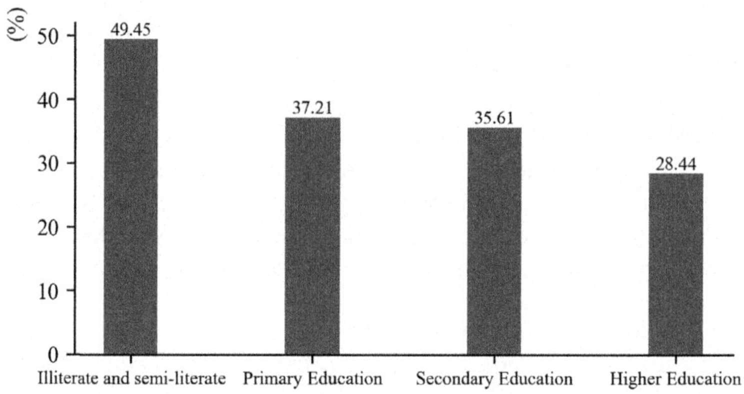


**Fig. 9** Coverage of the full sample of households receiving divorce/pension or old-age pension (education level of household head)

According to Fig. 9, as the education level of the household head increases, the coverage rate of households receiving severance/pension or old-age pension tends to decrease stepwise. The more educated the head of the household, the less likely the household head will retire early, and the lower the coverage rate of receiving a severance/pension or old-age pension.

According to Fig. 10, there is a 1.45% difference between the coverage rates of mid-high net worth households and non mid-high net worth households when the education level of the household head is illiterate/semi-literate, 3.17% when it is primary education, 8.48% when it is secondary education, and 20.76% when it is tertiary education. The difference between the two is 20.76% when the education level of the household head is higher education. In summary, the gap between the coverage rates of mid-high net worth households and non mid-high net worth households is the smallest when the household head has an illiterate/semi-literate education and the largest when he/she has a higher education. For different types of households, the effect of the education level of the household head is obvious.

The health status of the household head also affects household retirement and old-age decisions. This study analyzes the household head's health status to calculate the coverage rate of households receiving retirement/pension or old-age pension; the results are summarized in Fig. 11.

According to Fig. 11, the healthier the household head, the lower the coverage rate of the household receiving a severance/retirement pension or old-age pension. The unhealthier the household head, the higher the probability of leaving/retiring early, and the higher the coverage rate.

According to Fig. 12, the difference between the coverage rates of the medium–high net-worth-households and non mid-high net worth households receiving a severance/pension or pension is 5.21% when the household head is unhealthy, 10.59% when the household head is fairly healthy, and 11.89% when the household head

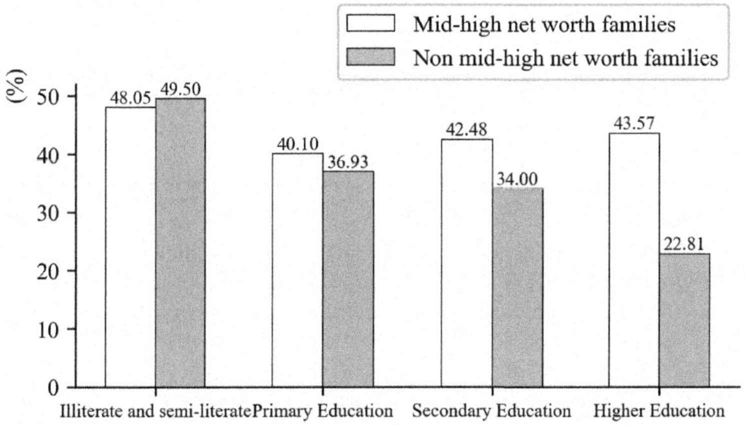


**Fig. 10** Coverage of mid-high net worth households and non mid-high net worth households receiving a separation/retirement or pension (education level of household head)

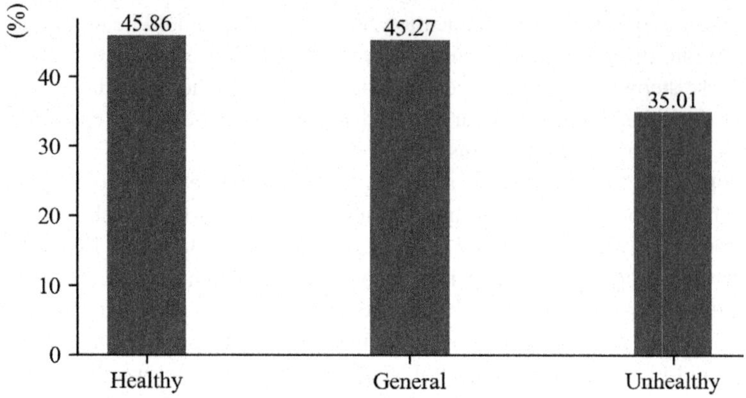


**Fig. 11** Coverage of the full sample of households receiving divorce/pension or old-age pension (health status of household head)

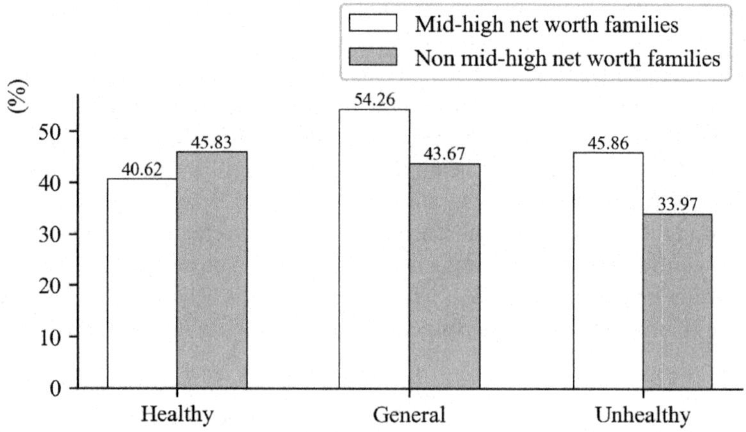


**Fig. 12** Coverage of mid-high net worth households and non mid-high net worth households receiving divorce/pension or old-age pension (health status of household head)

is healthy. In summary, the difference between the coverage rates of mid-high net worth households and non mid-high net worth households is largest when the head of the household is healthy, and smallest when he/she is unhealthy.

It is grouped according to the sex of the household head and calculates the coverage rate of the household receiving a severance/pension or old-age pension. The results are summarized in Fig. 13.

According to Fig. 13, the coverage rate of households receiving a severance/pension or old-age pension is higher when the household head is a female. However, overall, the difference in coverage rates is smaller, less than 3%, when the head of household is male or female.

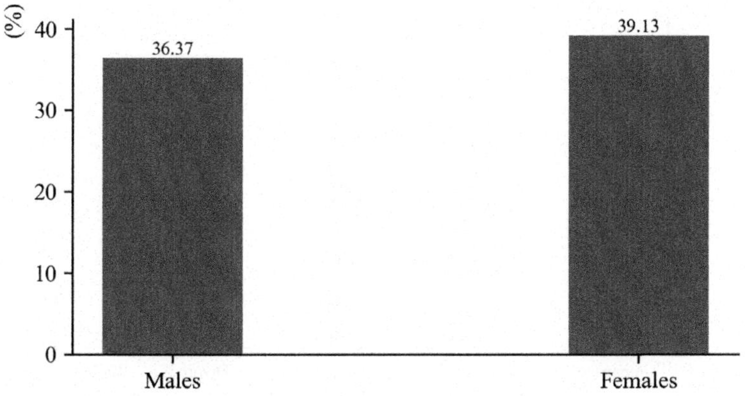


**Fig. 13** Coverage of the full sample of households receiving divorce/pension or old-age pension (sex of household head)

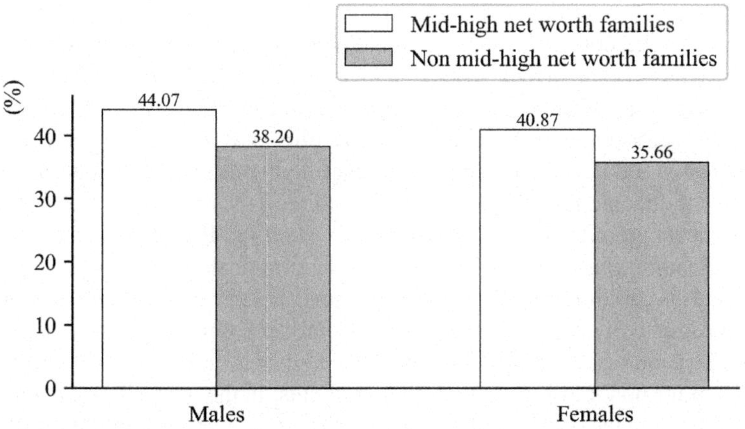


**Fig. 14** Coverage of mid-high net worth households and non mid-high net worth households receiving divorce/pension or old-age pension (sex of household head)

According to Fig. 14, there is a 5.87% difference between the coverage rate of mid-high net worth households and non mid-high net worth households receiving a divorce/pension or pension when the household head is a male and a 5.21% difference when the household head is a female. In summary, the difference between the two is greater when the household head is a male.

This study calculates the coverage rate of households receiving divorce/pension or old-age pension based on the marital status grouping of household heads, and the results are summarized in Fig. 15.

According to Fig. 15, the coverage of households receiving a divorce/pension or old-age pension is highest when the household head is widowed. The proportion of households headed by widowed older adults will be higher. Therefore, the

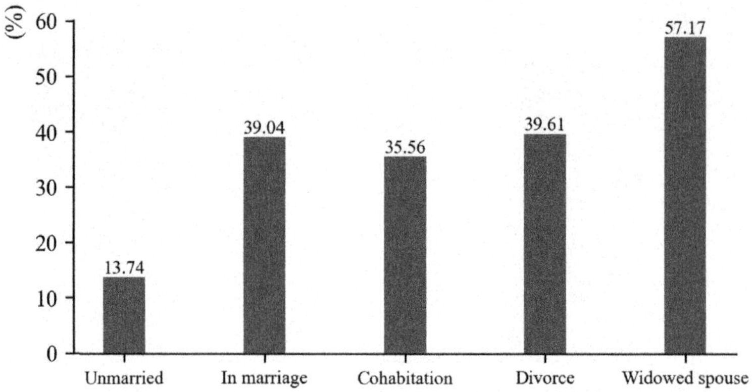


**Fig. 15** Coverage of full sample households receiving divorce/pension or old-age pension (marital status of household head)

coverage rate of receiving divorce/pension or old-age pension is higher for widowed households. The coverage rate of divorce/pension or pension is lowest when the household head is unmarried. Usually, unmarried individuals are younger; therefore, the coverage rate of family divorce/pension or old-age pension is lower. Another important factor related to marriage is the fertility rate. An increase in the fertility rate increases the future labor supply, promoting higher pension replacement rates and pension income [26]. Hence, it can be indirectly verified from this perspective that the coverage rate is significantly higher when the household head is married than when unmarried. This is because it is unquestionable that the fertility rate of households is certainly higher when they are married than when they are unmarried.

According to Fig. 16, when the household head is unmarried, the coverage rate of divorce/pension or old-age pension is 6.55% higher for mid-high net worth households than for non mid-high net worth households; in the married group, the difference is 5.89%; in the cohabitation group, the difference is 40%; in the divorced group, the difference is 21.54%; and in the widowed group, the difference is 18.08%. In summary, the difference between the coverage rates of divorce/pension or old-age pension for mid-high net worth households and non mid-high net worth households is highest when the household head is cohabiting and the difference is lowest when the household head is married.

## 3 The Total Amount of Retirement/Pension Benefits Received by the Family

The amount of severance/pension or old-age pension a family receives will not only directly impact the quality of life of that family's seniors after retirement, but will also affect the family's financial and investment behavior. Leaving/retiring is the process

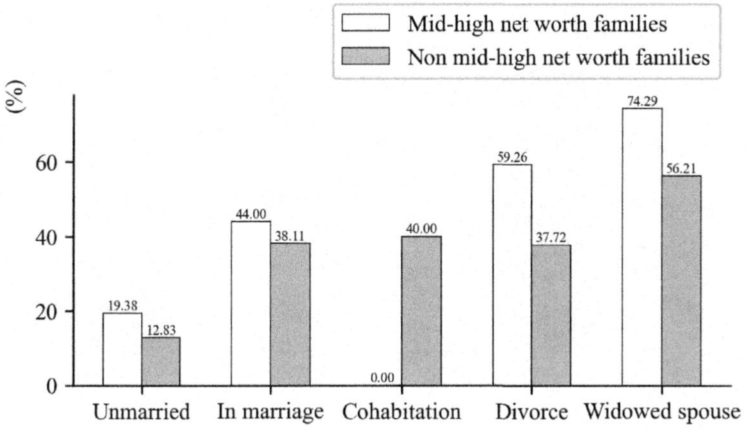


**Fig. 16** Coverage of mid-high net worth households and non mid-high net worth households receiving divorce/pension or pension (marital status of household head)

of realizing a potential severance/pension or old-age pension. This means that families can use this money for activities such as investment and financial management. Studies show that family members tend to sell their homes after retirement and purchase new properties, which is particularly evident in high-income households [27]. Mid-high net worth households are better off financially; therefore, they secure adequate retirement protection in normal times. The severance/pension or old-age pension money is a pure cash inflow and is, therefore, more likely to be used for property investment. Additionally, receiving a severance/pension or old-age pension increases households' healthcare consumption [28].

## 3.1 *Family Level*

The area in which a household is located affects the specific amount of severance/pension or old-age pension it receives. The impact of the community's nature on family pension insurance may be direct or indirect [29]. The community's influence on household decisions should not be ignored, as it is the most direct social space and time in which households exist. Therefore, it is necessary to analyze the influence of different communities. In this study, the total number of years a family receives a divorce/pension or pension is calculated according to the structure of the community grouping, and the results are summarized in 17.

According to Fig. 17, the total annual amount of retirement/pensions or old-age pensions received by households whose community structure is a neighborhood committee is 12,107.56 yuan higher than those whose community structure is a village committee, and the difference between them is statistically significant. This

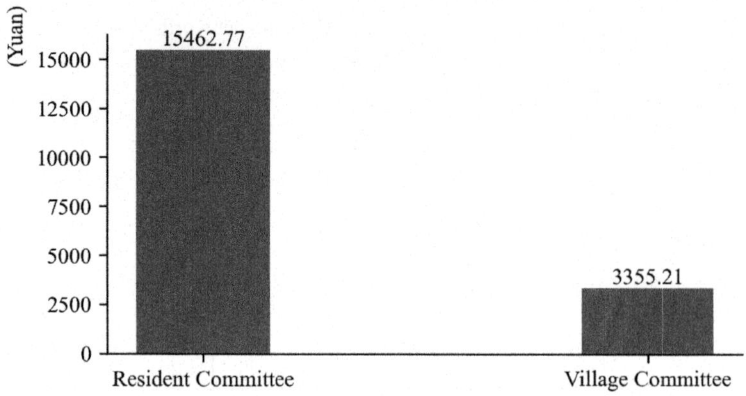


**Fig. 17** Total number of years receiving a severance/pension or old-age pension for the full sample of households (community-based structure)

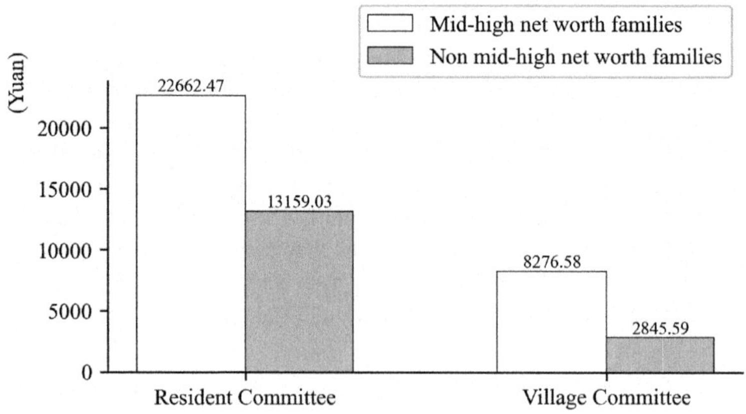


**Fig. 18** Total annual amount of divorce/retirement or pension received by mid-high net worth households and non mid-high net worth households (community-based in structure)

is an important factor contributing to the urban–rural gap in the post-retirement income of older adults [30].

According to Fig. 18, the total annual amount of retirement/pension or old-age pension received by the mid-high net worth households whose community structure is a neighborhood committee is 9,503.44 yuan higher than that of the non mid-high net worth households; the difference between the two is 5,430.99 yuan when the community structure is a village committee. The total annual amount of the separation/pension or old-age pension received by the mid-high net worth households is much higher than that of the non mid-high net worth households in the community committee. Moreover, this difference is also larger than that of the village councils.

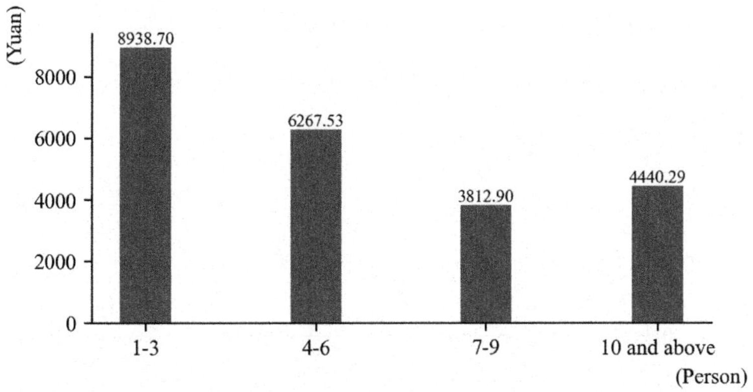


**Fig. 19** Total annual amount of separation/retirement or pension received by full sample households (household size)

This study calculates the total annual number of households receiving a severance/retirement or old-age pension based on household size grouping; the results are summarized in Fig. 19.

According to Fig. 19, the highest total annual amount of family pension or retirement benefit is received when the family size is one to three members, and the lowest when the family size is seven to nine members. The family size directly affects the total annual pension or retirement benefits received by a family.

According to Fig. 20, when the household size is one to three members, the total annual amount of the divorce/pension or old-age pension received by the mid-high net worth households is ¥8,921.79 higher than that of the non mid-high net worth households; when the household size is four to six members, the difference is ¥12,823.38; when the household size is seven to nine members, the difference is ¥8,995.57; and when the household size is 10 members and above, the difference is ¥5,304.26. The difference is 5304.26 yuan. In summary, the difference between the total annual amount of divorces/pensions or pensions received by mid-high net worth households and non mid-high net worth households is more obvious. In particular, the difference in the total amount of annual pensions received by mid-high net worth families and non mid-high net worth families is largest for medium-sized families (four to six members).

This study calculates the total annual number of households receiving retirement/pension or old-age pension according to urban and rural district groupings, and the results are summarized in Fig. 21.

According to Fig. 21, there is a difference of ¥10,043.52 between the total annual amount of retirement/pensions or old-age pensions received by urban households and rural households.

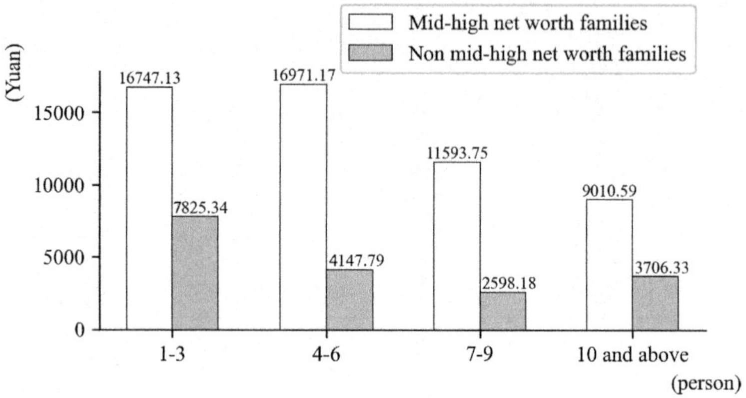


**Fig. 20** Total annual amount of divorce/retirement or pension received by middle and high net worth households and non mid-high net worth households (household size)

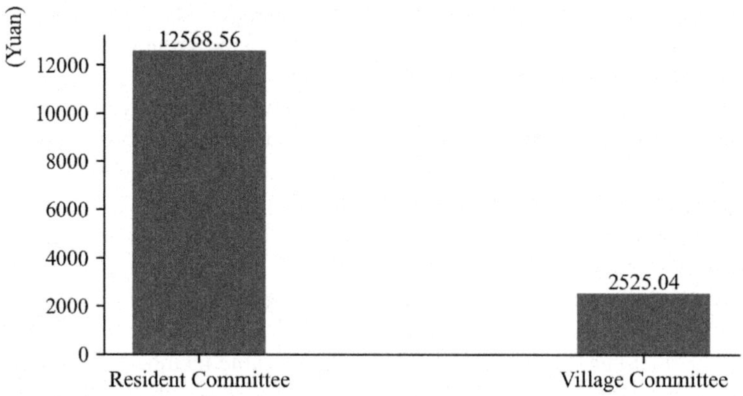


**Fig. 21** Total number of years receiving a retirement/pension or old-age pension for the full sample of households (urban–rural divisions)

According to Fig. 22, there is a difference of¥12,124.87 in the total annual amount of divorce/pension or old-age pension received by urban mid-high net worth households and non mid-high net worth households; and a difference of ¥7,583.48 when received by rural non mid-high net worth households.

The total annual number of households receiving retirement/pension or old-age pension is calculated according to the city type grouping, and the results are summarized in Fig. 23.

According to Fig. 23, there is a stepwise decline in the total annual number of families receiving a severance/pension or old-age pension as the city tier decreases. The largest total annual number of families receiving severances/pensions or old-age pensions is found in tier-1 cities, which exceeds ¥34,000. This amount is much higher than in other city types.

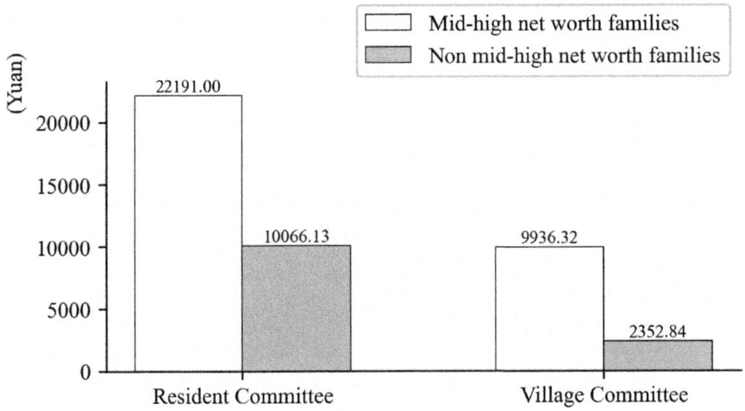


**Fig. 22** Total annual amount of divorce/retirement or old-age pension received by mid-high net worth households and non mid-high net worth households (urban and rural areas)

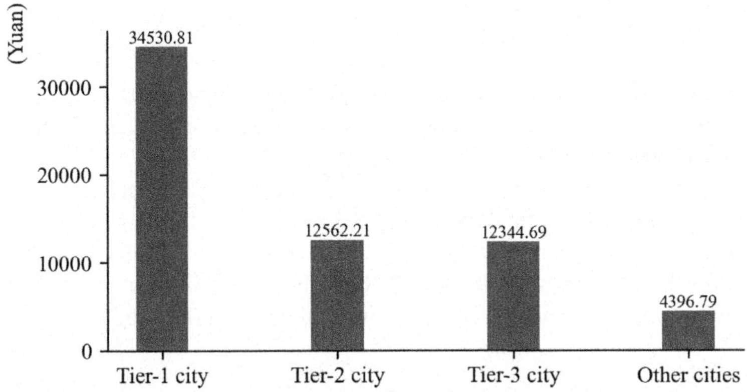


**Fig. 23** Total annual amount of divorce/pension or old-age pension received by the full sample of households (urban type)

According to Fig. 24, the difference between the total annual amount of divorce/pension or old-age pension received by mid-high net worth households and non-high- and middle-net-worth households in tier-1 cities is ¥15,029.03; the difference is ¥7,032.66 in tier-2 cities; ¥4,262.21 in tier-3 cities; and ¥4,038.65 in other cities. In summary, the difference between mid-high net worth households and non mid-high net worth households in terms of the total annual amount of divorces/pensions or old-age pensions gradually increases as the city level increases.

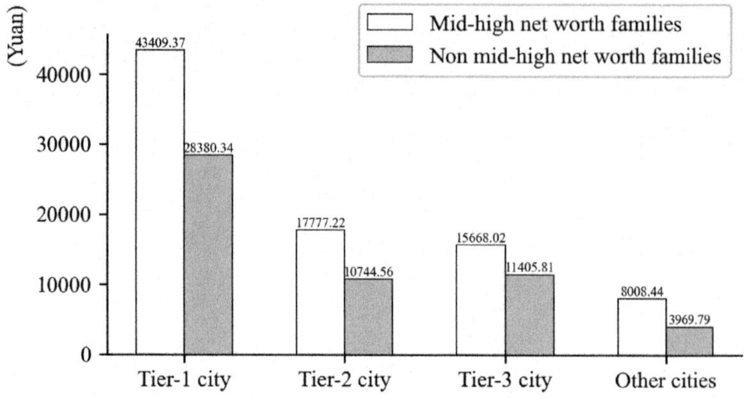


**Fig. 24** Total annual amount of divorce/pension or old-age pension received by mid-high net worth households and non mid-high net worth households (city type)

## *3.2 Head of the Household Level*

This study calculates the total annual amount of a household's receipt of retirement/pension or old-age pension according to the sex of the household head in groups; the results are summarized in Fig. 25.

According to Fig. 25, there is a difference of ¥10,396.67 between the total annual amount of divorce/pension or old-age pension received by mid-high net worth households and non mid-high net worth households when the household head is a male, and a difference of ¥10,691.34 when the household head is a female. In summary, the difference between the two is greater when the household head is a female.

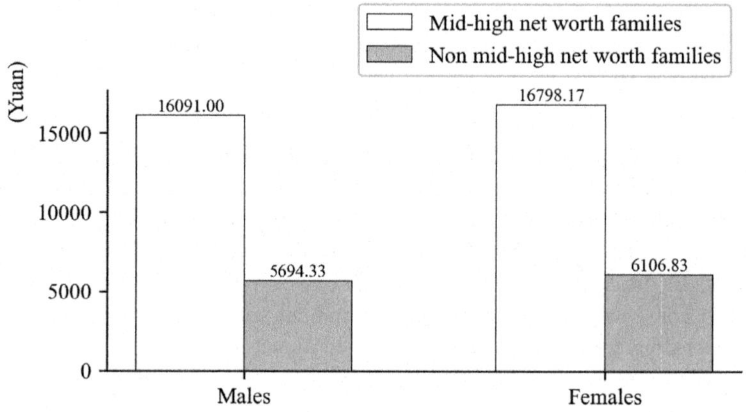


**Fig. 25** Total annual amount of divorce/pension or old-age pension received by mid-high net worth households and non mid-high net worth households (sex of household head)

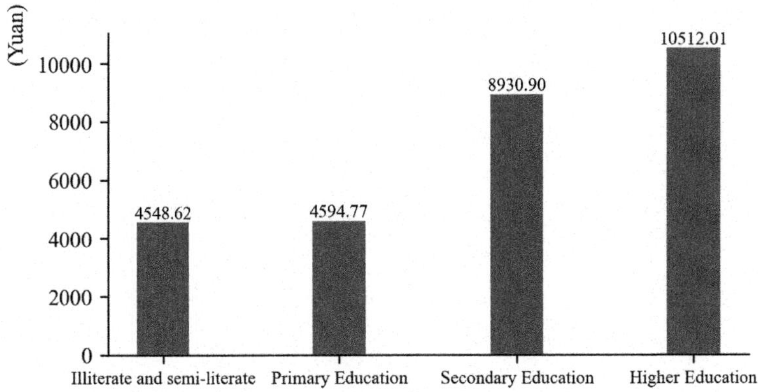


**Fig. 26** Total number of years of receiving divorce/pension or old-age pension for the full sample of households (education level of household head)

This study calculates the total number of years that a household receives a retirement/pension or old-age pension in groups based on the education level of the household head; the results are summarized in Fig. 26.

According to Fig. 26, the total annual retirement/pension received by the household gradually increases as the education level of the household head increases. The difference between the total annual pension received by households with secondary or higher education and those with less than primary education is significant. This is because the higher the education level, the better the workplace and job, and the higher the pension or retirement benefits provided.

According to Fig. 27, the difference between the total annual pensions received by mid-high net worth households and non mid-high net worth households is ¥5,300.25 when the household head's education level is illiterate/semi-literate, ¥3,645.96 when the education level is primary, ¥11,242.35 when the education level is secondary, and ¥8,885.64 when the education level is higher education. The difference between the two is RMB 8,885.64 when the education level of the household head is higher education. In summary, the difference between the total annual amount of divorce/pensions or old-age pensions received by mid-high net worth households and non mid-high net worth households is the highest when the education level of the household head is secondary and the lowest when the education level is primary education.

The total number of years that the household received a retirement/pension or old-age pension is calculated in groups based on the health status of the household head, and the results are summarized in Fig. 28.

According to Fig. 28, when the household head is unhealthy, there is a difference of ¥18,733.88 between the total annual amount of the divorce/pension or old-age pension received by the mid-high net worth households and the non mid-high net worth households; when the household head is in fairly good health, the difference is ¥14,777.33; and when the household head is healthy, the difference is ¥9,081.5. In summary, the difference between the total annual amount of divorce/pension or

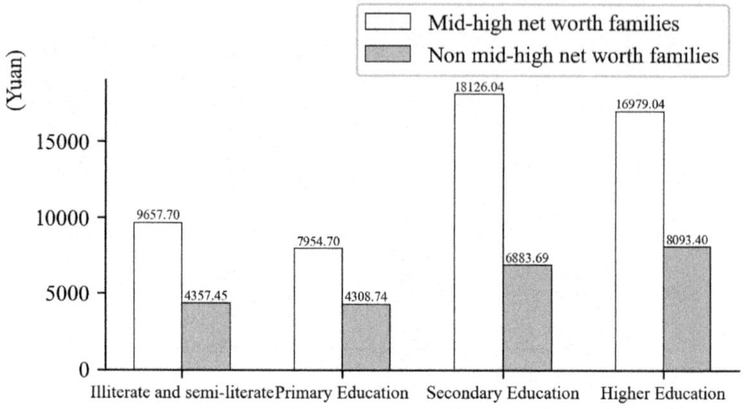


**Fig. 27** Total annual amount of divorce/pension or pensions received by mid-high net worth households and non mid-high net worth households (education level of household head)

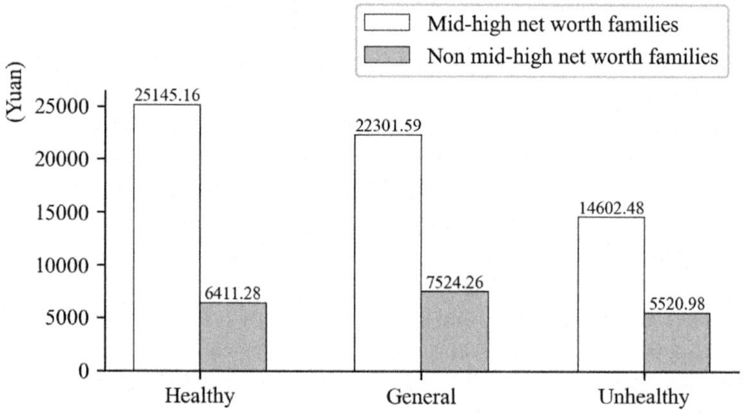


**Fig. 28** Total annual amount of divorce/pension or old-age pensions received by mid-high net worth households and non mid-high net worth households (health status of household head)

old-age pension received by mid-high net worth households and non mid-high net worth households is significant.

This study calculates the total annual number of households receiving divorce/pension or old-age pension based on the marital status of the head of the household group, and the results are summarized in Fig. 29.

According to Fig. 29, the total annual amount of divorce/pension or pension received by the mid-high net worth households heads who are unmarried is ¥4,891.58 higher than that of non mid-high net worth households; the difference between the two in the married group is ¥11,076.83, in the cohabitation group is ¥8,072.43, in the divorced group is ¥12,668.85, and in the widowed group is ¥15,863.35. In summary, the difference between the total annual amount of divorce/pension or old-age pension

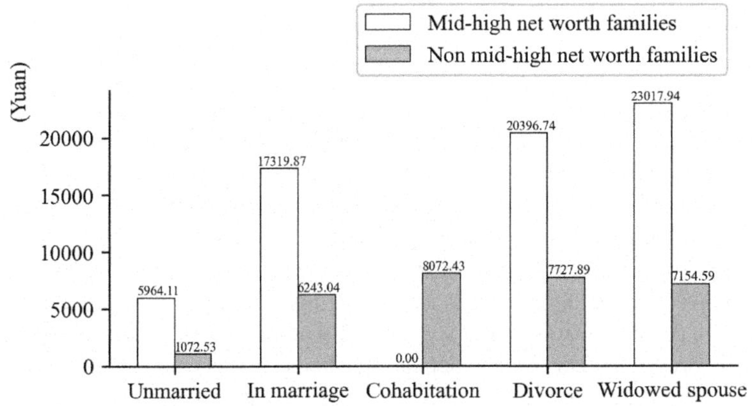


**Fig. 29** Total annual amount of divorce/retirement or old-age pension received by mid-high net worth households and non mid-high net worth households (marital status of head of household)

received by mid-high net worth households and non mid-high net worth households is highest when the household head is widowed, and the difference is lowest when the household head is unmarried. Foreign studies point out that if individuals live together as couples, their chances of receiving pensions and financial benefits during retirement increase [31]. However, this is different from the situation in China because each country is different regarding cultural and marital attitudes, and the impact of marital status on pension insurance.

# 4 Analysis of Family Pension Insurance Coverage

A previous study analyzed family pension insurance and security from the perspective of receiving a retirement/pension or old-age pension. We continue our analysis of family pension insurance and security from the perspective of family participation in pension insurance. These two components are, in fact, "two sides of the same coin." The former is the use side of pensions, while the latter is the input side of pensions. At the macro level, if the former is larger than the latter, there will be a drop in pensions. From a micro-household perspective, the latter is invested in the use of the former. Thus, there is a correspondence between the two at the micro level. Certainly, there is also the effect of time.

## 4.1 Family Level

The household pension insurance coverage rate is calculated based on the structure of the community grouping. The programs in which households participate in old-age insurance include those that receive divorce/retirement pensions from their institutions or agencies, basic old-age insurance, enterprise supplementary old-age insurance, commercial old-age insurance, rural old-age insurance (old farmers' insurance), new rural social old-age insurance (new farmers' insurance), urban residents' old-age insurance, and other types of old-age insurance programs. A household is covered by pension insurance if a household participates in any of the above pension insurance programs. This study calculates the household pension insurance coverage rate accordingly, and the results are summarized in Fig. 30.

According to Fig. 30, the family pension insurance coverage rate of a community structure as a neighborhood committee is 5.31% higher than that of a community structure as a village committee. Overall, the family pension insurance coverage rate is approximately 70%. The pension insurance coverage rate for neighborhood committees is significantly higher than that of village committees. Conversely, insurance companies and related departments have more publicity and promotion of pension insurance in neighborhood committees; in contrast, most residents of neighborhood committees work in enterprises and institutions, and the coverage of basic pension insurance and supplementary enterprise insurance is more extensive. For these reasons, the family pension insurance coverage rate in neighborhood committees is significantly higher than that in village committees.

According to Fig. 31, the pension insurance coverage rate of mid-high net worth households whose community structure is a neighborhood committee is 10.48% higher than that of non mid-high net worth households; when the community structure is a village committee, the difference between the two is 16.56%. Importantly, the pension insurance coverage rate of mid-high net worth households living in

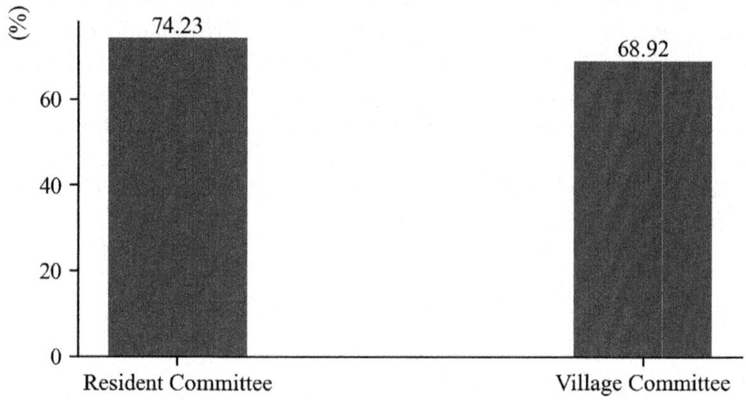


**Fig. 30** Household pension insurance coverage (community-based in structure) for the full sample

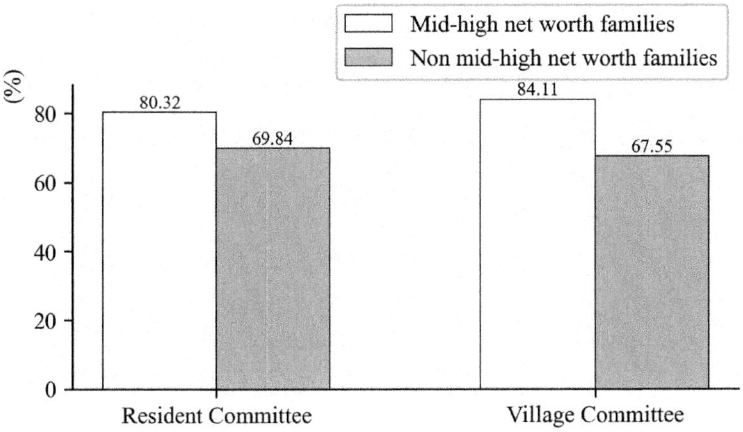


**Fig. 31** Old-age insurance coverage (community-based in structure) for mid-high net worth households and non mid-high net worth households

village committees is higher than that of mid-high net worth households living in neighborhood committees, with a difference of approximately 4% between the two.

This study calculates the pension insurance coverage rates for different households based on household size groupings, and the results are summarized in Fig. 32.

According to Fig. 32, the family pension insurance coverage rate is highest when the family size is four to six members and lowest when the family size is 10 members and above. Relatively, the family pension insurance coverage rate is higher for the size of four to nine members. Therefore, family size is a factor affecting family pension insurance coverage.

According to Fig. 33, generally, the pension insurance coverage rate of mid-high net worth households is significantly higher than that of non mid-high net worth households. Specifically, when the household size is one to three members,

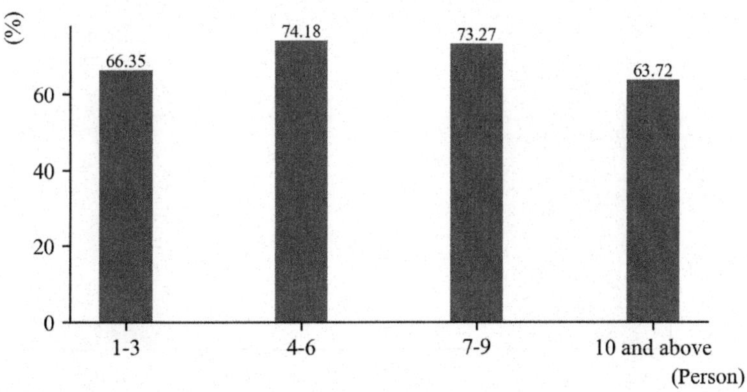


**Fig. 32** Pension insurance coverage of full sample households (household size)

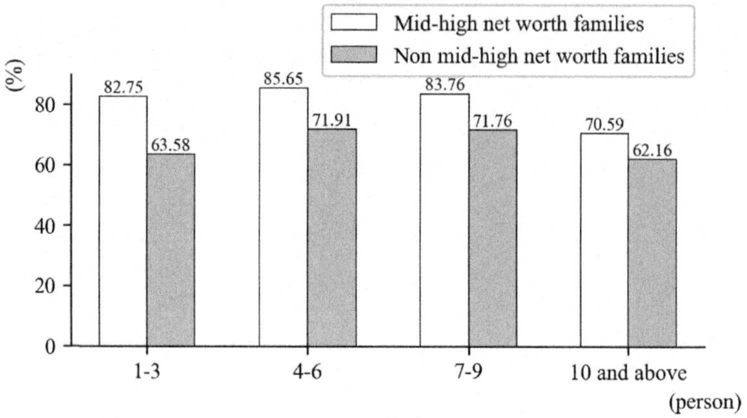


**Fig. 33** Old-age insurance coverage rates (household size) for mid-high net worth households and non mid-high net worth households

the pension insurance coverage rate of medium–high net worth households is 19.17% higher than that of non-medium–high net worth households; when the household size is four to six members, the difference is 13.74%; when it is seven to nine members, the difference is 12%; and when it is 10 members or more, the difference is 8.43%. In summary, the gap between the pension insurance coverage rates of mid-high net worth families and non mid-high net worth families gradually decreases as the number of family members increases.

This study calculates pension insurance coverage rates for different households based on urban and rural district groupings, and the results are summarized in Fig. 34.

According to Fig. 34, the household pension insurance coverage rate is approximately 70%; that is, approximately 70% of households are covered by pension insurance. Specifically, urban households have a higher pension insurance coverage

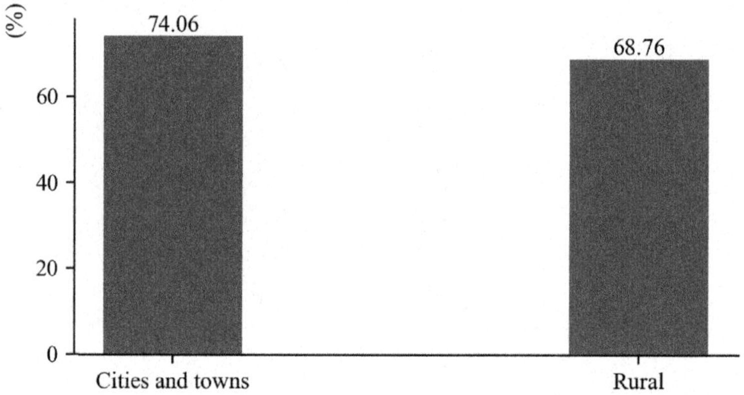


**Fig. 34** Full sample of household pension insurance coverage (urban and rural districts)

rate than rural households, with a difference of 5.3% between the two. This finding indicates that there is still a gap between urban and rural areas in terms of participation in family pension insurance [32]. With the gradual popularization of basic old-age insurance in rural areas, this gap generally shows a narrowing trend.

According to Fig. 35, urban households generally have higher pension insurance coverage rates than rural households. Specifically, there is a difference of 10.73% between the old-age insurance coverage rates of urban mid-high net worth households and non mid-high net worth households and a difference of 10.77% between the old-age insurance coverage rates of rural mid-high net worth households and non mid-high net worth households. In terms of pension insurance coverage rate, mid-high net worth households are roughly 10% higher than non mid-high net worth households. Pension insurance covers a higher proportion of mid-high net worth households. As some commercial pension insurance is included in commercial life insurance, the actual pension insurance coverage rate of mid-high net worth households should be somewhat higher than the above results.

This study calculates pension insurance coverage rates for different households based on urban and rural types, and the results are summarized in Fig. 36.

According to Fig. 36, the coverage rate of family pension insurance is the highest in tier-1 cities and lowest in tier-3 cities. Overall, the coverage rate of family pension insurance in tier-1 cities is approximately 80%, tier-2 cities are slightly lower than tier-1 cities, and the coverage rate in tier-3 cities and below is approximately 70%. This shows that in terms of the market potential of pension insurance, tier-3 cities and below have the highest market potential, followed by tier-2 cities. In contrast, tier-1 cities have the least market potential because the saturation of pension insurance is the highest. Therefore, tier-3 cities and below are the focus of market competition in the future of insurance companies. Insurance companies that dominate in tier-3 cities

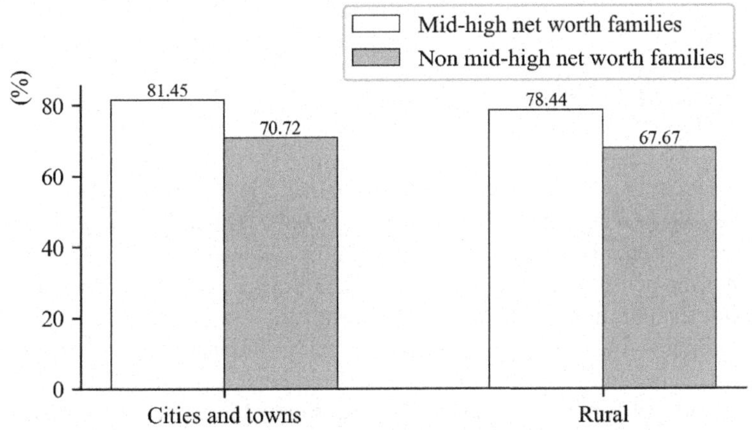


**Fig. 35** Old-age insurance coverage rates for mid-high net worth households and non mid-high net worth households (by urban and rural areas)

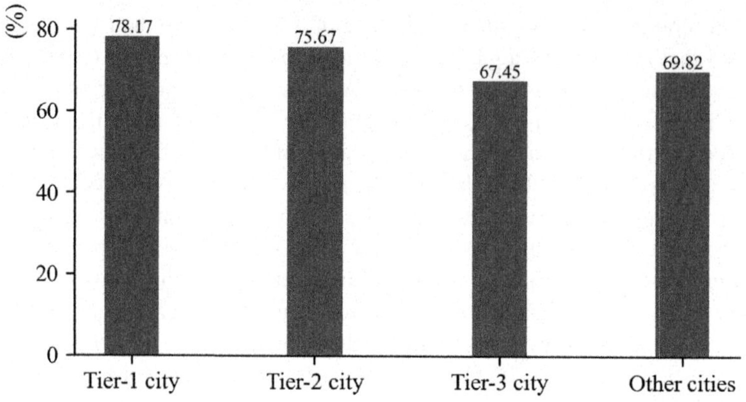


**Fig. 36** Household pension insurance coverage rate for the full sample (urban type)

and below have an overall competitive advantage. Hence, this is also a competitive strategy of "encircling cities in rural areas."

According to Fig. 37, the overall pension insurance coverage rate of mid-high net worth households is significantly higher than that of non mid-high net worth households, regardless of city type. The difference between the pension insurance coverage rates of mid-high net worth and non mid-high net worth households in tier-1 cities is 15.7%; in tier-2 cities, the difference is 18.35%; in tier-3 cities, it is 22.18%; and in other cities, it is 14.06%. In summary, the gap between mid-high net worth families and non mid-high net worth families in tier-3 cities is the largest. For insurance companies, the potential for non mid-high net worth households in tier-3 cities and below to participate in commercial pension insurance is relatively higher. This potential market for commercial pension insurance requires further development.

## 4.2 *Head of the Household Level*

The education level of the household head can have an impact on household participation in old-age insurance. The higher the household head's education level, the higher the household's motivation to participate in old-age insurance [32]. This study calculates the pension insurance coverage rate of different households based on the education level of the household head; the results are summarized in Fig. 38.

According to Fig. 38, the household pension insurance coverage rate gradually increases as the education level of the household head increases. This is consistent with the findings of previous studies [32]. The more educated the household head is, the more likely he or she is to plan for long-term household security and the more likely to participate in old-age insurance to ensure the quality of life in old age.

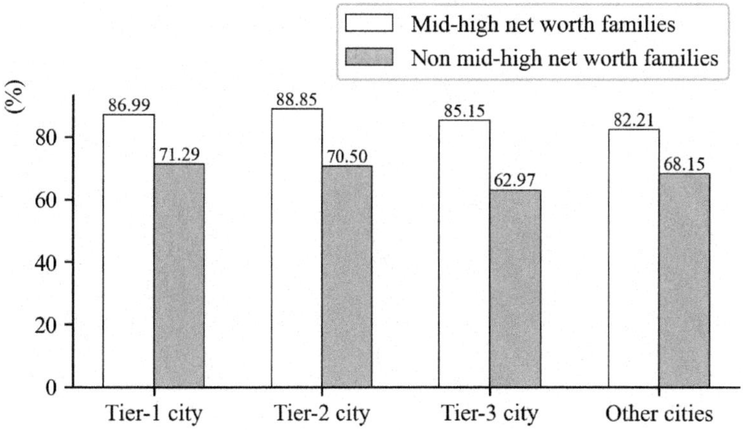


**Fig. 37** Old-age insurance coverage rates for mid-high net worth households and non mid-high net worth households (city type)

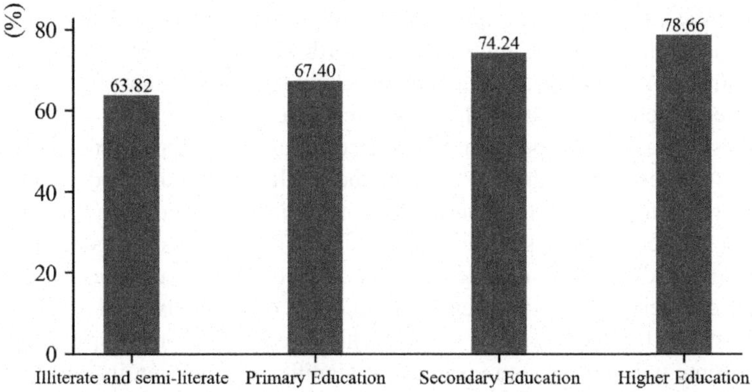


**Fig. 38** Old-age insurance coverage for the full sample of households (education level of household head)

According to Fig. 39, the pension insurance coverage rate is generally higher for mid-high net worth households than for non mid-high net worth households, except for households with illiterate/semi-literate heads. Specifically, when the household head is illiterate/semi-literate, the pension insurance coverage rate is 5.07% points higher for non mid-high net worth households than for mid-high net worth households. One possible reason for this phenomenon, which warrants further investigation, is that mid-high net worth households with illiterate/semi-literate household heads are more likely to develop a tendency to focus on current consumption and less on long-range coverage.

Additionally, the difference is 16.56% when the household head has primary level education, 15.26% when he/she has secondary level education, and 11.21%

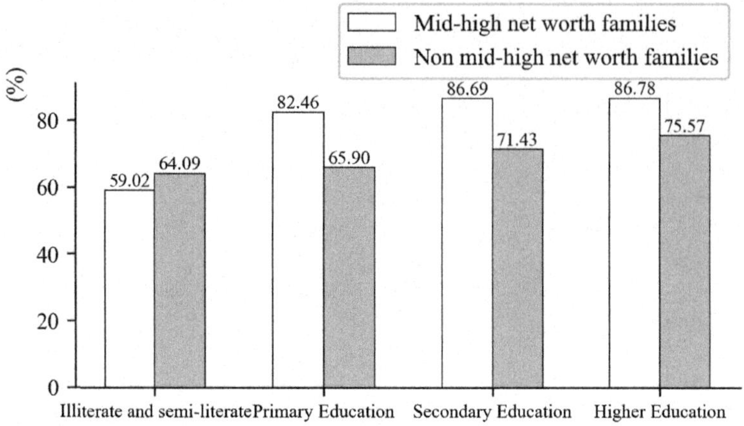


**Fig. 39** Old-age insurance coverage rates for mid-high net worth households and non mid-high net worth households (household head's education level)

when he/she has higher education. In summary, the difference between the pension insurance coverage rate of mid-high net worth households and non mid-high net worth households is highest when the household head has primary level education, and lowest when the household head is illiterate/semi-literate.

This study calculates pension insurance coverage rates for different households based on the sex of household heads, and the results are summarized in Fig. 40.

According to Fig. 40, the household pension insurance coverage rate is higher when the household head is male. However, the difference in coverage rates is lowest when the household head is male or female. Therefore, overall, household pension insurance coverage is not influenced by the sex of the household head. Existing studies show that the effect of the household head's sex on the purchase intention of some types of pension insurance is significant. However, its effect on urban

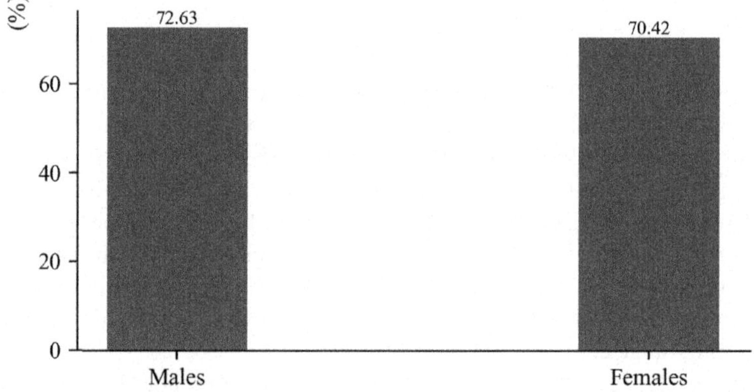


**Fig. 40** Pension insurance coverage for the full sample of households (sex of household head)

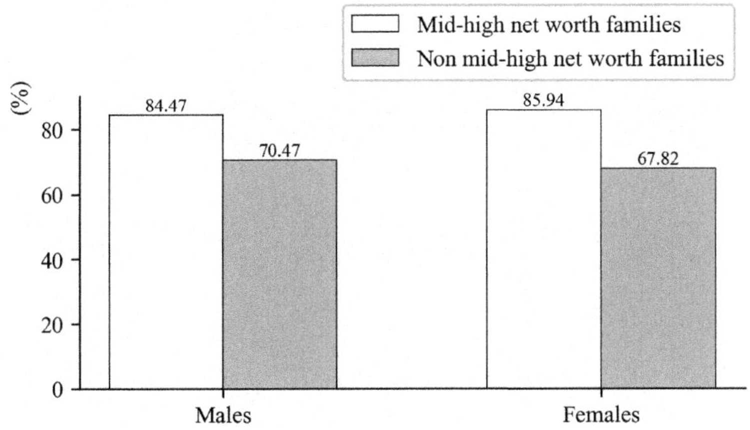


**Fig. 41** Old-age insurance coverage rates for mid-high net worth households and non mid-high net worth households (sex of household head)

workers' pension insurance and urban residents' pension insurance is insignificant [33]. Therefore, the impact of sex on the purchase intention and purchase behavior of specific pension insurance needs to be analyzed based on specific issues and cannot be generalized.

According to Fig. 41, there is a 14% difference between the pension insurance coverage rates of mid-high net worth households and non mid-high net worth households when the household head is male and an 18.12% difference when the household head is female. In summary, the difference between the two is highest when the household head is a female. It is worth noting that for mid-high net worth households, the pension insurance coverage rate of female-headed households is slightly higher than that of male-headed households. Women are more sensitive to future uncertainty [34], and are therefore more likely to plan ahead for their old age.

The relationship between health and old-age insurance is a common question in old-age insurance research [35]. The results of calculating the pension insurance coverage for different households based on the health status of household heads are summarized in Fig. 42.

According to Fig. 42, overall, household pension insurance coverage is highest when the household head is healthy and lowest when he/she is in fairly good health. Specifically, there is a difference of 15.49% between the pension insurance coverage rates of mid-high net worth households and non mid-high net worth households when the household head is healthy, 14.68% when he/she is in average health, and 17.32% when he/she is unhealthy. In summary, the difference between the pension insurance coverage rates of mid-high net worth households and non mid-high net worth households is highest when the household head is unhealthy and lowest when the household head is in average health.

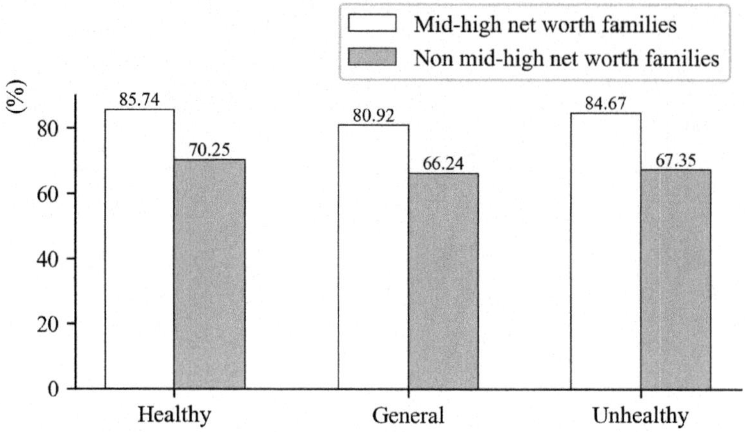


**Fig. 42** Old-age insurance coverage (health status of household head) for mid-high net worth households and non mid-high net worth households

This study calculates the old-age insurance coverage rates for different households based on the marital status grouping of household heads, and the results are summarized in 43.

According to Fig. 43, overall, household pension insurance coverage is highest when the household head is married and lowest when he/she is cohabiting. Additionally, regardless of marital status, the pension insurance coverage rates of mid-high net worth households are significantly higher than those of non mid-high net worth households. This again reflects that mid-high net worth households have a stronger demand for pension insurance and higher expectations for future life security and quality of life in old age. Certainly, it has been pointed out that marital status has different effects on men's and women's perceptions of old-age insurance [31]. This needs to be explored further using multiple regression models.

Specifically, when the household head is unmarried, the pension insurance coverage rate of mid-high net worth households is 20.81% higher than that of non mid-high net worth households; in the married group, the difference is 14.81%; in the cohabiting group, the difference is 28.57%; in the divorced group, the difference is 16.42%; and in the widowed group, the difference is 15.24%. In summary, the difference between the pension insurance coverage rates of mid-high net worth households and non mid-high net worth households is the largest when the household head is cohabiting, and smallest when the household head is married.

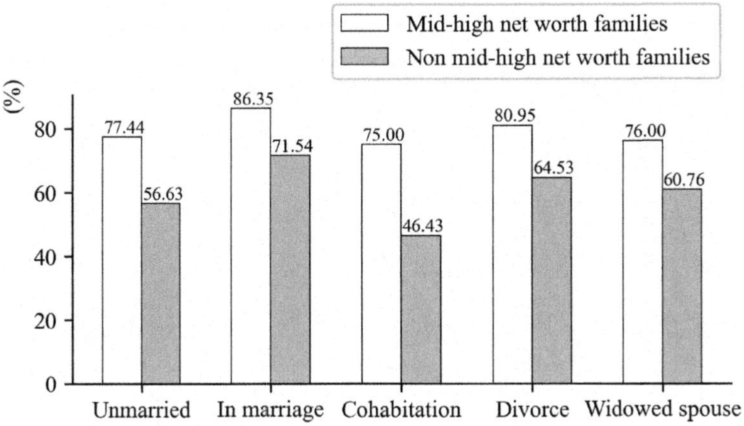


**Fig. 43** Old-age insurance coverage rates for mid-high net worth households and non mid-high net worth households (marital status of household head)

# 5 Analysis of Household Commercial Pension Insurance Coverage

As the name implies, commercial pension insurance is provided by insurance companies. In China, commercial pension insurance is the third pillar. However, in general, the proportion of commercial pension insurance is low, and there is much potential for development. At present, the third pillar of commercial pension insurance in China is in the primary stage of development, which is not fully developed, immature in all aspects, has not formed a perfect system, and has great development potential for further exploration [36].

## *5.1 Family Level*

This study calculates household commercial pension insurance coverage based on the communities by structure, and the results are summarized in Fig. 44.

Figure 44 shows that the overall household commercial pension insurance coverage rate is low. Even for mid-high net worth households in the neighborhood councils, the commercial pension insurance coverage rate is approximately 5%. The commercial pension insurance coverage rates of mid-high net worth households are significantly higher than those of non mid-high net worth households. The commercial pension insurance coverage rate of mid-high net worth households in a community structure is 3.46% higher than that of non mid-high net worth households; when the community structure is a village committee, the difference between the two is 1.41%, which is smaller.

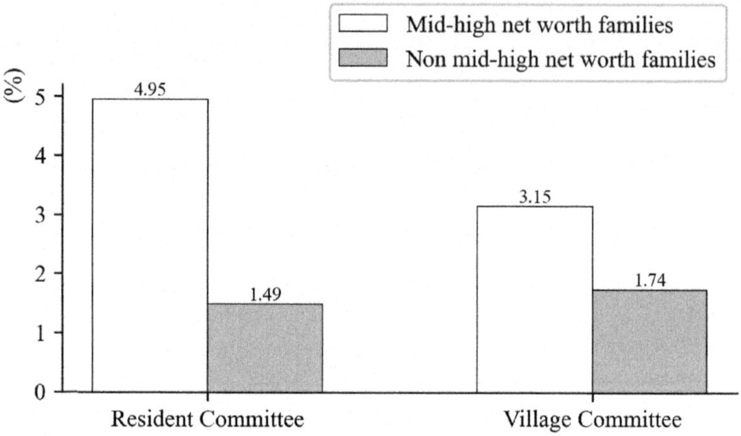


**Fig. 44** Commercial pension insurance coverage rates of mid-high net worth households and non mid-high net worth households (community-based in structure)

This study calculates household commercial pension insurance coverage based on household size, and the results are summarized in Fig. 45.

According to Fig. 45, the family commercial pension insurance coverage rate is the highest when the family size is seven to nine members and the lowest when the family size is 10 members and above. In other words, when the household size is less than 10 members, the household commercial pension insurance coverage rate increases with the expansion of the household size. This is because the larger the family size, the greater the probability of having older adults in the family and the higher the possibility of purchasing commercial pension insurance.

According to Fig. 46, the commercial pension insurance coverage rate of mid-high net worth households is 2.95% higher than that of non mid-high net worth

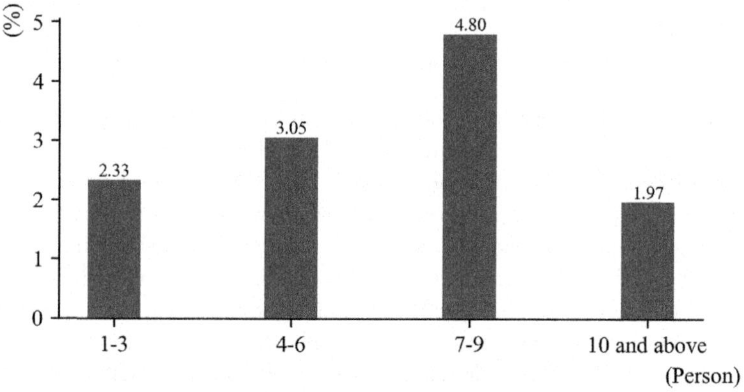


**Fig. 45** Commercial pension insurance coverage rate (household size) for the full sample of households

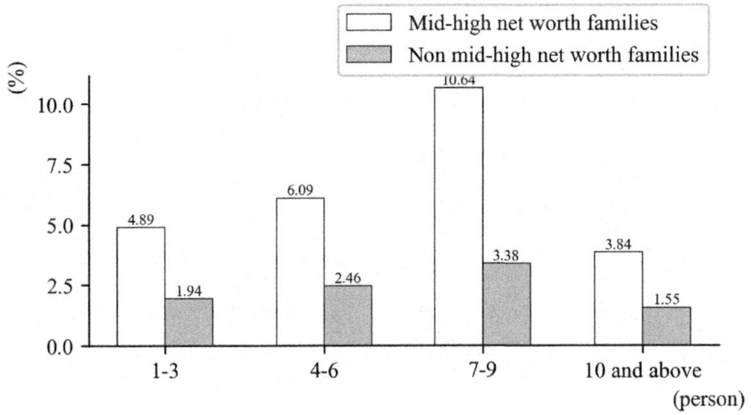


**Fig. 46** Commercial pension insurance coverage rate (household size) for mid-high net worth households and non mid-high net worth households

households when the household size is one to three members; the difference is 3.63% when the household size is four to six members; the difference is 7.26% when the household size is seven to nine members; and the difference is 2.29% when the household size is 10 members or more. Generally, the commercial pension insurance coverage rate of mid-high net worth households is higher than that of non mid-high net worth households; however, the difference between the two varies depending on the household size.

This study calculates household commercial pension insurance coverage based on urban and rural district groupings, and the results are summarized in Fig. 47.

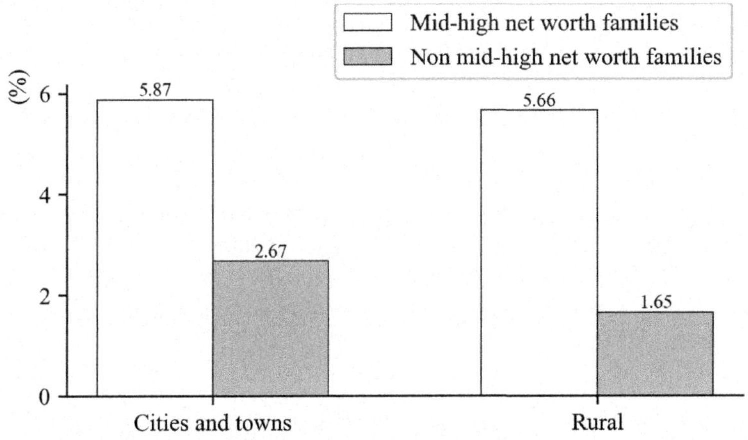


**Fig. 47** Commercial pension insurance coverage rates of mid-high net worth households and non mid-high net worth households (in urban and rural areas)

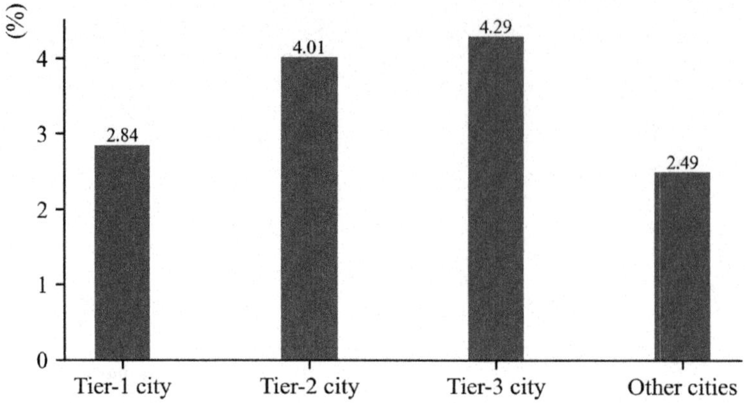


**Fig. 48** Commercial pension insurance coverage for the full sample of households (urban type)

According to Fig. 47, the commercial pension insurance coverage rate of mid-high net worth households is significantly higher than that of non mid-high net worth households in urban and rural areas. Specifically, there is a 3.2% difference between the commercial pension insurance coverage rates of urban mid-high net worth households and non mid-high net worth households, and a 4.01% difference between the commercial pension insurance coverage rates of rural non mid-high net worth households and mid-high net worth households. Comparatively, the difference between the two is larger in rural areas.

This study calculates the household commercial pension insurance coverage rate based on city-type, and the results are summarized in Fig. 48.

According to Fig. 48, the household commercial pension insurance coverage rate is highest in tier-3 cities and lowest in other cities. The higher coverage rate of commercial pension insurance in tier-2 and 3 cities is related to the business strategy adopted by insurance companies to sink into these cities over the years.

According to Fig. 49, overall, except for tier-3 cities, the commercial pension insurance coverage rates of mid-high net worth households in all cities are significantly higher than those of non mid-high net worth households. Specifically, there is a 4.46% difference between the commercial pension insurance coverage rates of mid-high net worth and non mid-high net worth households in tier-1 cities, a 5.31% difference in tier-2 cities, a 0.89% difference in tier-3 cities, and a 3.06% difference in other cities. The gap between commercial pension insurance coverage rates for mid-high net worth households in tier-3 cities and non mid-high net worth households is the smallest.

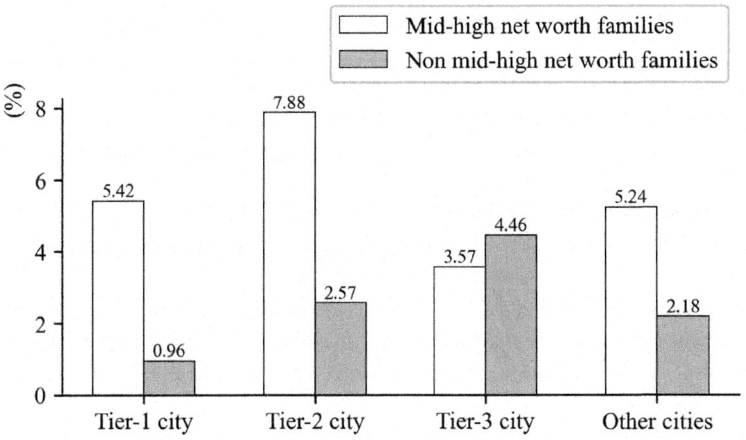


**Fig. 49** Commercial pension insurance coverage rates of mid-high net worth households and non mid-high net worth households (city type)

## 5.2 *Head of the Household Level*

This study calculates the household commercial pension insurance coverage rate based on the education level of the household head, and the results are summarized in Fig. 50.

As shown in Fig. 50, generally, the commercial pension insurance coverage rate of mid-high net worth households is significantly higher than that of non mid-high net worth households when the education level of the household head is primary or

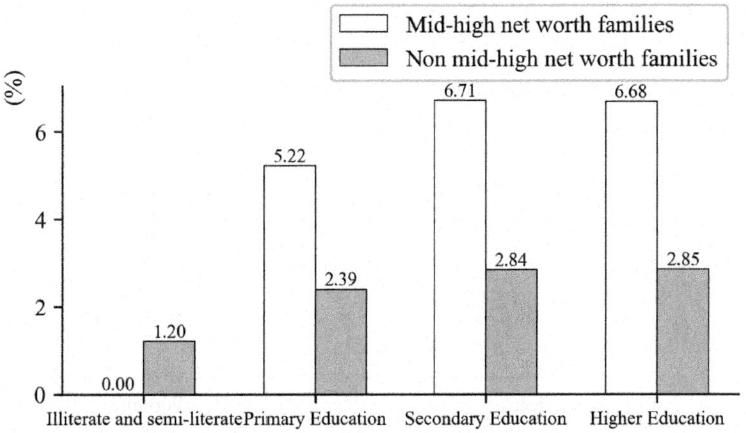


**Fig. 50** Commercial pension insurance coverage rate of mid-high net worth households and non mid-high net worth households (education level of household head)

above. Specifically, there is a 1.2% difference in the commercial pension insurance coverage rate between mid-high net worth households and non mid-high net worth households when the education level of the household head is illiterate/semi-literate, a 2.83% difference when the education level of the household head is primary education, a 3.87% difference when the education level of the household head is secondary education, and a 3.83% difference when the education level of the household head is higher education. The difference is 3.83% when the household head has higher education. In summary, the difference between the commercial pension insurance coverage rates of mid-high net worth households and non mid-high net worth households is largest when the education level of the household head is higher education; the difference is smallest when the education level is illiterate/semi-literate and the commercial pension insurance coverage rate of non mid-high net worth households is higher than that of mid-high net worth households. There are multiple reasons for this situation, which may be related to the relatively small sample size of this education level.

This study calculates the household commercial pension insurance coverage rate based on the sex of household heads, and the results are summarized in Fig. 51.

As shown in Fig. 51, generally, the commercial pension insurance coverage rate of mid-high net worth households is significantly higher than that of non mid-high net worth households, regardless of whether the household head is male or female. Specifically, there is a difference of 5.19% between the commercial pension insurance coverage rate of mid-high net worth households and non mid-high net worth households when the household head is male, and a difference of 2.12% when the household head is female. In summary, the difference between the two is greater when the head of the household is male. The sex of the household head impacts household participation and the purchase of commercial pension insurance to a certain extent.

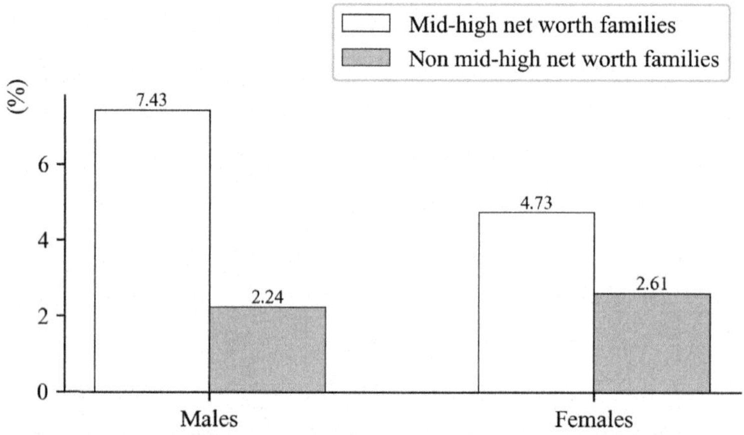


**Fig. 51** Commercial pension insurance coverage rate of mid-high net worth households and non mid-high net worth households (sex of household head)

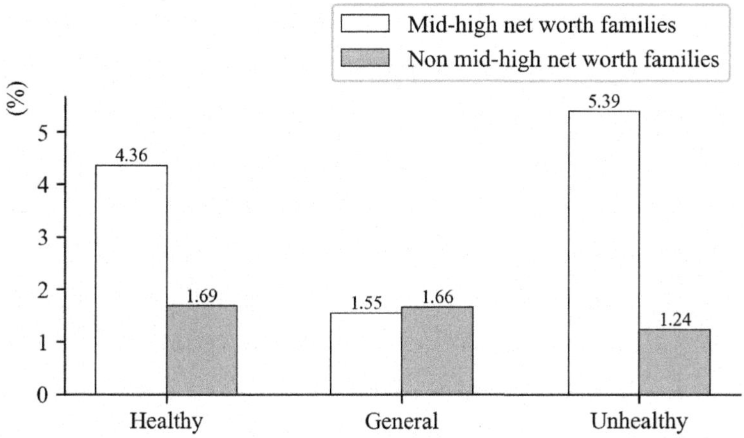


**Fig. 52** Commercial pension insurance coverage (health status of household head) for mid-high net worth households and non mid-high net worth households

Household commercial pension insurance coverage is calculated based on the health status of the household head, and the results are summarized in Fig. 52.

As shown in Fig. 52, when the head of household is healthy, there is a 2.67% difference between the commercial pension insurance coverage rate of mid-high net worth households and non mid-high net worth households; when the head of household is healthy, there is a 0.11% difference between the two, and there is basically no significant difference; and when the household head is unhealthy, there is a 4.15% difference between the two. In summary, when the household head is healthy or unhealthy, the difference between the commercial pension insurance coverage rate of mid-high net worth households and non mid-high net worth households is more significant, and the commercial pension insurance coverage rate of mid-high net worth households is significantly higher than that of non mid-high net worth households; when the household head is healthy, the difference between the two is smaller, and there is no significant difference.

This study calculates the household commercial pension insurance coverage rate based on the marital status grouping of household heads, and the results are summarized in Fig. 53.

As shown in Fig. 53, when the household head is unmarried, the commercial pension insurance coverage rate of mid-high net worth households is 0.56% lower than that of non mid-high net worth households; in the married group, the difference is 2.89%; in the divorced group, the difference is 1.56%; and in the widowed group, the difference is 2.23%. In summary, the difference between the commercial pension insurance coverage rate of mid-high net worth households and non mid-high net worth households is largest when the household head is married and smallest when the household head is unmarried. The marital status of the household head is also a factor that affects the purchase of commercial pension insurance.

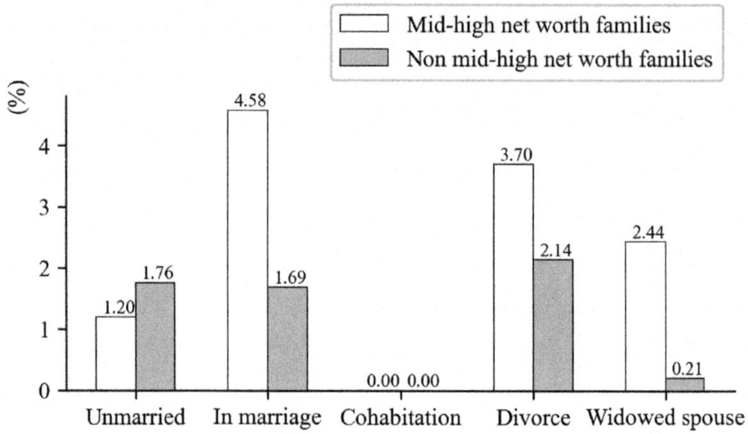


**Fig. 53** Commercial pension insurance coverage rate of mid-high net worth households and non mid-high net worth households (marital status of household head)

# 6 Analysis of Factors Influencing Family Pension Insurance

The pension or retirement benefits a family receives directly affect the quality of life of the older adults and the entire family. What household factors impact the receipt of severance/pension or old-age pension? This question requires empirical testing. This chapter uses regression analysis to examine the factors that influence households' receipt of retirement/pension or old-age pensions. It focuses on the impact of mid-high net worth households and the household's investable assets on the household's pension receipt. Additionally, this chapter examines the impact of household and head-of-household-level factors.

## *6.1 Data, Variables, and Models*

1. *Key Variables*

The explanatory variable is the household's receipt of a severance/pension or old-age pension. Based on the question in the CFPS household questionnaire, "In the past 12 months, what was the total amount of severance/pension or old-age pension received by all members of your household?" Define the variables. The value is 0 if no household member receives a pension or retirement benefit.

The core explanatory variables are mid-high net worth households (dummy variables) and household investable assets. The former consists of values 0 and 1. The former is a mid-high net worth household, and the latter is a non mid-high net worth household.

The remaining control variables include household-level and head-of-household-level control variables, with household-level control variables including household entrepreneurial decisions, household property investment decisions, household size, household income, bank loans, loans from friends and relatives and private individuals, human fees, and education and training fees, and head-of-household-level control variables including sex, age, years of education, marital status, health status, self-confidence level, and whether to access the Internet.

2. *Descriptive Statistics*

During data processing, samples with missing or incorrect values in the variables were eliminated, and 8775 valid samples were finally obtained. The definition and descriptive statistics for these variables are shown in Table 1.

3. *Model Setting*

This chapter examines the impact of mid-high net worth households and household investable assets on the household receipt of a severance/pension or old-age pension, as modeled by the following setup:

$$Pension = \beta_0 + \beta_1 \times MHW + \beta_2 \times ln(FIA) + \beta_3 \times X + u$$

where *Pension* denotes the severance/pension or pension received by the household, which is a continuous variable; *MHW* and *FIA* denote mid-high net worth households (dummy variables) and household investable assets, respectively; $X$ is a series of control variables containing household-level and head-of-household-level controls; and $u$ is the error term.

## 6.2 Empirical Analysis

1. *The Impact of Mid-High Net Worth Households on Household Receipt of Divorce/ Pension or Old-Age Pension*

Table 2 presents the regression results for the effect of mid-high net worth households on the household receipt of a severance pension or old-age pension. Column (1) considers only the explanatory variables of mid-high net worth households (dummy variable), column (2) adds household-level control variables, and column (3) adds head-of-household-level control variables to the household-level control variables. On this basis, province-fixed effects are added in columns (4) to (6), corresponding to columns (1) to (3). The results show that the regression coefficients for mid-high net worth households are significantly positive in all models. As shown in column (6), after accounting for household-level control variables, head-of-household-level control variables, and province fixed effects, mid-high net worth households received approximately ¥5,179 more severance/pensions or pensions than non mid-high net

**Table 1** Definition of variables and descriptive statistics

| Variable | Definition | Mean | S.D | Min | Max |
|---|---|---|---|---|---|
| Amount of retirement pension or old-age pension received | Amount of pension or old-age pension received by the family last year | 8550.997 | 22,024.447 | 0 | 400,000 |
| Entrepreneurship of the family | Number of self-employed or private enterprises | 0.104 | 0.349 | 0 | 6 |
| Investment properties | Number of properties other than current housing | 0.261 | 0.566 | 0 | 7 |
| Mid-high net worth families | 1 for middle and high net worth households, 0 for the rest | 0.155 | 0.362 | 0 | 1 |
| Household investable assets | Log value of household investable assets | 8.686 | 4.879 | 0 | 17.371 |
| Household size | Number of family members | 3.566 | 1.89 | 1 | 15 |
| Household income | Logarithmic value of household income | 78,668.465 | 93,924.659 | 0 | 1,600,000 |
| Bank loans | If the household has a bank loan, the variable takes the value of 1, otherwise it is 0 | 10.705 | 1.427 | 0 | 14.286 |
| Private loans from friends and family | If there is a family or private loan, the value is 1, otherwise it is 0 | 0.105 | 0.306 | 0 | 1 |
| Favor expenses | Last year's household spending on favors | 0.112 | 0.316 | 0 | 1 |
| Education and training fees | Spending on family education training last year | 3839.593 | 6008.965 | 0 | 120,000 |
| Gender | If the gender is male, the variable takes the value of 1, otherwise it is 0 | 4673.67 | 10,355.027 | 0 | 152,000 |
| Age | Age of the individual, in years | 0.562 | 0.496 | 0 | 1 |
| Year of education | Number of years of education received | 48.916 | 14.592 | 18 | 95 |

(continued)

**Table 1** (continued)

| Variable | Definition | Mean | S.D | Min | Max |
|---|---|---|---|---|---|
| Marriage | If the marital status is married, the variable takes the value of 1, otherwise 0 | 8.255 | 5.073 | 0 | 24 |
| Health | Health rating with a maximum of 5 and a minimum of 1 | 0.817 | 0.386 | 0 | 1 |
| Self-confidence | Self-confidence rating, highest 5, lowest 1 | 3.001 | 1.174 | 1 | 5 |
| Access to the Internet | Internet access is 1, otherwise it is 0 | 4.134 | 0.936 | 1 | 5 |

worth households. This indicates that mid-high net worth households receive more severance/pension or old-age pensions, which has a positive effect on securing a high-quality retirement life for older adults in the mid-high net worth households.

2. *Impact of Household Investable Assets on Household Receipt of Retirement/ Pension or Old-Age Pension*

Table 3 shows the regression results for the effect of household investable assets on the household receipt of a severance/pension or old-age pension. In all models, the regression coefficients of household investable assets are significantly positive. This indicates that the more investable assets a household has, the more retirement/pension or old-age pension it receives. The results in column (6) show that after considering household-level control variables, head-of-household-level control variables, and province-fixed effects, each 1-unit increase in the log value of household investable assets increases the severance/pension or old-age pension received by the household by approximately ¥377.

The results for the relevant control variables indicate that some control variables at the household level and the head of the household level have a more significant effect on the household's receipt of severances/pensions or old-age pensions. Overall, after accounting for province-fixed effects, household property investment decisions have a non-significant effect on household receipt of severances/pensions or old-age pensions. It is worth noting that household entrepreneurial decisions are significantly and negatively related to the household receipt of a severance/pension or old-age pension. The more entrepreneurial decisions a household makes, the less it receives as severance/pension or old-age pension. One possible reason for this is that household entrepreneurship extends the age of leaving/retiring, resulting in a smaller retirement/pension or old-age pension. The effect of household size on household receipt of retirement or old-age pensions is not stable; however, there is a significant positive relationship between household income and household receipt of retirement or old-age pensions. Both bank loans and loans from friends, relatives, and

**Table 2** Regression results for the impact of mid-high net worth households on household receipt of a severance/pension or old-age pension

| | Retirement or pension benefits | | | | | |
|---|---|---|---|---|---|---|
| | (1) | (2) | (3) | (4) | (5) | (6) |
| Mid-high net worth families | 11,164.1$^{***}$ | 9,591.788$^{***}$ | 7,933.721$^{***}$ | 6,869.409$^{***}$ | 6,398.904$^{***}$ | 5,178.552$^{***}$ |
| | (11.64) | (7.17) | (6.55) | (7.79) | (5.14) | (4.52) |
| Investment properties | | −1,459.305$^{**}$ | −1,319.992$^{**}$ | | −1,026.472 | −873.757 |
| | | (−2.04) | (−1.99) | | (−1.54) | (−1.41) |
| Entrepreneurship of the family | | −3,936.181$^{***}$ | −3,005.748$^{***}$ | | −2,511.546$^{***}$ | −1,988.394$^{***}$ |
| | | (−7.07) | (−5.60) | | (−4.79) | (−3.98) |
| Household size | | −933.364$^{***}$ | −483.792$^{***}$ | | −291.500$^{***}$ | −83.024 |
| | | (−9.08) | (−4.51) | | (−2.85) | (−0.77) |
| Household income | | 2,775.074$^{***}$ | 3,188.741$^{***}$ | | 2,007.610$^{***}$ | 2,441.558$^{***}$ |
| | | (14.74) | (13.56) | | (12.74) | (12.05) |
| Bank loans | | −5,069.442$^{***}$ | −1,575.586$^{***}$ | | −3,436.951$^{***}$ | −827.715 |
| | | (−9.18) | (−2.92) | | (−6.31) | (−1.56) |
| Private loans from friends and family | | −3,867.676$^{***}$ | −1,223.937$^{***}$ | | −2,852.904$^{***}$ | −607.189 |
| | | (−8.26) | (−2.58) | | (−6.03) | (−1.28) |
| Favor expenses | | 0.144$^{***}$ | 0.103$^{**}$ | | 0.034 | 0.016 |
| | | (3.12) | (2.50) | | (0.78) | (0.39) |
| Education and training fees | | −0.019 | 0.003 | | −0.068$^{**}$ | −0.036 |
| | | (−0.61) | (0.09) | | (−2.31) | (−1.27) |
| Gender | | | −2,293.569$^{***}$ | | | −1,863.569$^{***}$ |
| | | | (−5.42) | | | (−4.55) |

(continued)

**Table 2** (continued)

| | Retirement or pension benefits | | | | | |
|---|---|---|---|---|---|---|
| | (1) | (2) | (3) | (4) | (5) | (6) |
| Age | | | 728.549*** | | | 663.160*** |
| | | | (29.45) | | | (27.92) |
| Year of education | | | 617.456*** | | | 565.282*** |
| | | | (12.46) | | | (11.77) |
| Marriage | | | −568.652 | | | 6.992 |
| | | | (−1.18) | | | (0.01) |
| Health | | | 16.900 | | | −77.832 |
| | | | (0.10) | | | (−0.46) |
| Self-confidence | | | −226.676 | | | 24.338 |
| | | | (−1.04) | | | (0.12) |
| Access to the Internet | | | 6,517.281*** | | | 6,044.360*** |
| | | | (10.60) | | | (10.00) |
| Fixed effects of provinces | No | No | No | Yes | Yes | Yes |
| Constant | 6,821.992*** | −18,027.408*** | −66,875.147*** | 12,058.480*** | −8,379.402** | −50,908.724*** |
| | (32.00) | (−10.27) | (−20.31) | (3.14) | (−2.04) | (−11.81) |
| Observations | 8,775 | 8,775 | 8,775 | 8,775 | 8,775 | 8,775 |
| R-squared | 0.034 | 0.081 | 0.239 | 0.166 | 0.186 | 0.311 |

*Note* * $p < 0.1$, ** $p < 0.05$, *** $p < 0.01$

**Table 3** Regression results for the effect of household investable assets on household receipt of retirement/pension or old-age pension

| | Retirement or pension benefits | | | | | |
|---|---|---|---|---|---|---|
| | (1) | (2) | (3) | (4) | (5) | (6) |
| Household investable assets | 801.600*** | 432.765*** | 485.160*** | 535.712*** | 327.043*** | 377.161*** |
| | (16.95) | (8.90) | (10.60) | (12.65) | (7.14) | (8.61) |
| Investment properties | | 863.675 | 199.695 | | 386.160 | −65.987 |
| | | (1.54) | (0.38) | | (0.73) | (−0.14) |
| Entrepreneurship of the family | | −3,787.431*** | −2,945.255*** | | −2,412.565*** | −1,963.693*** |
| | | (−6.94) | (−5.55) | | (−4.69) | (−3.99) |
| Household size | | −955.923*** | −481.647*** | | −297.385*** | −79.260 |
| | | (−9.26) | (−4.49) | | (−2.89) | (−0.74) |
| Household income | | 2,719.837*** | 3,047.887*** | | 1,918.525*** | 2,300.071*** |
| | | (14.01) | (12.88) | | (12.07) | (11.42) |
| Bank loans | | −4,804.855*** | −1,148.221** | | −3,229.268*** | −501.032 |
| | | (−8.70) | (−2.11) | | (−5.93) | (−0.94) |
| Private loans from friends and family | | −3,504.768*** | −614.796 | | −2,527.431*** | −95.599 |
| | | (−7.43) | (−1.28) | | (−5.31) | (−0.20) |
| Favor expenses | | 0.172*** | 0.125*** | | 0.048 | 0.026 |
| | | (3.75) | (3.07) | | (1.10) | (0.65) |
| Education and training fees | | −0.011 | 0.009 | | −0.063** | −0.032 |
| | | (−0.35) | (0.29) | | (−2.15) | (−1.13) |
| Gender | | | −2,455.516*** | | | −2,002.190*** |
| | | | (−5.77) | | | (−4.86) |

(continued)

**Table 3** (continued)

| | Retirement or pension benefits | | | | | |
|---|---|---|---|---|---|---|
| | (1) | (2) | (3) | (4) | (5) | (6) |
| Age | | | 739.665*** | | | 669.933*** |
| | | | (29.62) | | | (28.09) |
| Year of education | | | 621.443*** | | | 563.923*** |
| | | | (12.41) | | | (11.63) |
| Marriage | | | −626.238 | | | −35.061 |
| | | | (−1.30) | | | (−0.07) |
| Health | | | 58.652 | | | −43.475 |
| | | | (0.33) | | | (−0.25) |
| Self-confidence | | | −229.927 | | | 31.250 |
| | | | (−1.05) | | | (0.15) |
| Access to the Internet | | | 6,475.420*** | | | 5,943.606*** |
| | | | (10.55) | | | (9.89) |
| Fixed effects of provinces | No | No | No | Yes | Yes | Yes |
| Constant | 1,588*** | −20,460*** | −69,512*** | 8,615** | −9,421** | −52,238*** |
| | (4.86) | (−11.09) | (−20.55) | (2.22) | (−2.27) | (−12.03) |
| Observations | 8,775 | 8,775 | 8,775 | 8,775 | 8,775 | 8,775 |
| R-squared | 0.032 | 0.074 | 0.238 | 0.167 | 0.184 | 0.311 |

*Note* * $p < 0.1$, ** $p < 0.05$, *** $p < 0.01$

private individuals have a less stable effect on household receipt of divorces/pensions or old-age pensions. Additionally, favorable expenses have no significant effect on household receipt of severance/pension or old-age pension. In contrast, education and training expenses show a less stable relationship with household receipt of severance/pension or old-age pension.

Sex significantly affects the receipt of divorces/pensions or old-age pensions, looking at the control variables at the head of the household level. Female-headed households receive more severance/pensions or old-age pensions than male-headed households. Age also affects households' needs for commercial pension insurance. It makes sense that the older the household head, the more the household receives as severance/pension or old-age pension. The higher the education level of the household heads, the more severances/pensions the household receives. The effects of marital status, health status, and self-confidence level on the household receipt of divorces/pensions or old-age pensions are insignificant. Internet access is significantly and positively related to households receiving divorce/pension or old-age pension.

## 6.3 Heterogeneity Analysis

1. *Heterogeneity of Mid-High Net Worth Households in Terms of Families Receiving Divorce/Pensions or Old-Age Pensions*

Based on the income level of the household head, the sample is divided into two groups with higher and lower household income levels and grouped into regressions. Columns (1) to (2) of Table 4 show the regression results based on income heterogeneity. The results show a significant positive effect of mid-high net worth households (dummy variable) on households with higher income levels receiving a divorce/pension or old-age pension, while there is no significant effect on households with lower income levels receiving a divorce/pension or old-age pension. This indicates that for households with relatively high-income levels, there is a significant difference in the receipt of divorce/pension or old-age pension between mid-high net worth households and non mid-high net worth households. However, for households with lower income levels, there is no significant difference in the receipt of divorces/pensions or old-age pensions between mid-high net worth households and non mid-high net worth households.

The sample is divided into two groups, urban and rural, and grouped into regressions based on the location of households in the sample. Columns (3) to (4) of Table 4 show the results of the regressions based on urban–rural heterogeneity. The results show that in urban areas, there is a significant positive effect of mid-high net worth households (dummy variable) on households' receipt of severances/pensions or old-age pensions; however, in rural areas, the effect is insignificant.

Based on the location of the households in the sample, the urban sample is further divided into four groups: tier-1, tier-2, tier-3, and tier-4 cities and below, and the

**Table 4** Regression results for the impact of mid-high net worth households on household receipt of divorce/pension or old-age pension (income and urban–rural heterogeneity)

| | Retirement or pension benefits | | | |
|---|---|---|---|---|
| | (1) | (2) | (3) | (4) |
| Income Heterogeneity | High income | Low income | | |
| Urban–rural heterogeneity | | | Urban | Rural |
| Mid-high net worth families | 3,028** | 1,810 | 4,807*** | 1,250 |
| | (1,334) | (1,320) | (1,512) | (954.0) |
| Household-level control variables | Yes | Yes | Yes | Yes |
| Control variables at household head level | Yes | Yes | Yes | Yes |
| Fixed effects of provinces | Yes | Yes | Yes | Yes |
| Constant | −102,682*** | −21,716*** | −73,729*** | −19,686*** |
| | (14,018) | (2,279) | (6,341) | (2,235) |
| Observations | 4,219 | 4,556 | 4,772 | 4,003 |
| R-squared | 0.362 | 0.245 | 0.349 | 0.206 |

*Note* * $p < 0.1$, ** $p < 0.05$, *** $p < 0.01$

regressions are conducted in groups; the results are summarized in Table 5. The results show that the effect of mid-high net worth households (dummy variable) on households receiving divorce/pension or old-age pension in tier-1 cities is significant, while the effect on households receiving divorce/pension or pension in tier-2 cities and below is insignificant.

2. *Regression Results of the Heterogeneity of Household Investable Assets on Household Receipt of Retirement/Pension or Old-Age Pension*

Based on the income level of the household head, the sample is divided into two groups with higher and lower household income levels and grouped into regressions. Columns (1) to (2) of Table 6 show the regression results based on income heterogeneity. The results show that the effect of household investable assets on receiving either a severance/pension or an old-age pension is significant for both. However, the effect is significantly larger for households with higher income levels than those with lower income levels.

The sample is divided into two groups, urban and rural, and grouped into regressions based on the location of households in the sample. Columns (3) to (4) of Table 6 show the regression results based on urban–rural heterogeneity. The results show that the effect of household investable assets on receiving a severance/pension or pension is significantly positive for both urban and rural households but is greater for urban households.

Based on the location of the households in the sample, the urban sample is further divided into four groups: tier-1, tier-2, tier-3, and tier-4 cities and below, and the regressions are conducted in groups; the results are summarized in Tables 7. The

**Table 5** Regression results for the impact of mid-high net worth households on household receipt of divorce/pension or pension (urban heterogeneity)

| | Retirement or pension benefits | | | |
|---|---|---|---|---|
| | (1) | (2) | (3) | (4) |
| Urban Heterogeneity | First-tier cities | Second-tier cities | Third-tier cities | Fourth-tier cities and below |
| Mid-high net worth families | 13,180.887*** | 2,944.398 | 5,357.633 | 622.632 |
| | (2.99) | (1.18) | (1.14) | (0.30) |
| Household-level control variables | Yes | Yes | Yes | Yes |
| Control variables at household head level | Yes | Yes | Yes | Yes |
| Fixed effects of provinces | Yes | Yes | Yes | Yes |
| Constant | −145,240.793*** | −76,370.921*** | −77,573.926*** | −63,682.578*** |
| | (−5.46) | (−6.52) | (−5.14) | (−8.29) |
| Observations | 584 | 906 | 391 | 2,891 |
| R-squared | 0.412 | 0.351 | 0.370 | 0.260 |

*Note* * $p < 0.1$, ** $p < 0.05$, *** $p < 0.01$

**Table 6** Regression results for the impact of household investable assets on household receipt of retirement/pension or old-age pension (income and urban–rural heterogeneity)

| | Retirement or pension benefits | | | |
|---|---|---|---|---|
| | (1) | (2) | (3) | (4) |
| Income heterogeneity | High income | Low income | | |
| Urban–rural heterogeneity | | | Urban | Rural |
| Investable assets | 447.1*** | 100.1*** | 501.6*** | 116.0*** |
| | (83.01) | (34.37) | (75.10) | (32.99) |
| Household-level control variables | Yes | Yes | Yes | Yes |
| Control variables at household head level | Yes | Yes | Yes | Yes |
| Fixed effects of provinces | Yes | Yes | Yes | Yes |
| Constant | −105,422*** | −22,001*** | −75,647*** | −19,937*** |
| | (14,300) | (2,266) | (6,367) | (2,249) |
| Observations | 4,219 | 4,556 | 4,772 | 4,003 |
| R-squared | 0.363 | 0.246 | 0.351 | 0.207 |

*Note* * $p < 0.1$, ** $p < 0.05$, *** $p < 0.01$

**Table 7** Regression results for the impact of household investable assets on household receipt of a severance/pension or old-age pension (urban heterogeneity)

| | Retirement or pension benefits | | | |
|---|---|---|---|---|
| | (1) | (2) | (3) | (4) |
| Urban Heterogeneity | First-tier cities | Second-tier cities | Third-tier cities | Fourth-tier cities and below |
| Investable Assets | 1,241.926*** | 435.714*** | 750.599*** | 280.437*** |
| | (3.54) | (2.63) | (3.14) | (3.07) |
| Household-level control variables | Yes | Yes | Yes | Yes |
| Control variables at household head level | Yes | Yes | Yes | Yes |
| Fixed effects of provinces | Yes | Yes | Yes | Yes |
| Constant | −153,445.008*** | −77,443.759*** | −81,270.164*** | −64,441.953*** |
| | (−5.74) | (−6.77) | (−5.45) | (−8.14) |
| Observations | 584 | 906 | 391 | 2,891 |
| R-squared | 0.409 | 0.353 | 0.376 | 0.263 |

*Note* * $p < 0.1$, ** $p < 0.05$, *** $p < 0.01$

results show that the effect of household investable assets on the household receipt of a severance/pension or old-age pension is significantly positive for all cities; however, the strength of the effect varies. Specifically, tier-1 cities have the largest impact, followed by tie-3, tier-2, and tier-4 cities and below have the smallest impact.

## 7 Summary

With China's rapidly growing aging population, retirement has become an important issue for economic and social development. Protecting the lives of the older adults after retirement is a family as well as a social issue. Thus, this study analyzed the situation of families receiving retirement/pension or old-age pension and the participation of family commercial pension insurance through Chinese household tracking survey data and obtained the following main conclusions.

First, the coverage rate of households receiving a divorce/pension or old-age pension is approximately 38%. Overall, the proportion of mid-high net worth households receiving pension or retirement benefits is somewhat higher than that of non mid-high net worth households. The coverage rate of households receiving pensions or retirement benefits tends to increase stepwise as household size increases. Except for households with one to three members, the coverage rate of mid-high net worth households is higher than that of non mid-high net worth households in all cases.

Households in tier-1 cities have the highest coverage rate of receiving a divorce/ pension or old-age pension; households in other cities have the lowest coverage rate. It is worth noting that the coverage rate of households receiving divorces/pensions or pensions in tier-3 cities is much higher than in tier-2 cities.

Second, as the education level of the household head increases, the coverage rate of households receiving retirement/pension or old-age pension tends to decrease stepwise. The healthier the household head, the lower the coverage rate of the household receiving a severance/pension or old-age pension. When the household head is unhealthy, the difference between the coverage rate of mid-high net worth households and non mid-high net worth households is 5.21%. When the household head is in average health, the difference is 10.59%. When the head of the household is healthy, the difference is 11.89%. When the household head is a male, there is a difference of 5.87% between the coverage rate of divorce/pension or old-age pension for mid-high net worth households and non mid-high net worth households; and when the household head is a female, there is a difference of 5.21% between the two.

Third, the annual retirement/pension received by households with a community structure as a neighborhood committee is ¥12,107.56 higher than that of a village committee with a community structure, and the difference between them is significant. The annual amount of pension or retirement benefits received by the mid-high net worth households whose community structure is neighborhood committee is ¥9503.44, higher than that of non mid-high net worth households; the difference between the two is ¥5430.99 when the community structure is a village committee. When the family size is one to three members, the annual amount of the divorce/ pension or old-age pension received by the mid-high net worth families is RMB 8921.79 higher than that of the non mid-high net worth families. When the family size is four to six members, the difference is RMB 12,823.38. When the family size is seven to nine members, the difference is RMB 8995.57, and when the family size is 10 members and above, the difference is RMB 5304.26. The difference between mid-high net worth families and non mid-high net worth families in tier-1 cities is RMB 15,029.03; in tier-2 cities, it is RMB 7,032.66; in tier-3 cities, it is RMB 4,262.21; and in the other cities, the difference is RMB 4,038.65.

Fourth, when the household head is a male, there is a difference of ¥10,396.67 between the annual amount of divorce/pension or old-age pension received by the mid-high net worth household and the non mid-high net worth household; when the household head is a female, the difference is ¥10,691.34. When the household head has a secondary education, the difference between the total annual amount of divorce/pension or old-age pension received by mid-high net worth households and non mid-high net worth households is ¥11,242.35. When the household head is unhealthy, the difference between the total amount of annual pension/retirement or old-age pension received by mid-high net worth households and non mid-high net worth households is ¥18,733.88. When the household head is in average health, the difference is ¥14,777.33; and when he/she is healthy, the difference is ¥9,081.5.

Fifth, the overall household pension insurance coverage rate is approximately 70%. The pension insurance coverage rate among mid-high net worth families is significantly higher than that of non mid-high net worth families. There is a difference of 10.73% between the pension insurance coverage rates of urban mid-high net worth households and non mid-high net worth households and a difference of 10.77% between the pension insurance coverage rates of rural mid-high net worth households and non mid-high net worth households. The difference between the pension insurance coverage rates of high- and non mid-high net worth households in tier-1 cities is 15.7%, in tier-2 cities it is 18.35%, in tier-3 cities it is 22.18%, and the in other cities it is 14.06%.

Sixth, the overall household commercial pension insurance coverage rate is low. Even for mid-high net worth families in the neighborhood council, the commercial pension insurance coverage rate is only approximately 5%. When the family size is one to three members, the commercial pension insurance coverage rate of mid-high net worth families is 2.95% higher than that of non mid-high net worth families; when the family size is four to six members, the difference is 3.63%; when the family size is seven to nine members, the difference is 7.26%; when the family size is 10 members and above, the difference is 2.29%. Except for tier-3 cities, the commercial pension insurance coverage rate for mid-high net worth households in all other cities is significantly higher than that of non mid-high net worth households.

Seventh, after considering both household-level control variables, head-of-household-level control variables, and province-fixed effects, mid-high net worth households receive approximately ¥5,179 more in severance/pensions or old-age pensions than non mid-high net worth households. This indicates that mid-high net worth households receive more severance/pension or old-age pension, which plays a positive role in ensuring a high quality of retirement life for older adults in mid-high net worth households. After considering the household-level control variables and the head-of-household-level control variables, and the province-fixed effects, each one-unit increase in the logarithm of the household's investable assets increases the amount of retirement/pension or old-age pension received by the household by about ¥377.

## References

1. Yang, Y., Zhang, X., Chen, J., Qian, L.: Blue Book on Healthy Aging: Report on Healthy Aging Index in Large and Medium-sized Cities in China (2019–2020). Social Science Literature Publishing House, Beijing (2020)
2. Yu, C., He, J.: Vulnerability concept, analytical framework and vulnerability analysis of farmers' pensions. Rural Econ., 88–91 (2011)
3. Xu, J., Li, S., Wu, Z., Liu, W.: Vulnerability assessment of rural older adults' household elderly care: an empirical study based on rural Anhui province. Popul. Stud. **43**, 91–101 (2019)
4. Liu, X.: The situation and path choice of social elderly service in china. Popul. Stud. **36**, 104–112 (2012)
5. Qi, P.: Research on the Promotion Strategy of Basic Pension Insurance for Urban and Rural Residents in China. China Social Science Press, Beijing (2021)
6. Luo, J., Wang, H.: Research on the Mode and Path of Urban-Rural Integration of Pension Insurance. Shanghai Jiao Tong University Press, Shanghai (2019)

7. Bönke, T., Grabka, M.M., Schröder, C., Wolff, E.N., Zyska, L.: The joint distribution of net worth and pension wealth in Germany. Rev. Income Wealth **65**, 834–871 (2019)
8. Zhang, X.: Research on the influence of pension insurance system on labor supply behavior—role mechanism, international experience and policy implications. China Price, 78–81 (2021)
9. Wang, Y., Xu, X., Chu, X.: A review of research on social pension insurance for urban and rural residents. Labor Secur. World, 117–119 (2015)
10. Liu, X.: Study on the income and expenditure gap and sustainability of china's pension insurance. China Indus. Econ., 25–37 (2014)
11. Wang, Z., Antoinette, H.: Social identity analysis of the rural "raising children for old age" security model and the new rural insurance system. China Rural Econ., 46–56 (2015)
12. Zhou, Y., Liang, H.: Study on the unsustainability of the traditional family old-age security model in rural china. Econ. Syst. Reform, 107–110 (2006)
13. Luo, Y., He, X., Ning, M.: The impact of the new rural social pension insurance system on the economic acquisition of rural elderly people. J. Hunan Agric. Univ. Soc. Sci. Edition **22**, 63–69 (2021)
14. Lv, Z.: Comparison of elderly care service needs between middle and high income groups. Gerontol. China **38**, 2780–2782 (2018)
15. Yue, J., You, Z.: A study on the happiness effect of pension insurance for low- and middle-income classes. Academic Digest of Liberal Arts in Higher Education, 44–45 (2019)
16. Wang, G., Huang, J., Wang, L., Wang, X.: A study on the contribution pressure of urban low- and middle-income households on pension insurance. Population Econ., 78–85 (2011)
17. Huang, L.: Secure retirement programs for high-income families. Import Export Manager, 74–75 (2008)
18. Hejun: Beijing Rim Quality Recreation and Wellness Consumption Insight Report; Hejun Group: Beijing (2021)
19. Lv, Z., Yuan, M.: Research on the transformation and upgrading of the elderly service industry under the background of "internet plus"—survey based on the elderly service needs of urban middle- and high-income people. J. Changsha Civil Affairs Vocat. Technical College, 8–11 (2016)
20. Hakola, T., Uusitalo, R.: Not so voluntary retirement decisions? Evidence from a pension reform. J. Public Econ. **89**, 2121–2136 (2005)
21. Rofman, R., Fajnzylber, E., Herrera, G.: Reforming the Pension Reforms: the Recent Initiatives and Actions on Pensions in Argentina and Chile. World Bank, Washington, DC (2008)
22. Shaw, S.: Network offering HNW pension leads. Money Marketing **000**, 17 (2005)
23. Zeng, H.: Exploring the wealth management of personal pension in China. China Insurance, 30–34 (2020)
24. Zhao, Y.: What does the launch of the personal pension system mean? School Bus., 13 (2022)
25. Ma, H.: Reflections on the third pillar personal pension system in the context of population aging. China Bus. Rev., 146–148 (2022)
26. Geng, Z., Sun, Q.: Delayed retirement age, endogenous fertility and pensions. Financial Studies, 77–94 (2020)
27. Zhao, Z., Wang, Y.: The impact of retirement on the housing and property of elderly households in china—a case study of CFPS data. World Econ. J. 72–88 (2020)
28. Xu, S., Xue, H.: The impact of retirement on medical consumption of urban and rural residents. Cooperative Econ. Technol., 156–158 (2020)
29. Brown, M.K.: In re marriage of stenquist: tracing the community interest in pension rights altered by spousal election. Calif. Law Rev. **67**, 856–885 (1979)
30. Huang, Z., Zhao, J.: How to enjoy an equal old age? --Pensions and the rural-urban income gap of the elderly. Populat. Econ., 74–86 (2022)
31. Yabiku, S.T.: Family history and pensions: the relationships between marriage, divorce, children, and private pension coverage. J. Aging Studies **14**, 293–312 (2000)
32. Zhao, X.: Analysis of the influence effect of urbanization on the full coverage of urban and rural residents' pension insurance. Youth Times, 99–100 (2017)

33. Meng, Y.: Study on the current situation of pension insurance participation and influencing factors of urban ethnic minority migrant population--based on the 2014 national migrant population health and family planning dynamic monitoring survey data. Soc. Secur. Res., 3–10 (2018)
34. Holden, K.C., Fontes, A.: Economic security in retirement: how changes in employment and marriage have altered retirement-related economic risks for women. J. Women Politics Policy **30**, 173–197 (2009)
35. Valset, K., Naper, S.O., Claussen, B., Dalgard, O.S.: Does mastering have an effect on disability pensioning independent of health, and may it explain divides of education in the Oslo Health Survey? Scandinavian J. Public Health **35**, 157–163 (2007)
36. Song, S., Wang, W., Luo, W.: Current situation and development suggestions of commercial pension insurance in china. Commer. Exhib. Econ., 50–52 (2021)

# Chapter 8
# Typical Family Analysis

**Abstract** The family is the most basic unit of society, and exhibits economic behaviors such as division of labor, production, consumption, investment, savings, education, and retirement protection. In this chapter, by following the principle of "structure follows strategy," we analyze and establish family's financial goals, optimize the asset allocation structure of the family under the guidance of these financial goals, and match the asset allocation structure of the family with its family development strategy. This, certainly, is the fundamental principle of family asset allocation. In the actual analysis for a particular family, a customized analysis should be conducted according to the situation of that family. To attain the family's financial goals, family financial planning should be conducted by optimizing the allocation of family assets to ensure sufficient support for the realization of the family development strategy.

In the opening lines of Anna Karenina, Leo Tolstoy wrote: "All happy families are alike; each unhappy family is unhappy in its own way." This is a literary description. However, from the perspective of scientific research, even seemingly similar situations must be further dissected to identify the differences, for which, the case study method is used. The CFPS family questionnaire can effectively reveal the fundamental household-level situation. Additionally, the CFPS family questionnaire can be correlated with individual questionnaires using the family codes, allowing for an in-depth analysis of family members and their profiles. All these provide the necessary details for studying typical families.

The asset allocation structure of households is characterized by diversity and dynamic adaptability. Specifically, the household asset allocation structure can be divided into the financial and non-financial asset allocation structures. The household financial asset allocation structure can be further divided into risk-free and risky financial asset allocation structures. The risky financial asset allocation structure can be further classified into low-risk and medium–high-risk financial asset allocation structures. The medium–high-risk financial asset allocation structure can, in turn, be classified as stocks, funds, bonds, insurance products, etc. The household non-financial asset allocation structure can be classified into property, real estate,

 
J. Gu, *Wealth Management Report for Mid-High Net Worth Families*, Spatial Demography and Population Governance, https://doi.org/10.1007/978-981-97-0387-6_8

consumer durables, etc. It can be seen that the asset allocation structure of households is complex and diverse; households dynamically adjust their asset allocation structure at different times—in response to different external environments, and based on different internal needs—to make it optimal to fulfill their needs. The analysis of a family's asset allocation structure should be based on the situation of a specific family and should not be carried out in isolation from the situation of a particular family.

In his book "A Treatise on the Family," Gary Becker created the "economics of the family" by systematically studying the family using an economic approach. He was awarded the Nobel Prize in Economics for this work. When analyzing the structure of a family, we should not only focus on its asset allocation structure but also analyze its demographic structure, including its marital status and fertility. In other words, family demographic structure and asset structure are often correlated. The analysis of the family in the household asset allocation structure has two levels—namely, broad and narrow. The broad structure includes factoring in marriage, population, etc., whereas the narrow structure is simply the asset structure, that is, the distribution of household assets among the different asset types. These two variables have a complementary relationship.

The asset allocation structure of households is dynamic; however, it is not irregular and exhibits certain patterns. Frequently, a correspondence exists between the household asset allocation structure and household development strategy; that is, the asset allocation structure of a household changes with a change in the household development strategy. This is the "structure follows strategy" law in family analysis. Family development strategy is a major choice, involving planning and strategy for the family's development direction, speed, quality of development, development point, and development capacity—according to the family's own strengths over a certain period of time in response to changes in the environment. In his book "The Seven Habits of Highly Effective People," Stephen Covey discusses the importance of family development strategies, saying, "Going with the flow means disaster for the family." The family that goes with the flow is actually the family that lacks a development strategy. Owing to the lack of a family development strategy, the family operates aimlessly, which can easily lead to the loss of family development and even the disintegration of the family itself. On the contrary, a family with a development strategy already has a "blueprint" for the family's steady growth and success. With a development strategy, families have greater direction in their financial management and insurance protection choices and are more likely to achieve optimal wealth allocation and appreciation.

The family development strategy determines the design of the household's allocation structure and the choice of assets. In turn, the process of implementing the family development strategy and its effects are constrained by the adopted household asset allocation structure. The relationship between the two is similar to the relationship between economic foundation and its superstructure: The focus of family development strategy determines the organization of family asset allocation, and any shift in the focus of the family development strategy requires an adjustment of the family asset allocation structure. In turn, the family asset allocation structure restricts the implementation of the family development strategy's focus. This is an important example of the "structure-following strategy" in the process of family asset allocation. In other words, the family development strategy plays a leading role in the family asset allocation process. The fundamental principle of family asset allocation is matching the asset allocation structure with the family's development strategy. Desirable family business performance can only be achieved when the two are matched.

In the family development process, family development strategy is concretely reflected in the family's strategic goals, which are the expectations of the primary outcomes of the family's development strategy activities. Family development strategy goals are reflected differently at different family functional levels. For example, in family asset allocation, there is a family financial goal. Based on this financial goal, households allocate assets and engage in various financial activities. When analyzing the family asset allocation, grasping the family's financial goals and using them as a guide to optimize its asset allocation structure is necessary. This is the fundamental method of household asset allocation analysis. This chapter analyzes the asset allocation of three typical families based on this method.

# 1 Case 1

## *1.1 Basic Information*

This is a typical family of three, including a husband, wife, and their boy child, living in Shanghai. The 38-year-old male partner runs a small personal business with an average monthly operating income of 12,500 yuan; the 38-year-old female partner holds a grassroots administrative position in the marketing department of a company with a monthly after-tax salary and bonus totaling 7,800 yuan and a year-end bonus of 5,800 yuan. The income generated by the duo's work accounts for 40.26% of the total household income, which is a relatively high percentage. In addition to business and work income, the household also earns rental and financial investment income. Financial investment income is the primary source of total family income, accounting for 48.43%, which indicates that the family has certain knowledge of financial products as well as certain investment and financial management abilities. The couple has a son in elementary school: The annual expenditure on education and training for the child is 110,000 yuan, which accounts for the highest share (36.18%) of the total household expenditure. The above data reveals that the couple attaches great importance to the growth process and the quality of education of the child. The woman's company pays "five insurance and one fund." It includes five social insurances (pension, medical, unemployment, work-related injury, and maternity insurances) and one housing fund. Additionally, the family has purchased commercial insurance, which indicates that the couple values the function of insurance, pays attention to the reasonableness of the insurance structure, and carries out certain risk-averse planning to provide the most comprehensive protection for the risks faced by the family. The annual expenditure on commercial insurance is 5,500 yuan, accounting for a relatively small proportion of the total household expenditure. In addition to these annual expenses, the annual general expenses of the family, medical and healthcare annual expenses, living (clothing, recreation, etc.) annual expenses, and other annual expenses totaled 188,560,000 yuan. The annual household balance rate is 50.91%, indicating that the family has good financial management skills and a reasonable income and expenditure structure. The household income and expenditures of Case 1 are summarized in Table 1.

This household has no debt, such as mortgages or borrowings from others and has a low financial burden. The family owns two properties: The value of the owner-occupied property is four million yuan and the value of the property rented out is seven million yuan. The total value of the properties accounts for the highest proportion (58.2%) of the family's total assets. However, with the implementation of the "no speculation in housing" policy, it is reasonable for property to account for less than 40% of the family's asset allocation; if it exceeds 40%, the asset allocation will be excessively concentrated. Although the couple has no time deposits, they have a total of 1.5 million yuan in cash and demand deposits for use in a family emergency or to continue their (financial education, etc.) investments. In general, their assets are more liquid. The total value of the financial products (stocks, funds, etc.) acquired by the family is six million yuan, which accounts for a large proportion (31.75%) of the total assets, and the family has a strong preference for financial investment. Usually, financial products have high risk, and high risks often accompany high returns. Hence the family can consider increasing the proportion of more stable products when selecting financial products. Overall, the household has a net worth of 18.9 million yuan, no debt, and a relatively favorable economic condition. Table 2 presents the household assets and liabilities for Case 1.

## *1.2 Financial Goals*

This family's financial goal is accumulating enough money for their child's college education by improving the protection of family members and reasonable planning for achieving good return on investment. At the time of this survey, the boy is only nine years old and is still in elementary school. However, the parents clearly had expectations for their child, hoping that he could attend college or even study abroad in the future. However, all of this requires a large amount of money. Therefore, the parents plan to accumulate sufficient funds for their child's future education. It is expected that when the child is prepared to attend college or study abroad, the family will already have sufficient money for the child to complete his studies. To achieve this goal, further optimizing the family's asset allocation in a reasonable manner is necessary, to generate a stable and sustainable income and save sufficiently for the child's education while fulfilling their current life needs.

**Table 1** Household income and expenditure of case 1

| Revenue | Amount (million yuan) | Percentage (%) | Expenses | Amount (million yuan) | Percentage (%) |
|---|---|---|---|---|---|
| Average monthly business income of the man | 1.25 | | Monthly housing expenses (water, electricity, gas costs) | 0.048 | |
| Monthly after-tax salary of the woman | 0.58 | | Monthly expenses for meals and daily necessities | 0.4 | |
| Monthly after-tax bonus for women | 0.2 | | Monthly postal and telecommunication expenses | 0.05 | |
| Year-end bonus for women | 0.58 | | Monthly transportation expenses | 0.03 | |
| Subtotal annual income from work | 24.94 | 40.26 | Subtotal general expenses for the year | 6.336 | 20.84 |
| Annual profit from home financial investments | 30 | 48.43 | Annual expenses for children's education and training | 11 | 36.18 |
| Gross annual income from rent | 7 | 11.31 | Medical, health care annual expenses | 0.7 | 2.3 |
| | | | Annual living expenses (clothing, recreation, etc.) expenses | 4 | 13.16 |
| | | | Annual expenses for business insurance | 0.55 | 1.81 |
| | | | Other annual expenses | 7.82 | 25.71 |
| Total annual revenue | 61.94 | 100 | Total expenses for the year | 30.406 | 100 |
| Balance of the year | 31.534 | | Annual balance rate | 50.91% | |

## 1.3 Implementation Strategy

For this family, the most important thing in financial planning is achieving stability while seeking progress: to continuously increase their family assets to fulfill the child's future education needs while maintaining the current standard of living. With

**Table 2** Household assets and liabilities for case 1

| Assets | Amount (million yuan) | Percentage (%) | Liabilities | Amount (million yuan) | Percentage (%) |
|---|---|---|---|---|---|
| Total cash and deposits | 150 | 7.94 | Home Loans | 0 | |
| Total value of financial assets | 600 | 31.75 | | | |
| Total value of real estate | 1100 | 58.2 | Loans from others | 0 | |
| Total value of consumer durables | 40 | 2.11 | | | |
| Total assets | 1890 | 100 | Total liabilities | 0 | |
| Net assets of the household | 1890 | | Liabilities/ total assets | 0 | |

a stable income and a certain amount of savings, the couple can use their financial management skills to diversify their investments to spread their investment risks while earning significant investment and financial returns to achieve family wealth appreciation. Specifically, the following strategies can be adopted:

1. *Increase the proportion of risky financial assets held*

The annual income of this family is relatively stable, with a relatively substantial annual balance of over 300,000 yuan. However, the family holds a relatively large amount of cash and demand deposits of 1.5 million yuan. Although holding such risk-free financial assets can ensure liquidity and preserve asset value, the ability to increase value is very limited. In this case, from the perspective of the existing asset allocation, reducing the amount of cash and demand deposits held and switching to fixed-income or equity funds or purchasing corresponding financial products from banks is appropriate. As this family is in the growth period (the child is still young and still has approximately 10 years to attend college), it is not recommended that this family select high-risk investment products, but they can select bank financial products with certain liquidity. For example, the family can take out one million yuan from the existing 1.5 million yuan in cash and demand deposits and invest in semi-annual bank financial products with an annualized return of 4%. This will ensure that this portion of the money will steadily increase in value and can be turned around within a few months in an emergency in the short-term.

2. *Improve insurance planning*

The purchase of insurance indicates that this family still greatly values the insurance function. Their annual expenditure on business insurance is 5500 yuan. This is done correctly. However, from the perspective of family protection, it is important to further examine the specific type of insurance, whether there is sufficient accident insurance and other additional insurance, and to confirm the reasonableness of the insurance structure to ensure that the annual premiums are spent on the "cutting edge" products. In terms of family income, the male partner is the breadwinner of the family, responsible for the greater part of the family's economic income. Therefore, the insurance coverage for the male partner should be comprehensive and adequate. In this way, even if the man loses his earning capacity in an accident, the family can receive enough insurance money to deal with the risks, such as accidents and diseases, continue to maintain and protect the existing quality of family life, and continue their child's education without disruptions. At the same time, it is also important to allocate appropriate accident and medical insurance for their child to effectively ensure his healthy growth.

3. *Reasonable allocation of emergency reserves*

Life is full of risks and surprises that can be overwhelming. In addition to insurance, families can have some emergency reserves. This family study has a strong sense of protection and the 1.5 million yuan cash and demand deposits it holds are actually the family's emergency reserve, which serves as a temporary emergency expense beyond the family's expectations. As the family does not have loans, it is not under pressure to repay them. In this case, it is generally sufficient to maintain a total household emergency reserve at a level that covers three to six months of the household's fixed expenses. This family's annual expenses are approximately 300,000 yuan; therefore, the family's emergency reserve of 150,000 yuan would actually be sufficient. The extra portion can be invested by purchasing money funds or wealth management funds. This type of investment has both liquidity and value-added characteristics, which can maintain the liquidity and safety of the funds, so that they can be taken out in time for use in case of emergencies. The family can also monitor the profitability of the investment expenses, ensuring that the assets steadily increase in value with a reasonable rate of return.

# 2 Case 2

## *2.1 Basic Information*

Case 2 is a family of four living in Guangzhou, Guangdong Province. The 35-year-old male partner is a professional operator of production and transportation equipment with an average monthly income of 12,500 yuan. The 32-year-old female partner works in a small private company and is a commercial and service industry worker with a monthly after-tax salary of 4,500 yuan and a year-end bonus of 2,000 yuan. Their annual work income accounts for 80.47% of the total household income and is the primary income source of the family. Only the mother of the male partner is alive, aged 66, and her retirement income and pension are 50,000 yuan, accounting for 19.53% of the total annual household income, which is the second source of income for the family. The male partner gives his mother 600 yuan per month in financial support. The couple has a son who is about to enter junior high school and is 12 years old. The annual expenditure for the child's education and training is 4,000 yuan, which accounts for only 5.23% of the total annual household expenditure. Compared with the education expenditure in first-tier cities, the family is in the middle range; however, when this family's education expenditure is compared with that of typical mid-high net worth families, a large gap exists, which reflects the fact that a family's economic condition has a certain influence on the level of education and training of the children. The family purchases commercial insurance, and the annual expenditure on commercial insurance is 800 yuan, accounting for a relatively small proportion of the total expenditure. Although the insured amount is small, it indicates that the family has a certain awareness of risk avoidance. However, probably owing to the limiting economic conditions, the family cannot afford the cost of fine insurance products. Owing to the presence of an older adult in this family, the annual expenditure on medical and healthcare accounts for a relatively high percentage (13.06%) of the total annual expenditure. Overall, the annual household expenditure is 76.55 thousand yuan. The annual household balance is 179,450,000 yuan, with an annual balance rate of 70.1%. The household income and expenditures for Case 2 are summarized in Table 3.

The respondent household has no debt, such as a mortgage or borrowing from others, and has a low financial burden. The family owns three properties: The value of the owner-occupied property is 1.5 million yuan and the total value of other two properties is 5 million yuan. The total value of properties accounts for the highest proportion of total household assets at 86.26%. The proportion of properties to total household assets is excessively high, and there is no rental income; hence, some unreasonableness exists in the asset allocation structure. Additionally, the couple has only 135,000 yuan in cash and demand deposits and no time deposits. In case of an emergency, the liquid assets available are too small and some of the properties may have to be considered for liquidation. The family has acquired few financial products (stocks, funds, etc.). The couple has a low-income level and no income other than salary; hence, it is recommended that they purchase low-risk and stable financial products to accumulate extra income for the family, which can relieve part of the financial pressure. Overall, the household net worth is 7.535 million yuan, with no debt and a relatively desirable economic condition. Table 4 presents the household assets and liabilities for Case 2.

## 2.2 Financial Goals

The family's financial goals are to maintain its current standard of living, take good care of its older adults, and build up a certain amount of money for their child's education. Their child is in middle school and will enter college in six years. Therefore, the family must set aside an education fund for the child's college education. To

**Table 3** Household income and expenditure of case 2

| Revenue | Amount (million yuan) | Percentage (%) | Expenses | Amount (million yuan) | Percentage (%) |
|---|---|---|---|---|---|
| Average monthly working income of the man | 1.25 | | Monthly housing expenses (water, electricity, gas costs) | 0.0325 | |
| Monthly after-tax salary of the woman | 0.45 | | Monthly expenses for meals and daily necessities | 0.415 | |
| Year-end bonus of the woman | 0.2 | | Monthly postal and telecommunication expenses | 0.03 | |
| | | | Monthly transportation expenses | 0.005 | |
| Subtotal annual income from work | 20.6 | 80.47 | Subtotal general expenses for the year | 5.79 | 75.64 |
| Annual income of the man's mother's retirement pension | 5 | 19.53 | Annual expenses for children's education and training | 0.4 | 5.23 |
| | | | Medical, health care annual expenses | 1 | 13.06 |
| | | | Annual living expenses (clothing, recreation, etc.) expenses | 0.25 | 3.27 |
| | | | Annual expenses for business insurance | 0.08 | 1.05 |
| | | | Other annual expenses | 0.135 | 1.75 |
| Total annual revenue | 25.6 | 100 | Total expenses for the year | 7.655 | 100 |
| Balance of the year | 17.945 | | Annual balance rate | 70.1% | |

achieve these goals, it is necessary to plan and allocate the family's wealth to better serve the functions of caring for older adults and nurturing the child.

**Table 4** Household assets and liabilities for case 2

| Assets | Amount (million yuan) | Percentage (%) | Liabilities | Amount (million yuan) | Percentage (%) |
|---|---|---|---|---|---|
| Total cash and deposits | 13.5 | 1.79 | Home loans | 0 | |
| Total value of financial assets | 50 | 6.64 | | | |
| Total value of real estate | 650 | 86.26 | Loans from others | 0 | |
| Total value of consumer durables | 40 | 5.31 | | | |
| Total assets | 753.5 | | Total liabilities | 0 | |
| Net assets of the household | 753.5 | | Liabilities/ total assets | 0 | |

## 2.3 Implementation Strategy

As this is a middle-income family, financial stability should be sought first in financial planning. Therefore, the family assets should be reasonably allocated to stabilize and grow the family's wealth. Specifically, the following strategies can be adopted.

1. *Optimize the allocation of risky financial assets*

The annual income level of this family is not very high, but it is relatively stable and is a typical of a middle-income family. Moreover, the family has adopted a relatively good strategy of being frugal and controlling unnecessary expenses well, so there is still a surplus of approximately 180,000 yuan per year. In terms of financial management also, the family is not conservative, holding 500,000 yuan worth of financial products. Thus, this family has relatively good financial management skills. However, the family's asset allocation structure can be further optimized. The family's risky financial assets are predominantly concentrated in stocks, funds, and bonds. However, the family's investment in insurance products is extremely limited. Investment insurance products are becoming increasingly mature, and these financial products not only provide insurance protection but also enable saving and investment. Investment insurance products protect against risk and manage the money insured and since insurance companies are generally sound in their operations, the risk of them not performing fully is very low. Therefore, this family can appropriately hold some investment insurance products and convert the funds from the stable risk-averse financial account to a more aggressive growth account to gain additional income.

2. *Reasonable increase in insurance investment*

The annual income level of the Case 2 family is not very high, and the family includes an elderly person and a child. Thus it needs to take care of both the "old age" and the "young age" functions. The family support ratio is 100%: two adults support one minor and one elderly person. Therefore, the family's life is still relatively stressful. The family's annual expenditure on commercial insurance is only 800 yuan, which is low, and its protection ability is insufficient. Therefore, the family's ability to cope with risks is weak, and it is often difficult to bear the blow if there is an unexpected situation. The most important things that a working family should buy is accident insurance and health insurance policies. As both the husband and the wife work outside their home, health issues cannot be ignored. Therefore, the couple should buy suitable health insurance after making sufficient provision for accident protection. For this type of middle-income families, when buying health insurance, the breadwinner of the family should be prioritized: Selecting an insurance product with a coverage of 100,000 to 200,000 yuan for the male member is more appropriate. Additionally, when this kind of family buys health insurance, paying attention to the female member is also necessary: Female special disease insurance may be considered. The older adult in the family does not require additional pension insurance. The couple should be provided adequate insurance and accident protection to avoid a possible "precipitous" decline in the family's economic income, due to an unforeseen accident that makes one of the couple incapacitated, thereby affecting family stability.

3. *Accumulate education funds*

"It is the common wish of parents to see their child become a dragon and their daughter become a phoenix." In this family, the child has almost finished elementary school and will soon start secondary school. Therefore, the family must prepare the child's education funds. Therefore, fund investment is a good choice for this family. Fund fixed investment is similar to a bank's zero deposit: it accumulates less into more, can avoid difficulties when choosing, amortizes the investment cost, reduces the investment risk, obtains a greater return with less investment, and can effectively achieve the purpose of accumulating funds. Specifically, for fund products, one can select a hybrid fund under a brand name fund company with a large-scale and more robust benefits. As there are only approximately six years until the child goes to college and the couple's combined monthly salary income is approximately 17,000 yuan, an investment 2,000 yuan per month is recommended. Thus, the accumulation over six years—plus the investment income—will be a substantial amount of education funds, sufficient to cover the child's potential college expenses.

# 3 Case 3

## 3.1 Basic Information

The family, in this case, lives in the lively and prosperous city of Shanghai. It is a family of five with three generations living together. The 38-year-old male partner works in a foreign, Hong Kong, Macau, or Taiwan enterprise in the commercial or service industry, with the monthly after-tax salary and bonus adding up to 8,000 yuan and a year-end bonus of 10,000 yuan. The 38-year-old female partner works in a private enterprise in the commercial or service industry, with a monthly after-tax salary of 6,000 yuan and a year-end bonus of 2,000 yuan. The income brought in by the duo's work accounts for 47.62% of the total household income and is the primary source of economic income for the family. The man's father and mother are both alive; the 64-year-old father being has a monthly after-tax pension of 2,000 yuan and the 62-year-old mother has a monthly after-tax pension of 2,000 yuan. The man's parents' annual pensions account for only a small percentage (12.7%) of the total family income. Since both of the man's parents have pensions, they do not need additional financial support, which removes the burden of retired parents. The couple has a son who is in high school and is 15 years old. The annual expenditure for the child's education and training is 35,000 yuan, accounting for 15.2% of the total annual household expenditure. The family has purchased commercial insurance, and the annual expenditure on commercial insurance is 20,000 yuan, accounting for 8.68% of the total annual household expenditure. This indicates that the family has a certain awareness of risk avoidance and can afford boutique insurance products that provide comprehensive protection against the family's unexpected risks. The proportion of annual expenditure on medical needs and healthcare of the family is relatively low at 1.3%, which may be because the insurance purchased can reduce some medical care costs. In addition to these annual expenses, the annual general expenses, annual expenses for living (clothing, recreation, etc.), and other annual expenses of the family totaled 172,320,000 yuan. The annual balance of the family is 147,680,000 yuan, and the annual balance rate is 39.07%. The household income and expenditures for Case 3 are summarized in Table 5.

The family interviewed took a bank loan of 4.8 million yuan when they purchased the property. Prior to that, the family had also borrowed 500,000 yuan from relatives and friends. These two items added up to a total of 5.3 million yuan. These borrowings were primarily for the acquisition of properties. The family owns three properties worth a total of 14 million yuan, and the total value of the properties accounts for the highest percentage (77.35%) of the family's total assets. These properties bring additional income for the family, and the annual income from rent is 70,000 yuan, accounting for 18.52% of the total income, indicating that these properties can bring considerable amount of other income. Additionally, the couple's cash and deposits total 2 million yuan, making the household assets highly liquid. The family has also acquired a large number of financial products worth 1.5 million yuan, which can earn 80,000 yuan per year. From the perspective of financial product profitability,

**Table 5** Household income and expenditure of case 3

| Revenue | Amount (million yuan) | Percentage (%) | Expenses | Amount (million yuan) | Percentage (%) |
|---|---|---|---|---|---|
| Monthly after-tax salary of the man | 0.6 | | Monthly housing expenses (water, electricity, gas costs) | 0.026 | |
| Monthly after-tax bonus of the man | 0.2 | | | | |
| Monthly after-tax salary of the woman | 0.6 | | Monthly expenses for meals and daily necessities | 0.75 | |
| Year-end bonus of the man | 1 | | Monthly postal and telecommunication expenses | 0.03 | |
| Year-end bonus of the woman | 0.2 | | Monthly transportation expenses | 0.1 | |
| Work year income subtotal | 18 | 47.62 | Subtotal general expenses for the year | 10.872 | 47.2 |
| Monthly after-tax pension for the man's father | 0.2 | | | | |
| Monthly after-tax pension for the man's mother | 0.2 | | | | |
| Subtotal annual income of the man's parents' pension | 4.8 | 12.70 | | | |
| Annual profit from home financial investments | 8 | 21.16 | Annual expenses for children's education and training | 3.5 | 15.20 |
| Gross annual income from rent | 7 | 18.52 | Medical, health care annual expenses | 0.3 | 1.3 |
| | | | Annual living expenses (clothing, recreation, etc.) expenses | 3.1 | 13.46 |
| | | | Annual expenses for business insurance | 2 | 8.68 |

(continued)

**Table 5** (continued)

| Revenue | Amount (million yuan) | Percentage (%) | Expenses | Amount (million yuan) | Percentage (%) |
|---|---|---|---|---|---|
| | | | Other annual expenses | 3.26 | 14.16 |
| Total annual revenue | 37.8 | 100 | Total expenses for the year | 23.032 | 100 |
| Balance of the year | 14.768 | | Annual balance rate | 39.07% | |

**Table 6** Household assets and liabilities for case 3

| Assets | Amount (million yuan) | Percentage (%) | Liabilities | Amount (million yuan) | Percentage (%) |
|---|---|---|---|---|---|
| Total cash and deposits | 200 | 11.05 | Home loans | 480 | 90.57% |
| Total value of financial assets | 150 | 8.29 | | | |
| Total value of real estate | 1400 | 77.35 | Loans from others | 50 | 9.43% |
| Total value of consumer durables | 60 | 3.31 | | | |
| Total assets | 1810 | 100 | Total liabilities | 530 | |
| Net assets of the household | 1280 | | Liabilities/ total assets | 29.3% | |

the household can adjust the financial products appropriately to obtain higher income at the existing higher economic cost. Overall, the household net worth is 12.8 million yuan, with some liabilities. However, the household debt ratio is 29.3%, meaning that the total household debt is approximately 30% of the total household assets. This indicates that the household leverage ratio is still within a reasonable range. Overall, the family is in a healthy financial position and has a strong sense of financial management. The household assets and liabilities for Case 3 are summarized in Table 6.

## 3.2 *Financial Goals*

The financial goal of this family is ensuring a high quality of life for the family. This is primarily reflected in the arrangement and protection of the high quality of life for the older adults after retirement and the advance arrangements and planning for the child's college life and study. Both the older adults in the family are retired and have a certain amount of pension. In this case, a steady growth in family wealth should be achieved to ensure that the elderly can enjoy a high quality of life after retirement. Meanwhile, as the child will enter the university in two to three years, they need to prepare sufficient funds for the education of their child, plan for their child to go overseas for further studies, and create financial reserves.

## *3.3 Implementation Strategy*

This is a middle-to-high income family, where there is a certain degree of security for the elders' retirement and the child's education. As the old saying goes, "A family should know its rituals when the granary is solid." The family's income is relatively stable and in addition to the couple's salary income, the older adults have a certain amount of pension income, and the family also has rental income. Therefore, in terms of family asset allocation, it is necessary to integrate salary, pension, and rental income for improved overall financial management and investment to ensure that the family's wealth can grow stably and faster. To this end, several strategies can be adopted as follows.

1. *Increase the allocation of medium- and high-risk financial assets as appropriate*

The annual income of this family is relatively stable and the sources of income are relatively diversified. Additionally, the family has some financial management experience and is able to make reasonable use of the family's leverage to realize the allocation of family assets to multiple properties to receive a stable rental income and dividends from the rising housing prices. This family also has a relatively unique financial strategy in terms of financial asset allocation, with the holding of financial products valued at 1.5 million yuan. Moreover, the family is relatively risk-controlled, with 2 million yuan in cash and deposits for emergencies. However, this asset allocation structure can be further optimized. First, the proportion of risky financial asset allocation can be further increased. This family could spend half of the 2 million yuan in cash and savings on stock and bond funds. Although the net value of the funds will fluctuate, if they opt to buy them when their historical performance is better and more stable, they can obtain an annual investment return of approximately 10%. Meanwhile, 10–20% of risky financial assets can be allocated to formal and reliable P2P lending platforms, and the annual return from this is also relatively substantial. Overall, the risk level after optimizing the asset allocation increases, but this new investment risk is still within the range that the family can afford. The increased risk means that the investment returns will also increase accordingly. In this way, with optimized asset allocation, the assets of the household can appreciate significantly faster than they do with the current allocation.

2. *Optimize insurance allocation structure*

The family is extremely insurance-conscious and spends 20,000 yuan per year on insurance. Overall, these insurance investments provide a good guardrail for protecting the family's property and personal safety. With the improvement of living standard, this family has a higher demand for the protection of its own safety, is no longer satisfied with the protection provided by ordinary medical insurance, and wants the protection of a larger assured amount and wider range of medical protection provided by the middle- and high-end medical insurance products. Therefore, in addition to the current basic insurance, the family can purchase a mid to high-end medical insurance product to ensure a high quality of life. Mid-range and high-end medical insurance products feature high coverage amounts, comprehensive coverage responsibilities, private hospital coverage, wide geographic coverage, and direct insurance payments (there is no need for the client to advance funds). In the event that a family member becomes unwell, he or she will be eligible to receive excellent medical treatment. Although the premium for this type of insurance product is relatively high, it is within the family's reach. Moreover, the family is based in Shanghai, which has many VIP-level medical resources. Therefore, after purchasing a mid-to-high-end medical insurance product, the family can receive VIP-level medical care if they become unwell, which is an important step in protecting their health.

3. *Education fund accumulation and protection*

This family's child is already in high school and is close to attending college. Currently, the family does not have a separate allocation for the child's education, probably because they believe that the child's college expenses can be sufficiently covered based on their current financial resources and have not given much thought to it. This perspective actually needs to change. Regardless of the family's financial resources, they need to plan ahead for their child's education. As a parent, one should not only care about your child's health, but also plan for his or her education. However, nowadays, the cost of raising children is high, and family assets can be seriously depleted due to unforeseen accidents. Therefore, to avoid any disruptions in a child's education and relieve any potential pressure on the family's finances, it is preferable to buy education fund insurance products, in advance, to avoid future uncertainties that may lead to depreciation of family wealth. An education fund insurance product is an annuity insurance product where parents deposit a premium in advance and the child receives an educational benefit at a specific stage of education in the future. It is flexible because parents can select when and how much they want to receive according to their child's education plan or expectations. It makes sense to purchase an education benefit insurance product for your child as it will secure your child's future education expenses. Considering the family's current income and the timing of the child's college education, it is recommended that the family opt for an education fund insurance product that starts at ¥50,000 in single payments.

# 4 Summary

The family is the most basic unit of society, and exhibits economic behaviors such as division of labor, production, consumption, investment, savings, education, and retirement protection. The family can be considered equivalent to a small-scale economy, where the resources, such as the human resources and other input factors, are limited. Every family faces the difficult question of how to allocate and utilize the existing limited family resources to enable the preservation and appreciation of family wealth and better realize the consumption and production of family members. In this regard, by following the principle of "structure follows strategy," we analyze and establish family's financial goals, optimize the asset allocation structure of the family under the guidance of these financial goals, and match the asset allocation structure of the family with its family development strategy. This, certainly, is the fundamental principle of family asset allocation. In the actual analysis for a particular family, a customized analysis should be conducted according to the situation of that family. To attain the family's financial goals, family financial planning should be conducted by optimizing the allocation of family assets to ensure sufficient support for the realization of the family development strategy.

## 4 Summary

The family is the most basic unit of society [illegible]

[illegible]

# Postscript

In 2019, we discussed the need to conduct research in this area, and in 2020, we started collecting relevant articles, reports, and publications on the research into mid-high net worth groups in China and abroad, which are introduced in the first chapter of this book. In early 2021, China Life Insurance Co. Ltd. initiated a major horizontal research project titled "White Paper on Asset Allocation (Insurance Protection) for Banks' Mid-High Net Worth Clients" (hereinafter referred to as the white paper), of which I was the presenter. After the project was established, the research team, from the joint project team formed by the Institute of Social Science Survey of Peking University and China Life Insurance Company Limited, devoted considerable effort to conduct systematic research and completed the research report in October 2021. The essence of the research report, the white paper, was released in Peking University in September 2022 and received attention and praise from people from all walks of life.

After submitting the study in October 2021, the author found that CFPS data could also be used to conduct further in-depth research on the wealth management of mid-high net worth households. This inspired the writing of this book. In terms of content, this book is an extension and supplement to the white paper. Unlike the white paper, this book conducts research predominantly from the perspective of family wealth management, although it includes asset allocation, insurance, etc. Therefore, the content of this book is different from that of the white paper. In terms of research methodology, this book adopts multiple regression analysis to understand the impact of the different factors on the wealth management of mid-high net worth families. As the white paper is not publicly published, many readers may not be able to access it. The publication of this book can effectively compensate for this and allow all readers to have a more comprehensive understanding of the financial management of mid-high net worth families, as well as provide valuable guidelines and references for their own families' and others' wealth management.

This research report could not have been completed without the care and support of many people. We would like to express our gratitude to the five experts who



J. Gu, *Wealth Management Report for Mid-High Net Worth Families*, Spatial Demography and Population Governance, https://doi.org/10.1007/978-981-97-0387-6

participated in this project: Professor Yu Hongjun, former Executive Deputy Secretary of the Party Committee of Peking University; Zhao Peng, President of China Life Insurance Company Limited; Zhan Zhong, Vice President of China Life Insurance Company Limited; Professor Jin Yunhui of the Guanghua School of Management of Peking University; and Professor Shi Yupeng, Vice President of the China Institute of Internet Economics of Central University of Finance and Economics. We are thankful to all the members of the project team: Chen Yi, Jia Fenglei, Li Qiang, Li Kecheng, Lyu Ping, Song Peike, Sun Yan, Yan Jie, and Wu Qiong. We also extend our thanks to all the leaders, experts, guests, and journalists who attended the white paper launch: Cao Deyun, Executive Vice President and Secretary General of the China Insurance Asset Management Association; Gao Shanwen, Chief Economist of Anxin Securities; Dong Yu, Executive Vice President of the China Development Planning Institute of Tsinghua University; Chen Daofu, Deputy Director of the Institute of Financial Research of the Development Research Center of the State Council; and Zhang Yaojun, Professor of the School of Applied Economics of Renmin University of China; as well as the representatives from Industrial and Commercial Bank of China, Agricultural Bank of China, Bank of China, China Construction Bank, China Postal Savings Bank, and several journalists from the financial media. We would like to thank Professor Zhang Zhixue, Director of Institute of Social Science Survey of Peking University, for his steadfast support of the project and our colleagues, including Ding Hua, Chen Xinxin, and Chen Minyan for their help. Additionally, students Chia-Ling Zhou, Rui-Xi Lyu, Rui Ding, and Pei-Coi Xu also participated in this study.

SPRINGER NATURE

# GPSR Compliance

*The European Union's (EU) General Product Safety Regulation (GPSR) is a set of rules that requires consumer products to be safe and our obligations to ensure this.*

*If you have any concerns about our products, you can contact us on ProductSafety@springernature.com*

In case Publisher is established outside the EU, the EU authorized representative is:

Springer Nature Customer Service Center GmbH
Europaplatz 3
69115 Heidelberg, Germany

The manufacturer's authorised representative in the EU is Springer Nature Customer Service Centre GmbH, Europaplatz 3, 69115 Heidelberg, Germany. If you have any concerns regarding our products, please contact ProductSafety@springernature.com

Printed and bound by CPI Group (UK) Ltd, Croydon, CR0 4YY
01/10/2026
02225853-0008